The Inconvenient Child

An abandoned
Australian child struggles
to survive and find
her American father

SHARYN KILLENS & LINDSAY LEWIS

First published by Miracle Publishing in 2009

Reprinted 2009

Copyright © Miracle Publishing 2009

Miracle Publishing Pty Ltd
Level 1, 80 Chandos Street, St Leonards, NSW, 2065, Australia
www.MiraclePublishing.com.au

National Library of Australia
Cataloguing-in-Publication data:

Killens, Sharyn, 1948-

The inconvenient child : an abandoned Australian child
struggles to survive and find her American father /
Sharyn Killens, Lindsay Lewis.

1st ed.

978 0 6464 8782 3 (pbk.)

Killens, Sharyn, 1948-
Women entertainers--Australia--Biography.
Entertainers--Australia--Biography.
Children--Institutional care--Australia--Biography.
Mothers and daughters--Australia--Biography.
African American fathers.
Fathers and daughters--United States--Biography.
Racially mixed children--Australia--Biography.
Australia--Social conditions.

Lewis, Lindsay.

790.209220994

Typeset in 12/15 pt Granjon by Bookhouse, Sydney
Printed and bound in Australia by Griffin Press

Front cover photos: Getty Images
Back cover photo: girls at the Havilah Little Children's Home. Source unknown.
Cover design: Nada Backovic Designs
www.TheInconvenientChild.com

For my father

Contents

All Souls' Day: A Prologue

MY GRANDMOTHER WANTED me dead even before I was born.

'Abort it. Adopt it. Drown it. Just get rid of it! That evil child is never coming into my home.'

Her vile words were revealed to me by my cousin a few years ago, after a couple of bottles of chardonnay.

Evidently, my grandmother had gone on to say to my horrified mother, 'You will ruin your life. A good and decent man will come along one day and want to marry you. But that will never happen if you keep this devil child. No man will ever want you! And besides, what will the neighbours think?' She had just heard what was to her an appalling confession from her youngest daughter: that she was pregnant with me, the illegitimate child of an American 'coloured' man.

My grandmother convinced my mother her life would be ruined if she kept this devil child: I was evil and the sensible thing to do was to get rid of me. And so my mother agreed. Well, almost.

I WAS BORN IN SYDNEY, Australia, on November 2, 1948, three years after the end of World War II, in Crown Street Women's Hospital. I emerged with chocolate-coloured skin, brown eyes, soft black curls, huge lungs and a spirit I believe was blessed by God himself. Fortunately, He also bestowed on me the gifts of strength, determination, persistence and willpower to guide me through the next gruelling years of my life.

There were no celebrations when I drew breath on that hot All Souls' Day. No baby shower or nervous father pacing impatiently in the waiting room. No tears of joy or relatives and friends rushing to visit with bouquets of flowers and teddy bears. I came into this world quietly and secretly. Few knew of my arrival and fewer still thought I was special. In fact, the doctor and nurses must have stared in astonishment when they delivered the tiny black baby to the fair-haired and delicate young woman with ivory-coloured skin. I imagine my mother would have considered this moment her greatest humiliation.

Later, back in her ward with the other new mothers, the nurse placed me into her arms. No doubt the embarrassment and shame was almost too much to bear as she took in the shocked expressions on the faces of the women in the other beds. What an incongruous sight, she would have thought. Blue eyes and blonde hair, and cradling a tiny brown-skinned baby. And to make matters worse, she didn't have a husband by her side! Where was that man? He had promised he would return. He'd promised her love and marriage. When he came back everything would work out, she was sure of it. They would be married. She would be his wife and he would take her to live in America. Wouldn't he?

I was born into a hostile environment because of the colour of my skin. Not only was it unacceptable to be born illegitimate in Australia in 1948 but to be born brown or black as well was unforgivable. In my mother's defence, frankly she had few choices. A backyard abortion was far too dangerous, not to mention illegal and extremely expensive, and adoption was just not an option. In that era, 'coloured' babies were not wanted by anyone, full stop.

Ignoring the whispers and sniggers surrounding her that hot November day, my mother stared into my little face. She knew the road ahead would be almost unbearable but she realised she had to try to take care of me. She had no choice. However, she couldn't take me home to live with her at her mother's house, so she decided she would find people to look after me, somewhere. And so I became my mother's secret.

My existence was to become the family's shame; one of those family secrets known by most but never mentioned.

CHAPTER ONE

The Dutiful Daughter

TOWARDS THE END of World War II, Grace Samuels and her girlfriends Rosa and Jeannie (like most young women of the time) tried to block out the sorrow and hardship the effects of war were having on the home front by enjoying Sydney's night life, particularly the company of visiting American servicemen. By June 1943, there were around eighty thousand American military personnel in Australia on their way either to or from the War in the Pacific. At age twenty-one, vivacious Grace thought the Americans were great fun and looked very handsome in their uniforms. Princes and Romano's nightclubs were for officers only, so the Trocadero nightclub was the place to go for civilians and non-commissioned forces and the Americans packed the venue every night. The band was Australia's version of the Glenn Miller Orchestra and considered to be the best in town, playing the popular music of the day: swing and jazz. The girls loved the atmosphere there, the big orchestra, the upstairs seating, and of course the dancing. Grace loved to dance. Each weekend she, Jeannie and Rosa would dance away their cares almost nonstop — particularly from Saturday afternoon through to the early hours of Sunday morning — and they weren't the only ones adopting the craze. In groups and pairs, even singles on their own, sometimes it seemed the whole city had come to the Troc. It was the place to meet new people and many romances began and blossomed on its vast dance floor.

In-between favourite numbers, they'd head to the bar for refreshments, which were strictly non-alcoholic since the Trocadero didn't have a liquor licence. Of course some would smuggle it in, inside a coat or jacket, but the security officers (or 'red coats') were ever alert in their search for contraband or intoxicated patrons among the crowd. It was a good thing too: the intense rivalry between the American and Australian servicemen fuelled many resentful clashes. Even in wartime, no self-respecting girl would venture out bare legged but because of rationing, silk and nylon stockings had become luxuries, as were cigarettes, and almost impossible for the Australians to obtain. The American boys, on the other hand, had easy access to these items and treated their dates to transport by taxi rather than bus or tram, so they were popular with the girls. Inevitably, fights broke out. The 'red coats' who tried to calm the situation until the police arrived, were not helped by the band who were ready with a repertoire of well-pitched satire for these occasions: the strains of 'Stars and Stripes Forever', 'Home Sweet Home' and 'I Love You Truly' would rise above the rabble until order was restored. The Trocadero was the place to be seen and these were busy and colourful times for the club.

Ensured of a loud, dramatic night of fun (and possibly romance), many girls went to the Trocadero straight from work or on their way to a nightshift. Social young women from the suburbs, like Grace, would make their way into the city by public transport. Less intense than London's blackout, Sydney's brownout would have given the journey a sober edge as the tram rattled down suburban shopping streets lined with darkened or dimly lit display windows, on its way into town. Passengers would ride the buses in darkness and you were lucky if the driver would turn on the dim interior light at your stop. Set down in the city under the ghostly light of shopfronts' half-strength neons, the excitement would build as friends joined up for the short walk to the Troc.

MY MOTHER, GRACE SAMUELS was born in Sydney in July 1924, the youngest of six children. She was an attractive child, with her golden curls, blue eyes and her polite, softly spoken manner; and she was obedient. Her elderly father had passed away when she was quite young which meant that, although she was a clever student and enjoyed school, the family's finances could not be stretched for her to continue on to matriculation. At fifteen she was obliged to leave school and begin work as a sales girl in a city department store. But her dream was to become a secretary so she studied shorthand and typing at night. Always the dutiful daughter, she took her unopened pay packet home to her mother and accepted whatever was left after the household bills were paid. She also helped her three older sisters by babysitting their children and cooking them treats, so she quickly became everyone's favourite aunt.

Grace was left at home as companion and carer for her mother in the small, semi-detached three-bedroom house they shared not far from the ocean near Maroubra Junction, a southern Sydney suburb. She adored her mother and happily sat with her each night listening to radio quiz shows and serials.

By her early twenties, Grace was a successful stenographer in the city with no shortage of good-looking young men lining up to take her dancing or out to the cinema. She was the epitome of a mid-1940s beauty: slim, blonde and beautiful. Her gracious manners made her popular, too. She dressed fashionably and always carried a white lace handkerchief scented with fine perfume. Her mother was determined Grace should 'marry well'. To earn her mother's approval, Grace's suitors were encouraged to visit on a Sunday and take both her and her mother for a drive to the country, or for lunch in the city or a picnic in the Botanical Gardens. Fortunately or unfortunately, her mother didn't know what her daughter did, or where she went, on nights out with her girlfriends.

One night, Rosa excitedly told Grace and Jeannie, 'I know where we should go! I've heard about this new nightclub only the coloured boys go to. It's supposed to be jumping with the best music and the best dancers.' So the three game girls decided to go and have a look.

The Booker T. Washington Club had been set up by the American Red Cross, together with McKell's State Government, for visiting 'coloured' American servicemen to avoid the embarrassing situation of Australia's Allies being refused entry into the city's whites-only nightclubs. The government recognised the need for these servicemen to have a place of their own to socialise and the Booker T. Washington Club in Surry Hills quickly became one of the most popular clubs in Sydney.

Grace and her girlfriends loved it and thought the 'coloured' boys were terrific dancers. The Australian musicians employed in the big band also had a great time playing the new boogie-woogie music; however, when they took a break, black American musicians would step in and play terrific jazz and swing while the crowd danced up a storm. Professional jitterbuggers were hired to entertain the crowd and show them how to do the moves. Grace quickly learned the steps, twirling and shaking her shoulders. She was born to dance and this was where she shone. Plus, the American boys could see she had rhythm and enjoyed partnering her and she was in her element, moving skilfully around the floor with them. As the music reached a crescendo, the crowd clapping and cheering her on and watching her jive, swing, twist and shake, she knew she was the best. Throwing back her long blonde hair, a smile on her radiant face, she felt like a film star dancing in step with her partner and the music.

The Trocadero orchestra was wonderful but the music at the Booker T. Washington Club was different, more exciting: it was the new music, popular in the United States of America's Deep South. The 'coloured' Americans and their music attracted the prettiest girls in Sydney and it quickly became the new place to be. It was almost a secret but drew a good-sized crowd.

IN THE ADJOINING SYDNEY SUBURB of Kings Cross, Dorrie and Ellie, two enterprising and vibrant West Indian women were living a very different kind of life. This shrewd mother and daughter pair were well known for holding fun parties in their home, a sizeable two-storey terrace they rented in narrow Womerah Avenue, only a short distance from the legendary Sydney Stadium which was renowned for boxing events.

Menial factory work or cleaning white people's homes was not for these two astute women. They decided there was a living to be made accommodating the black American servicemen who regularly arrived in Sydney on naval ships for rest and recreation leave and had turned their home into a 'safe house' for these GIs during the war years. They were in their element at the Booker T. Washington Club, where they spent most evenings dancing or networking with the fine young men and women. After the club closed each night it was customary to go on to Ellie and Dorrie's house and party through the early hours of the morning.

On board, the ship's complement of white and 'coloured', worked in close proximity; socially, though, it was a different situation. At each port of call they went their separate ways. Initially Ellie and Dorrie would meet the visiting ships, and be already waiting on the dock when the boys walked down the gangway. The old white terrace house soon built a reputation as the place to go for the best food and some of the prettiest ladies in Sydney. For a fistful of dollars, silk stockings and a couple of cartons of cigarettes, the pair took care of the boys' needs. Ellie spoilt them with her home cooking, played the music they loved and provided alcohol long after the hotels had closed at six o'clock. The house was always jumping and taxis would be pulling up outside all night long, overflowing with dashing men in uniform and girls in party dresses. The place became known as 'the party house' from Sydney to San Francisco and, before long, the boys would walk off the ships, hail a taxi and drive straight to Womerah Avenue.

Ellie was a boisterous, jovial and buxom woman with a hearty laugh. In her mid-twenties, she had smooth chocolate-brown skin, a large bosom and, when she smiled, a front-teeth gap and dimples in her cheeks. She was a tough broad — loud and opinionated — but inside beat a heart of gold. Dressed in brightly coloured flowing kaftans, turbans and high heels, big earrings and lots of noisy bangles of quality gold, Ellie always smelled of French perfume. She loved what money could buy and the Americans' dollars provided the beautiful silk scarves she craved, not to mention gold and diamond jewellery and good quality Scotch. She was a great cook and threw extravagant parties providing tasty food, the best liquor and great music. Her favourites were the top musicians and singers of the day:

Nat King Cole, Ella Fitzgerald, Lena Horne, Duke Ellington and Count Basie. Given the boys were in town for up to a week, these parties cost a lot of money but Ellie had all that organised. She knew how to obtain scarce and rationed items and exactly how to wrap 'her boys' around her little finger to make the most of their bulging wallets.

The boys were generous and whenever cash was needed it was provided. Ellie was their favourite bad girl, great fun, good company and wickedly flirtatious. When the men placed the cash in her soft hands, she'd smile and discreetly slide the money inside her brassiere to rest against her ample bosom, giving it a reassuring pat to make sure it was safe. Men loved Ellie and Ellie loved money.

Dorrie was the opposite of her daughter. In her mid-forties, she was very slim and tiny in stature with short curly hair. She always looked neat in tailored slacks, silk blouses, dainty jewellery and flat shoes. Homely and unpretentious, she was polite and quietly spoken with a husky voice and a rattly cough, possibly the result of her constant chain-smoking. She carried her cigarette case and lighter with her like fashion accessories wherever she went, indoors and out. Her alcohol of choice was beer. Although she enjoyed the music and the parties, Dorrie always had time to sit and listen to anyone's problems and, consequently, was loved for her compassionate and understanding nature.

Grace and her friend Rosa were intrigued and excited the first time they were invited to Ellie and Dorrie's 'party house' one night when the Booker T. Washington Club closed. Ellie had approached Grace and introduced herself as Grace came off the dance floor with a good-looking young man after an impressive jitterbug display. Little did they know it was to be the beginning of a significant friendship.

On the way home from the club, Ellie would coax the American boys to purchase a quantity of liquor from the open 'sly grog' shops in the back lanes — it was important to know where to buy alcohol after hours. Back at the house, they would lower the lights and play the music of the day on the gramophone, with enough seventy-eights stacked beside it to last for hours. The couples would dance, drink, smoke, laugh and do whatever they wanted to have a great time. It became an enterprising and very profitable business when Ellie expanded 'a great time' to include enticing some of the 'ladies of the evening' from Kings Cross to come and entertain the boys, for which she would take a percentage of whatever the boys were paying. This side-business was operated in a discreet manner and was not obvious to the girls from the suburbs like Grace — she was invited to the party to have a good time. Grace and Rosa formed a close friendship with Ellie and Dorrie and began attending most of their parties.

At last the war ended in late 1945 but still the American ships arrived in Sydney as cargo and Liberty ships carrying merchant seamen gradually replaced the warships. The decreasing number of 'coloured' Americans meant there was no longer a need for the Booker T. Washington Club, so its doors closed in 1946. But the Trocadero continued to thrive, as did various other nightclubs, and Ellie and Dorrie's party house.

GRACE'S WORLD CHANGED one evening in early 1948 at Ellie and Dorrie's when she was introduced to a young American merchant marine. The couple of weeks they spent together were a whirlwind of parties and dancing. He was tall and very handsome and she didn't care that he was a 'coloured' man. She was twenty-three years old and they were in love. She dreamed of a life together in America and, just before his ship sailed away two weeks later, he said he would come back for her.

She was shocked to discover, several weeks later, that she was carrying his child. She confided in Ellie and Dorrie who assured her he would return and that, until then, they would help her any way they could.

What was she to do? Abortion was illegal, and far too dangerous and expensive. And suppose he came back to find she had aborted his baby? He would never marry her and take her to America *then*. It was imperative to keep this child until he returned, so she would have to look after the baby herself. She felt sure everything would be alright.

Finally, after tea one evening as they sat companionably listening to the radio, Grace confessed to her mother, expecting her to support her plan. Perhaps her mother would even take care of the baby while Grace worked. But her mother was appalled.

'Abort it. Adopt it. Drown it. Just get rid of it! That evil child is never coming into my home,' she said, her voice rising as her face flushed and eyes narrowed to slits behind her thick-lensed glasses.

No matter how much Grace sobbed, pleaded and begged, her mother stood firm, fuming, as she began her tirade, 'You will ruin your life. A good and decent man will come along one day and want to marry you. But that will never happen if you keep this devil child. No man will ever want you! And besides, what will the neighbours think?'

As her pregnancy progressed and her emotions seesawed, Grace began to see the hopelessness of her situation. She had written many letters but had received no reply and, as the months passed, she realised he was not going to return. How dare he leave her to cope on her own in this predicament? What a mess!

It was far too late for an abortion now, so she was left with no choice but to have the baby. But taking it home was completely out of the question. Her mother had convinced her. If she were to have any sort of future, an illegitimate child would certainly be a hindrance and a burden. Adoption was the only choice left but the feasibility of that depended on the child's colour. She would have to wait and see before she could make those arrangements.

She dressed to hide her pregnancy and went about her business as though everything was fine. She dropped out of her social scene and told no one the true reason, particularly her friends. Ellie and Dorrie offered her their home and insisted they would care for the baby but Grace refused their offer. She didn't want to be beholden to these women and felt she could still consider other options. One person she did confide in was Rosa, who had also met an American and was planning to leave Australia and marry him in his hometown of Cincinnati. Grace was happy for Rosa. If only her own life could have the same happy ending.

MY MOTHER GAVE BIRTH to me on that All Souls' Day in 1948 and any options left to her immediately disappeared when I was born chocolate-coloured.

To fully appreciate the challenging circumstances of my birth and the social complexities of that era in Australia, I might need to explain. When I was born, the immigration laws of Australia were ruled by the White Australia Policy (first enacted in 1901 and kept in some form until 1973) which aimed to 'keep Australia white' by keeping the 'Asiatics' and 'coloured races' out of Australia. The policy was gradually dismantled in stages by successive governments after the conclusion of World War II but, in those times, most white Australians did not know nor had ever met any people of colour.

Socially, it was a time when young women like my mother were expected to remain virgins until they married. Unmarried pregnant girls were either forced into hasty unwanted marriages or dangerous, illegal and expensive backyard abortions. If neither could be arranged, it was common practice for the young woman to be sent away to a 'home for unmarried mothers'. There, they gave birth and 'in the best interests of the child' were forced to sign adoption papers and give up their newborn baby, often without even seeing their child, let alone holding it. The welfare authorities considered it to be the proper thing to do for the wellbeing of the child. The girls were then told to go home, resume their lives and never speak of the incident again.

Illegitimacy was a social disgrace that could not be afforded by decent households like my grandmother's. Wrongly, society branded young women who had a baby out of wedlock as sluts and cheap tarts. There was no sympathy for the mother or the infant. These women were supposedly wanton and felt society's wrath and scorn. Unfortunately, during this era there were hundreds of women giving birth to illegitimate children and not enough couples wanting to adopt them. Couples wanted to adopt a perfectly formed, white Australian child and even many white illegitimate children were deemed 'just not suitable', so children from mixed and unknown racial heritage were considered absolutely unadoptable!

I was illegitimate *and* 'coloured'. I had no chance.

MY MOTHER WAS TOLD about a type of babysitting business where couples took infants to live with them and care for them, as a form of unofficial paid foster care. It was this or an orphanage; she had to make a choice. A couple was found who had children of their own and lived on a farm past Liverpool, a Western Sydney suburb. They offered to care for the baby if Grace paid them an amount each week but she needed to move quickly.

Ellie and Dorrie visited the hospital soon after the birth and when Grace explained she had found a couple who would take care of the baby, Ellie helped to arrange a car to take them out to Liverpool to deliver the child. Ellie and Dorrie were very disappointed that Grace would not let them care for the baby girl — it seemed logical after all, considering the baby's colour.

Grace returned to her previous life, living with her mother and going to work each day. Her mother had been right. It was better this way. She needed to put this episode in her life well behind her and move on. She worked hard, took care of her mother, spent time looking after and spoiling her nieces and nephews, and before long began going out with her friends again. The Trocadero was still her favourite club for dancing but when she was invited out on dates, she was more wary. She kept in touch with Ellie and Dorrie and continued to attend their parties because she liked the attention she attracted. She had regained her figure and her cool persona, ivory complexion and coiffured blonde hair made her stand out amongst the other women. Americans! She should have listened when friends told her to just have a good time. She did hope to be married but look what had happened to her because of her thoughts of falling in love and marriage. No, she would just take each day as it came and wait and see.

She was ashamed of herself: she should have been more careful. Her friends gossiped about women like her, those having babies outside marriage. How could she have been so foolish? At least nobody knew and she wasn't about to tell them. She didn't speak about the baby and anyway, it was her business and her mistake.

The couple who were looking after the baby seemed like nice people. All she had to do was put the money in an envelope and post it to them each week. They didn't expect her to travel out there as it was a long journey on the train then the bus. Still, she would have liked to visit the baby once in a while, just to see how she was doing. But she knew this would anger her mother and she didn't want to upset her.

CHAPTER TWO

Ellie, Dorrie and Freddie Dawson

AT THE SYDNEY STADIUM in Rushcutters Bay on September 1, 1947, Australian lightweight boxing champion Vic Patrick was knocked out in the twelfth round by black American boxer Freddie Dawson. There were no cheers; no one moved or left the building. Just total silence from the fourteen thousand shocked spectators as their Aussie hero Vic Patrick, lay out-cold on the canvas. No one noticed as a bewildered Freddie Dawson left the ring. With a lot of assistance, finally Vic shakily struggled to his feet after three or four minutes and gave a feeble wave. The crowd erupted. The applause was long-lasting and full of warmth and relief as hats were tossed into the air. Meanwhile, after the long walk to his dressing room, Freddie Dawson turned to his trainer, old 'Silent' Bill McConnell and asked, 'What's wrong with them Bill? They didn't cheer me. They made no move to leave. They made no sound.'

McConnell filled him in, 'You just knocked out their idol, Freddie. You'll get full credit when they get over it.'

And he was right. Freddie became known as 'the Dark Destroyer' and fought frequently in Australia, defeating some of the best of that era. He was admired by all, including Vic Patrick, as a champion athlete and a gentleman and became part of Australian boxing culture. Australians loved the American and Freddie loved the Australian women.

For years Ellie and Dorrie had attended the fights down the road at the Stadium and consequently, many of the international black fighters frequented their home. Freddie was their favourite and had become a good friend and regular visitor — a popular ladies man who charmed these girls and brought them gifts from his travels.

Freddie Dawson was also to play a significant role in my life. In fact Freddie Dawson changed my life dramatically.

Ellie first told me this story and, over the years, snippets were verified by my mother. She actually had quite a dislike for Freddie Dawson because, according to her, on more than one occasion he'd called her names and abused her for sleeping with a black man and then not taking care of the resulting child herself.

Anyway, one evening in June 1950, Freddie, Ellie and Dorrie were discussing Grace's baby and the whole situation. The ladies told him they were concerned about the baby's welfare because she had been taken to a farm miles away on the outskirts of Sydney and was being cared for by strangers. On the spur of the moment they decided to go out to the house on an impromptu visit, just to check the baby was alright. Freddie volunteered to pay the cab fare out and back, so the three rugged up against the cold and walked around the corner to the main road to catch a taxi. When Freddie asked the driver to take them out to Liverpool the driver queried whether the three black people could afford the fare. Smiling sweetly, Freddie flashed a roll of notes at him.

The journey took well over an hour and then, because it was a country road with no street lighting, they had to hang the driver's flashlight out the window to search for a number on the letterbox. As they drove through the gate, the car headlights showed a shabby and run-down house in an unkept yard. Dorrie waited in the car with the driver while Freddie and Ellie picked their way through the long grass and knocked on the door. From behind the house a dog barked, then a second joined in, creating a commotion. It was late and the house was in darkness but they waited until a woman answered, peering apprehensively through the half opened door. Ellie explained they had come to see the baby girl the woman was minding for her friend Grace. The woman complained about the lateness of the hour, suspicious of buxom Ellie and the stocky black man standing beside her. Shivering, Ellie persisted, explaining they had driven all the way from the city and just wanted a few minutes with the child. Eventually the woman gave in and showed them through the messy, stale-smelling house to a small room at the back. In the dim light they could make out a small mound lying on a dirty mattress on the floor, covered only with an old grey army blanket. Freddie bent down and carefully picked up the little light bundle, turning the child in his hands to examine her.

He was shocked to see that her body seemed covered in lice and she had what looked like bruises on her thin legs. Exchanging a horrified look with Ellie, he carefully rewrapped the baby in the blanket, then abruptly pushed past the woman and, still cradling the infant, stormed out the front door, Ellie hurrying behind. After a quick explanation to the taxi driver, they sped off into the night leaving the stunned carer staring after them.

Obviously, the panicked woman contacted the police, who in turn contacted Grace; so, by the time the trio arrived back at the house in Kings Cross with the abducted child, the police weren't far behind. In the meantime, Freddie, Ellie and Dorrie had taken the chance to examine the baby properly and were sickened and enraged at her appalling condition.

Dorrie opened the front door in response to loud knocking from a police officer standing on the porch. Beyond him, standing on the path at the bottom of the stone steps, inside the front gate, was another policeman, and my mother. The officer demanded to see the 'minor by the name of Sharyn who is the 19-month-old daughter of Miss Samuels'. Freddie then appeared at the door behind Dorrie and a heated exchange of raised voices followed, between my mother at the bottom of the steps and Freddie at the front door. The police demanded I be handed over to my mother but now Ellie weighed into the argument and flatly refused, then disappeared. Once the neighbours started appearing, drawn out of their houses by the commotion, Dorrie begged for the dispute to be continued inside the house.

But Ellie reappeared at the door with the baby bundle, demanding the police and Grace come and have a look at 'what those people have done'. Grace climbed the steps to the front porch and peered at me as Ellie opened the filthy grey blanket. I was thin and dirty, my black hair was matted and lice-infested and there were bruises on my legs and back. My shocked mother burst into tears. Freddie began cursing her again so my mother wailed louder as the police tried to usher everyone inside.

Finally, Dorrie was able to close the front door and lead everyone into the living room. There, the shouting and name-calling continued until the police were able to reduce it to a heated discussion. Eventually a decision was reached. It was quite obvious the people who were supposed to be caring for me had neglected me terribly. My mother had been sending them money but had not visited to check on me, mainly because of the distance. It was decided and agreed I would live with Ellie and Dorrie, Grace paying them a small weekly fee towards my upkeep. The police officers eventually left, and my mother with them, when they offered her a lift home.

My mother walked away from me that evening; it was something she would do many times over the course of my life.

Boxing champion Freddie Dawson became *my* champion that night. He was my rescuer and continued to be my hero. I don't remember very much about my life before that but I do remember flashes of that evening, probably because there was a lot of arguing and people passing me around the room. I know that, whatever happened, it was the beginning of the happiest days of my childhood.

MY HEALTH and physical condition was Ellie and Dorrie's first priority. The lice were treated but I was still very thin and not very strong. Immediately, they noticed a problem with my legs because I would fall over frequently. After visits to various doctors, the words 'malnutrition', 'polio' and 'knock-knees' were mentioned, so I was fitted for callipers and wore those and built-up shoes for quite a while. (To this day, when I am tired my left leg drags a little as I walk.) Eventually, my legs became stronger, my skin improved and my smile grew bigger. Over the next three and a half years I grew into a healthy, happy little girl surrounded by laughter, hugs and joy in a home filled with music and loving people.

My new home was quite a large terrace house at the end of a row of five. There were three good-sized bedrooms and a bathroom at the top of a long flight of stairs that I loved to slip down on my bottom, giggling as I bounced. At the foot of the stairs was the lounge room, leading into another sitting room. The space underneath the stairs had been closed in to form a broom closet, creating a short hallway that led into the big kitchen with a table and chairs in the middle of it. The backyard was spacious and sloped uphill slightly, with a laundry plus an outside toilet over in one corner.

Aunty Ellie was noisy and affectionate. She would scoop me up in her arms, nearly smothering me in her bosom while she covered me with kisses. I would run to her room first thing every morning, climb into her big bed and snuggle into her while she told me what we would do that day.

Most mornings, Aunty Ellie dressed me and off we went for our morning walk to the corner shop to buy the daily newspaper and cigarettes. (She loved to comb my hair into ringlets and tie the curls in pink ribbons.) The street, long and narrow and lined with tightly packed terrace houses, had just enough footpath for a small person like me to walk next to my large 'aunt'. Ellie referred to me as 'the baby' and the neighbours would stop for a quick chat or doff their hat as they hurried along to catch their morning bus. It didn't take long for the whole street to know who I was and, as I grew older, I would call out neighbours' names as we passed by their houses.

Nothing fascinated me more than the wonderful thing they called the radiogram. Jazz music was played constantly and was a significant part of my early life. Ellie would carefully put on a record then, clicking her fingers, would sway to the joyous sounds as I sat on the floor letting the music envelope me, singing along with the tunes I'd heard played over and over again. Then Ellie would sweep me up and dance me around the living room, both of us giggling. The trumpet rhythms and velvet voices of the female singers were often my last memory as I drifted off to sleep, snuggled into fresh-smelling, crisp cotton sheets.

MY FIRST RECOLLECTION of my mother is of sitting on the top front step leading up to the house, at age three or four, waiting for her to arrive. She got out of a taxi wearing a long cream-coloured coat with high heels and a pearl necklace and earrings, her blonde hair soft and wavy. She opened the gate then walked up the front steps. At the top of the steps she leaned down so I could kiss her cheek. She was so beautiful that she almost took my breath away as I breathed in the smell of her. I reached up and encircled her neck with my arms, clinging onto her and not wanting to let go. She gently released my grip, then she smiled. My love for her was instant; I couldn't take my eyes off her. I held her soft hand and led her into the house.

I loved my time with Ellie and Dorrie but I especially loved it the Friday afternoons my mother visited. My normal bath routine became a special ritual with my 'aunties' fussing because 'You gotta look nice for Mummy'. All primped and preened, I would sit on the top step and wait for her taxi to arrive, jumping up and down with excitement as she came through the gate. She was never late and she never arrived empty handed but usually with lots of brightly wrapped presents and new clothes for me. Always beautifully dressed in her office suit and high heels, with a matching handbag, she would sit with me on the sofa and listen to my stories of what we had been doing. I would hold her hand, with its perfectly manicured nails, and gaze into her exquisite face, drinking in her soft blue eyes, creamy skin, shiny blonde hair and her trademark perfume. I adored her and was starstruck by the beauty that was my Mummy. To me, she looked like a fairytale princess so I named her the Princess Mummy. Sometimes she stayed for an hour, sometimes longer, and occasionally she stayed for dinner. Every now and then she would stay for the whole evening and, after dinner, Ellie would play jazz records and we'd all dance about the room. Princess Mummy was the best dancer of all and she taught me to shimmy and shake and do the Boogie Woogie. I would collapse on the floor with laughter as they all shimmied and shook around the room. It was such fun! Sometimes the Princess Mummy tucked me into bed, telling me not to forget to say my prayers. Then she would kiss my cheek and be gone when I woke in the morning. In the beginning I searched for her but I wasn't upset because she had never been there when I woke in the mornings, ever. I had never had a parent on a day-to-day basis, just my Aunty Ellie and Aunty Dorrie — had *they* disappeared unexpectedly, I would have been broken-hearted.

One thing I remember from my childhood is that I was always gorgeously dressed, people often commenting on my clothes and how lovely they were. The Princess Mummy would arrive with lace dresses in musk pink or the colour of lemon drops, new shiny shoes, fuzzy flannelette pyjamas and fluffy slippers, a new book to read or tickets to see the latest pantomime show. Also, she never left without first passing a little envelope to Ellie.

ELLIE WAS AS LOUD and boisterous as Dorrie was quiet. Dorrie would sit for hours doing crosswords, chain-smoking, with her reading glasses perched on the end of her nose. On Saturdays, she would study the horseracing form guide from her favourite chair positioned right next to the radio, tuned to the races all day long. Because there was no telephone in the house, if she liked a horse for a win, she would quickly throw on her cardigan and flatties and scurry down the road, cigarette in hand, to place a bet with the local SP bookie. She often won. Dorrie was very close to my mother and I believe she was the reason I lived there. She was a kind and sweet woman, very polite and popular.

In fact, it wasn't just Dorrie who liked to win: the two of them were great card players. Dorrie taught me how to play cards and Ellie taught me how to cheat. They also taught me how to be crafty. Once a month, the Walton's department store man would arrive for his payment. My aunts bought towels, sheets and furniture on time-payment and, when times were lean, they would coach me then get me to answer the door. I would look up at the man in his grey suit and say, 'There's nobody home,' then slam the door. The following month when he came, Ellie would go to the door and apologise profusely, explaining that she had been in the backyard, last time, and she would make two months' payments.

Ellie and Dorrie's income came from Dorrie's wins at the races and their party house business, which was still quite prosperous despite there being fewer ships. Each month, the occassional American cargo ship still arrived and docked at Garden Island or Woolloomooloo, bringing merchant marines in need of a few days of rest and recreation. By the time the ships reached Sydney, many of the sailors had been on board for months at a time and were ready for some fine home cooking and good loving from willing ladies. Ellie provided all of that and more, finding the best recipes and the classiest women to satisfy their needs. Her business had evolved over the years to include some 'regular ladies' at the parties but the principle was the same.

One of Ellie's ladies was a woman called Big Red. She babysat me one night and I don't remember the reason but she locked me in the broom cupboard under the stairs. No doubt I was being a little brat and she thought she'd teach me a lesson. I was terrified in the dark and imagined spiders and scary things crawling on me. I kicked and screamed but she left me there for what seemed a very long time. Ellie eventually came home and asked her where I was. When she realised what Big Red had done and saw how distressed I was, she tore strips off the woman, threatening to punch her if she ever did that again. One day, when Big Red was babysitting me again, she fell asleep on Ellie's bed so, in retaliation, I cut off her much-loved long red hair with a pair of scissors. She woke up screaming and crying and threatening to beat the living daylights out of me but Ellie just roared with laughter.

Life was busy for the three of us in the days leading up to a ship's arrival. Dorrie and I would spread out newspaper on the kitchen table and, our rags dipped in smelly Brasso and pink Silvo liquid, we would polish the silver candlesticks, cutlery and platters till they sparkled. I enjoyed rubbing until I could see my reflection in the big silver trays and jugs while Dorrie polished the brass with the sharp ammonia-based Brasso. The house was vacuumed and the big rugs thrown over the veranda railings or the clothes line out the back, where I would help a sneezing Ellie beat out the dust and watch it float away in the sunlight. The house shone and tablecloths were starched and ironed to perfection, ready for vases of bright flowers to be placed strategically throughout on the day. We would set off with large baskets on expeditions to the fish and fruit markets and struggle back with them nearly spilling over. The butcher supplied mutton, sausages and chickens and Ellie cooked up a storm in the days leading to the ship's arrival.

Early in the morning of the big day, the three of us would dress in our finery. Ellie was usually in a bright, loose-fitting dress with matching headscarf or turban, co-ordinating shoes and handbag, and far too much jewellery. I can still hear her jangling as she walked. The final touch was her signature perfume, a little of which she would always dab behind my ears. Dorrie dressed sedately, in black or another dark colour from head to toe, usually in slacks and a blouse. I would be wearing my favourite lemon-yellow guipure lace dress which Mummy had given me, shiny black patent-leather shoes and white socks trimmed with yellow embroidery, and my hair done by Ellie with matching yellow ribbons. Eager and looking resplendent, we would parade up Womerah Avenue and hail a taxi to take us to the wharves. It was exciting when the American ships arrived. There was always a carnival atmosphere on the docks as hundreds of people met the ships carrying sailors from all over the United States, keen to have a good time in Sydney. Ellie and Dorrie hugged various fine-looking black men with strange accents, reeking of exotic aftershave. Their deep voices and laughter were unforgettable. The regulars returning to Sydney got to know me well, so I had a lot of new 'uncles' who would swoop me up in their strong arms and shower me with gifts of nougat and candy and special American clothes, like stars and stripes capri pants. Sometimes we were invited onto the ship for a tour.

As the taxis arrived at the house and the first jazz trumpet sounds blared from the radiogram, the fun would begin. I loved those days of music, laughter and partying. Big men with strange names like Uncle Virgil or Uncle Elroy would sit me on their knee and tell me stories of a wonderful place called America. As darkness fell, sweet-scented pretty girls arrived and, as platters of food were devoured along with many bottles of alcohol, the party in the terrace house became boisterous. The Princess Mummy was often at the parties too, laughing and dancing and twirling in the smoky haze of exotic, aromatic cigarettes. Late in the evening Mummy or Dorrie would take my hand as I roamed the room for goodnight kisses, then bundle me up the stairs to bed where I would either fall into an exhausted sleep or overexcited, slip out of bed and perched at the top of the stairs, peer through the balustrade at the noisy party below. Sometimes one of the boys would catch me sitting there and throw me over his shoulder and carry me back down into the crowded living room for another Jitterbug dance. They were memorable and very happy times.

The first person to wake in the morning was me. If Aunt Ellie was alone in her bed I would go there for my morning snuggle or, if her door was shut after a party, I would sneak downstairs, carefully stepping over the sleeping bodies. The rooms, reeking of stale cigarette smoke and perfume, were a chaotic mess of empty bottles and glasses and overflowing ashtrays everywhere. Many times I picked up the stylus from a record and placed it back on its hook. Heading to the messy kitchen, though only four, I would get my special bowl and fill it with Cornflakes then move the debris out of the way and sit and eat my breakfast. Usually within minutes, a sleepy Ellie would appear, kicking bodies as she passed to wake them up and send them back to their ship. I would then get my morning hugs and kisses and Ellie would join me at the kitchen table with her coffee and the first of her Camel cigarettes for the day.

Dorrie would join us a bit later except she had coffee and her first Bex headache powder of the day. Dorrie was addicted to Bex powders. I would watch fascinated as she went through the procedure of opening the small oblong-shaped box (blue, black and yellow) to take out one of the individually wrapped, thin paper packets. Opening it carefully and shaping it into a V, she would put her head back and allow the pinkish Bex powder to slide down the paper onto her tongue. Sipping a glass of water to wash the powder down her throat, Dorrie performed this ritual several times each day. (Dorrie wasn't the only one. For years, Australian women took Bex powders for headaches, neuralgia, influenza, rheumatism and nerve problems. An analgesic containing forty-two percent aspirin and the same percentage of phenacetin, plus caffeine, in each dose, they were highly addictive and eventually caused kidney disease, renal failure and death in habitual users.)

Dorrie constantly complained of headaches. She was a heavy smoker and drinker and her chronic cough and rattly chest were just part of her personality. She was also a thin, frail and sickly-looking woman but she had a big heart.

With and without the Americans, quite often as a treat we would all eat at the local cafés and restaurants around the corner in cosmopolitan Kings Cross. I loved the Chinese food but not the chopsticks. Our favourite was an Italian restaurant with red-and-white checked tablecloths and dusty old chianti bottles hanging from the ceiling. The owner was big, loud and jolly like Ellie and he always made a commotion when we arrived, fussing over us all. His seafood was my favourite and I remember the Princess Mummy showing me how to peel the prawns. Occasionally I'd notice Ellie and my mother having angry words with each other back at the house. It was a strange thing to see and a bit frightening because I rarely saw people unhappy or raising their voices. As the years progressed it seemed to be happening quite often during my mother's visits and I was confused as to why they would be upset with each other. Usually Dorrie hurried me away so I didn't see or hear what was going on. Still, it was distressing.

MY IDYLLIC CHILDHOOD came to an abrupt end the day I witnessed my Princess Mummy arguing very loudly with Ellie and Dorrie. She had arrived unexpectedly early one morning after another rowdy party to discover the house in disarray and littered with dirty ashtrays, empty bottles strewn around the living room. She was extremely annoyed to find me sitting amongst the mess at the kitchen table eating my Cornflakes. After a heated exchange with my aunts, she dragged me protesting up stairs to my bedroom where she started pulling clothes out of drawers and stuffing them into a small suitcase. Ellie, puffing up the stairs after her, demanded to know what was going on.

'I am taking her away because the goings on in this house are not proper for her to see,' said my mother, as she pushed past Ellie and shoved me down the stairs towards the front door.

'Since when did you become the Virgin Mary?' snapped Ellie struggling back downstairs.

At the bottom, Dorrie put her arms around me and tried to calm the situation, begging my mother to see reason. 'Please, Grace, don't take the baby away from us. After all, she looks like us, she's so happy here and fits in so well that everyone thinks she's part of our family.'

But the Princess Mummy refused to listen and continued to push past my aunts, dragging me by the arm with one hand and the suitcase with the other. Confused, I began to cry. Ellie then pleaded with my mother but when that didn't work, she became very angry. 'How dare you do this to this child!'

Princess Mummy turned and stared into Ellie's face, eyes blazing. 'I am her Mother!'

'You don't know the meaning of the word. You have never spent a night with this baby since the day she was born!' said Ellie, her voice trembling with rage.

Princess Mummy pulled me down the outside steps and pushed me into the waiting taxi with Ellie and Dorrie struggling after us. By this time I was frightened and crying hysterically. Ellie was pleading again while Dorrie tried to lean in to kiss me goodbye but Princess Mummy slammed the door of the taxi and, as we sped away, she didn't look back. I stood on the seat to see out the back window and watched as my adored aunts clung to each other on the footpath weeping. Who knows what motivated my mother to move me at that time. Perhaps she was concerned for my moral welfare or perhaps she was envious of my close relationship with my aunts. Perhaps she was fearful I would grow up to make the same mistakes she had. Whatever her reasons, her action was to prove absolutely disastrous for me. My face pressed up close to the window, I waved and wept as Ellie and Dorrie faded into the distance.

CHAPTER THREE

The Sisters of No Mercy

AS HEARTBROKEN AS I WAS that day to leave my doting aunts, I still would have walked to the ends of the earth for the Princess Mummy. No matter where she took me, I always trusted and believed her when she told me I would be alright. It was January 1954 and I had recently turned five so I didn't understand everything she was saying but, in the back seat of the taxi, I listened as she explained I'd be living with the nuns and she would visit me every Sunday. Then she passed me her white lace handkerchief to dry my eyes.

I asked, 'What is a nun?' and she said they were sisters who dedicate their lives to God, 'they'll look after you when Mummy isn't here.' As she was not there most of the days of my life, I thought I must need a great deal of looking after.

I struggled to stem the tears, wiping and rubbing my eyes with clenched fists, trying desperately to stop them falling. I remember inhaling deeply the smell of her perfume on her lovely lace hankie, crumpled in my hands. I knew I had to be brave but I was terrified. Why was this happening? Where was I going? I remember gripping her hand tightly and staring into her beautiful face. Why did she not take me home with her to wherever it was she lived? I trusted her when she promised me that if I was a good girl, everything would be fine. At that moment I truly believed her with all my heart.

The taxi pulled up outside a big gate at the end of a high dark brick wall. My mother paid the taxi driver, grabbed my little suitcase, took my hand, and we walked together through the gate and along a cement pathway down the middle of what seemed a large, ordered garden filled with roses in full bloom. I remember the heady scent of jasmine and the black wrought iron gate with the shiny gold bell and buzzer at the end of the path. I was certainly not prepared for the apparition who greeted us, dressed from head to toe in long flowing brown robes which were pulled in by a thick, black leather belt with strings of black beads looped on it. I was fascinated with the sparkling gold cross with the man on it hanging from the beads. I looked up at the kind round face with the lovely smile. Still, I squeezed Mummy's hand tighter as the apparition, who introduced herself as Sister Agnes, led us through two heavy oak-panelled doors and into an office with polished wooden floors and an enormous desk. Everything about this place was so shiny and clean and smelled of polish.

As we entered the room, another nun, who had been seated on a chair behind the massive desk, rose to greet us. She shook hands with Mummy then proceeded towards me, crouched down to my eye-level and welcomed me to Saint Martha's. I remember looking into her eyes — they were bluer than Mummy's. She too was pretty. However, what I noticed about both nuns was that they smelled like nobody else I had ever met. It was a fresh smell — I've never forgotten it. I later learned it was scented holy water.

I was very frightened and sad but I felt safe with the lady in the brown robes with the lovely blue eyes. I had to have something to hold on to. My small world had just crashed down around me and my sense of security was gone. I was just a little girl trying desperately to do what the Princess Mummy wanted me to. I just had to be brave.

The lady with the Princess-Mummy eyes was the Mother Superior. She held my hand as I kissed my mummy goodbye and, with tears again welling in my eyes, I promised her I would be good for the sisters. I really did try hard not to cry. It had been a big day for me. I hadn't had a chance to kiss my beloved Ellie and Dorrie goodbye and now I was left standing in a big house with funny-smelling strangers in long brown robes. But I was so brave as Mummy waved goodbye. I held back the tears as long as I could, my clammy hand trembling in the Mother Superior's. As soon as Mummy was out of sight I dropped to my knees and, wracked with shock and deep despair, sobbed into my hands, holding Mummy's lovely hankie. Mother Superior just stood quietly beside me until I was finished. Then, because I had promised to be good, I wiped my face dry and Mother Superior helped me to my feet. She said it would be just a few days until I saw Mummy and that made me feel a bit better. I would be good until then.

Another sister appeared and told me to follow her as she strode off, her long veil flapping behind her. Several times I had to run to catch up with her as she walked quickly around the huge buildings, her heavy footsteps echoing on the highly polished timber floors. As she showed me each classroom, the dining room, the main bathrooms and the laundry building, I wondered how I would ever find my way around. Upstairs, downstairs, along dark corridors; this was much bigger than Aunty Ellie and Aunty Dorrie's house. Finally, telling me to hurry up, Sister marched up another staircase to a place she called a funny name. I stood in the doorway of a long colourless room with plain walls and shiny timber floorboards, staring at the rows of neatly made beds lining the walls. Each was covered with a well-washed and faded blue chenille bedspread covering a pillow and a worn towel hung on a rail at the end of each bed. Neatly folded on a straight-backed timber chair between each bedhead, was a small pile of night clothes. It looked so cold and unwelcoming but I remember the warmth of the afternoon sunlight streaming in through three tall, curtain-less windows in the small alcove off to the left. Sister walked me down to show me the modest bathroom, with just a basin and toilet, at the end of the room. She said mine was the first bed back inside the main door, and gave me a navy-blue tunic, a blue short-sleeved blouse, white socks and sturdy black shoes to change into.

Back down the stairs she took me back to the dining room, which she now called 'the Refectory', where the same straight-backed wooden chairs surrounded long timber tables already set for the next meal. I was grateful to be shown the main bathroom again, with its rows of cubicle toilets and basins, then Sister hurried me along to a large hall, known as the Recreation Room, and there she introduced me to the other girls.

There were so many girls, and so many names to remember, I felt bewildered and dazed. A girl with red plaits and freckles bounded over to me, 'Hello. My name's Sally and I'm seven years old,' then she took me by the hand and led me around for the rest of my first day. Not only was I the youngest but, from what I remember, the only black child in the place, so I became a bit of a curiosity. The older girls made a fuss of me, feeling the velvet texture of my skin, my hair, and called me 'cute' and 'adorable'. All the younger girls were assigned a big girl guardian and mine was Elizabeth, fifteen years old with brown curly hair and a gentle nature, who told me she enjoyed playing basketball. She showed me off to her envious friends who all made a fuss, calling me 'a little doll'.

The rest of the day is just flashes of painful memory but I know that as I lay in my hard bed after lights out at seven o'clock that night, I felt completely overwhelmed by the day's events. I buried my face in Mummy's lace handkerchief, which I'd hidden in my singlet, and breathed in the sweet smell of her. As tears welled in my eyes again, I wondered what Ellie and Dorrie would do without me. How long was I going to be here? When would my Princess Mummy come to get me? As I fell into an exhausted sleep, I had no idea this would be only the first day of the next seven years of my life at St Martha's Home and Orphanage.

I WASN'T THE FIRST GIRL to have to get used to St Martha's. Established in 1881 with the encouragement of Cardinal Moran, St Martha's was originally set up by Mother Mary of the Cross (Mary MacKillop, founder of the Sisters of Saint Joseph) who appointed four Catholic nuns to form a community and establish what was known as a workhouse. Originally called Elswick House, it was later renamed Saint Martha's Home and Orphanage, Leichhardt, when it became an institution of care and religious education for underprivileged and homeless adolescent girls in addition to providing an orphanage for female Wards of the State.

By the time I arrived in 1954, the orphanage housed approximately one hundred girls from the ages of five to eighteen. Covering roughly two acres of land, it had expanded into five attached three-storey buildings in various stages of disrepair. Set amongst established gardens, these monastic-style buildings, in the rough shape of the letter H, were of solid dark brick with slate roofing and a row of open cloisters running either side of the main centre building. At one end was quite a large high-ceilinged chapel which backed onto a solid, imposing building with small windows that housed the nuns' living quarters.

Ask anyone who has been raised in an institution what's the first thing they remember, apart from the heartbreaking loneliness and feelings of isolation, having no family around on a daily basis — it's the ringing of bells. I can still hear their incessant clanging and the sense of panic in my chest because I was late getting to wherever I was supposed to be. Bells rang at Saint Martha's to summon us girls to wake, to the Refectory to eat, to attend class, to chores and to sleep but most often, to go to prayers and chapel.

After the carefree and undisciplined life I'd been living with my two precious aunts, this was certainly a rude awakening. No more fun, loud parties with glamorous sweet-smelling ladies, my beloved music and smoke-filled card-playing nights with handsome American sailors. Now it was down on my hands and knees on cold hard wood floors, cleaning and praying with Sister Aloysius and Father Flanagan.

WE GIRLS WERE DIVIDED into Juniors and Seniors with separate dormitories and classrooms, dependant on the age group. I was a Junior, as was my friend Sally, and Elizabeth was a Senior.

It was a harsh, Spartan and strict way of life. Institutions are run like clockwork and there is a rhythm to the regimentation. Rules were always adhered to, regardless and without question. The nuns were never to be disobeyed, punctuality was paramount and protocol was strictly enforced. Lining up in silence in a long line, we walked sedately from each activity of the day to the next.

Good manners were expected, without exception. Before each meal, we stood behind our chairs, hands clasped in prayer mode, heads bowed, and recited grace in unison, 'For what we are about to receive may the Lord make us truly thankful. Amen'. All meals were eaten in silence. We were drilled in how to sit at the table properly — with a straight back, feet placed together, the serviette folded neatly across our thighs and our hands resting in our laps, until the cue was given to pick up our fork in our left hand and the knife held correctly in our right hand. We were to slice and eat one forkful of food at a time and to place the knife and fork down between mouthfuls. Chewing was done always with a closed mouth. All food on our plates was to be eaten; no excuses. Then the knife and fork placed straight and side-by-side on the empty plate. 'Please' and 'thank you' were essential parts of our vocabulary. Disobedience, insolence, bad manners and selfishness meant punishment by strapping with a thick leather belt, administered immediately across the open palm of the hand. It was common for one of the nuns to pull out her strap and prepare to administer six excruciating strokes across the hand without any warning. The offending girl was dragged to stand in front of the entire dining room full of girls while the rest of us were ordered to stop eating. The strap was then thrashed across the girl's hand, causing her to cry out in pain. She had to leave her hand outstretched until the six lashings were administered, then take her place and finish her meal. Crying was inevitable but discouraged.

During the day, playtime was kept to fifteen minutes at morning tea time and thirty minutes after lunch. We were allowed to run, jump, skip, hop and chase each other in the playground but we were always careful not to be too noisy or boisterous as this was unladylike and therefore punishable. Evening activities included listening to music on the old wireless in the Recreation Room. We read books, played snakes and ladders and other board games, or did jigsaw puzzles, which were often left unfinished on tables to be continued the next evening. Many times we spotted one of the sisters furtively adding a piece or two to the half-finished puzzles as they hurried by throughout the day.

We all showered after five o'clock supper in the evening and before we went to the recreation room. We would collect our neatly folded nightie and dressing gown from the chair beside our bed, plus our small wash bag, which hung on the back of it (and contained our own soap, face-washer, toothbrush, toothpaste and hairbrush) then our towel from the rail on the bed, and calmly walk down to the main bathroom at the allotted time for our dormitory. The shower room in the basement was a cavernous, frigid room underneath the convent, accessed from an outside entrance. It had ten shower and toilet cubicles, each with a wooden half-door open at the top and bottom. There was a row of washbasins along the far wall but no mirrors. The floor was smooth concrete and the walls were painted institution-cream which had yellowed with age. Once showered and changed, the ritual was reversed and we'd place the towel on the rail and our wash bag and neatly folded uniform on our bedside chair, ready for the morning.

We were given clean bloomers every day but a clean blouse and fresh socks only mid-week. On Saturdays we all wore a light-brown cotton shift dress because that was cleaning day. Sunday was visiting or going out day for those lucky girls blessed with a parent or relative. We were allowed to wear our going out uniform, which meant adding a blazer and a hat. Some parents arrived with play clothes or dresses for girls to change into.

Mother Superior had told me it would not be long until I saw Mummy again so, Sunday after Sunday, desperately hopeful, I sat in the playground with the other girls who were expecting visitors. As each little girl's name was called and the number of us waiting diminished, so my distress and sense of abandonment grew. Eventually, my mother did come to see me but not for many months after the day she left me, and infrequently after that.

Children ultimately accept and adapt to their surroundings and, once I found my way around with the help of Sally and my guardian Elizabeth, I got used to the discipline and routine and settled in.

For a few hours each day, we had school lessons of English and Maths but mainly, Religious Study. My class teacher was a kind-faced Irish nun named Sister Theresa and I idolised her. She taught me to love literature and reading. Every morning we wrote the letters 'AMDG' on the top page of our work sheet, next to the day's date. Sister said the letters stood for 'All My Deeds To God', which meant we should dedicate each day's endeavours to God and try to do good work. I was a willing student and thrived with my patient and gentle teacher as she filled me with her messages of inspiration. She'd say, 'God helps those who help themselves,' 'Never be afraid to work hard', 'Be kind to each other', and my favourite 'You can be anything you want to be. It's up to you.' She instilled them in my mind, my heart and my soul and I believed her. I was a little girl in need of love but it was not at this address. The most I could hope for was a little kindness, so my soft place to land was with Sister Theresa. If ever God had left a saint on this earth it had to be her. In this dark convent with its strictness, cruelty and harsh rules, she was a shining light.

Punishment for any broken rule was severe, plus we lost privileges such as movie night that we would all look forward to. Television had not yet arrived in Australia so going to our makeshift cinema in the Refectory on special Saturday nights was a real treat. There was always great excitement and expectation as the tables were moved, the projector and screen set up and those hard wooden chairs lined up for the sisters and us girls to sit on. When it was Father Flanagan's choice of a film, which seemed quite often, we would watch Westerns with John Wayne, his favourite actor. I was usually on the side of the Indians.

From my first day, even though I was only five, I was expected to make my bed perfectly every morning with envelope corners and without a bump or crease. Other daily duties included scrubbing floors, toilets and basins. There was a roster system for all daily duties and no one was exempt, no matter what age. Immediately after each meal the nuns on duty supervised the dining room girls to remove, stack and wash the plates. Working in the kitchen after each meal meant washing hundreds of glasses, dishes and dozens of pots and pans. Several girls would be assigned to dry the tableware with tea towels and place the crockery inside the cupboards, the cutlery into the designated baskets and drawers. All benches were scrubbed and floors swept and mopped and the tables wiped down and set for the next meal. This was the procedure after every meal.

Preparation duty for each meal meant peeling and chopping mountains of potatoes, pumpkins, turnips, parsnips, carrots, shelling peas and cutting up dozens of oranges and apples for morning tea.

Sometimes cakes were baked for Mother Superior and the priests and served on a tray with a pot of tea. Plump Sister Hazel was in charge of the kitchen and happily cooked hundreds of meals a day for hungry girls and the sisters or baked a few scones for Father Riley's morning tea. She was jovial and loud and sometimes stole a bit of time to teach us to cook. The best times were when we helped her bake a cake because she would turn away discreetly to give us time to lick the bowl. She was a stickler for order and cleanliness and taught us to properly scour saucepans, to scrub wooden and stainless steel bench tops and polish them until they shone, and to mop the tiled floors and leave the kitchen spotless and shiny. Sometimes she'd let us sing while we worked, which suited me because I had a song in my head all the time and loved to sing out loud. Sister Hazel was a big fan of Doris Day and loved to hear us singing her songs, especially 'Que Sera Sera'.

The list of convent household duties was endless, consistent and done daily in addition to our school lessons. It was drilled into us that work was a necessity and was to be performed energetically with enthusiasm and without complaint. While the nuns were hard workers, they were also good at delegating, instructing us through tasks, no matter how heavy or dirty. They were also inflexible and strict disciplinarians, slapping our hands and the backs of our legs with canes, thick rubber straps and sometimes whatever else was handy at the time: belts with hard buckles, wooden spoons and coathangers were used to whip our bottoms. The nuns kept us busy washing, scrubbing, mopping, dusting, sweeping, cooking, gardening and weeding. Child labour at its worst (or so I thought then).

Saturday was the worst day of the week. All we did was work — from breakfast until dinnertime, with a break for Confession in the afternoon. Each chore had its own ritual to be adhered to. Outside surfaces were swept with a straw broom and inside floors with a soft broom, and the endless timber floors were scrubbed and polished on hands and knees. No one was ever excused from scrubbing the floors, down on all fours with a bucket of warm soapy water. Tins of thick, smelly polish were issued and carefully applied with a soft cloth, inch by inch, square by square, allowed to dry for a few minutes and then buffed with another cloth. Hard rubbing over and over until our hands and arms ached and the floor shone. No excuses, no exceptions. All interior floors were swept, washed, waxed and polished every Saturday morning and sometimes in-between, for punishment in the middle of the night, particularly for the older girls. The floors were gleaming and pristine. The cloisters or verandas, of which there were many, were also mopped then, once every few weeks, polished until they shone. Occasionally, if the nuns weren't around, we would quickly take off our shoes and skid up and down the polished floors in our socks, bumping into each other and falling over laughing.

Little girls and young teenagers worked side-by-side in the laundry building out the back, sweating over the boiling coppers filled with the convent's huge quantity of sheets, towels and clothes. These big tall tubs, set on a metal frame, came complete with a lid and a sturdy wooden copper-stick that we used to poke the steaming cauldrons of soapy linen. The wet copper-sticks were also used to flog us across the backs of our legs by one of the nuns when we made the mistake of giggling or talking as we worked. Corporal punishment was swift, severe and cruel, and a common occurrence.

Laundry duties entailed rinsing hundreds of heavy sheets and towels in two separate sinks, carefully feeding them through a treacherous hand-wound mangle and hauling them onto the lines to dry. The same was repeated for the clothes. It was backbreaking work. Occasionally, we were allowed to use the industrial washer and dryer but most days the nuns preferred us to wash and dry by hand because it taught us obedience.

In the basement shower room, no matter how hard we scrubbed the concrete floor it always looked grey and dirty, the greenish rusty water stains in the basins where the taps constantly dripped never seemed to fade and the walls always looked grubby.

Some nuns were kind. Sister Catherine was the gardener among them and she was mighty proud of her exquisite roses and blooms. No doubt she had to say plenty of Hail Mary's as penance for that bit of vanity. She taught us everything: how to prepare the soil, plant rows of flowers and vegetables then nurture them. Even back then, she insisted we wear our hats in the hot Australian sunshine, but had no qualms about sending us out to do hours of weeding as punishment.

Religious study was top priority. We all went to the chapel every morning before breakfast with either Father Flanagan or Father Riley saying the Mass in Latin. We studied and were drilled in our little catechism until we could recite it backwards. We were obliged to pray regularly throughout the day, Hail Mary and the Lord's Prayer, which came in handy for me because as soon as I was baptised at seven and made my first confession, I spent a lot of time saying prayers for my penance. The Lord's Prayer became second nature to me.

As a five-year-old I was fascinated with the religious side of convent life; it was all so unfamiliar and confusing. I discovered the man on the gold cross was Jesus. I marvelled at the Bible stories of his life but got very upset when I was taught the Stations of the Cross and learned how the people had crucified him. The stories of the different saints were also touching but, more than that, religion gave me something to believe in. I prayed every day and sometimes my prayers were answered. I told God all my troubles and thanked Him for the few good things in my life. Every day I asked Him to take care of all of the other children and some of the nuns. I even asked Him to take one of the cruellest nuns away as quickly as possible, which He did, eventually, but it took six years for that prayer to be answered. Now, as I look back, I doubt I would have been able to survive my life had I not believed in God.

OUTSIDE SCHOOL HOURS, Sister Thomas took care of the Seniors and Sister Lucifer (my name for her) was in charge of the junior girls. This Sister was a solid woman; a cold, sour-faced, middle-aged nun who had taken an instant dislike to me and was hell-bent on making my life as miserable as possible. She obviously didn't think I was 'cute' or 'a little doll', as some of the other nuns did and she particularly disliked the attention I received. I really did try hard to be good but nothing endeared me to her. She simply did not like me and took perverse pleasure showing it when she knew no one else was around.

I know I had never wet the bed in my years with Ellie and Dorrie, yet from almost my first night at Saint Martha's, I woke to a wet bed. And from that first time, Sister Lucifer made an exhibition of me, pulling back my top sheet and announcing in a loud voice so the whole dormitory full of little girls could hear, 'Filthy girl! Dirty filthy! Pull those sheets off immediately!'

Shivering in my wet nightie, confused and humiliated, I did as she commanded. I piled my sodden sheets on the end of my mattress with the stain in the middle; mine now the only unmade bed in the dormitory. I was so ashamed. Not knowing what else to do, I quickly washed my face and dressed, put my wet and smelly nightie on top of the pile and ran after the other girls to Mass, breakfast and school.

I was mortified when we all returned to the dormitory at the end of the school day to find my urine-soaked mess still piled up on my bed. Watched by Sister Lucifer, and in front of all the other girls, I struggled to turn the mattress over, wrap a thick rubber sheet around it, make the bed with the clean sheets she had flung at me and then, in front of the whole school, I had to walk all the way down the stairs, out of the building and over to the laundry carrying my smelly bed linen and nightie.

Every time, there would be a loud, embarrassing scene as Sister Lucifer made a commotion about my wet bed. The more attention she drew, the worse my problem became, so it wasn't long before I was a chronic bed-wetter. But the mental anguish was the most damaging. Several other girls had wet beds some mornings but I was the one she picked on and made an example.

Because I was young and had no one to tell me otherwise, I became convinced there was something wrong with me. If I was normal like everyone else why couldn't I stop? Every morning Sister Lucifer told me what a filthy dirty little girl I was; that I was smelly and no one wanted to be near such a foul-smelling individual. Each morning I would try to wash myself as best I could in the little bathroom basin, as we were only allowed to shower each evening.

I knew I still smelled and that, if I could smell me, others could too. I thought I must have done something very bad so I prayed constantly, asking God what the terrible thing was so that I could fix it and be able to stop.

As my bed-wetting continued, Sister devised a punishment for me. The first time, she barked at me to follow her down to the shower room in the basement. She filled a bucket with cold water, threw a scrubbing brush at me and stood over me as I scrubbed the hard concrete floor on my hands and knees. As my bed-wetting was now a daily event, this became my regular punishment, summer and winter. My grazed knees bled and I developed chilblains on my fingers in the cold months.

As with everything else in my life at St Martha's, this punishment became routine and, as with other chores, I would sing loudly to pass the time. The basement shower block echoed with me singing 'Ave Maria' or whatever new hymn I had learnt in Chapel, but whoever may have passed by that basement paid it little attention.

One day as I sang and scrubbed on hands and knees I didn't hear Sister Lucifer creep up behind me. She grabbed me by the hair. Startled, I yelped as she struck me across the back with something. The pain was intense. As I twisted around in her iron grip, I caught a glimpse of a wooden coathanger in her hand just before it slammed into my bony back again, almost taking my breath away.

'No Sister, please, no Sister,' I screamed as the wood cracked across my ribs. 'Stop! Sister, please' I begged, trying to wriggle away as the stinging blows continued. Her face turned an angry red-purple, the colour bright against her tight, white wimple. She picked me up and threw me across the wet slippery cement floor, my body slamming into the shower-recess wall. As I cowered on the floor, she strode over and began again to thrash me with the coathanger; white foam in the corners of her mouth and an expression of pure hatred on her face as the blows rained down.

'Sister, please stop,' I sobbed but the beating continued until she had exhausted herself. Then she straightened up, smoothed her habit and walked away.

'Oh, God' I whimpered. 'Oh God help me.'

Distraught, I stayed huddled against the shower recess for what seemed hours, my thin body aching. I tried to get up but I was so sore I fell down. My back was on fire, my legs were bruised, I couldn't stop crying and I couldn't stop the pain. I was trembling, with terror. This was madness I had never experienced before.

Frightened she would return, eventually I stiffly picked up the empty bucket, refilled it and finished scrubbing the shower room, groaning in pain. By the time she returned I had composed myself, though I ached all over. I returned with her to the dormitory to continue getting ready for the rest of the day. Of course I wet the bed again that night.

Some mornings she made me stand beside my bed, shivering and humiliated in my wet nightie while the other girls washed, dressed, made their beds and went to Chapel. I was ordered not to move. Sister would escort the girls to the chapel, return to me and drag me whimpering into the dormitory bathroom where she'd plunge my head into the toilet bowl and pull the chain. Other mornings she'd grab me by the back of my head and, with a brutal shove, force my face into the centre of the stinking urine-soaked sheet, rubbing my face into it until I was suffocating and gasping for breath. Calling me filthy and dirty, she'd tell me the Devil was waiting for me in Hell, as she viciously pushed my face again into the acrid, soggy sheets. Turning to leave, she would hiss, 'Get yourself dressed quick smart. If you are one minute late for Mass you will scrub the shower room.'

Knowing what that meant and holding back tears, I'd quickly dress then frantically run to Chapel and mostly I'd manage to make it before Father Flanagan walked out to the altar.

Sister Lucifer beat me many times over the years, each beating progressively worse. She'd grab me by my hair and physically throw me across the shower room floor. In a frenzy, she'd drag me back across the concrete, smashing my body into the walls. She would pour the bucket of cold water over me then kick it across the room in a maniacal rage, her face purple and ugly. She'd then beat me around the legs and the back with the big wet scrubbing brush. Like a mad woman, spitting foam she would rant that I was 'a filthy beast who'll burn for all eternity in Hell.' Some days she whipped me with a leather strap, forcing me to cower against the wall and cover my face and head with my hands as I yelped in fright with each stinging blow. The welts that woman left on my body bled for days. I was just seven years old.

Occasionally I made some excuse that I had fallen so I could request a Band-Aid but it would be years before anybody responded to that evil sister's abuse of me. I know the shower room echoed. I know someone outside must have heard something but nothing was ever done and no help came for me over the years that demented, cruel woman tortured me. The more she did, the worse my bed-wetting became.

The cruelty of this woman was so frightening that I often wondered if other nuns behaved the same way with the girls. Were other girls subjected to Sister Lucifer's violent temper? Probably not because they were faultless and I was the only one who was evil, dirty, filthy and smelly. Sister said so. I never discussed her behaviour with anyone ever, especially not the girls. I was much too frightened of her. Sometimes I was tempted to tell Mummy or perhaps my lovely teacher Sister Theresa but if Sister Lucifer found out, the consequence would be just too terrible. Some mornings when I'd rush into chapel late and quietly slip into the back aisle seat Sally had saved for me, she would furtively give my hand a gentle squeeze. I knew it was her way of letting me know she understood and to keep strong.

I became determined to stop wetting the bed. I tried staying awake all night by humming silently and pinching myself when I felt drowsy. I tried getting out of bed and sitting in the bathroom after I was sure Sister Lucifer had done her last round, hoping the cold would keep me awake. Though I was frightened of the dark, and the creaks and groans of the old building, I often sat on the wooden floors under the big windows in the alcove and listened to the passing traffic, wondering what my aunties were doing and if they missed me. Eventually I would give in to fatigue and drag myself back to my bed and sure enough, by the time I woke the next morning, my bed was wet and the nightmare would begin again.

Sister Lucifer decided the answer was to deny me fluids from four o'clock in the afternoon. Afternoon tea would be my last opportunity to have anything to drink until breakfast the next morning after Chapel. Sixteen hours! Everyone was under instruction and I was to be watched, particularly during dinner. At bedtime I felt alright but, by the early hours of the morning, I remember I woke feeling parched. I lay there, mouth dry, tongue thick, imagining I was drinking a glass of cold, clear water. I could picture the little sink in the bathroom at the end of the dormitory and all I had to do was turn on the tap. But I couldn't because Sister might hear the water running and come to investigate.

Searing thirst eventually drove me out of bed to the dark bathroom where I sat on the toilet, contemplating whether the consequence of being caught was worth the risk of turning that squeaky tap handle. My courage failed me. I finished my business and flushed the toilet.

I stood riveted to the spot as I heard the rush of fresh, clean water splash into the bowl. I flushed the toilet again. Then quickly knelt on the cold cement floor, cupped my hands under the stream of fresh water and gulped as many mouthfuls as I could, before the flow stopped. The relief was instantaneous and so was my utter disgust in myself. How could I do that? Drink from the toilet! Sister was right, I was a dirty, filthy wicked girl and I deserved to go Hell. I crept back to bed. In the morning, my wet bed and Sister's abusive tirade only added to my self-loathing.

Each night I would pray to God, 'Please don't let me be thirsty tonight,' but thirst would drive me to the bathroom, to the toilet and to deeper selfdisgust. Sister Lucifer could not understand how her plan had failed, so her bullying and maltreatment became more intense. She persevered in denying me fluid for a few months but I continued to wet the bed. Eventually she allowed me liquids again — a small victory for me.

Sometimes, I would survive the morning with verbal violence only, but the threat of Sister's rage bursting into a beating always hung low in the air like a black cloud. It was like playing Russian Roulette every day of my young life.

At one stage Sally joined forces with some of the other girls in my dormitory and decided whoever woke up to go the bathroom, would wake me so I could use the toilet as well. It worked for a while and some mornings I was dry but not many. The nightmare continued.

THERE WERE SOME FUN TIMES in the convent, too, especially the days we challenged the nuns to a rowdy game of basketball. I can still see those laughing young nuns, who also happened to be good sportswomen, racing around looking quite undignified with their habits flapping around their legs and their veils flying. They played a mean game but they could rarely beat our team. We were good and our best team were the Under 16's who had never been beaten in their games against other schools. The Sisters had to play hard to try to win against them and although the young nuns were excellent, they didn't have the opportunity to train as often as the girls. Still, it was fun to watch the nuns versus the girls.

I also loved going to Chapel because that's where the choir was. I desperately wanted to be in the choir and would bail up the choir mistress Sister Bernadette and beg her to let me join. To placate me, she said I could but I must first learn all the mass in Latin. So I studied and, with Sally's help, practiced until I knew it by heart.

I was finally accepted into the choir when I turned eight years old. I was so excited. I loved choir practice and singing in the chapel on Sundays and celebration days, and Sister Bernadette was kind and encouraging. Sometimes she would even whisper a 'well done' or 'nicely sung, Sharyn' and I'd beam with pride. It wasn't all hymn-singing though; occasionally the nuns lead us girls in some rowdy Irish singalongs and Australian bush ballads.

Then I was given the job of cleaning the chapel. Each day as I swept and dusted the honey-coloured timber pews, threw out dead flowers and polished brass door handles, I sang loudly, my lone voice bouncing and echoing in the high vaulted ceiling. The chapel became my sanctuary, the one place I felt safe and loved. It seemed to glow on sunny days when the sun cast warm hues of colour across the pews as it streamed in through the simple stained-glass windows.

Sister Mary Brigid, a very elderly nun, sat up in the alcove every day saying her rosary and praying, often with her eyes closed and head bent. When I first started chapel duties, the sight of her frightened me a little. I decided she was a hundred years old. All wrinkled, with gnarled hands holding her rosary beads, she never spoke, not even when I sang loudly. I deliberately sang as loudly as I could without taking my eyes from her but she never moved. I came to the conclusion that if she left me alone I would leave her alone and, anyway, she was probably deaf. Most mornings I would acknowledge her presence: 'Good morning, Jesus. Good morning, Sister!' I would call out loudly. No answer, so I would launch into the first of my hymns.

I was the chapel girl for a long time and Sister Mary Brigid was always there. So it was a surprise one morning to find her missing. The following morning when we arrived at the chapel for Mass, near the altar was an open coffin. As we filed into the chapel we were told to lean into the coffin as we passed it and kiss the wedding band on the hand. I had no idea what they were talking about. As my turn at the coffin arrived, I stood on tiptoe, leaned forward and screamed. Lying there was Sister Mary Brigid! I screamed again, shocked and frightened. My guardian Elizabeth rushed over and hurried me, traumatised, out of the chapel and as I passed Mother Superior I remember her shaking her head, no doubt at my irreverent reaction to poor Sister Mary Brigid's death. I had never seen a dead person and it scared the living daylights out of me. I missed the dear old nun after she died though. I had grown quite fond of her.

But I was often in the chapel for another reason. I turned to God and begged him to help me stop wetting the bed. I sat up night after night praying to God to help me but my prayers were never answered. I couldn't make it stop and I couldn't restrain Sister Lucifer. I was at her mercy. I prayed to God to make her stop beating me. After a particularly bad flogging, I looked at her across the playground and I prayed to God to make her die!

With thoughts like these I became a regular participant in Saturday afternoon Confession. 'Bless me Father for I have sinned.'

'Yes child, what sins have you committed?'

'Oh, Father, I told three lies, swore twice and wanted to commit murder!'

'Are you having such a problem with somebody that you would think such thoughts?'

'No, Father, I just want them to die and very soon if possible.'

'Well, my child, think pure thoughts and say ten Hail Mary's.'

'Yes Father.' Some days, Father would give me twenty Hail Mary's and thirty Glory Be's, so I started saying my penance in parrot fashion. I became very fast at praying. The faster the better!

ONE RAINY MORNING after a few years of abuse, I just couldn't take it any more. I was still sore from yet another beating, I was exhausted from lack of sleep and I had woken in a wet bed again. I was hurrying along the veranda towards the chapel when on the spur of the moment I made a detour and barged into Mother Superior's office. As usual she was sitting calmly at her desk. I limped around to her, looked into her lovely blue eyes and wept, 'I want Mummy!' I was so very sad and completely heartbroken. This lovely nun gathered me into her arms and allowed me to sob on her shoulder.

The truth of my situation was: I was a little girl who was in the world on my own. There was no love or warmth, just institutional care. Little did I know this was where I would see out my childhood.

CHAPTER FOUR

Do I Have A Father?

SUNDAYS WERE SPECTACULAR. I lived for the intermittent Sundays my Mother came to take me out. I refused to allow Sister Lucifer to upset me on that day. After her customary morning tirade and bullying, I would strip my wet bed, wash, dress and throw my soiled sheets and nightie into a pile, quickly remake my bed, then scoot down to the laundry before heading off to Mass. I would sing my favourite hymns loudly and revelled when Sister Bernadette gave me a wink as I sang the harmony accurately or all the lyrics correctly. She was very proud of her youngest choirgirl and sometimes patted me on the head, telling me how well I was doing. It made me feel very special.

After breakfast I would sit in the playground watching the front gate and wait for what seemed like hours for Mummy to arrive. The minute I saw her coming through the gardens I'd dash across the playground to the waiting area outside Mother Superior's office, always being told not to run by the playground-duty nun. Standing impatiently I'd hop from one foot to the other, anticipating the announcement my mother had arrived. Then, like a boisterous puppy, I'd bound the rest of the way down the long veranda to her where she'd bend down and offer me her cheek. I'd reach up and kiss her and breathe in the smell of her. God, she was so beautiful! Then I'd clutch her hand and chatter nonstop about everything I'd been doing. But never about Sister Lucifer.

My mother rarely arrived alone on her visiting Sundays. Over the years Princess Mummy arrived in the car of different Uncle Johns or Uncle Charleses, or 'uncle' whoever was her current friend. They were mostly pleasant fellows, not particularly interested in me but certainly keen on my mother. We had fun on Sundays. Sometimes they would take me to the Tivoli Theatre to see the live vaudeville shows and pantomimes or to the cinema in the city to see a musical, where I'd sit spellbound watching the singers and dancers. Most Sundays we spent at the beach or the park having a picnic and playing games. In Australia in the early fifties, most Australians did not know, nor had ever met, any people of colour and I remember the interest sparked by my presence with two white adults. People would stare at me and our little threesome, then turn away and talk behind their hands while my mother would fuss and tell me to ignore them. I guess it was the beginning of my awareness that I was different.

One Sunday on an outing, driving through the seaside suburb of La Perouse, we passed the houses of its Aboriginal community; dilapidated, shanty-style houses with broken and boarded up windows, peeling paint and overgrown yards. Sitting in the back of the uncle's car in a sundress, a hat and matching shoes, I looked at the laughing, barefoot and ragged children. Surrounded by their family and friends, the little black kids were running about chasing a football in the street and appeared to be so carefree and full of joy, I no longer noticed their scruffy clothes and homes of poverty. I sat in the back of the shiny car dressed like a black Shirley Temple, wishing I could join in.

'Am I one of them?' I asked hopefully, craning my neck to peer out the window.

'Do not be ridiculous! Of course not!' declared my mother, shaking her head in disbelief. I didn't understand why not because the Aboriginal people looked the same as me.

Occasionally we visited my mother's friends at their homes. Some had children to play with and those who didn't usually tried to entertain me by bringing out board games and colouring books. But my mother *never* took me home to her place.

Mummy and my latest uncle would also take me to restaurants and cafés, but it would all end too quickly when five o'clock came around and I'd have to return to the orphanage and wave goodbye to her once again.

I remember, I'd be brave and wait for her to disappear through the gate. Then, slumped with my head in my lap, I would let the tears fall. My mother never knew how heartbroken I was every time she left me. I'd never cried when she said goodbye at Ellie and Dorrie's because that was my home. But here I was left with strangers who didn't hug or kiss me, read me bedtime stories or play cards. Here there was no love, no compassion and little caring. The damage done in these early years of my childhood has left deep scars and has continued to have an impact on me, for the rest of my life. The emotional and physical abuse was debasing and humiliating. It undermined my confidence and self-worth because I was constantly told I was wicked and worthless.

It was after these visits that we would sit around the Recreation Room on a Sunday evening and chat about where we had gone with our parents that day. Some girls never had visitors, some had occasional visitors and some had parents who simply did not turn up. These little girls would wait eagerly, hoping in vain for a family member to appear. I always brought back bags of lollies or chocolates for the girls who had no visitors that Sunday because often I was amongst that group. Some girls' days out were similar to mine with visits to the beach, an amusement park or a trip to the circus. Then one day, one of the girls said she had spent the day with her father. I didn't know what that was and when I said I didn't have one, she told me I did because everyone had a father.

The next Sunday as I sat in a taxi with mummy I asked, 'Do I have a father?'

'Of course you do! Everyone has a father,' she said irritably.

'Well, where is he?'

'Your father is dead,' she said. Remembering poor old Sister Mary Brigid, I knew what dead was, so I was curious.

'Dead?'

'Yes.'

'Why is he dead?'

'He was an American. He came here on a big ship from America. When the ship sailed away it sank and he drowned. So he is dead. We do not talk about it,' she said with finality.

That came as a big shock. I remember looking at the Princess Mummy intently, thinking about what she had just said. Her words stayed with me for a long time and, although I've forgotten what else happened that day, I know that even as a seven-year-old I simply did not believe her story.

I do know I was fascinated by her explanation and determined to find out what happened to my father. Where was this place called America? I remembered hearing about it at Ellie and Dorrie's too, so I asked Sister Theresa who showed me on a map. Little did I know then that my curiosity about my father's identity and whereabouts would cause endless trouble.

DURING CHRISTMAS SUMMER HOLIDAYS, the nuns encouraged those parents who could to take the girls home or away on holidays. The convent virtually closed down during these weeks, while the nuns used this time to renew their devotions. Some girls were orphans and state wards and obviously had no place to go so a few were always left behind. My first two Christmases and summer holidays were spent at the orphanage with these three or four other girls and it certainly was not the joyous season the rest of the children were enjoying with their families. The convent routine changed and there were no school lessons. In their place, we prayed constantly or played in the playground or the recreation room with board games and books, supervised by a nun. We never had dolls or toys; in fact no personal items were ever allowed. We were moved into the nuns' quarters to sleep and eat, and we sat at the end of the same table as the remaining nuns. The only blessed relief was respite from the constant scrubbing, polishing and washing. The strictness was relaxed temporarily but boredom and loneliness were accentuated. I don't remember Sister Lucifer being around during those times, so maybe she was sent on retreat with the other nuns.

Christmas was a non-event for me as a child; in fact, I don't remember receiving any Christmas gifts until I was eight years old.

As convent life revolved around religion and so many Saints days were celebrated each year, Christmas at the convent seemed like any other religious celebration day. I didn't realise its significance; for me, it just meant more praying.

My mother had explained to Mother Superior that it was inconvenient to have me over the Christmas summer holidays. She had to work during the day and there was simply no room where she lived with her mother. Mother Superior accepted this for the first two years. However, she insisted my mother take me out of the convent for the third Christmas holidays in 1956. I'd just turned eight. After a meeting with Mother Superior in her office, my mother sat me down and explained I was going to spend my holidays at the house where she lived. I would meet her mother, my grandmother, and I must be good, polite and obedient and not run about making noise. I promised I would do whatever I had to: anything to be with my Princess Mummy. I was overjoyed. I had always wanted to go home with her and I couldn't believe my dream had finally come true. At last I was going to Mummy's house and I would be with her all the time.

Mummy picked me up from St Martha's in a taxi on a sunny morning in late December. I remember chatting excitedly all the way there until we pulled up outside a small red brick house joined to the one next door. Behind a low brick wall in the narrow front garden, there were rose bushes in a bed under the front window, against the house. So this is where my Mummy lived. I followed her up a short side pathway to the front door, each step full of anticipation. As my mother turned the key in the lock and pushed open the door my eyes fought to adjust from the bright sunshine outside to the darkness of the hallway. I was used to shining timber and the fresh smell of polish so, to me, this house seemed gloomy and smelled stale and musty. My mother ushered me into a living room so crowded with large pieces of furniture I almost didn't see the silver-haired women seated in a large tapestry-covered chair. She was wearing a floral dress with a shawl draped around her shoulders, a necklace of pearls and heavy black shoes with opaque lyle stockings. Her steel-blue eyes appeared huge, magnified behind her thick-lensed glasses. Standing on the shabby floral carpet nearby were two children: a girl I guessed to be a little older than me and a boy who looked about my age.

'Sharyn, this is your grandmother and your cousins, Stuart and Kathy,' said Mummy.

'Hello,' I said, with my best smile. My grandmother nodded curtly so I knew she wasn't pleased to see me. Her look was cold and stern and she frightened me. I had seen the same look on Sister Lucifer's face and I wondered why she didn't like me. My cousins came over and each kissed my cheek.

'That's a pretty dress,' said Kathy.

'Thank you,' I answered.

'Come on. Can we go outside and play?' asked Stuart.

'Yes but not out the front, only in the backyard,' said my mother. The children led me through the dark house into a kitchen (also crammed with too much furniture, including another dining table and chairs and a large dresser partially covering a hole in the ugly worn linoleum on the floor) then out through a laundry to a small but tidy backyard. We sat on the path under the Hills hoist and played a game of jacks until we were called in for lunch. My grandmother was abrasive and unfriendly and obviously not happy with this arrangement.

Living with my mother was all I had ever wanted since the day she had dragged me away from my precious aunts Ellie and Dorrie and dumped me in the orphanage. It was my fantasy, my dream, and I desperately wanted Mummy and me to live in a sweet little house where she would love me; just the two of us. In reality, I was an embarrassing and unwelcome presence in my grandmother's house, already an over-crowded three-bedroom dwelling.

MY GRANDMOTHER, ADELE SAMUELS, was short in stature and temper, and of medium build with long silver hair that she wore twisted into a tight bun. She dressed in calf-length dresses, usually adorned with a sparkling diamond brooch, and wore what appeared to me to be diamond and ruby rings. Inside her wardrobe were well-worn fox fur coats and shiny leather shoes. One night, I was horrified to see she had removed her teeth and left them soaking in a glass of fizzy water on her bedside table. She was a woman of contradictions. She drank black tea from a fine bone china cup and saucer but at night, she would climb out of her bed, hoist up her long white nightie and pee into a big white chamber pot she kept under her bed, even though the bathroom was only a few steps away. First thing each morning, she took her teeth out of the glass, put them in her mouth, picked up the potty and emptied its contents into the toilet.

Apart from my grandmother, my mother and me, there were also my two cousins and my uncle living in the house. My mother shared my grandmother's bedroom when she was home but Mother was away often, leaving me at the mercy of this unpleasant and bigoted old woman. My two cousins Kathy and Stuart shared the second bedroom with me and were my saving grace. Occassionally they would return home to their parents, only to come back again a few days later. Uncle Jack, a sedate and softly spoken man, occupied the third bedroom and was never home during the day. He left very early for work and returned promptly at tea time, his meal already prepared and waiting on the kitchen table.

'Hidy hody, everybody,' called Uncle Jack every evening as he came through the front door.

'Hidy hody, Uncle Jack,' we'd call back from the living room, as we sat in front of the radio listening to the evening serials and game shows after tea. He would eat his meal alone then promptly go to his room off the kitchen and close the door. We hardly ever saw Uncle Jack except on Friday nights when, as a treat, he brought home hot fish and chips wrapped in newspaper. He would spread the paper over the kitchen table and we'd crowd around, grabbing at the pieces of golden battered fish and the mountain of steaming chips. It was a delicious and welcome change from Grandmother's overcooked and boiled corned meat, tripe and tongue and stinky, transparent cabbage and soggy vegetables.

In the absence of my mother and cousins, that first holiday, my grandmother would quickly usher me into the bedroom whenever visitors arrived and firmly close the door. She insisted on total silence and threatened me with a beating if I came out or made a noise.

These visits could be hours long so I would either lie on my bed reading, which was my favourite pastime, or just fall asleep. Often desperately needing to go to the bathroom before she came to let me out, I would slip out the window, drop to the grass below, pee then climb quietly through the window again. I knew the reason I had to stay away from grandmother's visitors; she was ashamed of me — so ashamed to introduce me to people, it was easier to keep me out of sight to save herself the embarrassment. I was never allowed to play in the front garden and very rarely taken on any outings outside the house during that first Christmas holiday. (Many years later at an aunt's funeral, a cousin came rushing up to me saying, 'Oh, it's you! So you're the one they used to lock up in the bedroom when we came over to visit!' I felt humiliated and embarrassed, suddenly thinking I still should not have been there. Fortunately another relative standing nearby said, 'Well she's here now, aren't you love?')

A year later, during the next Christmas holidays when it had become too difficult to keep me a secret any longer, my grandmother finally and gradually introduced me to family and friends. She would loudly state that her caring daughter had adopted and brought home a little black American girl. 'Meet our little friend from America!' she would say, pointing at me.

No one ever questioned my grandmother and I had no idea what she was talking about and didn't understand the implications of 'adopted' or what it meant. And I certainly wasn't about to ask her to explain.

Grandmother was extremely unhappy with me staying in her home and told me so at every opportunity. She cared a great deal what the neighbours might think of her having a 'coloured' child living there and why, so I tried very hard to please her without much success. I needed to find a way to gain her acceptance so I wouldn't be sent away from my mother again. The answer came to me one rainy afternoon when we were home together.

I was reading while Grandmother played the organ, a large, square piece of shiny timber furniture that took up a sizeable section of wall in the cramped living room. It was a Hammond type organ which she played very well, making full use of the double keyboard, pull-out stops and the long foot pedals. She began playing 'Danny Boy' and, as the nuns had taught me this song, I stood up and sang it with her. She smiled. And so it became a ritual, when we were home alone, that she would teach me Irish folk songs, my favourite being the 'The Blue Velvet Band'. After that, when visitors came she introduced me with the classic line of 'Our little friend from America will sing now' and the two of us would perform our collection of songs.

I realised that to remain there I would have to win her over, so I appealed to her vanity and indulged her. Standing behind her chair, brushing her long hair, I would encourage her to tell me the story of her life.

'In 1837, my ancestor John Rice was born in rural Devon, a large county in southwest England,' my grandmother would often start. He was *my* great-grandfather. Apparently, at twenty-one he set off to seek his fortune and migrated to Australia, landing in Sydney in 1858. He'd come, having caught the gold fever sweeping the New South Wales gold fields. Grandmother told me how he had travelled over the Great Dividing Range on foot, a long, dusty and hazardous journey taking quite a few weeks in those days, to the thriving gold rush township of Tambaroora, a mile or two from the diggings at Bald Hill settlement (later renamed Hill End). Tambaroora had a swelling population of two thousand and because it had the first stamper battery in Australia (a machine used for extracting gold from the quartz rock) it became the centre of business and commerce for the area. By April 1860, John had done well and married a local merchant's daughter, seventeen-year-old Lucy Jane Davis. Resettling further west near the town of Orange, John and Lucy prospered on the land and over the next twenty-four years, Lucy gave birth to eleven children, of which the tenth was my grandmother Adele, born in 1881.

In 1885, there was a bit of a scandal when John Rice's head was turned by a twenty-six-year-old widow by the name of Charlotte; she gave birth to their daughter Alice in 1886 (John's twelfth child). When my great-grandmother Lucy died three years later in 1889, after a suitable period of mourning, John then married thirty-year-old Charlotte in 1890. Charlotte took on the five of John's children still at home and gave birth to his thirteenth child, a boy Edward, in 1891. Great-grandfather John Rice died in June 1900, leaving the remaining children in the care of Charlotte and my grandmother Adele, then an eighteen-year-old. Without John, the two women struggled to bring up the children, leaving Adele with few prospects of finding a husband.

In 1902, businessman John William Samuels moved to Orange from Victoria with his wife and five children. His ailing wife Agnes died shortly afterwards, in 1904, and at twenty-three and unmarried, Adele was employed to look after and school their children. A genteel young lady with correct manners who spoke with cultured diction, Adele was a fitting housekeeper and governess for the children of John Samuels.

In January of 1907, twenty-six-year-old Adele married forty-six-year-old John Samuels and became stepmother to his five children. Almost immediately, the family moved from the country to Daceyville, a fairly new garden suburb in southeastern Sydney and, by the end of that year, Adele had given birth to the first of eight children. Six children survived infancy, giving John a total of fourteen. Grandfather John gained employment at Way's Department Store as a floor manager and over the years, as her children were born and older children married and moved out of the charming brick bungalow, the constant strain of raising her large family began to take its toll on Adele. My mother Grace, born in 1924, was the last child.

Although she'd been stoic and resourceful through the Great Depression, my grandmother Adele's resilience was pushed to the limits when John died in 1937, leaving her and thirteen-year-old Grace alone in a rented, more modest home in Kingsford.

Now my grandmother was raising her children's children as well. Since her own life of hardship and compromise had left its mark, she had made sure her daughters were well educated and demanded they marry well — they would not struggle as she had.

Unfortunately, not every daughter's life had turned out as she had intended. Her eldest daughter and son-in-law had a large family, and shared a larger drinking problem, so she assisted, where she could, to raise some of their children. Her son, my Uncle Jack, remained unmarried and lived with her and her other daughters appeared settled in their married lives, so her top priority was my mother Grace, on whom she relied heavily.

I enjoyed her stories and often asked questions but, as I brushed and listened, I was always carful to keep my grandmother in the distant past. I didn't need to remind her of my unwanted presence in recent events.

MY MOTHER WAS ABSENT for the majority of the time. So much so that whenever she pulled up in a taxi my cousins would scream excitedly 'Aunty is home!' and we'd all rush out to the front gate to greet her. Always immaculately dressed, she would step from the taxi laden with goodies and groceries for my grandmother and gifts of clothing and treats for me and my cousins. For the next day or two, the house would become a hive of activity as we stripped all the beds and washed and cleaned and polished the place until it sparkled. Delicious baking aromas wafted through the house as she prepared meals but the best part was, I got to spend two whole days and nights with her. I would constantly ask her if she was home for good, to which she would smile and say, 'One day'. Then she'd be gone again.

Obviously, she worked during the day and my grandmother certainly relied on her daughter's pay packet to run the house and feed all the occupants. However, she was not there most nights either. She was glamorous, very social and, I assume now, looking for a husband, which was probably the reason my grandmother did not object to her lifestyle.

Over the years there were a few uncles. Uncle John I met most frequently as he would drive her to the convent on Sundays, wait in the car till we both came out and drive us to his very neat and tidy flat in Rushcutters Bay. He was a 'mummy's boy' who had inherited his flat from his mother and also her frugal ways. He had money but was tight and very boring, according to my mother. He worked in the city and would take her out for a drink after work, then insist on cooking her dinner at his flat rather than eating out. He never danced or did fun things but took her to museums, art galleries and sometimes the theatre. Uncle Charles, on the other hand, was good-looking, older than my mother and married (his wife was chronically ill, so he would never leave her). He and my mother liked to drink and he took her to clubs and fancy restaurants. He was more sophisticated and spoilt her with lovely jewellery. I liked Uncle Charles — he smelled of alcohol and we laughed a lot.

Mostly, my mother liked the Americans and I saw photos of her with many in uniform, both black and white. She continued to go out with them even after she severed her relationship with Ellie and Dorrie. She liked their good-time attitude, their social ways and sense of fun, their skill on the dance floor — and of course, they were very generous to the Aussie girls. My mother was an attractive woman so she had her choice of suitors but she hardly ever went out with Australian men, except Uncle John and Uncle Charles.

MY GRANDMOTHER rarely left the house; however, on the few occasions she did, my cousins and I, left alone, would get up to mischief. We loved to parade around in her bedroom wearing her rouge and red lipstick. We'd raid her large and musty wardrobe, draping ourselves in her fox furs or feather-trimmed hats and pinning or clipping onto ourselves as many of her jewels as we could. The finishing touch would be her heavy leather shoes. We would giggle and prance in front of her large mirror, always petrified she would arrive home and catch us, which was probably part of the excitement.

The family had a relaxed routine that I rather enjoyed each holidays, after my strict institution life all year. Breakfast was cereal with milk and burnt toast with Vegemite, followed by tidying the house and hanging the washing on the line. For me this was easy work. After a sandwich for lunch we were free to play. Eventually, over the next few years, as my grandmother's attitude toward my colour relaxed a little, we were allowed to go to the local park. We'd kick a ball around with other neighbourhood kids or play in the sand hills where my cousins were the cowboys and I was always the Indian who they killed with toy guns. Sometimes Stuart played soldiers where he was the captain and Kathy and I the enemy, which meant we were blown up by gelignite or slaughtered by the cavalry. At twilight we often played outside the house on the quiet street: hopscotch, or cricket with garbage bins turned upside down as the stumps.

That first Christmas, my mother gave me a doll. The trouble was, having never had toys but only books and puzzles, I didn't know what to do with it. The doll herself was lovely. She had creamy skin, brown curly hair, a pink floral dress, little white shoes and she stood about a foot and a half high. Long eyelashes framed her blue eyes, which opened and closed. What fascinated me, though, was how her limbs moved and what puzzled me most was that she said 'ma ma' when I bent her forward. Eventually, curiosity got the better of me and I prised open the small panel set into the middle of her back, covering her voice box. I pulled out the rods, bands and discs inside in an effort to see how she worked. Unfortunately my mother caught me.

'What have you done you ungrateful child?' she yelled, grabbing the doll and the scattered mechanisms. 'You don't deserve her so I'm taking her away.' I never saw my doll again, nor was given another.

In the back garden, Kathy and I played with her dolls, complete with a tea set; a new experience for me. Kathy's most treasured possession was her doll with a porcelain face that she named Rosemary, who was considered part of the family. As kids do, sometimes to be horrible, Stuart and I hid Rosemary and sneakily watched poor Kathy searching frantically for her. But mostly she and I played 'ladies' with her dolls while Stuart swung himself around on the squeaky Hills hoist clothesline. We didn't do that while grandmother was in earshot, knowing she had threatened to 'thrash us around the legs' if we were caught. Stuart never ever did get thrashed. He was Grandma's favourite, so he was warned hundreds of times while I was told only once before feeling the sting of that damn cane around my legs. Even though my grandmother and I had a connection with the musical intervals, it didn't stop her, when I had committed some childish misdemeanour, from rushing out with a long, thin, flexible cane and thrashing me, while she hissed through clenched teeth, 'You are a wicked, evil thing. Somebody should have drowned you at birth!' Each word was emphasised with a whack of the cane.

It was Sister Lucifer all over again. I couldn't escape these cruel women; they were everywhere in my childhood. I grew up being told continually I was useless, worthless and dirty, a filthy beast and an evil child who should not be on the planet.

Kathy was three years older than me, an innocent and at times shy girl with a great smile. Stuart and I were the same age, which was part of the reason our mothers were so close, both having been pregnant together. Their mother, Aunt Laura, was my favourite aunt. She was a sweet woman with a drinking problem who would get well and truly sloshed at family gatherings. She loved to sing, so she and I would often burst forth into songs like 'Take Me Home Again, Kathleen' and 'Show Me the Way to Go Home', singing energetically and in full voice. All us kids enjoyed singing along with her.

During these holidays, Stuart and I became close friends. He let me play with his toys, especially his precious fort from where he led his cavalry charge of toy soldiers to kill me and my Indians. I loved the Indians, either watching them at the movies or playing with Stuart. He was a terrific playmate and great company and together we would trek over to the sand hills near our suburb. We played great games of make believe, running and rolling down those hot sandy hills.

I treasured those holidays and, to me, they were the best ever. Returning to St Martha's towards the end of each January was always traumatic. I had no choice. I submitted to my strange, harsh and regimented way of life but my dream of living with my mother, just the two of us together, never left me.

CHAPTER FIVE

Running Away to Home

WAKING IN MY SOAKED SHEETS at the convent on a particularly cold and rainy day, I was not in the mood to see Sister's angry face and suffer another humiliating tirade. I quickly got up, stripped my bed and, with lightning speed, ran down to the laundry with my wet linens and hurried back to the dormitory.

Although I moved fast, the other girls had already left and gone to Chapel. I was leaning over the little sink cleaning my teeth, so I didn't hear Sister sneak up behind me. With one swift movement she grabbed me behind my neck and viciously hauled me over to the toilet then forced my head down into the bowl and flushed. I struggled to get my breath but the water whooshed up my nose and into my mouth and eyes. She finally released the pressure on the back of my head and dragged me away from the toilet. Coughing and gagging, I vomited all over the floor, water and vomit streaming from my nose and mouth.

'The Devil is waiting for you in Hell you disgusting child. Now clean up that filth immediately then get yourself to Chapel,' she spat as she strode out of the bathroom. I grabbed a towel from the laundry basket and proceeded to clean up my vomit.

Later that same morning I was sitting quietly under the covered veranda with the other girls while they chatted during the morning tea break. I felt dejected, humiliated and somehow distanced from everybody.

The duty nun asked if I was alright. Looking up at her, my eyes filled with tears as I felt a wave of hopelessness wash over me.

'She feels sick, Sister,' said my friend Sally.

'Well, down to the infirmary you go. You tell the Sister I sent you.'

'Yes, Sister.'

The infirmary nun had me lay down on a trolley bed, covered me with a blanket then put a thermometer in my mouth as she held my wrist, taking my pulse. 'Everything seems normal. Are you worrying about something, Sharyn?' she asked.

'Only that I'm going to burn in Hell for all eternity. I'm a very bad girl and that's what happens to bad girls. They go to Hell to live with the Devil,' I said.

'No, that's not going to happen to you. If you were really naughty you might not get to go to movie night, that's all.'

'But what if I was really bad? What would happen to me then?'

'The worst thing that ever happens, dear, is if you run away you will be expelled.'

'What's expelled?' I asked.

'Expelled means you'll have to leave St Martha's and probably not be able to go to another Catholic school anywhere. Now rest and stop worrying.'

It had never occurred to me to run away. Whenever I asked Mummy if I could live with her she always said, 'Not yet. One day. Now we won't discuss it any more'. No matter how many times I asked, the answer was always the same.

It was 1958, I was nine years old and I had already spent two Christmas holidays at my grandmother's house. Although I knew I wasn't really welcome and was only tolerated for the brief holidays I spent there, my dream was to live with my wonderful Princess Mummy. And I had to get away from Sister Lucifer somehow. Anyway, I was sure that once I got to Mummy's house, she would be happy I was there and would let me stay.

On impulse one night after lights out and Sister's last rounds, I waited till her torchlight disappeared and the dormitory was left in darkness. I waited a few more minutes then got out of bed, pulled on my dressing gown and slippers and crept quietly out the door, then down the stairs and out into the night, running through the grounds to the back gate. I had never realised how big and tall it was until I tried to climb it but I managed to clamber to the top. As I looked down in the semi-darkness, I knew the only way was to jump, so I did. Landing awkwardly, I turned my ankle. I felt a bit discouraged but I was not about to give up — I was outside on my own and it was thrilling. Now all I had to do was to find the Princess Mummy's house.

I limped across the dimly lit street, making my way past the row of small houses to the lights of the main road at the end. Parramatta Road was busy with cars rushing by so I stood on the corner wondering which direction to go. Unfortunately my determination was stronger than my sense of direction. Unaware of the dangerous situation I was in, luckily it wasn't long before a police car pulled up beside me and I was delivered back to Mother Superior, who wasn't happy to be woken in the middle of the night to find one of her charges had escaped. I wasn't expelled but I was given garden duty, pulling weeds for what seemed like months. Mummy was extremely cross when she heard what I had done and I was distraught I had upset her, so I promised never to do it again.

Still, by the following year, and after more beatings, I was more determined to get away from Sister Lucifer and go to live with my mummy. I was sure if I ran away enough times I would be expelled. The problem was, once I was over the back gate I had nowhere else to go but to head towards the main road. One night I had just managed the long drop from the top of the gate to the ground when the heavens opened and freezing rain pelted down. I wanted to get back over the gate but there was no way in. Drenched, I ran down to the corner in my pyjamas and waited for a passing police car to notice and pick me up.

As I grew older I became more organised and stashed a pair of pants, a top and shoes in a hole near the grotto in the gardens. I would kneel in front of the Virgin Mary's statue in the grotto and, staring into her serene face, pray for her to help me find my way to Mummy's house. As she was Jesus' mother I knew she would understand and help me go home to live with my Princess Mummy. But the police always found me before I could get very far.

Many times Sister Theresa sat quietly with me, explaining the dangers of running away in the middle of the night. I listened patiently but had no intention of changing my mind. I was on a mission now and nothing was going to stop me. I begged my mother almost every visiting day but her answer was always the same: it was inconvenient and not possible yet, but one day. Well, 'one day' was too far away for me. I knew I would be stuck in the convent until I was eighteen if I didn't get out before. If I ran away enough times, expulsion was a certainty. The only place left for me to live, then, would be my mother's house — I would do whatever I had to do to make that happen.

As I continued to run away I became more street-smart. I would slip in and out of back streets, climb over people's fences and run through their backyards. When I was thirsty I looked for bottles of milk left on people's doorstep by the milkman in the early hours of the morning. I would pass an Italian man with a fruit barrow who loved to sing Italian songs and arias. Occasionally I crept up and stole an orange or an apple and by the time I was eleven he would call out to me, throwing a piece of fruit through the air.

'Good morning! Here, catch!' Then he would laugh, '*Ciao, Bella.*'

I wonder who he thought I was.

It wasn't all rosy on the streets of Sydney in 1959. I had a dreadful fear of the dark and was paralysed with fright whenever I saw someone approaching me. I'd crouch down on a doorstep, cowering and wishing for the warmth of my bed in the dormitory. Noises in the night would have me blindly running in terror and often I imagined spiders crawling and jumping on me. Plus, the weather wasn't always my friend; the raw winter winds whipped at my face and icy rain often chilled me to the bone.

I was followed by men in cars and men on foot, not to mention the dogs. They chased me, barking and yelping as I ran headlong in fear. I learnt how to avoid cruising police cars; however, there were many times when I wanted to call out to them for help. I was a streetwise kid on the lookout for danger and there was plenty out there. It was my fierce determination to find my mother's house that kept me going. Another problem was my poor sense of direction and frequently I was lost. That led to confusion and frustration, not to mention exhaustion. I was a frightened little girl desperately needing to be loved. It really was that simple.

WHEN I WAS ELEVEN, one Sunday in February, Mummy found the welts on my back and bruises on my body as she helped me try on a new swimsuit she had bought me. Weeping and hiccuping, I poured out six years of pain as I told her about Sister Lucifer's beatings. All she did was hand me her lace-edged handkerchief and tell me to dry my eyes; she would sort it out with Mother Superior when she took me back at five o'clock. All the adults in my life showed appropriate concern but not one of them counselled me in any way. There were no words of kindness, compassion or therapy. No comforting either. My mother felt she had done the right thing by reporting my injuries but once done, that was that. The bruises on my body healed but my soul never did and my heart was broken. After all those years of beatings, pain and humiliation, nobody even bothered to give me a hug. I felt I was of little significance. Nobody mentioned it again, not then, not ever. That was the last time I saw Sister Lucifer though; she disappeared faster than my bruises. So did my bed-wetting.

I asked my mother each time she visited, could I live with her, but she still refused. I would follow that with questions about my father: who was he? Where was he? What did he look like? But she would become irritated and snap at me. 'He is dead. There is nothing left to be said about that.' Then she'd change the subject.

My fantasy was for my Princess Mummy to welcome me with open arms. We would live in a sweet little house together, just the two of us, to make up for all of the years we had been apart. As I wandered the empty streets of Sydney's suburbs, in the dark or as dawn was breaking, I dreamed. If I could just make it to Mother's house then my life would be perfect. But nothing in life is perfect. I hadn't yet learned to be careful of what you wish for. Sometimes wishes come true.

AS THE YEARS PASSED I had watched many girls come and go. By September 1960, I was almost twelve and the longest-staying resident at Saint Martha's. Elizabeth had graduated at age eighteen and had been gone since I was nine. Sally's mother's situation had improved the year before, so an excited Sally had deserted me and fulfilled her dream of living with her mother. I missed Sally terribly and envied her happy life. Then a cheeky, fun girl named Denise started at St Marthas and became my new best friend.

Denise laughed when I told her about my adventures, walking for miles and getting hopelessly lost. By now I knew my mother lived in the suburb of Kingsford, about eleven miles away.

'What! You walk?'

'Yes,' I said. Silly girl — how else did she think I would get there?

'Why do you walk?'

'To get where I'm going, dummy.'

'Shaz, nobody walks!'

'Of course I walk, how else am I going to get there?'

'You catch a tram, dopey,' said Denise, laughing.

'A tram? I don't know anything about trams,' I said.

'Well, I'll show you. When are you going again?'

'You'll runaway with me?' I asked excitedly.

'Yep. As long as we don't walk!' She laughed and we shook hands.

'OK. Now what's your mother's address? We need a tram timetable for which tram numbers to catch. Instead of walking all night, we'll be there in half an hour!'

'Are you serious?' I asked.

'Yes, nobody walks. I can't believe you are walking!' She just kept laughing.

So we ran away together and her plan worked beautifully. In the early mist of a spring morning we walked down to my mother's house from the tram stop. Then Denise hugged me goodbye and headed in the opposite direction. Her mission was not to go home, she had just wanted to get away from the convent and it had been convenient to have me as company. For me, she knew all about trams, which had made my escape so much easier and safer.

I sat patiently on the brick front fence of the house, waiting for some movement inside before I announced my arrival. I noticed my grandmother peek through the front curtains then disappear, no doubt to tell my mother (who would have been getting ready for work) that I was sitting on the fence.

My mother and grandmother were not at all happy to see me. Nobody was having a good day that day, except me. After the police arrived at the house, they drove my mother and me back to Saint Martha's. Mother Superior explained to my mother I would now be expelled because they could not be held responsible for my safety while I roamed the streets of Sydney by myself, plus the nuns had run out of ways to keep me in. Mother pleaded and cried but Mother Superior stood firm.

Though I kept a straight face I was secretly delighted. At last I was going to live with my mother! I was careful not to show my excitement and sat quietly, looking remorseful.

I did cry when I said goodbye to my friends and my favourite nuns, especially saintly Sister Theresa who hugged me and made me promise to be a good girl. She then whispered my favourite saying: 'You can be anything you want to be. It's up to you. God bless you Sharyn.'

'God bless you too, Sister,' I answered as tears ran down my cheeks. I hugged my choir teacher Sister Bernadette who had steadfastly refused many times to remove me from the choir as punishment each time I ran away. She had encouraged me to sing, repeatedly telling me over the years what a lovely voice I had.

As the taxi drove away I looked back with little remorse at the convent, yet Saint Martha's had been my home for so many years. I had arrived the youngest and now left as the longest staying student of them all. I had lost my innocence in that place; my childhood had been taken away from me. But I had survived it. I was so excited to be leaving.

On our way back to my grandmother's house, sitting in the back seat of the taxi with my mother, she fumed and chastised me all the way. Over and over she kept exclaiming how inconvenient this was, how uncaring I was of her situation, and how was she going to sort out this disaster, as she called it.

I HAD FINALLY FORCED MY MOTHER'S HAND. There was no alternative for me but to live permanently with them in the house. My grandmother was not at all happy with the situation and quite hostile but decided that if she maintained the story, that I was adopted from America, she would save face with the neighbours and relatives and preserve my mother's reputation. Meanwhile, as in the school holidays, my mother continued to be absent most of the time.

I was immediately sent to the local primary school. It was October 1960, the final school term for the year and my last few months of primary school before starting at an all-girls high school the following January.

Life with my grandmother was not ideal but certainly better than the convent. She only just tolerated my presence and didn't hesitate to tell me so. I tried hard to win her approval by helping to prepare meals, cleaning the house and doing the washing: all the chores that were second nature to me. Still, it didn't stop her whipping me across the legs with that stinging cane when she considered I had misbehaved.

'I'm not going to let you ruin my daughter's life anymore than you already have, you ungrateful thing,' she'd screech at me; or her favourite, which she always fell back on, 'You are the worst thing that ever happened to my daughter. Someone should have drowned you at birth.'

I endured days of icy silence so I spent most of the time in my room reading and waiting expectantly for those occasional evenings when my mother came home for the night or stayed, sometimes for a day or two. My uncle Jack continued to live there and Stuart and Kathy came and went every few weeks, which I looked forward to because their company was a welcome respite from my grandmother's cold disdain.

I WAS NOW TWELVE but I easily looked fifteen. I was tall for my age, had matured early and was well developed. Due to my extremely sheltered upbringing in the convent, however, my emotional development was well behind. I was completely naïve when it came to contact and experience with boys, except for my cousin Stuart who was like a brother. Any knowledge I had, I had learned from my idols Doris Day and Sandra Dee by watching their cheesy movie romances of chaste kisses and innocent flirting.

Each Saturday afternoon, my cousin Stuart and I caught the bus to the cinema to watch the news of the world, two cartoons then two feature films. Sundays, it was skating at the local ice rink — where I first met Ronny, who winked at me one day as I skated by. He was much older, about eighteen, and had already left school and was working at a local stables tending the horses. I was incredibly shy and blushed whenever I saw him.

'Do you like horses?' he asked one day, catching me off guard as I was leaving the rink to go home.

I shrugged. He smiled and said, 'Meet me next Saturday and I'll show you the horses.'

I visited the stables a few times and he showed me how he groomed the horses and cleaned out the stalls. My cousin Stuart did not approve, and told me so, but I was smitten with Ronny and he made me feel very special. Some of the girls at my high school talked about their boyfriends and I so wanted to be just like them. When Ronny paid attention to me I felt I had a boyfriend too and I was sure he felt the same way.

For my thirteenth birthday my mother had taken me shopping and bought me a special dress. It was called a Brigitte Bardot dress, the must-have dress of that summer and a change from my blue jeans and T-shirt.

The following Saturday afternoon, on my way to the cinema with Stuart, I felt good in my new dress. I had not expected to see Ronny leaning against his car outside the theatre. He gave me a wolf-whistle as I walked past.

'Shut up creep,' said Stuart and headed toward the ticket booth. Ronny laughed and called me over.

'Meet me here outside in half an hour,' he whispered in my ear. Blushing, I hurried to join Stuart as he purchased our tickets for the show.

'What did he want?' asked Stuart.

'Nothing.' I said too quickly, feeling guilty for misleading Stuart.

'Stay away from him — he's no good,' said Stuart. What would he know, I thought.

Just after the news of the world was shown, I told Stuart I had to go to the bathroom.

'Hurry up,' he whispered.

'Won't be long,' I whispered back, soon picking my way out of the darkened theatre and hurrying outside to Ronny waiting in his car. We drove the short distance to the stables, where he led me by the hand inside.

'There's something up there I want to show you,' he said, pointing to a wooden ladder leading to a platform. Then he climbed up and disappeared over the top. 'Where are you?' he called out. I remember how the heat from the November sun, beating down on the barn's tin roof, had mingled the acrid smells of hay and horses in the steamy atmosphere.

I looked up in the direction of his voice then scrambled up the ladder to the loft. As I climbed onto the platform I could see he was propped up on one elbow, stretched out on a small bed covered with a grey blanket. He whistled again at the sight of me.

'You look real good,' he said.

'Thanks. Mum bought it for my birthday.'

'I didn't buy you anything,' he said, patting the bed for me to sit beside him, a puff of dust rising as he did so. I walked over and sat down. He sat up, leaned over and kissed my cheek, then held my chin in his hands. 'Happy birthday pretty lady,' he said softly.

He leaned forward till our lips met. I had never been kissed before and it was nice. I felt just like Sandra Dee in one of her movies and I really liked Ronny. Now his mouth was on my neck and it didn't take long for the soft kisses to become more intense. He pushed me back on the bed, feeling my breasts. I started to protest but he whispered, 'Let me look at you baby. It's alright,' kissing me again as he started removing my dress and shoes, leaving me with just my bra and underpants on. His hands were all over me. I felt confused but he kept kissing me so I kissed him back. Now his hands were stroking my thighs then his fingers were between my legs. I pushed him away, my senses telling me this was wrong.

'No, please don't,' I said.

'Hey I won't hurt you, I promise. You ever done this before?' he asked. I shook my head. 'That's OK, I'll be gentle.'

By now he had removed my bra and underpants and I was lying naked on the bed. His fingers were inside me, his breathing was heavy and his mouth was wet, kissing me. In one quick movement he was on top of me, pushing my thighs apart and before I realised what was happening, there was a shock of searing pain as he penetrated me. I could hardly breathe for pain and the weight of his body as he hammered his penis into me, again and again. His breath was hot and loud in my ear then, abruptly, he was moaning then laying still, his weight pushing me into the hard bed springs and scratchy blanket. A male voice called out as the sound of footsteps came up the ladder, 'Hey Ronny, you here?' It was David, a friend of Ronny's who I had also met at the stables.

'Oh, sorry,' he said as he saw us. 'Mr Watson wants you straight away.'

Ronny jumped off the bed, quickly pulled on his jeans and hurried towards the ladder saying, 'I'll be back in a minute. Look after my girl for me will you, mate?'

David's eyes travelled over my body as I struggled in my confusion to grab my lovely new dress, crumpled on the floor, and cover myself. I stared numbly at him as he sat down on the bed next to me.

'Sure, I'll look after you. Don't you worry, love,' he said, 'I've got sisters.'

Shaking my head and mumbling protests, I was trying to put the dress over my head when he reached up and pulled it away. 'Hey, don't worry about covering yourself. You're real nice.' He leaned over to kiss me.

His breath smelled of cigarettes. I tried to jerk away but he pushed me down on the bed. Pinning me with one hand, he quickly unzipped his jeans with the other. Suddenly he too was on top of me, forcing himself into me. I fought to get my breath and cry out but he kept ramming himself inside me, hurting me. The pain was so intense I thought I was going to pass out. I wish I had! Then I heard another voice.

'Hey, what are you doing?' said a man, pulling David off me. They began to argue then David ran to the ladder and was gone.

'It's OK love,' said the stranger.

Dazed, I got off the bed and was struggling to pull on my underpants when the stranger put his arm around my shoulders and led me to sit down on the bed again. Someone is going to help me finally, I thought.

But he was all over me too. I pushed him away and tried to stand but this was a strong man. He pushed me violently into the bed, shoving my face back with his hand. He smelled and was rough and didn't have much to say. I lay pinned under his weight with my eyes tightly shut, willing the nightmare to stop, as he penetrated me and ejaculated quickly. Now I was crying, struggling, shocked and frightened. What was happening? Where was Ronny?

I heard voices below.

It was my cousin Stuart, 'Get my cousin down here now or I'll get the police!' he yelled. The man on top of me got off, looking down at me as he dressed and said with a smirk on his face, 'All you black sheilas are the same, Midnight.'

Weeping uncontrollably, with trembling hands I tried to put on my clothes. My lovely new birthday dress was crushed and my underpants were sodden from wiping away the stickiness from between my legs. I couldn't stop shaking. The throbbing pain between my legs made me feel sick and I was so frightened. What had just happened? Who were they? Where was Ronny?

Trying to compose myself as I gingerly climbed down the ladder, I saw David and the stranger running away from the stables.

Stuart rushed over to me. 'Are you alright? You shouldn't have disappeared like that. I've been searching for you. What did those blokes do to you?'

'Nothing. They did nothing. Promise you won't say anything?' I pleaded.

'I'm going to tell Aunty.'

'No! Please don't. I'm alright. Nothing happened. They just talked to me.'

He stopped and looked into my troubled face, 'Cousin, what happened?'

'Nothing! Nothing happened and you promise me you will say nothing. I will get into big trouble if you say anything. Promise?' He nodded and helped support me with his arm through mine as we hurried to the bus stop.

Warily, I walked into my grandmother's house then straight to the bathroom and locked the door. I was still in shock and felt completely filthy. I carefully climbed into the shower and began scrubbing at my skin with soap and a brush under the hot water, crying and shaking. I felt so dirty no amount of scrubbing would ever clean me again. Then I sat on the floor of the bathroom and wept. Eventually I wrapped myself in my dressing gown and, careful to put on a good act, walked sedately into my bedroom. As I sat on my bed, I could hear Stuart in the living room with my grandmother. Suddenly she thrust open the door, her face flushed red and eyes narrowed.

'You been sleeping with boys in your petticoat?'

'No, Grandma,' I answered quickly, shaking my head.

'You had better keep your dirty self away from any trouble, do you hear me? Don't you go giving this family a bad name!'

My life had changed forever. I felt depressed and blamed myself for what had happened. Sister Lucifer had been right all along: I was a bad girl, a dirty girl, and I deserved what I got. I considered myself a tramp and a slut and I hated myself.

I had just turned thirteen.

During those years of abuse in the convent I had remained positive and always tried to find the smallest joy in most situations but now any self-confidence I had left was completely gone. I never mentioned the rape to my mother and was glad she didn't speak to me about it — that meant my grandmother hadn't mentioned it either.

Anyway, my mother was preoccupied with her own life. She was planning a wedding. Hers.

CHAPTER SIX

Trying to Belong

THE WEDDING TOOK PLACE at the Sydney Registry Office on a cool autumn day in May, 1962. A small family party of Aunt Laura, Uncle Jack and my stepfather's brother and his wife, celebrated at the simple ceremony. I felt very sophisticated in my new dress and very grown up as I tasted my first pink champagne.

My stepfather Lars was a gentle and quiet businessman. I first met him when I went to live with my grandmother. I realised he was not just another 'uncle' because he obviously cared for my mother and also took an interest in me. Some evenings we'd sit on the back steps of my grandmother's house where he'd help me with my homework, particularly maths. I had been living with Grandma for a year when Lars rented an apartment a mile or so away in Maroubra, the neighbouring beachside suburb. Although they were not yet married, Lars moved my mother and me in to live with him. It was the best thing that had happened to me — plus I was finally free of my Wicked-Witch-of-the-West grandmother.

I remember the evening we left her house in December 1961. Lars packed the last of our belongings into his car and drove the ten minutes to our new home, the three of us laughing as they blindfolded me by tying a scarf around my eyes. Finally we stopped and my mother and Lars led me across the road and up a winding path, giggling as Lars fumbled with the keys to open the front door. They stood me at the doorway of my new bedroom and undid the blindfold. I whooped with joy when I saw it. The bed was covered in a pink chenille bedspread and next to it stood a small dresser holding magazines and a record player. I was thrilled and hugged and thanked them both. The first thing I did was put up two huge posters of my favourite stars, Elvis and The Beatles. For the first time, I had my own room and I was sure this was the beginning of the life I had always dreamed of with my mother.

The apartment was sunny and comfortable and had a combined living and dining room, a modern bathroom and two bedrooms. Although a quiet man and softly spoken, Lars was a high-achieving corporate executive. He made time for me and talked to me about the ways of the world and the subtleties of politics. He also taught me to play chess and would take me on outings to interesting educational places like the State Library and the museum. In his home country of Norway, he was an accomplished gymnast so he encouraged me to enjoy exercise and, most evenings after dinner, he and I would go for a jog around the block. Due to his Scandinavian conservatism, he was not overtly affectionate but I felt safe and trusted him. By this stage I was a damaged youngster; traumatised, very insecure, with no self-esteem and smack-bang in the middle of puberty. I think perhaps if he had come into my life earlier it may have been different. When a stepparent takes on the responsibility of a teenager it can be challenging.

NOT LONG AFTER we settled into the apartment, I remember seeing my mother standing at the front door talking to someone. Looking at her standing side-on in the doorway, I noticed her stomach bulged. As she shut the door, I turned to her and asked disbelievingly, 'Are you having a baby?'

She looked me in the eyes, her hand resting gently on her stomach and she said with a smile, 'Yes I am.' Then she turned on her heel and walked away.

I stood there incredulous. My dream was shattered again. I thought I finally had my happy family of my Princess Mummy, Lars and me — but everything changed again that day.

When my mother had the baby it was a difficult birth; in fact she almost died — all the more reason for her to dote on her new offspring. Everything was all about the new baby. He really was a beautiful baby boy who, with his Nordic complexion and blue eyes, looked exactly like his parents. They called him their little prince. My mother was besotted with the tiny baby who brought a look of love to her face that I didn't recognise. Often I would catch her unaware as she leant on the rails of his cot gazing rapturously down at the gurgling baby. Confused, I would sulk in my room, anxiety tying a hard knot in my stomach as I wondered why I had never seen that look when she looked at me. Other times Lars and my mother would sit together on the lounge exchanging tender glances, the baby cradled between them in her arms, the picture of them burning itself into my memory where it rankled and festered into resentment. Even more confusingly, I loved him too.

I became a hurt and angry thirteen-year-old teenager. I was jealous of the attention the baby received and felt isolated and cast aside. All along I'd thought I was finally going to spend time alone with my mother. Instead, after all those years of separation from her, she had sent me to live with my wicked grandmother then married Lars and given birth to a new baby.

I enrolled in a different high school, within walking distance of our new home. I was the only black kid in the school again and I felt I had nothing in common with the blonde surfie girls who, to me, all looked the same. I felt as though I was nearly invisible to my classmates. They weren't being unkind, it was just that I was the new girl and not part of anything. Plus by now I wore glasses. Coming from a strict and sheltered life in a convent filled with nuns, what did I know of the latest fads and fashions and their beach culture? Nothing! Living near the beach, surfing and swimming were the most popular pastimes, and of course shopping. The girls loved to shop and the boys rode surfboards. I couldn't find common ground with them and felt lost in this teenage world. I was the black sheep again which made me more difficult to live with.

Sometimes on Saturday mornings my mother took me shopping for clothes at the local shopping centre. She bought me jeans with T-shirt tops and fashionable dresses and ornaments for my room. I loved those days, just my mother and me, even though I would often see my classmates shopping in groups together, laughing and talking and having fun.

My cousins Stuart and Kathy came for visits on Sundays and often the three of us would go down to the beach for the day. I had just turned fourteen when we decided it would be a good idea if I asked for a surfboard for Christmas so we could all ride it. Although my stepfather had insisted I have swimming lessons first, I almost drowned in a rip after falling off my new board. I had to be rescued by a lifesaver: there I was in my brand new swimsuit, looking very uncool. Most weekends my surfboard, all ten feet of it, and I would struggle up and down the steep hills of the street to the beach. Gidget I was not. And no one was paying me any attention, so my attitude worsened.

I had no idea I was likely traumatised from the years of abuse and abandonment, plus I had never spoken of the rape to anyone. My grandmother had warned me not to bring shame on the family. Because I was so desperate to belong, I was frightened that if I told, everyone would know and think less of me, and she would find out and have me sent back to a convent, or worse. I was sure the rape was my fault. After all, I liked the boy and had let him kiss me so I must have led him on. But when he got out of control, I couldn't make him stop. When the other two followed, I blamed myself for allowing that situation to develop even though I hadn't understood what was happening. Now I was what my grandmother called 'soiled goods': a slut and a tart. It was my fault because I was a bad girl, so I kept my shame to myself.

I was awkward and shy around the kids at school but longed to make friends. I felt out of my depth and didn't quite fit in; and also, I hardly ever saw another black person. I wished I could go to school down the road at La Perouse with the Aboriginal kids — at least I would look similar — but here I was a half-caste kid with no culture. I felt isolated.

OUR SMART BLACK-AND-WHITE TELEVISION took pride of place in the living room, its square varnished-timber cabinet looking too heavy for its four spindly legs. Each night Lars sat, captivated by news and current event shows, while my mother liked fashion and cooking demonstrations.

In August 1963, Lars and I watched a television news report of Martin Luther King standing on the steps of the Lincoln Memorial in Washington. He made his historic 'I Have a Dream' speech, advocating racial harmony as part of the March on Washington for Jobs and Freedom. Lars tried to explain discrimination and the significance of Dr King's speech, the racial problems in America and the meaning of 'civil rights'. Although I realised this was important, I didn't yet understand how it related to me; it was my introduction to the Civil Rights Movement.

I was drawn to music and dance shows and *Bandstand* was my absolute favourite. Every Saturday night without fail, at six-thirty I'd turn on *Bandstand* to watch Bobby Rydell, Brenda Lee, Lesley Gore, Neil Sedaka, Paul Anka and a whole lot of young Australian singers perform their current popular songs. Singing along with them, I'd dance around the room trying to copy the latest steps.

Maroubra Beach, like most Sydney beaches in the early sixties, was packed with bronzed sunbaking bodies, especially on the weekends. Each Sunday afternoon a very popular weekly dance was held at the surf club for all the local teenagers. The trouble was, it drew a large crowd of kids in from all over Sydney, including motor bikers from the western suburbs. Arriving on noisy, highly polished, chromed motorbikes, the bikers in black leather jackets and slicked-back hairdos would often clash with the bleach-blond surfers, causing fights between the 'Rockers' and the 'Surfies'.

Australia's top bands and singers performed live at these Maroubra Surf Club dances, including my latest idol, blonde teenage singer, Little Pattie. She also regularly appeared on *Bandstand* and led a dance craze created by her song 'Stompin' at Maroubra'. I would stand in front of the stage and study every move she made, then race home and imitate her in the mirror using my hairbrush as a microphone.

By the time I was fifteen, I had made a few friends — not with the in-crowd girls but friends nonetheless. They included a little blondie named Charmaine and a beak-nosed, funny Jewish girl named Ruth. They were great girls who, like me, idolised The

Beatles so we'd sit in our little group in the playground and sing their latest songs.

Ruth, Charmaine and I had the time of our lives when our parents bought us tickets to see The Beatles concert when they appeared at the Sydney Stadium in 1964. We didn't hear them sing because we screamed hysterically throughout their entire performance, along with the thousands of other girls, but at least we were there and could say we had seen them. This was of course, one of the highlights of our young lives.

ONE AFTERNOON on my way home from school, I heard music coming from the garage of a house in my street. I stopped and listened to the sound of a band playing very well but a guy singing very flat. I mustered up enough courage to bang on the door and the music stopped. A boy not much older than me poked his head out the door.

'Hi,' he said.

'Hello,' I said, 'I came to ask you could I sing with your band?' He looked at me as though I was mad. 'No thanks. We don't need a singer.'

'Sounds to me like you do' I said, rudely.

He looked at me impatiently then said, 'Hold on a minute.' He disappeared then returned, 'OK, you get to sing one song.'

I smiled as he introduced me to Andrew and David, two guitar-playing brothers. He was James, the drummer. I looked around; the garage was set up with a half-decent-looking PA system.

'OK so what are you singing?' asked impatient James, who I think was the singer I'd heard.

I suggested a few rock and roll songs they were sure to know. When I'd finished singing 'Be-bop-a-Lula', 'Johnny Be Good' and 'Rock Around the Clock', they were impressed and by the end of the afternoon I had joined my first band and made arrangements to rehearse every Saturday.

I was beside myself with joy. I picked ten favourite songs, wrote out the lyrics in a special book and locked myself in my bedroom playing the songs on my record player repeatedly, then practiced them on my baby brother.

Saturdays became a big deal for the local kids and neighbours who enjoyed sitting on their front fences listening to us rehearse. Before long we had a following, including an enterprising young man who elected himself our manager and proceeded to get us gigs. Within months our little band had a few bookings. We played at church dances in draughty old scout halls but we didn't mind, as long as we had an audience who were enjoying themselves.

Even though word had got around school, I was surprised to be voted by my peers onto the school Social Committee. One of the main tasks was to organise the annual school dance. I immediately booked our little quartet to play as support act to one of the better-known bands who were appearing — just a few songs. Still, I was very nervous but excited. The big night arrived and the assembly hall was packed, dressed up with tables covered in white tablecloths, festive lights across the hall and a DJ to play between band sets.

My mother had bought me a floral knee-length dress, sleeveless with a round-necked bodice fitted to the waist and a generously gathered skirt. For extra flounce, I wore a starched rope petticoat and two stiff tulle petticoats. I paired the dress with kitten-heeled, white sling-back shoes and put a flower in my hair. The boys in the band wore white shirts and black trousers. When I walked onstage I noticed that the crowd of girls I had most wanted to impress left the room and went to the bathroom. Darn! By the time we had started our first song they were back talking loudly, giggling and flirting with some boys.

Sensibly, a few bars into the song I focused and concentrated on what I was singing. The boys were playing well and singing harmonies and suddenly the whole crowd was joining in, bopping and dancing, and by the end of the song, the students were cheering. I introduced the other band members and the most popular guys and girls cheered us on. It felt wonderful. They loved me! We played three more songs and, at the end, the enthusiastic response was overwhelming. I helped the guys to quickly pack up the equipment while the next band set up. Ruth and Charmaine were delighted, jumping up and down and giggling with me when we'd finished.

On Monday morning I walked into Biology class and received a standing ovation from my teacher and classmates. Wow! Right away, invitations were extended to go to parties, to sit with the most popular girls at lunchtime and, best of all, to join them on their Saturday morning shopping trips. Now I was one of the in-crowd!

AS LIFE AT SCHOOL IMPROVED, life at home became very strained. Mother and I argued constantly and I found little joy in being around her. Hers and Lars' lives seem to revolve around my two-year-old brother and the house was scattered with photos of their happy family threesome. Letters, cards and gifts constantly arrived from Lars' family overseas, addressed to my mother, Lars and the baby but never to me. For Lars' relatives, it was as though I didn't exist. My mother would make such a fuss, reading out their latest letter or card and parading their gifts in front of me, exclaiming how generous Lars' family were. I felt hurt and confused and didn't understand why she never hid them from me. My feelings of isolation increased as I began to realise in my heart that, no matter what I did, I was not really wanted. I continually questioned her about my life and why she had abandoned me and sent me to the convent, which would invariably start an argument, and she still would not answer when I asked about my father.

There was a side to my mother she never showed to the rest of her family. When she couldn't get her own way with me, she would dissolve into tears and, to make me feel guilty, look at me pleadingly, saying things like, 'How could you do this to me?' or 'Why do you want to upset me so much?' As a child, this had always had the desired effect because the last thing I ever wanted was to upset my beautiful Princess Mummy. But now I was older and smarter, her tears and pleading had little effect. Instead, she would throw a tantrum. These were quite dramatic and would start with her flouncing around the room, accompanied by wild gesticulating as her voice grew louder, higher and more shrill. Funnily enough, the words hadn't changed over the years, just the delivery. Eventually she would just be screaming at me.

One day, as punishment for starting an argument, she refused to allow me to go to rehearsal with the band. I couldn't take anymore. I walked out and didn't come home till the next day. When I did return, I refused to tell her where I'd been because she wouldn't give me the answers I wanted. This started the whole cycle again. I would go and sometimes not return for a couple of days, grabbing the pocket money I'd earned from doing chores on the way out. She tried locking me in my room and, after I'd climbed out the window a few times, Lars nailed it shut to try to keep me in; but even that didn't always work. Then the boys in the band became annoyed because I was not turning up for rehearsal. I loved my singing (it was my only passion) and I felt terrible letting them down but it was how my life had become. I let everyone down — especially myself, which made me angrier. My life started to unravel.

Sometimes, when my mother was not home, I'd rummage through her drawers trying to find any information I could about my father's identity. One day I found my birth certificate and discovered my name 'Sharon' was actually spelt with a *y*. I also noticed a black line right through the space for the father's name, with no information entered. When my mother came home, I demanded to know why.

'It's none of your business. Your father is dead. I have told you that many times.'

'What would you know?' I retorted. 'You don't even know how to spell my name so how would you know if he is dead or not. You don't even know who I am!' With that, I did not escape out the window in the dark of night — I simply walked past her out the front door and, again, did not come home. Each time, I secretly hoped she would come looking for me but she didn't.

WHEN I TOOK OFF, I always headed to the city and the bright lights of Sydney's red light district, Kings Cross. The area was vaguely familiar to me but it had changed quite a bit since I'd lived there with Ellie and Dorrie, more than eleven years earlier.

Located about ten blocks from the city centre, the Cross had started as a wealthy suburb. In the 1800s, land grants were issued to the socially prominent who built prestigious and stately mansions with sweeping harbour views and grandiose gardens, establishing the area as exclusive and stylish. As I wandered past these big old mansions, I'd often imagine the families who might have lived there and the balls and elegant parties they must have had. By the late 1890s, many of those estates had been subdivided, first for substantial houses and later for apartments, creating Sydney's most fashionable leafy suburb. By the time I knew it, the Cross was full of pre-war apartment buildings, people and life. It had been Sydney's bohemian heartland since the first apartments were built and, when my mother was a child, was the home of poets, actors, musicians and artists — a kind of bohemian melting pot, not unlike Paris' Montmatre with its cosmopolitan and sophisticated ambience. Black market trading and prostitution evolved during World War II, when the Cross was also full of nightclubs entertaining the American servicemen, which had transformed an area of the precinct into a red light district attracting girls, gangsters and crooked police.

During the 1950s, an influx of immigrants from Europe and the Mediterranean found their way to Kings Cross bringing their social and culinary traditions, so it became *the place* to eat out in Sydney. The espresso machine had also arrived and, by my childhood, there were around fifty coffee shops and tourists everywhere. The coffee culture had brought music and, towards the end of the 1950s, Jazzers flocked to subterranean jazz cellars to listen to non-commercial jazz and daringly order cappuccinos and raisin toast, the latest craze.

By 1964, the Beatniks and jazz culture had given way to rock 'n' roll and Kings Cross was filled with people of all tastes and persuasions, the common denominator being a love of the night life. When the sun went down, the place came alive with glitz, glamour and neon. The strip of businesses, shops and restaurants along Darlinghurst Road sparkled and fizzed with excitement. Servicemen from the large Garden Island naval base at the bottom of the hill, curious suburbanites on a night out, tourists, people of all sexual perversions, musicians and working girls filled the nightclubs, strip clubs, brothels, restaurants, cafes, Italian coffee houses and hotel bars. Everyone came looking for fun or to make easy money and alcohol was the obvious drug of choice at the time.

It seemed every kid who ran away in Sydney headed to Kings Cross and I was no different. It was a place where I felt comfortable. I belonged there. No one wanted me to 'be good' and no one asked anything of me. I would sit at the El Alamein fountain and ponder my life. I was only fifteen years old but no one was asking me my age either. Fifteen and sixteen-year-old girls were a common sight in the Cross but, of course, if one had any altercation with a police officer, we automatically became eighteen. I was tall, slim and well proportioned, with black curly hair and an air of arrogance, and could easily pass for eighteen.

I joined a crowd of youngsters who were living the same life. Leaving unhappy homes in the suburbs, some had been molested and abused, beaten, raped or both; some came from parents who were alcoholics, some had been kicked out of home and others just lived on the street. But it was the music and atmosphere that kept luring me back to the Cross. There were plenty of bars and nightclubs but my favourite was Surf City. An historical former theatre had been transformed into a live music venue in the early sixties and could hold up to two thousand sweaty dancers at any one time on the enormous floor. All the seats had been removed and the whole ground floor transformed into an unusual dance floor that sloped slightly towards the stage. The name came from a Jan & Dean hit, because the surf-music craze had been a major musical force when it opened. The interior walls were painted black with white cartoon drawings of surfers, illuminated by black fluorescent lights which made the lint on your cloths glow white, your teeth yellow and bleach-blond hair look green. Surf music and rock 'n' roll bands played each night plus all afternoon on the weekends. Hour after hour I danced, longing to get up on the stage and dreaming of a time it might be me in a glittering gown singing and the crowd dancing to my music.

We all slept wherever we could, in railway stations or on the floor of someone's place. To get money for food, shoplifting and theft were most kids' ways of surviving. I would spend a few days with them, enjoying the freedom and the sense of belonging but mostly, when my pocket money ran out, I headed home again to face my mother's wrath.

Late one night some of the boys broke into a store and stole an amount of women's clothing. They brought it to where we were staying and gave us girls first choice of the dresses, coats and whatever else we wanted. A couple of days later, dressed in our finery, two of us were parading down the road when we were spotted by a couple of Italian women who chased us when they recognised the clothing stolen from their store. Obviously, looking back, I'm horrified at this scenario but I was young, confused and easily influenced and this was fast becoming a way of life for me.

We found ourselves in highly dangerous situations, too, especially the day one of the boys came by in a shiny new car to take us for a ride. We were cruising along listening to a popular DJ on the radio when one of the boys heard a police siren behind us. 'Cops!' he called out. Immediately the driver sped up, screeching around a corner on two wheels, smashing into the curb and fishtailing almost out of control, with the police right behind us. I clung on in the back seat, petrified, praying the driver would stop. After narrowly missing pedestrians, he pulled over and left the car running as he bolted down a laneway with the police in pursuit. I just sat there, trembling. One of the officers pulled me out and threw me in the back of the police car. My heart was pounding: I thought we were going to die in that car.

After a lecture back at the police station, I was let off with a warning and sent home with my mother. She berated me all the way in the taxi. 'How could you do this to me after all I have done for you? How can you be so ungrateful and uncaring of my situation? I have a husband and a baby to look after and I have tried to make you part of the happy home I've created.'

Funny — that's not how I saw it.

MY FAVOURITE AUNT Laura still had a drinking problem. At family gatherings when she drank too much, she would either start singing or abusing everyone within hearing. Although she and my mother were very close, often she was heard loudly berating my mother for 'locking me up'. My mother considered me ungrateful and disruptive but Laura would defend me, saying what a wonderful kid I was and that I deserved so much more than what I had been given.

One rainy afternoon, Aunt Laura informed me the father my mother had declared was dead was not really dead at all. Out of loyalty to her sister, she would not tell me his name but she promised me that 'One day, you will show the bastards just how brilliant you are . . .'

'Your name is going to be up in lights,' she said then swore me to secrecy about my father.

Well, that lasted about an hour before I marched over to my mother and demanded she tell me who my father was. She and Aunt Laura argued and above their raised voices, I pleaded again with my mother to tell me his name.

'He is dead and it's none of your business,' she screamed.

Once again, out the door I went on my usual path of self-destruction. Within a few days I was picked up and returned home by the police. I had never actually been arrested, just had my details noted and been delivered back home.

By this time I had become well and truly street-smart. I was popular with boys and able to manipulate them for the things I needed to survive on the streets like dinners, clothing and a roof over my head. I'd had a couple of boyfriends but I'd been looking for love and affection and didn't realise all they were offering was sex.

I may have been on a path of moral self-destruction but I always took pride in my appearance and was fastidious about my personal hygiene. I remember a woman police officer remarking, after picking me up one evening, that I was the cleanest runaway she had ever seen. Every day I made a special trip down to the women's amenities centre in Hyde Park, which I think may have been run by the Country Women's Association. This was a low brick building on the corner of Park Street in the city where, for two shillings, I could have a shower and wash my hair. I would also wash my bra and pants then iron them dry. I would do this every morning, putting my clothes back on even if they were damp, and this kept me clean all day.

Although still fifteen, I left school towards the end of 1964, having passed my Intermediate Certificate the year before. Due to the disruptive life I was living and my absences from school, my mother finally agreed to my leaving, provided I got a job. I was interested in nursing but ended up with a position as a clerk with a government department.

NOT LONG AFTERWARDS, my mother announced she, Lars and my little brother were going away on a holiday to New Guinea for six weeks. I was not asked or invited, just told; I was to go to my elder cousin Jean's to stay with her family. I couldn't understand why I wasn't included in this family holiday. Once again, my mother's actions showed I was not considered part of her family, which played havoc with my sense of security.

As it turned out, I got to experience a truly happy family life — something I'd never had until I went to stay with them. I realised they had what I'd been desperately seeking: I loved this family and they made me feel part of it. My cousin Jean and her husband Charlie had three wonderful children and I shared the bedroom of their only daughter, who looked up to me like I was her heroine.

My cousins included me in their summer camping holiday at the beach, north of Sydney on the Central Coast. We played on the beach all day, returning to the campsite for lunch and dinner. In the evenings the other campers came over and gathered around as the adults shared cups of tea and told long funny stories. It was great fun.

In self-destruct mode, even in this happy family atmosphere, I couldn't stay out of trouble. I met a boy. He was a tanned, good-looking surfer type with bleached hair and, after a day or two of getting to know each other, I agreed to sneak away in the middle of the night, while everyone slept, to meet him at the beach. Poor Jean and Charlie woke to find me gone and spent hours frantically searching the area with torches. When they did find me, in the early hours of the morning, I was making out with my surfie in the sand. They were absolutely furious. My surfie sheepishly slunk off as they shunted me back to the campsite.

'We were desperate with worry. What if something had happened to you?' said Jean, on the edge of tears, her voice raw with anxiety.

'I'm very disappointed in you Sharyn,' said Charlie. 'We care about you and thought you cared about us.' I did, so this made me feel worse than being caught; I loved them so much and hated to upset them.

Our happy life continued when we returned to their home. Unlike my mother, they never held me to ransom. Once they'd scolded me and I'd promised to be good, that was the end of it. We all had chores to do around the house and I loved the happiness and peace of this family's life. It was so wonderful that one night I sat them down and begged Jean and Charlie to let me live with them. Of course they said no, that my mother would be sad if I left her. I said she wouldn't care — still they stood firm.

My mother, stepfather and brother were returning the next day, January 25, and the plan was to meet them at Sydney's Mascot Airport. I asked Jean if I could visit a friend. When I didn't return home, she and Charlie spent the night searching the streets looking for me. They called the police. By the time they met my mother's plane, they were so worried and upset to have to tell her they didn't know where I was that Jean was on the verge of a nervous breakdown.

After spending a couple of weeks back on the streets with my friends, I was eventually arrested when the police found me in a hotel room with a man well known to them. Although he had a long criminal history, he had not done anything to hurt me. The police questioned us both and I said we had just been sitting and talking, which was true. I believe the police had been after him for quite a while; they were far more interested in him than me. They arrested and charged me with being exposed to moral danger and drove me to the Glebe Children's Shelter. I was detained there a few days before my court appearance, during which I was processed and interviewed by various court officers. My psychiatric report completed by the medical officer states:

> *... She has suffered emotional deprivation throughout her childhood but although her self concept is very poor her strengths are good and she is strongly motivated to improve and make something of herself. She has many anxieties and conflicts related to her background and colour.*

> *Her present home environment is good but the relationship with her mother is strained ...*

On February 22, I appeared before the magistrate in the Sydney Children's Court and was charged with being 'exposed to moral danger'. I had no idea what he was talking about. I felt I had been exposed to danger of every description my whole life, moral and otherwise. I'd been given to strangers at birth, then raised in a brothel, beaten by a sadistic nun, lived in a family with my raving-racist grandmother as its matriarch, not to mention having been raped, so I held little hope for myself. I was placed on twelve months' probation on a good behaviour bond and sent home with my mother who, as I'd predicted, berated me all the way home.

On March 5, my mother telephoned my probation officer to tell her that, although I had run away again, she'd found me — at the Woolloomooloo Hotel, partying with sailors and my runaway friends. My mother's main concern was that she was unable to keep me away from my 'old associates of bad influence' as she put it. I then spoke to my probation officer to tell her I'd been accepted as a nurse's aid at St Vincent's Hospital in Darlinghurst, a job I was looking forward to starting in four days. She reminded me of the terms of my probation order which, if breached, meant I would be brought before the court again.

MEANWHILE, THREE DAYS LATER on March 7, 1965, rebellion on a disturbing and dehumanising scale was taking place in the US. Lars and I watched on television a report on the latest racial violence in

America. I cried as I watched the footage of peaceful demonstrators being brutally attacked by State Troopers and sheriffs from Dallas County. Some six hundred Civil Rights marchers had wanted to march from Selma, Alabama, to the State capital Montgomery to raise awareness of racial violence and discrimination — Dr Martin Luther King had made the request himself — but the march had been banned by the Governor of Alabama, citing public safety issues. The marchers went ahead anyway but, as they crossed the Edmund Pettus Bridge, the troopers were waiting for them; they had billy clubs, bull whips and tear gas that they used to attack the peaceful demonstrators as they came off the bridge. The coverage showed marchers left bloodied and severely injured. It was horrific and shocking. Bloody Sunday may have been a major turning point in public support for the Civil Rights Movement in the United States but the violence, cruelty and humiliation left me deeply distressed.

None of these images helped my self-esteem and, from what I could see, there was no cause for pride in the colour of my skin. Why were black people hated so? What was wrong with us and what was wrong with me? Here I was, a young teenage black girl living in a white society where no one looked like me and there was no one to talk to about it. Even as my stepfather and I discussed the Civil Rights Movement and the injustice felt by black people in America, he was complicit in the racial discrimination happening in my own home.

'So this is what you want? Who you want to be — one of them?' was my mother's only comment through a forced, bitter laugh.

I felt I didn't belong in this family and began to believe it was shameful to be a black person.

I started work at St Vincent's Hospital on the late shift, as a nurse's aide in the sterilisation unit, sterilising instruments for surgery and delivering them around the hospital. While I found the work interesting, the hospital was only a few blocks from Kings Cross. My relationship with my mother had deteriorated even more, so at the end of my shift a few days later, the temptation was just too great. I was off, back to the Cross. Again, I was reacting to my circumstances, trying to find a place to belong.

Ten days later I was picked up and arrested in a private hotel in Kirribilli where I had been staying in a room with a girlfriend. She was friendly with some boys who lived there and we'd been having a good time and generally hanging out. At one stage I had pawned my glasses and my camera to get money. This was my second breach of probation and more serious than I realised. According to my probation records, my mother had reported me missing and '. . . wishes her to be charged as an uncontrollable young person and has asked for a warrant to be issued.'

The police delivered me to the Glebe Children's Shelter again, where I was processed and assigned a court date. Then they called my mother to let her know I had been located. It was the end of the line for her. She'd had enough.

My mother sat in court a few days later on March 29, sniffling into her lace handkerchief, my stepfather by her side. She stood and announced to the magistrate, 'We have tried everything possible to give her a nice home and provide a good education.'

I remember thinking she hadn't given me what I craved most: love, affection and acceptance. 'There is nothing more we can do,' she said. 'As far as we are concerned, she is uncontrollable and it would be better for everyone if she was placed in an institution until she is eighteen.'

My mother's apparent distress won the magistrate's sympathy. He charged me as 'uncontrollable' and sentenced me to six months incarceration in the Training School for Girls, Parramatta, commonly known as Parramatta Girls' Home — a reformatory. I stood in the dock, devastated. How could she do this to me? As I was escorted from the courtroom sobbing, I turned back and yelled at my mother, 'Are you happy now? You've locked me up again. Just what you wanted!'

Now I was in real trouble and I was just sixteen years old.

My Princess Mummy

My mother Grace Samuels, circa 1948

My confirmation at
St Martha's, aged about nine

Me, aged about seven, on a Sunday outing
in the park with Princess Mummy

Me in late 1961,
just turned thirteen

In a very stylish dress I'd made
in sewing class in junior
high school, 1963

Morning Muster beyond the Covered Way at Parramatta Girls' Home.
On the right was our dance area and notice the in-girls' steps on the left.

Looking down the Covered Way, the scene of so much misery
yet also joy, with dancing and family visits

My first glimpse of Parramatta Girls' Home:
the main building and high wall

A girl arriving at Hay Institution for Girls, a brutal maximum-security
institution for teenage girls

Inside the cell block at Hay Institution for Girls. 'Eyes down, quick march.' We never walked but marched everywhere.

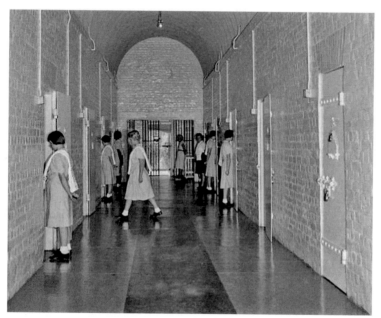

Standing 'at ease' at our cabin doors, waiting for our turn in the ablution parade. I am last in line, at top left, aged only sixteen.

Hard labour, harsh discipline and extreme punishment
were standard at Hay

'Eyes down, knees high, elbows in, on the double!' I should have been
punished severely for surreptitiously adjusting my glasses without permission.

Free at last. In my mother's kitchen
in Townsville, 1966.

Nurse Sharyn: during my nurse's
training in Townsville, 1966

'Georgia' and 'Sheeba' in the Paradise Club, Kings Cross, 1973

CHAPTER SEVEN

Prison or Purgatory: Parramatta Girls' Home

TWO POLICE OFFICERS marched me out the back of the courthouse with three other girls, to a large black police wagon. One of the officers ushered us inside, locking the door with a bolt and padlock. The back door had a small grill set into it, which let in some extra light and air to the otherwise dim interior. We sat on metal bench seats opposite each other, all trying to show signs of bravado as the van started its long and jarring sixteen-mile journey to Parramatta. Out of the back window I caught glimpses of people hurrying along the city streets, going about their daily lives. Only then did I realise that I had truly lost my freedom. It hit me like a punch in the chest. I looked around at my three companions; two seemed about my age but the third looked only about fourteen. We all knew Parramatta had a reputation for being a strict juvenile prison with harsh discipline and hardened female inmates. The youngest girl told a story she had heard about the Parramatta girls being rough, tough lesbians who shoved broom handles inside the new girls for initiation. All of a sudden we didn't feel so brave.

Sitting on the cold bench, being jolted by each bump, I thought back over the day's events. After my outburst in the courtroom, I was led to the holding cells below, where a policewoman came to see me. As I cried into the handful of tissues she'd given me, she comforted me and talked to me about my situation. She suggested I use my time in Parramatta to think about my life, and how I wanted to live it in the future.

Then my mother and Lars came to the holding cells to see me. We had another endless, useless argument about whose fault this was and how, according to them, I needed to grow up, wake up and get my life in order. As I looked at my mother I tried to understand why she thought that yet another institution, namely a reform school, was going to help sort out my problems. I knew I needed help — but surely locking me up wasn't the answer. Her rationale was that I needed to be punished for my behaviour but did she fully understand the harshness of Parramatta Girls' Home and what was going to happen to me there? I knew she'd breathed a sigh of relief when I was sentenced: now she could get on with her life. It was heartbreaking to consider that my mother didn't want me. Why wouldn't she answer my questions, instead of making the circumstances of my birth some frightening, mysterious damned secret no one ever spoke about? Now I was sitting in the back of a van on my way to juvenile prison. I resolved to stop feeling sorry for myself. I sat up straight, took a deep breath and made a pact with myself and God: no matter what happened, at the end of six months when I got out of this place, I would never run away again!

The van finally lurched to a stop, the door was unlocked and we were ushered out and told to stand in a line. As a guard locked the huge iron gates behind us, I looked around to get my bearings. We were standing in a gravelled area beside a stone wall so high it seemed to block out the sun. Behind it, I could see the top storeys of menacing grey buildings; they reminded me of a workhouse or something, from a Charles Dickens novel. A portion of one building met the wall at a right angle and had a sign over the doorway: *Administration Office*. On its own over in a grassed area, was another tall and imposing old two-storey, red brick building with a slate roof. As we were led to this building called *Admissions*, my heart began to race.

The guards ushered us into a vestibule where paperwork was handed over and our personal details checked. We were each given an identification number and told that each of us would now be known by our name and number. A female prison officer shepherded us into another room and told us to remove all our clothing and jewellery. 'These will be returned on the day you are released,' she said as she shoved them into separate packets.

She was joined by another officer and, standing naked in front of them, we were body searched then handed a grey, sack-like cotton uniform; a plain cotton bra and large white bloomer pants; socks and black shoes without shoelaces; and a small bag containing soap, toothpaste, a toothbrush and a sanitary napkin. We were marched naked to a shower block of cubicles without doors and given a cake of lye soap to wash our hair and every part of our body. I remember the strong-smelling soap: it felt harsh and stung my skin. After the shower, another officer examined our hair. She poured kerosene on our heads and covered each one with a turban-like cap, telling us not to remove them until instructed.

'You will be here in Admissions for a few days while you are processed, then you'll be moved to the big house,' said one of the officers. 'Tomorrow morning you will all have a check-up with the doctor to determine if you have any venereal diseases, scabies or are pregnant. Now, follow me ladies.'

She led us into a small hall where about ten other girls were sitting around, some playing cards. Feeling numb and confused, I kept to myself and followed along with the others for the remainder of the day. New girls had looked lost during their first few days at St Martha's and now I knew how they felt.

The doctor's visit the next morning was brutal. I was instructed to remove all my clothes and lie on a flat table with my knees bent, feet together, legs apart and knees over each edge. As the doctor pushed my legs wider apart, in his hand I glimpsed a large stainless steel instrument shaped like a duck's bill. He forced it into my vagina, tearing my skin and making me scream with pain.

'Be quiet. Hold very still,' he ordered. I gritted my teeth until he had finished scraping, poking and feeling around, my eyes watering with the burning pain. I felt humiliated and frightened. I'd never had an internal examination and didn't know what was happening. Turning my head sideways, I glanced over at the female officer standing at the door but she had turned her back to me. Then the doctor started examining my breasts, kneading and squeezing, his head so close I could smell his rancid breath. I pulled away and jumped off the table. The officer turned to look inside the room.

'Are you finished with this one, Doctor?'

'I am now,' he said, giving me a hard stare. I pulled on my clothes and left. Later, I found out the girls' name for him was Doctor Fingers.

When the turban cap was removed a few days later, my scalp felt sore and tender and the skin below my hairline was red and angry. Any head lice would have been long dead by then — but I'd never had them to start with. This place seemed a bit like St Martha's, so I settled into the routine thinking, 'this is OK'. But it did not prepare me for what was to come. All my tests must have come back with a clean result because, a few days later, I was transferred 'over the other side' to the 'big house': the main buildings, inside the high walls. This is what I had been dreading.

BACK THEN, most people in New South Wales knew of Parramatta Girls' Home. Under various names, it had been a brutal and cruel institution for the incarceration of young women for more than 125 years. First built by convicts in 1841, the original main building was still in use when I was sentenced. A Georgian-style barracks comprising a three-storey dormitory block and schoolrooms with a basement or dungeon, the place had opened (in 1844) as the government-funded Roman Catholic Orphan School and first housed destitute and vagrant children and orphans. There was a residence for the salaried superintendent, matron and teachers at the rear, within the walled grounds. Several new buildings were added over time, including a kitchen block and dining room (with staff quarters above) and a chapel. These buildings, all still existing, were linked to the main building by a long covered walkway and two additional dormitory wings had been added to the main building by the time I arrived.

The place had been re-assigned as an Industrial School for Females, when the NSW Government took it over (and built the high walls). It was intended as a home for destitute and vagrant girls but in reality it was a reformatory for delinquents, operated along the lines of a prison. The first inmates were young girls relocated from the Biloela Industrial School, another harsh reformatory institution on Cockatoo Island, in the middle of Sydney Harbour.

Then in 1905, the official emphasis changed from reformatory to training and education as a means of 'developing acceptable behaviour in young women' as they described it, in those times. In 1912 the Industrial School was renamed the Girls' Training Home, intended for girls of an uncontrollable character but not of immoral tendencies. Repairs and alterations to the buildings were carried out in the 1920s and more isolation cells were built during the Depression, in 1934.

Names like 'Industrial' and 'Training School' sound innocent enough but don't be fooled — these were not schools as we know them but prisons where harsh and oppressive conditions were concealed under the guise of child welfare philosophies, to justify their creation. These institutions were intended for two groups: the first being delinquent children put into reformatories; the second, destitute children put into industrial schools. Eventually, this difference became unclear and the children were identified and treated as one group: delinquents.

In 1946, it was re-established as the Parramatta Training School for Girls for the reception, detention, maintenance, discipline, education and training of young women. It then became known as Parramatta Girls' Home but the name belied its function: it was no home. In reality, it was a prison where young girls were stripped of their dignity and liberties and punished frequently with physical force.

By the 1960s, when I got there, it was staffed by career public servants. These male superintendents and deputies had received their training in boys' institutions and were selected because they were tough disciplinarians. All the subordinate staff officers were female. Parramatta's inmate population fluctuated, at any time housing between one hundred and one hundred and sixty girls from all social, ethnic and economic backgrounds and including state wards. We all shared a common background of some type of neglect or abuse by parents or State authorities, many having spent their entire childhood in a series of institutions or foster care. Around ten percent were Aboriginal (Koori) girls. A girl like me need present only a minor challenge to the authorities to be remanded to Parramatta as an uncontrollable or delinquent teenage girl. Although most of us were sentenced to the mandatory six to nine months, this did not guarantee our release; it was up to the Child Welfare Department and the superintendant.

Mostly, we girls were incarcerated for welfare rather than criminal matters. These could be: 'neglect' (the girls were the ones neglected, meaning their parents were incapable of looking after them); 'uncontrollable' (my situation of having committed a series of misdemeanours such as playing truant from school or running away from home) and certainly, the most extraordinary reason for imprisoning a girl, 'exposed to moral danger', meaning they were likely to be raped. Unfortunately this was sometimes the case, once they'd arrived there.

There were also a large number of pregnant girls in Parramatta, housed in separate quarters to the general inmate population. I believe that, at the end of their pregnancy, these girls were transferred to Paddington or Crown Street Women's Hospital where they gave birth, in many cases shackled to the rails of the bed; their babies were then taken from them, never to be seen again. All under the age of eighteen, the girls' state ward status was then imposed on their babies. The girls were returned to the main inmate population at Parramatta, many showing the signs of extreme grief at their loss, which was interpreted as resistant behaviour and resulted in further punishment.

A PRISON OFFICER led me toward the high walls and the door marked 'Administration'. This is it, I thought. Inside a shabby but pleasant room, I was introduced to the superintendent.

'Sharyn, you have been assigned to dormitory three,' he said. My heart sank. I'd heard they were the toughest girls.

'Behave yourself and your time will pass quickly and easily. It is up to you.' He handed me over to a dark-haired female officer.

'Follow me.' She had a pleasant voice and appeared to be a caring kind of person, so I relaxed a little.

It was an old building with high ceilings, and as I followed her down the corridor of creaking, polished wooden boards, I noticed all the doors were closed. Each time we needed to pass through a closed door, she reached for her large bunch of keys and unlocked it, then locked it again once we had passed through. She led me outside, down a long covered walkway with timber benches running each side of it, to an assembly hall at the end of it where about twenty girls were sitting around in groups talking. Some girls had fierce-looking tattoos on their arms and other girls looked just plain mean. In the corner, a group of dark-skinned girls were playing cards so, looking to protect my own interests, I bravely walked over, pulled up the nearest chair and sat down.

'G'day love,' said a female giant with a toothless grin.

'Hi,' I said in a meek voice, hiding my trembling hands in my lap, 'can I sit here?'

'Yep. You're better off here than anywhere else in this room!' She laughed loudly. I nervously smiled back. A sweet-faced black girl about my age leaned over to me.

'You Koori?' she asked. 'What's ya tribe? You a blackfella?'

Having absolutely no idea what she was talking about, I answered 'Yeah!'

'Good. I'm Rosie, what's your name?'

'Sharyn,' I said. Rosie pointed to the laughing toothless giant, 'This is Joyce, and Karen and Betty.'

Now I felt safe. I hadn't met people with my skin colour before, except my West Indian aunties and their American servicemen friends, so this was good.

Joyce was winning at cards. She looked over at me, 'You scared, love? First time in?' I nodded, my eyes darting over her left shoulder. She followed my gaze to a tattooed girl.

'You scared of Sammy?' I nodded again. Joyce laughed. 'She's not the one you should be scared of, love.' Leaning towards me, she pointed as she whispered, 'She's the one you have to worry about.' I looked where she was pointing — straight at the nice officer who had brought me here! 'The girls are OK. It's them you gotta watch!'

EVERY DOOR WAS LOCKED. As we moved from one activity to another, we had to wait for the routine unlocking and locking of doors. We were continually locked in and locked out.

We were also controlled by a points system, both individually and as dormitory groups. The degree of discipline, punishment and privileges dished out to us depended on this point system. There was no warning. The slightest misdemeanor like walking too fast or too slow, or giggling at the wrong time, and you lost points.

'That's ten points off,' they'd say. If you questioned or argued, you lost additional points or were more severely punished — with isolation or segregation. Four rankings of 'privilege' correlated to the number of points acquired; the more points you had, the better. Ranking one girls were allowed out under supervision, to go swimming at the local pool or to play soccer on the open grassed areas outside the walls. Ranking two were allowed to listen to the radio in the evenings and watch movies shown in the main recreation room. Rankings three and four were degrees of 'unprivileged', which meant you spent evenings in your dormitory — scrubbing, cleaning and turning beds — or in the kitchen scullery scrubbing pots and pans and peeling vegetables in readiness for the following day's meals. Also, in the 'unprivileged' rankings, you were not allowed visitors or mail (which was censored: incoming and outgoing). The officers were always riding us, pushing us to make a mistake so they could punish us and at times girls were beaten with leather straps and batons.

There were periods during the day when we were not permitted to speak and there were frequent musters where we were counted. Access to other areas was restricted, particularly in the main building. It was a three-storey building with five or six dormitories, counting the top two floors, but I was only allowed access to my dormitory and the staircase leading up to it.

Most of the girls in my dormitory were a tough lot, yet they proved to be the hardest workers. We usually had the most points at the end of every week for the best-made beds, the most highly polished floors and the highest standard of general neatness and tidiness. The same girls, me included, were at the bottom of the individual points system every week for insolence, questioning the officers and general disobedience.

My dormitory was similar in layout to the one I'd been in at St Martha's, with the addition of a couple of windows which were barred and quite high off the floor. It was a plain room with rows of iron beds arranged down the walls, each with a rail at the foot where we hung our towel and clothes at night. Our underpants had to be placed on the top, turned inside out with the crutch showing as each girl's menstrual cycle was recorded. Halfway down the length of one wall there was a small bathroom containing a toilet and basin. We were locked in the dormitory each night around eight-thirty and the lights turned out, except for a row of night lighting embedded in the floor. There was an internal window towards one end of the room, with a viewing room beyond, that allowed the officers to see into the dormitory without having to unlock the door and come in. Regularly, they would drag us all from our beds in the middle of the night to 'stand out', meaning we stood to attention for hours facing the wall in the freezing hallway, dressed only in our nighties. This punishment was used frequently for, say, a couple of girls heard whispering to each other after lights out. Standing there, you would try to switch off your mind as your feet slowly went numb, followed by your legs. Then your back and neck would ache and the cold would penetrate your bones. If you fell asleep on your feet or swayed slightly, an officer would suddenly jab their fist into your back. If you cried out you lost points and you didn't dare look around when anyone was being beaten. You stood motionless, facing forward listening to the thuds and cries of pain. They would demand to know, over and over, who was talking but we would never tell. After a couple of hours they would start to let some go back to bed — 'Stand. Stand. Stand. You can go. Stand . . .' — playing us off against each other. The discipline was cruel and brutal.

Lying in the semi-darkness, that first night, I wondered what was to become of me. The girls with their tattoos and attitudes of bravado were intimidating and frightened me, and Joyce had said the officers were not who they seemed. I was trying to work out how I could fit in, when I heard whispering and rustling along the floor near my bed. I had expected some sort of initiation but now I was petrified. The dormitory lights blazed and keys jangled in the lock. Girls fled quickly and silently to their beds, lying absolutely still. The officers flew into the dormitory and strode up and down, ordering everyone to stand at the end of their beds. Then the yelling and intimidation started. When no one would answer, an officer came up to me and shouted in my face, 'Who was out of bed Sharyn? What were they doing? Who was it? Tell me right now.' I could feel her spittle spray my face. I tried not to flinch.

I was the new girl and she thought I'd blab immediately but I just stood there, trembling. Finally, in a shaky voice I managed to say, 'I don't know what you mean. I didn't hear anything. No one was out of bed.'

As punishment, for the next few hours we were made to 'stand out'. The next day during lunch break, a perky blonde came over to me and introduced herself.

'Hi, I'm Sandy,' she said. 'That was really good what ya did last night. Ya did good, lovie. Don't worry, I'll look after ya.' And she did. From that day on she watched my back and we became good friends.

Our lives were ruled by ringing bells and our day started with the six-thirty bell. The dorm lights blazed and an officer strode up and down yelling 'Get up, get up'. Within a few minutes we would be up, washed, dressed, and, our beds made perfectly, lined up in the dorm. We were then marched downstairs to line up for breakfast. Along the painted brick walls of the dining room, were four tall barred windows, hung with curtains of a metric design. The tables were covered with checked tablecloths and each had seating for six girls. A large teapot and cups sat in the middle of each table. Breakfast was porridge, often with weevils or semolina (with weevils) and thick wedges of bread with a little jam.

Immediately after breakfast we marched to the muster yard and lined up for Assembly, which was taken by the superintendent and

Matron. Matron walked with a strut like a Nazi soldier and it seemed her only job was to take Assembly. She was a heavy-set woman with a European accent and wore sturdy lace up shoes with thick stockings, old-fashioned, ugly dresses and bulky cardigans, and no make-up and tied her grey hair in a bun. She was quite strange and made us all laugh, not because she was trying to be funny but because no one could ever understand a word the woman said. Matron would muddle her English and sort of talk backwards, addressing us as 'My good girl just.' We had to stifle the laughter behind our hands or pretend to be blowing our noses into a handkerchief to disguise the giggling. During assembly one morning, we were sure we saw a fly go in one ear and out the other. Our giggling became almost uncontrollable that day. I don't think she knew anyone's name and none of us knew what she was doing there. Actually, she was the school nurse but few ever saw her in that capacity.

After a lecture from the superintendent each morning, an officer would take us to our rostered job for the week. No real attempt was made to provide a basic education; the so-called 'training' was kitchen duties, laundry work, sewing, endless cleaning and scrubbing, painting, gardening and general maintenance — none of which had any real relevance to job opportunities. Instead, the aim was to ensure each girl's time was completely occupied.

Some jobs were 'privileged' and others, like peeling hundreds of vegetables and continuous scrubbing in the scullery, were punishment. 'Privileged' girls cleaned the administration offices and carried out sewing and mending work. The work in the dorms was endless. After scrubbing and drying the floors, we applied thick coats of beeswax polish, which is extremely difficult to shine off. We wrapped a cloth around a scrubbing brush and kept rubbing till the floors shone. This would take hours. Each day, the officers ran their fingers along every surface and round any ledges checking for dust. Behind the dining room was the laundry, a long and very old sandstone building where we would stand for hours — freezing in winter and sweating in summer — over rows of ironing boards, washing tubs and basins. Long clotheslines were strung up beside it. All this work was familiar to me after the years at the convent, particularly the laundry chores.

The next break of the day was lunch. We were marched from our jobs back to the dining room. Lining up, we'd file past the girls ladling out typical prison slop, then sit in our designated seat. The hot lunch of stews with vegetables always looked unappetising. The meat was usually tough and the green vegetables were overcooked and grey. There was mashed potato and mashed pumpkin and always plenty of weevils. No special care was taken, it was just cheap institutional food made to a strict and tight budget. Saturday night was my favourite meal though, meatballs in tomato sauce with rice.

THE HOUR AFTER LUNCH was the one time in our day at Parramatta that we could be teenage girls. We were allowed an hour of music and dancing on the Covered Way. This long pergola-style walkway linked the main buildings and ran adjacent to the muster yard. One girl would be the DJ on the supplied record player, spinning the records we received as gifts from visiting family. We behaved like normal teenagers, singing along with The Beatles and Elvis — but fifties rock 'n' roll was our favourite. To this music, we would dance out our frustrations. We were good dancers and we loved it. We had our own dance style called the Parramatta Jive, a form of rock and roll with our own steps. Eventually I graduated to DJ, picking all my favourite songs to keep the girls dancing. Some would watch, or sit and talk on the grassed area in the middle, but mostly we danced. When the bell rang, we all went back to work knowing a small part of us had been free, if only briefly.

Sandy showed me around and let everyone know she was my protector. She was funny and made me laugh and it was good to have a friend, especially one of the in-girls. She had been in Parramatta for quite a while and knew everyone. She wasn't afraid to say what she thought, often to the officers. This always resulted in lost points and her being 'unprivileged'. She would be dragged off to Isolation or Segregation and would disappear for days and sometime weeks.

I noticed Sammy lurking around me quite a lot so I asked Sandy what she was like.

'Oh she's just a crazy lesbian. Just ignore her. She'll get the hint you're not interested!'

'Oh great!' I said sarcastically.

'Then again maybe you are interested!' laughed Sandy.

Shower time was around four o'clock and as there was only one shower room and more than a hundred girls, it was run like a military operation. An external stone staircase gave access to the bathroom, which was underneath the main building. This was the original dungeon: a cavernous, cold and menacing place. Although the ancient walls of hand-hewn sandstone blocks had been painted institution cream, they ran with chilly moisture all year round. At some time, a smooth concrete floor had been laid; a barred window at the end of the room acted as a ventilation shaft, rather than providing any light. Four toilet cubicles and ten shower cubicles lined one long wall. The toilets had small half-doors but the showers had no doors at all. Down the centre of the room ran a long timber bench seat with a rail above. On the opposite wall were four washbasins, then a door to the adjoining laundry room beyond, and another to the laundry office.

In our dormitories we undressed, then, wrapped only in our towel, summer and winter, we lined up one girl to a step down the long timber staircase from our dorm. The line snaked all the way to the dungeon steps below and, as girls went in, the line progressed and the next dorm joined it. Held in front of us on upturned palms were our clothes, neatly folded in a pile with our underpants, turned inside out, on the top. I hated shower time and I hated the uneasy feeling that place gave me as we reached the dungeon door, ready for pants parade.

We went in, ten at a time. 'Next ten,' the officer at the door would count us in as we filed over to the laundry office door to show the crotch of our underpants to another female officer. Clean underwear was handed out only three times a week. If our pants were stained in any way and it was clean underwear day, we had to quickly wash them by hand at a sink and after re-inspection, were allowed to place them in the general laundry basket. When required, and only with an officer's approval, we were given a clean sanitary napkin after the soiled one was produced. We found this ritual humiliating and shameful. Adolescence is difficult enough but to be stripped of all dignity and privacy, and treated as worthless, has a lasting effect.

Lining up along the bench, we'd hang our towels on the rail, put our clothes on the seat and then dash into the shower, where the water was turned on for approximately two minutes, quickly washing our bodies and hair with the cake of hard white soap. When the order was given for 'water off', if our hair was still soapy it was too bad. If we complained or objected we were given points or punished and sometimes hit. After a quick wipe-down, we stood naked while our legs, our arms, between our fingers, then our whole bodies, were inspected for scratches or fresh tattoos. Unfortunately, self-mutilation was common; if you could get into hospital, there might be a way to escape.

Picking up our clothes, we'd file, shivering, into the adjoining gloomy laundry room, while the next ten girls repeated the ritual. We would hurriedly dress in our uniform and dirty or clean underwear and socks, depending on the day, then walk single-file back up to the dormitory to hang our towel at the end of our bed, before filing down for dinner.

Dormitory Four, next to Dorm Three, had been converted into a large common room so after dinner, 'privileged' girls were allowed to read, listen to the radio and talk before being rounded up and sent to their dorms for lights out at eight-thirty. 'Unprivileged' girls, more often than not including me, peeled vegetables, scoured pots and pans and had bed drill as punishment instead. This involved stripping your bed, turning the mattress then making the bed perfectly again, over and over. This punishment could go on for hours and often we didn't get to bed till well past midnight.

Eight-thirty is a ridiculous bedtime for teenage girls and of course, most of us couldn't sleep. We would lie in silence waiting for the officers to finish their rounds and, once sure they had gone, we'd start whispering to each other. Sometimes, someone would smuggle sweets into the dorm. We'd quietly creep out of bed and sit on the floor eating and whispering, our ears attuned for the sound of footsteps. I loved these night-time feasts, the camaraderie and sense of belonging. And just being typical teenage girls. Unluckily for us, the officers were adept at sneaking around and catching us unawares. Suddenly, the lights would blaze and we'd be up, scampering back to our beds in fright, trying to lie still as our hearts pounded.

'Stand out. Stand out!' Striding up and down, the officers demanded to know who was out of bed, but of course we never told.

'Line up. Line up. Now, downstairs all of you.'

Scrubbing the Covered Way was a cruel and popular punishment with these officers. We would be marched downstairs, given buckets of cold water and scrubbing brushes and made to scrub the concrete pathway in the dark. Often we were given only a toothbrush for scrubbing! Hour after hour on our hands and knees in the cold, dressed in our nighties, we scrubbed till our fingers and knees bled. If we cried or complained we were kicked. Often we could hardly stand when the punishment was over, our joints stiff with cold. The concrete path under the Covered Way was shiny and smooth from years of girls' scrubbing as punishment.

VISITING DAY WAS SUNDAY and very important to us. Each Saturday afternoon was clean clothes day and we were handed a different uniform, a pink-and-yellow polka-dot dress to wear the next day. This is how we knew which day of the week it was. Sunday morning we went to church services, in different rooms depending on our religion. After lunch we waited impatiently in the main recreation room at the end of the Covered Way. Lots of girls never had visitors so, to keep us all occupied, the room was turned into a make shift cinema and a film was shown. If your name was called, you were escorted down the Covered Way to sit with your visitors for an hour — immediate family only. They were allowed to bring us records, toothpaste, cakes and sweets, which we shared with each other during the following week. The officers paced up and down, watching every move. When the hour was over, we handed in our gifts and were taken down to the shower room where we were stripped of our clothes and, standing there naked, ordered to spread our legs. An officer would then check us internally to make sure nothing was hidden. Mostly they were looking for cigarettes and other objects wrapped in plastic. Our gifts were returned when we went back to the rec room, where we stayed till shower time.

My mother visited me only twice. The first time was two weeks after my admission. I was excited to see her and wanted so much for her to hug and hold me but, as usual, she offered her cheek. At least she had brought me some records and cakes. I tried to tell her how horrible it was here and what was happening to me. All she said was, 'The magistrate said you would benefit from the discipline. Surely it can't be as bad as that.' Then she changed the subject.

The second time she came was a couple of weeks later, to tell me they were moving to Townsville (interstate, in Far North Queensland). 'Your stepfather has been given a promotion. It is a great opportunity.'

'Congratulations,' I said. 'Will you still come to visit me?'

'No.' I looked at her in disbelief.

'It's a long way away, Sharyn. I will write to you. You are more than welcome to live with us when you leave here, as long as you have made up your mind to turn over a new leaf and be good.' I nodded, blinking back tears as my mind raced. My mother was leaving me in this God forsaken place! She was deserting me. How could she do this?

But she did. Did she understand the effect her rejection had on me? I knew my stepfather had to further his career and I accepted that; I was just sad my mother was never there for me. All her decisions centred on her mother, her husband, her son and mostly, herself. When it came to me, her decisions were about locking me up in institutions — putting me away — separating me from her, and her life. She had broken my heart again.

Now, I had nothing to look forward to and nothing to strive for. Feeling angry and deserted, I wanted to lash out at someone, so I did. An officer. A big mistake. I was on dormitory duty, polishing the floor on my hands and knees. I had polished the same area over and over and the officer was pushing me.

'Keep going. That's still not good enough,' she said.

'It looks OK to me.'

'I said it's not good enough.' I could hear the impatience in her voice but I was past caring.

'What's the point? It's only going to be walked on later.' The tension in the room was palpable. The other girls polished faster, careful not to look up or in my direction.

'That's it. I've had it with you,' she said and reached down and dragged me to my feet. 'Isolation. Now!' She marched me down to the cell block situated between the main building and the muster ground. A second officer grabbed me by the arm and shoved me into one of the small, dark cells, slamming the heavy door shut and securing it with a large bolt.

'Oh my God. What have I done?' I whispered.

The isolation cell block was built in 1934. It contained six cells and a small courtyard at one end, with a cold-water shower attached to the wall and open to the elements. Each cell was about twelve foot square. A heavy wooden door secured each cell, each door with a small observation window of thick glass with mesh embedded in it. The punishment never fitted the crime. Something trivial like walking too fast or too slow, your socks falling down, whispering or giggling, or simply not having enough points at the end of a week, could earn you twenty-four hours in Iso. Insolence, questioning an order, or any type of threatening behaviour earned you forty-eight hours. Try to escape from Parra and you could be put into Segregation for weeks. I was one of two thousand, one hundred and sixty girls who were placed in Isolation, just between the years of 1959 to 1966.

My cell was cold and completely empty except for a tin bucket with a lid. High on the wall opposite the door was a small barred window. A piece of timber with drill-holes had been placed between the bars and the glass so there was very little light. I sat on the wooden floor and cried, feeling very sorry for myself. This time I only had myself to blame.

I lost track of time.

The sound of the bolt on the cell door made me jump.

'Come on, here's your dinner. Hurry up.' I took the offered metal tray and stared in disbelief as the door thumped shut. Bread and water! The bread was stale and dry but the water tasted good.

Keys jangled. 'Get your mattress.'

I followed the officer past other cells to a room at the end of the corridor. Inside was a stack of canvas mattresses. 'Go on. Grab one.'

I don't know what it was filled with but, for a thin mattress, it was heavy as I dragged it back to the cell. The officer threw in a blanket, a pillow and a nightdress. 'I'll be back for your clothes and tray,' she said. When she returned, she handed me four squares of toilet paper. In the morning the ritual was reversed. I dragged the mattress back to the pile and was given back my clothes. Bread and water continued; however, I was eventually given one hot meal, which I gulped down.

I could hear the daily routine outside the cells — girls' voices, the music at lunch break and orders barked by officers. There was nothing to do except sit on the floor and think and sing. I sang every song I knew, to help pass the time. I was supposed to feel repentant but I wasn't. I felt angry. Two days later I was released, after a lecture from the superintendent.

I became my own worst enemy. Feeling abandoned and unloved, instead of reforming I became more belligerent and insolent. Consequently, this was not my only detention in Isolation. The best and worst aspect of Iso was the five-minute showering time — best because the courtyard was open, so for a few minutes each day you smelled fresh air and saw the sky; also the worst because winter was approaching, it was a cold-water shower and everyone looked down on you from the dormitories as you stood naked.

On my second stint in Isolation I got to know Deanna. She was in the cell next to mine and as sound echoed, it was possible to be heard between cells. The officers left us on our own between meal times, so we were able to keep each other company talking and singing. Deanna was also in Dormitory Three but as she was one of the tough or in-girls, I had been wary of her. Over that couple of days we formed a friendship. This was good. I was being accepted by those who mattered.

From the Covered Way you entered the main recreation room, which was the original chapel, built in the nineteenth century. The outside entrance doors were permanently locked and the four steps leading to them were the exclusive domain of the in-girls. At lunch break, if they weren't dancing, the in-girls would sit here to chat casually and survey the scene. In our own hierarchy, these girls were admired and revered. From the day I arrived I had wanted to sit with them — I knew immediately what those steps represented. Now, because I had been accepted by Sandy and Deanna, I could walk over and tentatively nudge my behind onto the edge of the bottom step. I knew it was only a matter of time before I worked my way up the steps.

The bond between us girls was the core of our survival. I was not a 'flip', our word for nerds or girls who were weak or good; you never 'lagged' or told on anyone and never 'gave anyone up' to an officer. If you did, the other girls would retaliate sooner or later and if any girl became too friendly with an officer, she was ostracised. We had our own special sayings. 'Send My Love' was an expression we used constantly. It meant just what it said; however, we spoke it to each other in normal conversation. Instead of 'see you later' we would say 'send my love'. 'ILWA' meant 'I Love, Worship, Adore'. This was scratched onto walls, doors in isolation cells and tattooed on some girls' bodies. We also used it in letters and notes to each other, not necessarily in a romantic or lesbian way but as good friends.

Some of the girls were memorable characters, especially Lillian. Aged about fifteen, she was a beauty. I admired her white skin, almond-shaped eyes, full lips, white teeth and her white-blonde hair, so long that it touched her behind. She loved to comb and style it — the only thing she did love. She despised all the officers and told them regularly, often screaming at them, 'You f—ing bitches, leave my things alone! Don't you even think of touching me you f—ing freaks. I'll smash you from here into tomorrow!'

Her screeching and screaming could be heard echoing through the buildings. As we listened to her, we would try to stifle our laughter by holding our sides. Secretly we all wished we had the guts to do the same, but this girl was reckless. She was hard to get close to because she didn't like any of us either. Another time in Isolation, she was in the next cell. I wanted to talk, to keep each other company. Not Lillian. All was quiet from her side, so I left her alone.

SAMMY, THE TATTOOED GIRL, who Sandy called 'the crazy lesbian', was still hanging around me. This day I was in a foul mood. I had finally received a letter from my mother but it was all about their wonderful life in Townsville and how happy they all were. Sammy was following me everywhere, driving me crazy. I turned on her and yelled,

'Piss off and leave me alone.'

Walking away with tears in my eyes, I hadn't noticed Lillian sitting nearby. As I walked past her she said, 'You know the best way to treat your enemies? Ignore them. Make them invisible. It drives them insane.'

I turned towards her, expecting those cold grey eyes. Instead, I saw a compassionate and soft girl who was smart. (I carried her words with me and to this day it works! Ignore them — it definitely drives them crazy.)

I received no mail, except for the occasional letter from my mother, which only intensified my feeling of abandonment and rejection. One lunch break, after dancing to Little Pattie's 'Stompin' at Maroubra', I hit on the crazy idea of writing to her. I sent the letter care of her record label and, to my surprise and delight, a few weeks later I received a reply! It was quite newsy, sharing details of what she had been doing. I felt so special that the most famous teenager in the country would take the time to personally write to me — a nobody fan in Parramatta Girls' Home. It only strengthened my resolve to one day be a singer, just like her. I wrote her two more letters and received replies both times.

Sandy signed me up for basketball. It was good exercise and the games helped us get rid of pent up emotions but I was not a good player because I tired easily. Each dormitory had their own team and we played against each other in our in-house competition. Our best players were also in a team who played in competition with outside schools. Our team did well in this competition and had a reputation as tough players. The schools were afraid of us — understandably — we always played a challenging game!

A 'privileged' position was working in the kitchen with an officer we nicknamed 'Birdie'. In her little apron, she looked like a grandmother. As we prepared the meals, she taught us to cook and let us lick the bowl when she had mixed up scones or a cake. She would make hot chocolate for us, and coffee for herself, then sit and talk with us as though we were her grandchildren. What a pleasure and a breath of fresh air that woman was! The kitchen was also a place of punishment but working with Birdie was a privilege.

Deanna walked by the kitchen one afternoon; on maintenance detail, she was wearing her work overalls and her deep pockets were too good to resist. We quickly passed out fresh sandwiches left over from the staff tray, along with freshly baked cookies. She stuffed her pockets to the point of overflowing and somehow managed to smuggle the stash into the dormitory. Late that night we sat huddled on the floor, whispering and devouring the illicit treats. They were delicious and worth every mouthful — we were caught.

This time, we were all marched out to the asphalt muster yard in lines, given a metal bucket filled with water and a toothbrush and ordered to scrub the playground. It was a rainy night in early winter. We shivered uncontrollably in our cotton nightdresses as the material became soaked and clung to our bodies in the freezing wind. Hour after hour, on our hands and knees, we scrubbed. The officers shone torches on us as they stood around in their warm coats under umbrellas. Drinking mugs of hot tea, they laughed amongst themselves while twenty young girls wept silently and hopelessly into their buckets. Our knees and shins were torn from kneeling on the abrasive asphalt, our fingers frozen and our scraped knuckles raw and bleeding. We were there so long the officers had a change of shift. At handover, checking her watch one officer said, 'This lot have been here for a few of hours. Another hour should do it.'

When the punishment was over, many of us could hardly move we were so stiff with cold. We helped each other up and shuffled back to the dormitory.

I lay in bed, thinking I would never feel warm again. I couldn't understand how we deserved this cruel treatment. We were not criminals: we were children. All under the age of eighteen and most branded as 'uncontrollable runaways' by the court, we were left in the care of the Child Welfare Department's sadistic men and women. They succeeded in making teenage girls feel worthless, useless, depressed, suicidal, homicidal, and as though we were just plain rotten to the core. To them we were all bad girls; evil and vile creatures, we deserved the harshest punishment. Rarely a kind or encouraging word was spoken to us for the length of our sentence. For most of us, the sentence has lasted a lifetime. Our crimes? Who can remember? For the majority, it was something trivial.

SOME GIRLS PLOTTED and planned their escape and who could blame them? It was called 'absconding'. The penalty, when caught, was usually a period of incarceration in the hellhole institution called Hay Institution for Girls. Almost six hundred miles away in the country, a one-hundred-year-old jail had been resurrected by the Department of Child Welfare to teach the really badly behaved girls how to conform. We knew a girl had absconded if we found one of us missing at early-morning Muster. Everyone, girls and officers, would whisper about it throughout the day. The girl was usually brought back within a few days or sometimes weeks. But they were always brought back. They would be locked up in Segregation, waiting to be assessed by the visiting psychiatrist. Within a week, in the middle of the night we would hear the girl being taken away, her screams cutting the silence. We'd rush to our dormitory windows and see the shadows of officers walking quickly, escorting the distraught girl to the superintendent's office. Once there, the girl would be told she was going to Hay. The whole scene reminded me of prisoners on death row being taken to their final destination.

My friend Sandy tried to abscond. She was on painting detail outdoors and the tall and sturdy ladder she was using was too much of a temptation. As soon as the officer had turned her back, Sandy picked up the ladder and ran the twenty feet to the big wall, intending to clamber over it. She slammed the ladder against it and had cleared the first few rungs but the officer was too fast — Sandy was caught by the ankle and the hem of her overalls, yanked down off the ladder and marched away to the main office. We didn't see her again until three weeks later. She wasn't sent to Hay that time, but the fading yellow and purple smudges around her eyes and nose told us the story.

I was relieved to see her and we never really discussed in detail what had happened but, over time, I pieced it together. There was a particular male officer who wore Bermuda-style shorts with long socks. She'd been standing in his office being reprimanded when he'd walked over to face her, then bent down and pulled up his socks — as he stood he'd punched her hard in the stomach. She was winded. Then, as she collapsed forward, he gave her an uppercut in the face, breaking her nose and blacking her eyes. She had been put into Segregation for three weeks until the signs of her injuries healed enough for her to return to our dormitory.

These things you pretty much kept to yourself. Plus, you needed to keep up an appearance of being tough — to cultivate an outward brittleness — or you'd never survive.

Sandy was funny and cheeky and always had to have the last word. She couldn't help herself. It was a continuing battle of wills between Sandy and the officers. They would push her till she reacted. She was always being dragged off to Isolation; then she'd reappear a few days later, unrepentant. Eventually she was sent to Hay.

Every once in a while we came across a good officer, like the young housewife who really did try to show a bit of kindness to us. She didn't last long. Also, there was an older officer who would turn off the lights at night in the dormitory and tell us scary stories. We all liked her a lot. She disappeared — she went home from work one night, never to return.

BASHING AND SEXUAL ASSAULT of the girls by male supervisors was never, I believe, recorded in any official documents or inquiry at the time. However, according to many girls' testimonies to an official senate enquiry, years later in 2004, it certainly did take place.

In January 1961, the girls' situation had become so desperate that they rioted. I wasn't there at the time, but we heard about it. Academic Peter Quinn's thesis, written in 2004, told the story:

In January 1961, the Assistant Under Secretary, Alan Thomas, received an anonymous letter saying the place was in turmoil and asking the Deputy Superintendent be removed. Thomas disregarded it. A month later, things came to a head when the Deputy Superintendent was suspended for misconduct (he was later dismissed). Within a matter of hours of this event, the first of three riots started when twenty girls climbed on the roof of the hospital block, screaming obscenities and hurling roof tiles at police. They were removed after midnight by the use of fire hoses.

The next day an even bigger riot took place, with a hundred girls climbing on the roof, and hundreds of people gathering in the street outside to watch. The girls stripped naked and tore tiles from the roof, smashing windows, destroying furniture and causing thousands of pounds worth of damage. A particularly wild riot occurred ten days later, during which nineteen girls escaped over the wall, using building materials being used to repair the earlier damage. A series of riots then took place over the next few months. The response of the Department was coercive. Initially, a special squad of male officers was sent there to keep order. Girls, who were inmates at the time, later alleged they had been beaten with rubber hoses during the riots.

The *Daily Telegraph* newspaper's editorial (from March 3, 1961, quoted by Peter Quinn) suggests the official reaction:

Mr Heffron (NSW Premier) has decided there will be no open inquiry 'at this stage' into the conduct of the Training School for Girls. He is satisfied the departmental action will set matters right. It may be; but the public — in particular those unhappy parents who have children committed to the school, cannot be certain of it unless a full and open inquiry is held. Mr Heffron brushed aside the requests for an inquiry in the face of disturbing facts and even more disturbing allegations. The facts are that a senior officer has been suspended, that Child Welfare officers have been asked to take over from those in charge of the institution, and that there have been three outbreaks of rioting at the school in four days. The allegations are of immorality and brutality within the school. The Premier says that when he was Minister for Education he built up the institution from a 'shambles' to a modern school.

Peter Quinn tells of the consequences for the girls:

The ringleaders were taken before the Children's Court and sentenced to prison terms ranging from a month to three months. In the period from March to the end of 1961, thirty-six girls were so dealt with. Some went to prison twice, one girl three times.

As a result of these events, Hawkins announced a special institution for girls would be established at Hay.

Four years later, screams pierced the silence at night and only made us more terrified of the men who were our supervisors. It seemed to us that they were protected by authorities who turned their backs to what went on behind locked doors. We would gather around the barred windows, whispering in the dark as we listened to those screams from one of our girls.

'What's happening?' asked a new girl.

'Another bashing probably, or worse,' said Joyce. The frightening female giant I'd met on my first day had turned out to be a caring and wise Senior. She was a repeat offender and now nearly eighteen. 'You new lot have got it easy. If you'd been here a couple a years ago, it was really bad. We were being raped and bashed a lot.'

There was a sharp intake of breath. It was the new girl.

'That's why we did the riots in 1961. It was the only way we could think of to try to stop it. No one was listening to us. The officers were molesting us girls and bashing us senseless and getting away with it. So we rioted to get attention. Some of us climbed up onto the roof.' As I pictured the tall buildings in my mind, I could only imagine the desperation those girls must have felt to put themselves in such danger. 'Reporters came from the newspapers and the television, so we used that chance to tell them as much as we could. Trouble is, no one believed us.' I looked at Joyce. Tears were glistening on her cheeks, caught by moonlight coming through the window. The new girl's eyes were wide with surprise.

'Most of the girls involved were sent to Long Bay Gaol but nothing happened to the officers. Not a thing. There was an inquiry but they kept their jobs. After the ringleaders had been sent to jail, the department decided to really punish us all and opened up that Hay place. In the middle of nowhere, out in the country. So now when you play up in Parramatta they send you to Hay. Watch out, girls!' She paused. 'Things still aren't right but it's not as bad as it was.'

We stood quietly, some with our heads down, the new girl was crying softly. 'The screaming's stopped now' said Joyce. 'Yep, this place is like a holiday camp compared to what it used to be.' She turned away from the window and went back to her bed.

'It might be like a holiday camp compared to the old days but it still ain't right,' said a voice behind us. 'Those men are still having their way with us girls.' We turned to see who had spoken. It was a girl called Beth. We could see the terror in her eyes, 'It's far from over.' she said.

GIRLS WERE SENT TO HAY for 'a period of training' after so-called misbehaviour at Parramatta Girls' Home; repeated insolence and disobeying any kind of order were the main reasons, after a psychiatric test. Girls who failed to settle into the routine of Parramatta were also transferred to Hay.

We didn't know much about the place. Our unspoken code said there were things you didn't talk about and Hay was one of them.

But we saw the effects of Hay on returning girls. They would appear unannounced at early morning Muster, stamping their feet to attention and marching everywhere. They were zombie-like, brainwashed, and their regimented behaviour was very strange. We didn't understand what had happened or what they had been through. We never asked and the girls never told. We looked after them, treated them gently and offered a word of sympathy when we could. They were damaged and traumatised and it was too terrible to talk about.

After our stint in Isolation, Deanna and I had become good friends. We danced at lunchtime and generally spent our free time together — me respectfully pushing my way onto the in-girls' steps to chat with her or hanging out in the rec room in the evenings when we weren't 'unprivileged' turning beds and doing punishments, which we often did together as well. Unfortunately we were not a good influence on one another. We encouraged each other to be rebellious and insolent, one egging the other on to be reckless and not thinking of the consequences. I was continually told I was a bad girl and had no self-worth, so I acted accordingly. My mother had deserted me, no one loved or cared about me and, I believed, I had nothing to lose. I was wrong again.

By now it was late July and only two months from my release date set by the magistrate — but I had no way of knowing this. I was angry and in pain. I had a nagging toothache. I had reported it to several officers a couple of times, to no avail. No one would take any notice, my nerves felt raw and I felt ill.

At lunch I looked at the meal of tough meat and overcooked vegetables on the plate in front of me and decided it was too hard to chew. An officer noticed I was not eating. She was the one I had thought was so nice when I first arrived but I had since discovered she was as cruel and spiteful as the rest of them.

'Eat your lunch. Now.' I declined. She hit me hard in the back with her fist. I turned and vomited all over the floor.

'The minute you've cleaned that up, get back here and finish your lunch.'

'Miss, I'm feeling sick,' I said. Whimpering, I tried to wipe up the vomit with a cloth.

'I didn't ask about your health. Get up and eat,' she yelled at me, turning red in the face. Her temper, explosive in its sudden intensity, took me by surprise.

I guess it was the way I was feeling that day — I was not well — or perhaps it was just the years of abuse. Nobody gave a damn how I felt or what was happening in my pathetic life! I was sixteen years old and enough was enough. I slowly stood up and looked into the face of this woman who was supposed to be taking care of me. I was fed up with being spoken to as if I didn't matter — so I picked up the plate of stew and vegetables and threw it at her.

'F—ing eat it yourself, bitch!' I screamed back at her. Lord knows where that came from — I startled myself! It was not the way I usually spoke. But I had said it and she reacted accordingly. She grabbed a handful of my hair and pulled it hard. I lurched forward, off balance, and she put out her foot, tripping me. As I fell to the floor heavily, my hands flew to my face to protect my glasses. Then Miss dragged me across the dining room floor, up the long Covered Way and into the superintendent's office. He immediately agreed the segregation cell was the best place for me.

'You've done your dash now, girl. Oh yes indeed,' she said, panting with rage. I could see her hands shaking as she fumbled to find the correct key.

Knowing I was at the point of no return and definitely not caring, I replied, 'Oh f—k off!'

Segregation was a misery. This particular segregation cell was underneath the main building in the dungeon, near the shower room but entered by a different staircase. The walls were the same large sandstone blocks but were raw and unpainted. The floor was cold concrete, the thick walls muffled all sound and seeped moisture and seemed to hold a dank smell of years of despair. An overhead light cast a dirty yellow glow twenty-four hours a day, because the barred window was completely blacked out. Again, there was nothing, just a can to pee in. I hated it. I was sure I heard rats and could feel spiders crawling on me. God help me.

I sang to try to convince myself I wasn't frightened. I sang in defiance of the rules. When I wasn't singing I was praying. Angry prayers. Begging prayers: 'Come on God, help me.'

My prayers remained unanswered. What had I done to deserve this? Full of self-pity and hating everyone and every moment of my life, I ranted, sang and prayed. I was given a couple of hot meals but mostly each day it was dry bread and lukewarm milk; the milk, to me, was a bonus. The mattress each night was rock hard.

I was never bashed or abused in Segregation, as others told me they had been, but I believe one time I came close. I was sitting on the floor singing loudly when the door opened without warning. Standing in the door way was the officer in the Bermuda shorts and long socks. He didn't say a word, just stood with his arms by his side; but the fist he'd made with one hand gave away his intention. In a heartbeat I knew what was going to happen. The little girl inside me who had been beaten and degraded all those years by the nun was not going to let it happen again. This time I didn't cringe. I sprang to my feet in a defiant stance. Slightly side-on, I stood ready with my legs apart, my arms crossed, my hands forming fists and rage welling up in my chest, and I stared, challenging him. My sudden movement startled him. As he took a step inside, I brought up my fists and yelled as loud as I could, 'Get away from me. Don't you come near me! I'll scream, I'll yell and I'll tell. I'll tell everyone. The newspapers, the television and they *will* listen this time.'

Before he had time to react, a voice behind him said, 'Everything alright here Sir? Is there a problem?' It was the superintendent. God had answered my prayers after all.

'No problem, Super. I'm finished here.'

The superintendent closed the door, locked it, and they walked away. I shrank to the floor trembling; then I burst into tears. I believe the superintendent had seen the officer heading down to the dungeon, suspected his intention, and followed him.

A few days later those rattling keys were back. I was taken to the shower room and allowed a three-minute shower, which felt like a luxury. In a clean uniform I was taken to an office, next door to the superintendent's. A man wearing a suit and tie, glasses and brown leather shoes indicated for me to sit in the chair opposite his desk.

'Good afternoon Sharyn. My name is Doctor Forbes. I am here to have a talk with you about what happened the other day in the dining room. I have read your file. I see you were living in the southeastern suburbs with your mother and stepfather. Is that correct?'

What did my home life have to do with what had happened in the dining room? I nodded.

'Did you not like your home?' He looked over the top of his glasses waiting for my answer.

'The house was nice. It was the people in it I had a problem with,' I said.

'What was the problem?'

'We just didn't get along.'

'I see here you hadn't been out of St Martha's Convent very long before you were sent here. Do you like it here?' I looked at the idiot. Was he mad? Did he know what went on here?

'No,' I said. He leaned back in his chair and stretched out his legs.

'What do you like to do? What are your hobbies?' Now he was being ridiculous — there were no hobbies in Parramatta. What was the point of these inane questions anyway? I wasn't in the mood to give him any intelligent answers.

'I like to watch ants' I said, determined to make this as difficult as possible for him.

'Ants! Why is that?' asked the university-trained moron.

'Because they are very busy going about their business and they do it quietly.'

'You are not cooperating, Sharyn. Why is that?' Have you only just worked that out, I thought?

'Because I have absolutely no idea what it is you want,' I said.

Exasperated, he shuffled his papers and asked me to do a series of tests, mostly identifying what looked like blobs of black ink, and filling in missing words — a definite psychiatric test. The mood I was in, I was bound to fail miserably. I completed the paperwork and passed it back across the desk where he studied it for a minute, then pushed it into a manila envelope.

'You are quite an intelligent girl. It's a pity to see someone like you wasting your young life,' he said. I looked at him, searching his face for a trace of compassion.

'Would you do something for me?' I asked.

'Certainly.'

'Would you tell the superintendent I have a toothache?' He looked at me, feigned a smile and nodded, then stood up and called to an officer to take me back to my segregation cell. After she had locked the door, I sat on the floor and wept.

The following night they came to take me away.

CHAPTER EIGHT

Hell and Hard Labour: Hay Institution For Girls

KEYS JANGLING in the lock startled me. I looked up at two officers silhouetted in the doorway, one indicating to me to step out. They escorted me through a heavy door and up the stone stairs outside. It was cold and dark and quiet, so why was I was still in my uniform? My stomach turned the instant I realised what was happening. I was going to Hay! As they escorted me into the main building, I yelled into the silence as loud as I could, 'They're taking me! They're taking me!' in the hope some of the girls would hear. I stood, trembling, in front of the superintendent, seated at his desk. I guessed it was my file he had open, reading through the loose pages, turning each one slowly. Eventually he looked up.

'Regrettably you have failed to conform, Sharyn. This week you have been subversive, insolent and, finally, have refused to obey instructions.' He clasped his hands on top of the papers. 'Your continuing unsatisfactory behaviour has indicated a need for further strict disciplinary training so you are being transferred to Hay, for a period of three months. You will benefit from the less permissive atmosphere there and, I hope, return a more responsible person.' With that, he closed my file and stood up. 'Thank you officers.' It was August 12, 1965.

IN THE MIDDLE OF THE NIGHT I was handcuffed and taken away by a man and a woman escort, he wearing a gun. We travelled by car to a railway station where we waited in the cold for the train.

In the superintendent's office, a dose of Largactil was most likely administered. It's a liquid sedative that I have since discovered was fairly standard practice in these transfers. And I was certainly drowsy. The overnight train trip was long and uncomfortable and I dozed, sitting with my cuffed hands in my lap, covered by a blanket and an officer either side of me. I don't remember much else except eating a sandwich.

Eight hours later we arrived at Narrandera Railway Station in southwestern New South Wales, where we were met by two Child Welfare officers. In the car park, my handcuffs were taken off and I was put in the back of an old van. It was empty except for a long metal bench. There were some ventilation slits high up on each side panel and a small sealed window in each of the narrow back doors. The gloom of the inside was a relief from the bright sunlight, which hurt my eyes. I felt dazed, giddy and thirsty. I asked for water but was ignored.

Over the next two hours I slid, slipped and was thrown around the back of the airless van as it lurched and jolted along the rough country roads. I caught glimpses out the back windows of desolate country, dry and flat, with a few trees shimmering on the horizon. The van finally stopped inside the entrance of the Hay Institution for Girls and the van doors opened. All I could see was the back of two enormous, closed timber doors. Exhausted and petrified of what lay ahead, I was dragged through a door marked 'Office'.

I stood while my paperwork was checked by two women and a tall man. 'I'm the superintendent. Welcome to Hay. Eyes to the floor,' he said.

I didn't understand what he meant, so I looked at him, a question forming on my lips. He yelled so suddenly I jumped with fright. 'Eyes to the floor I said!' I jerked my head down, looking straight at my feet. He strode around me, hands clasped behind his back. I remember the sound of his boots thudding on the timber floor.

'There will be total silence. You will do what you are told, to the letter. From now on you will stand straight, shoulders back, head up and eyes down. You will never look any officer or any other person in the eye again. You will not look up, left, right or around. Your eyes are to be down at all times, no matter what happens. Do you understand?'

'Yes.' I squeaked.

'I can't hear you. Do you understand?'

'Yes, Sir!'

'If you want to do it the hard way, we will break you. Or you can do it the easy way. It's up to you. Miss will take you to your cabin. You will be drilled in the routine and put to work. You will benefit from the strict discipline here.'

'Yes, Sir!'

As I followed Miss out into sunlight I caught a glimpse of a large, square lawn area with a narrow cement path around the edge. On adjoining sides of it, long single-storey brick buildings with sloping corrugated iron rooves faced into the grassy area. A long solid-brick building with tiny high windows formed the third side and, in the middle of the fourth side, there was a small square building. It looked sinister standing on its own. Running behind the buildings was an unbroken, sixteen-foot-high brick wall with watchtowers on two corners. What was this place? I looked for the cabins. At least I'll have my own little cabin, I mused.

'Look around while you can,' said Miss, 'this is your last chance. And don't think about trying to escape from here either. You're out in the middle of the desert, hundreds of miles from anywhere. If you did get out, you'd be bitten by a snake or die of thirst before anyone ever found you.'

We stood in front of barred double doors while she selected a big iron key from the large ring hanging from her belt. I stared in shock into the gloom. It was a cell block! Ahead was a long corridor with six cell doors set into the painted brick walls down each side. Each door was open and had a small semi-circular drop-down hatch, a peep-hole and a large sliding bolt on the outside. The brick ceiling was curved like a cave, and the cement floor was so smooth and polished that the sunlight reflecting from it created an eerie glow.

Miss pushed me into a cell, banged the door shut and slammed the bolt across. She opened the hatch a few minutes later and passed me a sandwich and a mug of milk. I was ravenous. I'd had nothing to eat or drink for hours. Two officers returned with a chair and I was ordered to sit while one roughly cut my hair; clipped short and straight round, it would have looked as though someone had placed a bowl over my head except that I had curly hair, so it looked even worse. I was too traumatised to protest. Then one of the officers brought me a bucket of water, a wire brush and a brick.

'Stand to attention by the bed, your back to the door — eyes down. You will do this immediately you hear an officer coming to your cell door.' I did as I was ordered. 'Now, you will scrub the paint off the walls, back to the raw brick with this brush and this brick.' I didn't move. I was trying to work out what to do with the brush and the brick. 'The brick will help break the surface of the paint,' she explained. 'You will do this until the walls of this cell are completely clean, no matter how long it takes. If I can't hear the brick and the brush, you will be punished,' Behind me I heard her walk to the door. 'And do not speak or make a sound. From now on you will live in complete silence, unless otherwise instructed.' She slammed the door shut and bolted it.

I was trapped in a nightmare, I told myself; it was the only explanation. Surely this couldn't be real? I looked at the brick. What? How? I heard footsteps so I quickly picked it up; it was heavy. Gingerly, I rubbed it on the wall. Nothing. I rubbed again, this time harder, and the paint surface started to bruise and crack. I rubbed harder and harder as hopeless anger rose in my body, giving strength to my already aching arm. Tears of frustration and self-pity blurred my vision but I knew I must keep rubbing and brushing or I would be punished. God knows what other frightening punishments they deal out here, I thought to myself.

I scrubbed for the rest of the day. The paint was shiny and thick and seemed impossible to remove. I was so tired and confused. Later, as the light faded from the barred opening high up in the wall, I heard stamping and shouting and the banging of cell doors. What is this place, I asked myself, for the umpteenth time that day. Sleep did not come easily that night. I lay in the cold cell, shivering under the thin grey blanket, whimpering. I had never been so afraid. This was Hell.

FREEZING IN WINTER and sweltering in summer, the small country town of Hay is situated seven hundred and twenty-five kilometres southwest of Sydney, on the remote Hay Plains. I believe these plains are amongst the flattest terrain in the world, covering over forty thousand square kilometres.

The old Hay Gaol colonial prison complex was purpose-built during 1879 and has changed little to this day. It closed in 1915 and — apart from a brief period housing a maternity hospital in 1921 — didn't resume operation as a prison again until 1930, when it doubled as a lock-hospital for the insane. Parra Girls weren't the first to be incarcerated here under questionable circumstances. During World War II, it was used as a compound for prisoners of war: Italian, then Japanese — a number of whom were actually Australians from Broome but were descendants of Japanese-born pearl divers; some had never even been to Japan. Closed in 1946, the Hay site was left derelict for fifteen years until it was re-opened as an annex to Parramatta Girls' Home. The first girls were transferred to the facility by the NSW Department of Child and Social Welfare in September of 1961, just after the riots. As Hay Institution for Girls, the site's history as a place of pain and suffering continued in its new purpose as an experimental disciplinary centre for incorrigible girls (those aged between thirteen and eighteen).

The ringleaders from the Parramatta riots were sent to Hay ostensibly for three months of constant observation, supervision and extremely strict behavioural and dress codes. In reality, it was a brutal maximum-security institution for girls: a place of cruel and extreme punishment for the teenage girls who would not comply with the strict routine of Parramatta. They were subjected to a militaristic regime of State-sanctioned harsh discipline and hard labour designed to crush their spirits through brainwashing and programming. Behind high walls, and a long way from the Sydney-based authorities, many abuses occurred over the years. Hay's disciplinary practices and routines were modelled on a similar institution for boys, which operated from 1945 in Tamworth, another rural town in NSW.

Incredibly, the NSW Government of the day was presented with a completely different description of the place by its own authorities, as the plan outlined by the Minister for Child Welfare (NSW Legislative Assembly, November 8, 1961, p.2297) shows:

The present facilities at Parramatta do not permit a satisfactory segregation of those girls showing serious behavioural problems from those who are more amenable to the training situation. This undesirable state of affairs has been rectified by the opening of the Institution for Girls at Hay. The buildings had been unoccupied for many years and when taken over by the Department, were shabby and unkempt, with a general air of neglect and decay. It has now been completely transformed. Broken paths, rank grass and accumulated rubbish in the grounds have been replaced by trim lawns, gay flowerbeds and flourishing vegetable gardens. Inside there is a pleasant dining and recreation room, a large well equipped kitchen, a sewing room, modern surgery and the girls' cabins, all freshly painted in pastel colours.

In fact, it was the girls' backbreaking labour that had wrought the marvellous transformation: the place was virtually derelict when the first girls had arrived. The rationale given for this program of slave labour (let's call it what it was) was fanciful:

Each girl is treated as a special case and given individual training. This is one of the three main principals underlying the Institution's regime. The second is strict discipline, many of the girls come from homes where discipline was entirely lacking and in later years they had learned to defy or evade all attempts at control. Such a background tends to produce instability, and the firm discipline at Hay not only teaches a respect for law and order, but also helps to counter the insecurity that lies behind so much delinquent behaviour. The third principle is that all the girls should be kept occupied with a full programme of work and recreation. Emphasis is on productive activity of a kind that will encourage a sense of achievement. Thus much of the indoor painting has been done by the girls themselves: they do the cooking, laundry and housework and make all their own clothes. Physical exercises are given daily, while for recreation there are indoor games and an ample supply of reading matter. The girls also tend the gardens and pick and arrange the flowers in the living room and in each of the girls' cabins.

The Minister made it sound like a holiday camp! But I would quickly learn what it was really like.

THE LARGEST BUILDING comprised a cell block containing twelve cells called 'cabins' — a nautical term I believe, carried over from the era of convict and prison ships. My cabin contained a single iron frame bed, a thin horsehair mattress and a small narrow bench and seat; both had only one leg, the other end attached to the wall. There was no heating or cooling. A metal can with a lid and handle was provided for defecating and urinating, along with four squares of toilet paper and a Bible.

The maximum number of inmates held at any one time was twelve, with five or six officers on duty at all times. These officers were mainly untrained local Hay residents, (female staff were subordinate to male staff) and all were permitted to have keys to our cabins.

We had to remain six feet apart from any girl or officer — without exception. We were not permitted to speak without first signalling for permission and walking was not allowed; we had to march and often, 'on the double'. We always stood to attention unless otherwise instructed, with our eyes to the floor; again, no exceptions. The daily routine involved very hard physical labour designed to dehumanise us. They'd have us breaking up concrete paths then relaying them, digging and planting gardens, scrubbing paint from brick walls and concrete floors with a wire brush and a brick, hand-sewing leather and canvas. Plus, all institution washing was done by hand. Excessive exercising was also carried out at predetermined intervals during each day. All of this was designed to break us down to the point where, at the end of a day, we hardly cared about anything. The routine never altered, seven days a week.

Half-hourly checks were conducted all night, each time turning on our cell light, which deprived us of sleep. We were made to sleep on our side, facing the door, so our face could be seen through the peep-hole. If we rolled over during the night, we were dragged out of bed, made to strip and make it again, then ordered to stand to attention until the officer returned. This was repeated all night, every night, until each of us was conditioned not to move in our sleep.

No education or schooling was provided, only conditioning through control and punishment. If we resisted or showed any form of attitude or disobedience we were placed on a half-meal ration called a 'bounce', or locked in the isolation cell: that solitary, sinister-looking building in the middle of the yard. In Isolation, we were given stale bread and water and had our sentence extended — one month for each time.

The other form of punishment was Practices. Practices were exercises and other disciplines. According to the *Official Routine Procedures Hay 526*:

> PRACTICE *entails the repetition of a particular activity in which the individual inmate is below the required standard or that she has neglected i.e., having failed to answer* YES MRS *when spoken to, she will now spend her* PRACTICE *time answering* YES MRS *in a clear voice at regular intervals.* PRACTICES *also include marching, turning, break off, clothes folding etc. Note girls on* PRACTICES *do not forfeit their issue of fruit.*

The reality was harsh and relentless conditioning. Other forms of 'Practice' included repeating an activity over and over or standing at attention, facing a wall or with your hand up, for as long as the officer chose. If you moved, you were punished again.

Typically, the teenage girls sent to Parramatta and Hay had not committed a criminal offence. We were simply the lost and forgotten children of Australia's welfare system. In fact, each of us was subjected to the barbaric and inhumane treatment at Hay as punishment for committing the offence of disruptive behaviour at Parramatta: insolence, backchatting, complaining, throwing tantrums, arguing, absconding, self-damage and frustration at the injustice life had thrown our way.

Unfortunately, the female officers in charge of us girls were misled regarding our status, as shown in this address to the Hay Historical Society, delivered by a female ex-officer in August, 2004: 'Some of the girls were really, really bad; murderesses but they had dreadful beginnings to their lives, a lot of them. Of course some of them did not, they were just plain bad. In other words, the ten worst girls in New South Wales.'

Local Hay residents also had this impression, having been told that we were hardened criminals and they should stay away because most of the girls were quite mad and 'will stab you in the back'. Other residents had little or no idea of what went on behind the high walls. They were grossly misinformed by the local newspaper, *The Riverine Grazier*, as this extract from an article that appeared on Thursday, April 19, 1962 shows:

Each girl occupies her own room which she has tastefully painted in gay pastel colours. They are responsible for the tidiness and cleanliness of their own quarters and to enhance the appearance of their surroundings, each girl picks two bunches of flowers each week from their own gardens, for her own room.

I WAS CONFINED to 'the scrubbing cell' for several days, until I had completely scrubbed the paint off all the walls. Each night I was passed a lightweight nightdress and each morning I was passed the same shapeless, short-sleeved cotton uniform, white ankle socks and lace-up shoes. Buttons had replaced the hooks and eyes on the bras, to prevent us straightening them out and using them to scratch ourselves or self-mutilate. It was August, the middle of winter and very cold, so I was given a thin, red cardigan for warmth.

Before being moved to my permanent cell, I was drilled in procedure, marching up and down the cell for hours: swing straight arms forward to shoulder height, then a strong swing back; fists clenched with thumbs pressed into hands and fingers wrapped around; large strides and knees lifted high; back straight, head up — and eyes down! Always eyes down. To halt, lift knee high, foot fourteen inches off the ground, then a loud stamp down. I was ordered never to walk. I was to march everywhere like a soldier, and occasionally double-time. I learned to call out, 'Report to you, Sir,' and 'Report back to you, Sir,' — a strange language. If I needed to attract an officer's attention, I was forbidden to speak. I had to stand to attention and raise my hand in a military fashion; starting with my arm by my side, I had to quickly touch my shoulder, then put my arm up straight, beside my ear, keep my eyes down. And wait. Wait to be acknowledged. If my arm wavered I would be punished.

OUR DAY STARTS at six o'clock. My cabin's light blazes and the sound of keys rattling and door hatches clanging echo through the cell block.

'All rise!' I jump out of bed and stand to attention at the end of my bench-table, my back to the cell door. If I am not in position by the time the officer reaches my door, I will be punished (a bounce usually, which is half a meal). I listen as the footsteps come closer. The flap on my door is dropped and my name called, 'Good morning Sharyn.'

'Good morning, Miss. Report back to you, Miss.'

'Carry on Sharyn.' I've been here about a month by now, so I know the drill. I about-turn and march forward to my cell door. Through the flap she passes me my roll of day clothes. I take them, saying, 'Thank you, Miss. Report back to you, Miss.' I march back to my bench-table, stand to attention and wait.

'Carry on, Sharyn.' The flap is closed and I dress quickly, carefully folding my nightdress into a perfect, neat roll. Then I strip my bed and make it again. I take great care to make sure each fold is perfect and each corner is on a right angle, measured exactly by my four fingers; there's not one crease or ripple. My bed will be inspected by an officer and, if it isn't perfect, it will be stripped and I will have to make it again and again until I get it right.

I hear the shunting of bolts and know the cell doors are being opened. I stand to attention inside my cell by the head of my bed, my back towards the door.

'Kneel. Judy, lead prayers.' I kneel on the concrete, knees together, back straight, palms pressed in prayer position and eyes down. This morning, Judy has been selected to lead the prayers and we recite in unison. 'Our Father, who art in Heaven . . .' Then we recite the Apostles' Creed. Every sound in the cell block echoes so it's easy to hear the prayers and keep my voice with the others. An officer walks up and down the centre aisle, listening. If I don't say my prayers loud enough, or I don't know them, I will have prayers for Practice.

It's time for morning ablutions so a male officer now takes over. 'Company, stand.' I snap to attention, my back to the door and wait.

'Cans and night attire up! To cabin doorways. Move!' I grab my towel hanging at the end of my bed and toss it over my shoulder, pick up my rolled nightdress and take two steps forward to get the metal can from the middle of my cell, which I have used during the night. I march the remaining two steps through the open doorway, about-turn and snap to attention, facing into my cell.

'Cans down. At ease.' I put down my can and stand at ease, toes on the line, legs apart, my body straight, shoulders back, head up and eyes down. My hands are held behind my back in a V shape. Standing rigid, we wait for our names to be called. The six cell doors down each side are not positioned opposite each other but are staggered, so that at no time can any girl come face to face with another. The ablutions routine is performed in pairs and eventually it is my turn.

'Sharyn, Sue. Attention!' We both snap to attention, bringing our knees up then stamp down.

'Yes, Sir. Report back to you, Sir,' we call in unison.

'Cans up, two paces back. Right or left turn. Quick march!' Eyes down, I pick up my can, step back two paces into the centre of the aisle, I right turn and march to the enclosure at the end of the cell block, then stamp to attention in front of a female officer, my eyes to the floor. I can hear Sue marching and stamping behind me.

'Report to you Miss,' we both call. She hands me four squares of toilet paper.

'Thank you Miss. Report back to you Miss.' I wait.

'Carry on Sharyn. Carry on Sue.' I put my rolled nightdress on the shelf allocated to me and collect my toothbrush and brush, then quickly empty and rinse my can and put it with the other cans for the girl on can duty that week, who will scrub them out. Now I only have two minutes to use the toilet, wash my face, clean my teeth and brush my hair. I love the feeling of clean teeth, so I quickly urinate then move to the basin to splash my face, hoping there is plenty of time left to clean my teeth, but I'll do it carefully. I still have that damned toothache. My hair is short and curly, after that haircut, so brushing takes no time at all. If I take too long I will be punished with a bounce, so I hurry. Sue has caught up with me now as I march back to my shelf, replace my toothbrush and hairbrush, pick up a cleaning bucket and fill it with water, a scrubbing brush and a cloth and take big strides back to Miss, stamping to attention in front of her, my eyes down.

'Report back to you, Miss,' we call. She checks her watch and my heart pounds.

'Carry on Sharyn. Carry on Sue.' I've made it in time — phew! We turn and march down the centre aisle then mark time when we are aligned with our cell doors.

'Halt,' Sir commands and we stamp to attention. 'Right or left turn, two paces forward, buckets down.' I turn right, take two paces forward, put down the bucket.

'Report back to you, Sir,' we call.

'At ease, Sharyn. At ease, Sue.' I stand rigid as before, facing into my cell with my eyes down, until all the girls are finished.

'Attention! Party, two paces backward, march, left or right turn.' We snap to attention in unison and take two steps backward from our cell doors then turn. This lines us up, six feet apart, down the middle of the cell block and ready for morning exercises.

'One hundred push-ups, now!' he yells, 'One, two, three, four . . .' Every morning this male officer takes great pleasure in drilling us in a punishing exercise routine. We quickly get down, palms flat on the floor and start our push-ups. 'Back straight Judy, keep up.' Sometimes he presses his foot in your back to make you push harder.

'One hundred star jumps. Now!' Keeping our eyes down, we jump and throw our arms in the air and try to stay in sync with each other. I can hear his foot steps echo as he paces up and down the line. 'Not high enough Susan — a practice. You can have one too Judy.'

'Yes, Sir. Report back to you, Sir,' they call. I'm panting heavily now but it's not over.

'One hundred chicken squats. One, two, three . . . Elbows out and keep those hands in your armpits,' he barks. Now we do one hundred 'touch your toes' except our palms have to be flat on the floor — always one hundred, always with eyes down.

'Attention! Left or right turn. Two paces forward, march, halt. At ease.' We do as we're commanded and I stop at my open cabin doorway, facing in. Now I hear the clattering of the breakfast trolley as it's wheeled into the cell block.

'Buckets up, three paces forward, march.' We pick up the cleaning buckets, march into our cells and the doors are slammed shut. I begin to clean till I hear the trolley stop outside my door. I snap to attention, my back to the door. The flap opens.

'Breakfast, Sharyn.'

'Thank you, Miss. Report back to you, Miss.'

'Carry on, Sharyn.' I turn and march forward to my cell door. Through the flap, Miss passes me a bowl of porridge and a cup of weak tea. I take the cup, bowl and spoon and call out, 'Report back to you, Miss.'

'Carry on, Sharyn.' The hatch is closed and I sit and eat my breakfast. Then I continue cleaning, repeating the reporting procedure when I pass back my bowl, spoon and cup. I scrub and wipe down every square inch of my cell, taking care to clean right into the corners. The smooth cement floor shines. Good. I am sure this will pass inspection but you never know; they are always looking for the tiniest thing. They push you to make you crack; then they pounce. Some of the women officers are as bad as the men, if not worse. I'm sure they take callous pleasure handing out punishments and watching us suffer. Taking away our food is the worst deprivation because we are ravenous all the time. Sometimes the 'bounce' is no desert or half a piece of fruit at morning break but mostly, it is literally half of a meal.

I hear the bolt slide on my door. I snap to attention, my back to the door, and wait for Miss to inspect my bed and my cabin. A male officer waits at the door while she comes in, checks the folds on my bed, runs her finger along surfaces and checks the corners. I pass today but I didn't yesterday, so I had to do cleaning as Practices.

'Carry on, Sharyn.' She walks out.

'Yes, Miss. Report back to you, Miss.' I stand rigid in my cell, waiting until all cells have been inspected.

'Buckets up! To the door. Move!' I march to my doorway carrying the cleaning bucket, about-turn and put toes to the line, facing into my cell and wait. I snap to attention when we are called again, in pairs.

'Yes Miss. Report back to you Miss,' This time Sue and I march up to the enclosure, empty then put away our buckets and march back to our cell doors to stand facing in and 'at ease'.

It's eight o'clock and time for exercises on the path around the yard and Sir is back again.

'Party, two paces back! Left or right turn. Quick march — left, right, left right . . .' he calls. We snap to attention in unison and take two steps backward from our cell doors. We turn, then march on the double towards the front door, every step in time, our arms swinging, knees up, eyes down, and each taking care to stay six feet behind the girl in front. We mark time on red dots marked on the path outside.

'Running on the spot, one hundred times. One, two, three . . .'

It's freezing this morning: it must be minus four degrees. There is frost on the grass and an icy breeze is blowing through my uniform.

'Elbows in — get those knees up. In order, get them up!'

My lungs feel as if they will burst and I have a pain in my chest. I keep gulping the freezing air but this seems to make the pain worse. I lose co-ordination for a moment and he is right there, screaming in my ear, 'Can't count Sharyn? Can't keep up? You can have a Practice.'

'Yes, Sir. Report back to you, Sir,' I gasp while I'm still running. I'm fighting to get air into my lungs. Then I realise. Oh no! Not a Practice! The punishment of practices is Hell.

'Party, around the block six times. On the double. Eyes down, knees up!'

'Yes, Sir. Report back to you, Sir,' We run around the prison yard, for six laps, and I'm careful to keep six feet from the girl in front of me. I can feel him watching me closely so I'm on my guard, determined not to lose concentration.

'Mark-time. Halt! At ease.' We stand at ease on our red dots, sweating and puffing, waiting for the next instruction.

It's time for work detail. Usually in pairs, girls will be allotted specific jobs and be supervised by an officer.

'Attention. Sharyn, Judy, two paces to the left. Miss, you can take these two and break up that cement path over there.' Miss snickers.

'Yes, Sir. Report back to you, Sir,' Judy and I call in unison. As we march over to the shed with Miss shouting orders at us, the other girls are allotted their officers and jobs for the day. 'Judy, get that sledgehammer and crow bar. Sharyn, get that wheelbarrow and shovel.'

'Yes, Miss. Picking them up as ordered. Report back to you, Miss.'

'Carry on.' We march to a corner of the yard to a cement path we finished laying only a few days ago. It is beautifully smooth and straight and I am proud of my achievement.

'Start breaking up that path. Now.' Judy picks up the sledgehammer and swings it down with a crack, onto our new path. Six feet away, I am chipping at the edges with the crow bar. As the path breaks up, we bend from the waist and pick up the chunks and load them into the barrow. We are not allowed to bend our knees, squat or sit down as this is considered resting. Of course we make no sound; everything is done in complete silence. Over the next few days, once we have broken up the path, we will dig it out down to the foundations, smooth and pack the new bed, then mix and lay the concrete path again. This is hard labour. These jobs are designed to break a girl's spirit and destroy her sense of pride or achievement. These are jobs designed to show us we are worthless and that, no matter what we do, it isn't good enough.

Toilet Parade — it's ten minutes to ten. You can't go when you want to. You have to wait for the allotted times and go then, two at a time.

'All girls fall in,' shouts an officer. We put down our tools and quick march with Miss, over to red marker spots where we line up in cell-number order. The toilets at the end of the cell block also have an outside entrance and this is where we are now marking time. We are joined by an additional male officer.

'Knees up, keep those fingers out of sight. Halt. Attention! Jill, Shirley, two paces to the left. On the double — to the toilet,' he commands.

'Yes, Sir. Report back to you, Sir,' they call in unison. They run, knees up and elbows tucked into the waist, to the toilet entrance where the other male officer is located.

'Report to you, Sir.' The officer hands Jill four squares of toilet paper. He repeats the routine with Shirley. 'Carry on Jill, Shirley.' Meanwhile, we all take four paces forward, in line with one another, and stamp to attention. Jill and Shirley reappear two minutes later and report back to the toilet paper officer, run to the end of the line and stamp to attention. 'Report back to you Sir,' they say to the original officer. Eventually, I am next.

'Sharyn, Sue.'

'Yes, Sir. Report back to you Sir,' we answer in unison. We run to the toilet entrance, to the toilet paper officer. I hate this man. He is particularly cruel and delights in sadistic punishments.

'Report to you, Sir.'

I have my period and to get a clean pad I have to show this officer my soiled one. I feel completely humiliated. I have been exercising and working; by now the pad is bloody, broken and smelly but I have no option. The pads are large, bulky wads we wear stuffed uncomfortably into our underpants, which are bloomers with ties on each side. Ugly and unfeminine, the bloomers also cause chafing between my legs. Eyes down, I show the dirty pad. The officer examines it unnecessarily, then hands me a clean one, along with four squares of toilet paper.

'Carry on, Sharyn.' There is no door on the two toilets. I am in full view of the officer while I urinate. I am only allowed two minutes, no matter what my urge, so I must hurry.

'Report back to you Sir.'

'Carry on Sharyn, Sue.' We run to the end of the line, report again and stamp to attention as the next girls go in.

Morning break — fruit and Practices. It's ten o'clock and this is one of the two most precious times of the day.

'Sit! Practices, fall out.' I have exercise Practices so I march over to an officer, along with two other girls, delivering the obligatory, 'Report to you, Sir,' as we stamp to attention.

'Running on the spot. One hundred times. Now.' The three of us run on the spot and exercise for the next ten minutes while the other girls are handed their piece of fruit and sit, six feet apart, along the path, leaning against a wall.

Twice a day we are allowed to sit for ten minutes and talk. We cannot look at each other but we can look straight ahead. We can talk quietly but only about the birds and the bees — literally. We can talk about the weather, the flowers, the gardens and the trees. No personal questions, nothing about ourselves, or our families, or why we are here. We sit with our backs straight and our legs together, out in front of us. The officers walk up and down listening to our conversation, waiting for our knees or ankles to part so they can punish us with half a meal. Some girls, on a bounce that break, have been given only half a piece of fruit.

While the girls are on their morning or afternoon break, those with practices as punishment exercise instead, or practice their neglected activity. For example, if you haven't answered loudly enough you will call out the required answer over and over again. 'Report to you, Sir. Report back to you, Sir. Report to you, Sir. Report back to you, Sir,' all the while, stamping to attention. Or repeat an about-turn action or an attention command, over and over again. Useless and senseless.

'All girls from Practices, fall in,' barks Sir. It's ten past ten and morning break is over so we line up, call out our responses to the respective officers and march back over to resume our jobs. I'm exhausted from the exercises and desperate for a piece of fruit.

Toilet Parade — ten minutes to twelve.

'All girls fall in,' shouts an officer. We put down our tools and, again with Miss, quick-march over to line up in cell-number order on the red dots outside the toilet entrance for the second time. We perform the toilet parade drill then it's time for lunch.

Lunch — twelve o'clock. We march in with an officer yelling 'left, right, left, right . . .' then we each mark time near our chair. Each girl has her own small rectangular table, covered with a checked tablecloth. The eight tables are placed in a U-shape, with us girls sitting six feet apart. Set at the open top of the U is a larger table where two officers sit facing us. The dining room walls are painted brick and the polished timber floor shines. An attempt has been made to make the room look homely but nothing they do can disguise the horror of this place.

'Halt. One pace forward. Sit.' We sit. Two girls are ordered to report to the servery.

'Report to you Miss. Report back to you Miss.' The meals are placed in front of us while an officer calls out who has a half meal and who has no dessert as punishment. We say Grace in unison. We are sitting with backs straight, hands in our lap, eyes down, and waiting to be told we can eat. We wait. The two officers are chatting and laughing. They are taunting us, trying to catch one of us looking up to see why we haven't been given the order. The food smells wonderful and I am desperate for my first mouthful but we wait. Finally we are told to eat. I cut my food and push a small amount onto the fork, placing my knife and fork down while

I chew. They are watching and, if I gobble my food, I will lose half a meal next sitting. We're always given a hot lunch and dinner and the food is delicious — succulent country meat and fresh vegetables from our gardens — but there is never enough.

I have finished my main meal now and I'm waiting for the order to eat my desert. It's steamed pudding covered in smooth yellow custard. The portions seem small for the amount of physical labour we do and I am hungry, even after a full meal. We finish eating and the plates are taken and the cutlery counted by the girls on this duty. We say grace again. The two girls are also on kitchen detail and required to stay and help clean up, while the rest of us are ordered to stand and quick-march outside, back to our red dots.

Toilet Parade — twelve-twenty. We repeat the toilet parade drill.

'Resume work details.' It's twelve-thirty.

'Report to you, Sir. Report back to you, Sir. Report to you, Miss. Report back to you, Miss.' We all march off with our respective officers and Judy and I march back with Miss to continue destroying our cement path. A cold wind is making my eyes water and because I wear glasses, they are dirty with dust and tears. Plus I need to cough. I snap to attention, eyes down and raise my hand, touching my shoulder on the way, my arm straight up beside my ear and wait to be acknowledged. Finally, Miss says, 'Yes Sharyn.'

'Report to you, Miss. I need to clean my glasses and cough, Miss.'

'Carry on.' I cough and clean my glasses on my uniform skirt.

'Report back to you, Miss. I've cleaned my glasses, Miss.' I stand to attention, eyes down till I am acknowledged.

'Carry on Sharyn.' I put my glasses back on and continue to demolish the cement path.

Afternoon staff handover is at two o'clock. A male officer walks over and chats to Miss.

'Sharyn, Judy. Sir will take over now.'

'Yes, Miss. Report back to you, Miss,' we call in unison.

'Carry on with what you are doing,' he says.

'Report to you, Sir. Report back to you, Sir,' we again call in unison then continue working.

Toilet Parade — ten minutes to three.

'All girls fall in,' shouts an officer. We put down our tools and quick-march with Sir, to line up for the toilet parade drill then its time for afternoon break — three o'clock fruit and Practices. This is the other precious time of the day.

'Practices fall out. The rest, sit. You may talk.' I have survived the rest of the day without another practice punishment so I can sit with the remaining girls and eat my piece of fruit. It's such a pleasure to be able to look straight ahead. Careful to keep my head to the front and not get caught, I let my eyes dart up to the sky. Once the frost melted this morning, I could feel the warmth of the winter sun on my back as I worked. But it is overcast and getting cold now. I glance at the billowing cloud formations and enviously at a bird, soaring in circles, free. I wonder what my mother is doing in the warm Queensland sunshine. I haven't heard from her because we aren't allowed mail or outside contact — we are completely isolated.

I can hear the other girls talking quietly. I listen for my friend Deanna's voice; her place is further down the line. She is here too. Our misbehaviour at Parramatta has earned us both a place in Hay. I'd been here a few weeks when I heard her name called and I couldn't believe it. Although I don't know the other seven girls, there's the sense of camaraderie, an intuitive, spiritual bond. To experience this Hell together creates a unique closeness. Deanna and I have a sign, despite the officers' efforts to prevent any signalling: if we pass each other on a work detail or in a line, and the officers are out of earshot, I softly hum three notes and she clears her throat. Inside our heads we are giggling and laughing — still rebellious.

Now I can hear the girls doing their Practices. 'Report back to you, Sir,' a girl yells. She would be standing at ease only to immediately stamp to attention again and yell, 'Report back to you, Sir.' I hear her doing this over and over and over again. Obviously she had forgotten to report back to an officer at some stage during the day.

'Left turn. Left turn. Left turn. Left turn,' another girl is calling out. She would be making a left turn around the yard, over and over again.

'Eyes down. Eyes down. Eyes down,' a third girl is yelling out while stamping to attention again and again. She must have looked up!

'Resume work details. Practices fall in.' It's ten past three.

'Report to you, Sir. Report back to you, Sir.' We all march off with our respective officers and Judy and I march back with Sir to continue smashing up that path.

'All work details: cease work.' It's four o'clock and the end of our work day. I'm relieved because it's really cold now and it will be dark soon.

'Judy, Sharyn. Collect your tools and follow me.'

'Yes, Sir. Picking them up as ordered, Sir. Report back to you, Sir.' We are marched over to the shed, where the tools are counted as they are put away.

'Report to you, Sir. Handing you the crowbar, Sir. Report back to you, Sir.' This is repeated until all tools are accounted for, then Sir marches us over to join the others in cabin-number order, on the red dots.

'Party, forward. Quick march, left, right, left, right.' We march through the back door of the cell block and mark time in the centre aisle, each girl opposite her cabin.

'Party halt. Left or right turn, two paces forward, at ease.' We halt, turn, step forward then stand at ease facing into our cell. Each pair of girls waits till they are called to march back to the enclosure, collect a change of clothes, hairbrush and toothbrush from their shelf, and march back to their cell door, all the while parroting the programmed phrases.

'Party. Two paces back, left or right turn. Quick march.' We march out of the cell block front entrance to the bathroom near Matron's office, to go and shower. Here there are two shower cubicles with no doors and one toilet cubicle, again with no door. We line up and repeat the toilet parade ritual, stepping into the room two at a time, while the others move up two places. Again, I report to the male officer who examines my pad and the crotch of my underpants before issuing me with fresh items. I have only three minutes to strip off my clothes, soap myself and wash my hair, then dry off. He is able to walk into the shower and dressing area at any time, and he does. While I'm undressed, Matron performs medical parade; I must hold my arms up and out, spread my legs, turn around. She is a brusque, unsympathetic woman and seemingly indifferent to our situation. Shivering, I quickly dress in my uniform and clean my teeth, then rejoin the line. Those already showered stand brushing their hair for one hundred strokes. At least my hair shines, if not my soul.

'Quick march, left, right, left right, arms straight, get those knees up, mark time.' We march back through the rear entrance to the enclosure and repeat the ritual of placing our toothbrush and hairbrush back on our shelves. By this time it is five minutes to five, time for our evening meal, so we march through the cell block, out the main door and over to the dining room.

'Quick march, left, right, arms straight, get those knees up. Not high enough Sharyn. Practice for you.' Sh—t! Practice again in the morning. I can't take much more of this! Now we're marking time at our chairs.

'Halt. One pace forward, sit.' We sit. Two girls are ordered to report to the servery. The meals are served and the officer again calls out the names of those on half-meal bounces. Judy leads the saying of grace. As we wait for permission to eat I look at my meal — it's offal — lamb's fry and vegetables. I hate liver but I'm so hungry I'll eat anything. I tell myself to be thankful it's a full meal — I feel sorry for the girls on half-meals. It's so cold tonight; to go to bed feeling hungry as well as cold would be terrible.

The meal is finished, the plates are taken and the cutlery counted again. Judy leads again with grace. We remain seated, hands folded in front of us on the table, feet and knees together and eyes down, while two girls are ordered to help Cook clean up the kitchen. Matron and another officer sit at their table talking and laughing but watching, trying to catch us looking up so they can give a punishment. Because it's Sunday night, while we're waiting, they sometimes turn on the radio, which is usually tuned to the local station 2QN Deniliquin. This is my only indication of the passing of time, the day of the week. Tonight the radio reception crackles with interference, ruining the music that is playing. An announcer reads a weather warning for frosts and freezing temperatures, then an advertisement for sheep drench. This is our recreation time.

Eventually, Cook returns the girls to the group and we march from the dining room in reverse cabin-number order. It's dark outside now but the watchtower and perimeter's lights are so bright, it's like day. We enter the block through the main door then mark time and halt in the centre aisle, opposite our cabins.

'Left or right turn, two paces forward. At ease.' I turn left and take two steps forward then stand at ease facing into my cell. We wait until we are called in pairs to march back to the enclosure to use the toilet and collect our rolled nightdress from our shelf and collect our can. Sue and my names are called.

'Yes, Miss. Report back to you, Miss.' I step back, turn right and Sue and I march up to the officer in the enclosure. 'Report to you, Miss,' we say again and she hands me four squares of toilet paper.

'Thank you, Miss. Report back to you, Miss.'

'Carry on Sharyn.' I quickly use the toilet, collect my rolled nightdress and night can and march back to the enclosure officer, report to her, then march back to my cell door and turn right to face into the cabin, taking care to toe the line in the doorway.

'Report back to you Miss,' I then yell to no one in particular, but I know there is an officer beside me, I can sense it.

'Can down Sharyn.' I report back to her, then bend forward, keeping my back straight, and place my can on the floor in front of me. I stand rigid again with my hands behind my back, looking down. I wait. My night can sitting inside the doorway catches my eye and seems to mock me. I hate using that damn thing. It's less than two feet high and uncomfortable and difficult to use. I'm tall and have long legs so squatting down that low and accurately in the dark is almost impossible. I'm petrified I'll overbalance and make a mess on my cabin floor — then I'll really be in trouble; probably get dragged off to Isolation. The next order snaps me out of my musing. I stamp to attention.

'Attention. Cans up, three paces forward, cans down. Change!' I stamp to attention, bend and grab the handle of that rotten night can, take three paces into my cell then put it down. It has to remain in this exact spot all night and can't be moved — the officers must be able to see the can at all times through the peep-hole. I change into my nightdress, taking care to fold and roll neatly my uniform, shoes, socks and bra, then I step back to my cell doorway, facing in, toes on the line. Now we are again called in pairs to march back up to the enclosure to put our roll of day clothes on our shelf. As I report back to the enclosure officer, she hands me four squares of toilet paper, my ration for the night. Given clearance, I march back to my cell door and wait for the order. Standing in my thin nightdress, I shiver as the chill of the cell block creeps into my bones.

'Into cabins, move! Stand to bed!' I march into my cell, place my precious four sheets of toilet paper beside the Bible on the bench-table then stand to attention by the bed.

'Kneel. Judy, lead prayers.' I kneel on the concrete with knees together, back straight, palms pressed in prayer position and eyes down.

We all pray in unison with Judy. 'Our Father, who art in Heaven . . .' Then, the Apostles' Creed.

'Stand.' I stand to attention with my back to the door. I can hear the doors banging shut. I wait for the officer's voice at my cell door.

'Goodnight Sharyn.'

'Goodnight, Miss. Report back to you, Miss.' She bangs the door shut and wrestles the bolt across. Keys rattle as I'm locked in. Its six-thirty.

I would love to stretch my aching muscles, to throw my head back and turn it from side to side, but it's too cold, so I grab the Bible and jump into bed. I am not allowed to leave my bed now till morning, except to use that dreaded can. It's lights out at seven o'clock, so I have a little time to read. The Bible isn't new to me after all those years at St Martha's, but it is difficult to understand in places. I'm at a confusing part with lots of 'begats' so I try to concentrate. In what seems no time at all, my cell goes black. I place the Bible and my glasses on the floor and turn onto my side, facing the door. God, please don't let me roll over again tonight, I think. They'll wake me and make me strip and remake my bed, then leave me standing shivering for hours before I'm allowed back into bed. It's already happened too many times. I hate the dark so I wait for my eyes to adjust. Finally I can make out a faint glow coming through my small, high window from one of the bright lights at the perimeter wall. I have now heated my body shape in the bed with little help from my thin blanket. There is icy coldness either side if I move, so I lie rigid and still. My body is aching all over and I cry silently at the hopelessness of my situation. I don't really know how long I've been here or how long I will be here. I don't know when I will see my mother again or when I will hear music. Each day is exactly the same: that is the only certainty. The repetition is mind-numbing but you can't relax because they will catch you out if you're not concentrating. I'm only sixteen and I haven't done anything wrong but they tell me I am bad and keep punishing me for little things. I just can't seem to get on top of this. I drift into sleep.

My cell light is blinding and someone is banging on my cell door! I've rolled over in my sleep again. Oh God — help me. I can't do this again!

ALL DAY, EVERY DAY, the rote phrases and mindless routines were exactly the same. The object was to crush our spirit and reprogram us into subservient, fearful robots. Complete silence, no physical contact, exhaustive exercise and solitary cells, locked up and bolted in each night. No joy, no laughter, no fun, no eye contact; just orders, humiliation, shame, abuse and hard labour. They took away my voice, my eyes and my dignity but it was a while before they broke my spirit.

The merciless exercise program was torture. No matter how hard I tried, I could not keep up. Short of breath, I was often doubled over in pain, gasping and panting. Sir would kick me hard, screaming at me to get up and then increase the runs I had to do. Eventually,

I would run until I almost passed out. Still, the more I resisted, the more Sir persisted. One morning during punishment Practices, I couldn't go on. We were running around the yard on the path, Sir screaming at me, 'Lift those knees. Higher. Higher! Not high enough. Another Practice.'

My legs were like jelly, I couldn't get them to work, let alone lift my knees higher. I glanced at the lawn beside the path and decided I'd had enough. I threw myself onto it, rolling a few feet before stopping, my heart hammering in my chest. *If I lie here he'll think I'm dead*, I thought.

'Get up!' he yelled, standing over me. I didn't answer. He kicked me hard. 'Get up I said!'

'No,' I said, panting hard and careful to keep looking at the grass, not up at him.

'Get up you lazy bitch!' He kicked me again.

'Make me.' I knew the other girls were listening and could see me because it was morning break and I was right in their line of sight. I hoped this would restrain him in his actions and it did, to a certain extent.

'Isolation, twenty-four hours. That will teach you some manners.' Without warning he bent down, grabbed my arm and dragged me the full distance across the lawn. The friction of the grass burned patches on my legs and the cement path bruised my hips when we reached other side. He yanked me to my feet and pushed me up two steps into a dark, narrow passage then gave me a brutal shove right, through the cell's open doorway. My glasses clattered to the floor as I fell onto my hands and knees, adding to my bruises.

'You've just added another month to your sentence. Welcome to Hay.'

I remembered noticing that small square building standing alone near the edge of the yard. So this was what it was: the isolation cell. By now I'd seen a couple, but this was the worst. There was not a thing in it. The walls and floor were painted cement, dirty and chipped, and the ceiling was sheet-iron with no insulation and very high. It was a shocking place to be. The meals each day were stale dry bread and water, the mattress at night was hard and smelly. I was eventually brought a can and an old grey blanket. I had contact with no one, except the hands passing my meals through the door hatch. I listened to the routine of the jail during the day: the shouts of the officers, the sing-song replies of the girls and the stamping of feet. But it was the night when I felt so desperate. This really was isolation. It was deathly quiet and cold. Freezing in fact. I could see my steamy breath in the bright glow of the perimeter-wall light, shining through the open barred window near the roof. My prayers were still angry but they were silent this time. I knew if I made any sound I would be punished further.

After a day and a half, I was released at shower time. As the officer marched me back across the grass to join the line, I felt a bit like Steve McQueen in *The Great Escape*, walking back from the Cooler — unrepentant. And I was. But I was dreading exercises the next morning.

If we wanted to attract an officer's attention we could not make a sound, not even a polite 'excuse me'. If you needed to go to the toilet, you stamped to attention and raised your arm, and left it there till you were acknowledged. Once your arm was up you could not put it down. It had to remain straight and still — any movement and you got a bounce. And of course, eyes down. Under no circumstances could you look up or around to see if the officer had noticed. They had, of course, but they would deliberately ignore you, sometimes for up to an hour. By that time, the urine or blood was running down your legs and you couldn't do a thing about it. You just stood there, humiliated and shamed. It was part of the physical and mental torment; after all, when you look into another's face you acknowledge their essence of being. You couldn't brush the flies away from your face, even if they crawled up your nose. Where they landed, they stayed. I wore glasses and could not adjust those either, without permission.

INSTITUTIONS WERE NOTORIOUS for neglecting the education and health of their charges but I became one of the few girls allowed time out of this one, when I was eventually taken to the dentist in the town of Hay. My nagging toothache had become unbearable so, after standing with my arm up for what seemed like hours before an officer acknowledged me, I asked permission to see Matron. Off I was sent, running on the double, my elbows tucked into my waist and my knees high, to Matron's office. I could feel the side of my face was swollen and knew the throbbing pain signalled more than a regular toothache and Matron agreed. So, the following day, I was escorted by a male and female officer, through the small door set in the huge gates and into the outside world. I had realised in the first weeks that the institution wasn't in the desert as I'd been told because I'd heard the occasional car horn and general town noises at those times I'd been toiling in the gardens.

I was ordered to sit between Sir and Miss on the long front seat of his family car and driven down the main street of Hay. I suppose they thought I would try to escape if I sat in the back. I sat with my knees together, my hands in my lap and my eyes down but I was dying to look around. Sir parked the car and I got out and stamped to attention on the footpath.

'It's alright dear,' whispered Miss. Not knowing what she meant, I strode up the street between them, marching in my best attitude: back rigid, arms straight and swinging, knees high and eyes down. Heaven knows what the shoppers standing in the main street of Hay thought of me!

'Try to relax and walk normally, Sharyn,' said Miss.

'Yes, Miss. Report back to you, Miss.' I barked, scaring more shoppers. I tried to walk normally but it had been so long and took such great concentration that in the end I gave up and marched into the dentist's surgery.

It turned out I had an abscess under a back tooth, so the dentist pulled it out and drained the abscess. Now my face was even more swollen. As I half-marched, half-walked out of the surgery, I certainly wasn't ready for what happened next. They bought me an ice cream to help soothe my mouth and drove me around the town, showing me all the places of interest! 'That's the library and that's the council chambers, a lovely historic building . . . and that's the historic railway station . . .'

I was too stunned to say anything. I just sat between them, looking around and sucking the soothing ice cream, sure that at any minute they would revert to being the monsters I knew they were. Which is exactly what happened when we pulled up, back at the jail.

'Attention. Quick march. Left, right.' Following orders, I crunched up the gravel driveway between the rows of fragrant rose bushes. My hour of freedom was over, and their hour of humanity, too. The following morning Sir was as brutal as ever with the exercise regime and Miss was just as cruel in the laundry. At least my face had stopped aching.

ALL OF THE INSTITUTION'S LAUNDRY was washed by hand, by the girls' allocated that job for the week. We stood at big tubs set six feet apart, under constant surveillance by an officer. The white socks were the most difficult. We gardened, worked and exercised in those socks so they were usually filthy with ingrained dirt. They had to be scrubbed white again using only our knuckles, so by the end of the day our hands had absorbed so much water, the skin was soft and translucent and our wrinkled prune-like fingers were left raw and bleeding. Miss inspected every item and if there was the slightest mark you lost half a meal. The second or third day of laundry duty, it was almost impossible to stop blood from our cracked and bleeding hands from getting on the sheets or uniforms. On laundry detail we lost a lot of food to bounces.

A stint in the sewing room was sought after because you could sit down. Using foot-long needles and thick thread, we sewed large canvas laundry bags and rubbish bags. We used a leather palm protector but the sharp needle would go through it easily, straight into your hand and fingers, causing them to swell. It was treated with a Band-Aid and the order 'keep working'.

Right from the time we entered the 'scrubbing cell', new arrivals began their nightmare. Every inch of paint had to be scrubbed off the walls using the brick and a wire brush. This initiation usually took around five days or longer, depending on your attitude. When finished, you were transferred to your permanent cabin and the cell was then repainted, ready for the next arrival.

Often, girls cracked under the strain of the brutal discipline. Some nights I could hear screaming or yelling and knew a distraught girl couldn't take it anymore. It was a girl either rebelling or being beaten or worse, as some girls said happened. I was never bashed or sexually abused in Hay but you could never be sure of the cause of a girl's anguish or pain. I would lie in my bed, wide-eyed and grateful it wasn't me. I was tempted to jump out of bed and scamper over to the peep-hole in the door to try to see what the cause of the commotion was, but I was frightened — more of what I might see than of getting caught. So I lay there trembling instead. Any sort of rebellion usually got you a stint in Isolation. If a cabin door remained closed one morning when all the others were opened, I assumed that the girl was either locked in for the day, repeating endless chores, or in that atrocious isolation cell in the middle of the yard. And that she'd had a month added to her sentence.

We didn't know it at the time but sometimes the local residents had heard the screams. On August 10, 1962, the *Riverine Grazier* ran the headline 'Reports of "Pitiful Screaming" from Girls' Home'. This extract of the article tells the story.

Reports from residents of east Hay stated that 'pitiful screams' had been heard last Saturday from the Girl's Institution, established a year ago in Hay. This week the Department of Child Welfare acknowledged . . . that such screams did not take place, but that her screams were not caused by ill-treatment but were an example of a previously common pattern of response from this girl when frustrated or subjected to ordinary stress.

The newspaper article mentions at least half a dozen people who heard these screams. It goes on to say:

A workman engaged on a building project near the gaol said that he had heard screams during the morning from the direction of the gaol, but was unable to say what they were exactly, nor to define

if there was anyone being ill-treated. He could not distinguish
any of the words used and had been upset by the noise and had
turned his radio on so that he could not hear it.

THE TIMING OF MY NEXT PUNISHMENT in Isolation was significant. It
was my seventeenth birthday. I knew this only because two nights
previously, during our occasional Sunday night recreation activity of
listening to the radio, the announcer had mentioned the date before
reading the news report. Since hearing it, I'd been overwhelmed by
renewed feelings of desperation and resentment at being deserted
and forgotten in this hellhole. Things had gone from bad to worse
when I hadn't been able to keep up the pace in punishment Practices
the previous afternoon.

'Get those knees up! Keep up!' Sir had screamed in my ear.

'Please Sir — I can't,' I begged, gasping for breath. This time
I didn't fall to my knees or throw myself onto the ground. I just
stopped. Gave up.

'Get going now you worthless piece of sh—t or it's Isolation.'

'I can't, Sir.' I wasn't going to put up a fight and risk being
dragged across the yard again. Instead, I marched obediently with
Sir as he escorted me to the isolation block. This time I was prepared
for his parting words. 'You've just added another month to your
sentence. Welcome to Hay,' he said, just like the first time, as he
pushed me into the cell.

Waking the next morning on my seventeenth birthday, I looked
around the rank cell at the dirty floor and walls and the brown-
ringed stains on the mattress ticking. Hands passed me my breakfast
of stale bread and water — no celebration here. What was I doing
here? What was this place? I wanted my mother. Did she even know
I was here? If she did, why hadn't she come to get me? I couldn't
work it out. Most nights I cried myself to sleep feeling helpless and
terrified. Silly mistakes earned terrifying punishments.

Now I could hear the girls outside in the yard, being berated by
an officer. This life was so sad. Suddenly I didn't care. They could
do what they wanted with me. In defiance, I started to sing 'Happy
Birthday' — softly at first; then, as my voice bounced around the

empty walls of the cell, I sang louder and louder, disturbing the peace of the place and loving the echo of my voice.

'Happy birthday to me,' I sang as loudly as I could. The officers came running, keys jangling noisily.

'Who told you, you could sing?' roared Miss, standing red-faced at the door.

Defiant, I eyeballed her. 'God did,' I said.

She didn't have an answer for that one. She ordered me to be quiet and locked me in again. The girls later told me they thought it was hilarious; however, I was given another night in Isolation for my insolence.

Sitting in the cell later that day, I realised I had to toughen up. In that evil place, I felt under great pressure, and full of anxiety, self-hatred and shame. I knew that to save myself I had to get out of these institutions once and for all. I made a pact with myself to conform, not to question. I decided I had to find the positive aspects of my situation and not let the place get to me. For instance, brushing my hair for one hundred strokes after washing it made it shiny and, though exhausting, the exercise in the fresh air was good for me. When I was marched over to the shower line the next afternoon, I didn't feel like cocky Steve McQueen this time — I had repented.

WE WERE ALL TOILING in the garden on a hot December day, when screams from a familiar voice pierced the silence. 'You f—ing bitches! Keep your f—ing scissors away from my hair. I'm warning you, bitch, touch my hair and I'll cut your f—ing throat!'

Without looking up or saying a word, seven teenage girls knew Lillian had arrived and, secretly, we were all throwing our heads back and laughing. Of course, we hadn't dared to do it but now seven minds came together in one thought: thank God someone has come to shake this place up.

The swearing and cursing about her hair continued for half an hour, then she screamed about the uniform. 'You f—ing fat pig! If you think for one second I am going to put that piece of shit on my body, well think again, honey. You're the ugly bitch, you wear it!'

Next came the marching routine. 'What? Are you f—ing mad? I am not marching. I am not a f—ing Nazi soldier! F—ing piss off!'

She refused everything. While she was screaming, they held her down and cut her beautiful hair, which made us all sad as Lillian's hair was so long she could sit on it. That was a really cruel thing to do, so our girl kicked, punched, swore, fought, cursed and yelled louder in protest. Apparently, it took four officers to wrestle her into the uniform. By this time, she was refusing everything else so they put her in Isolation where, for the next three days and nights, she screamed obscenities.

'You f—ing wait, you bastards. Wait till I tell the newspapers, the radio, the television about what you arseholes are up to. You f—ing wait!'

We worked around Lillian's screams through the day, secretly smiling to ourselves. At night as we listened to her curse, I could imagine all the other girls lying in their cells and like me, laughing and quietly cheering her on.

Eventually, the officers moved Lillian, still fighting and screaming, out of Isolation. She was taken to Matron's office. Whatever they did or said to her in there had worked. She came out of the office and fell into step with us. I figured her behaviour had probably given her an extra couple of months on her time, so she had probably wised up and decided to just get on with it.

Interestingly, when Lillian was good, she was better than everyone. She worked harder, she ran faster, she exercised like a gymnast — but as we now knew, every once in a while when she was bad, she was wicked! What a character!

On the occasional Sunday, after breakfast, we'd have the pleasure of the Salvation Army coming to say prayers with us. Under the officers' supervision, we sang hymns, clapped our hands and listened to stories. I loved the opportunity to sing and have contact with 'the outside' and took great comfort in their benevolence. Thank God for the Salvos! They may not have saved our souls but they sure saved our sanity.

LYING IN THE DARKNESS one evening, I was listening to crickets singing in the warm night silence outside my cabin wall when I heard the distant sounds of Christmas carols. I sat up in bed, straining to hear until I was sure. I realised with sadness that it must be Christmas. I lay down and wept quiet tears of loneliness and despair. I hadn't celebrated Christmas until I went to live with my mother and, the last couple in particular she had made special with a decorated tree. Yearning for my mother, I cried myself to sleep listening to the carols and bells.

In the morning, I stood to attention beside the bed as usual, my back to the door. The hatch opened and I was passed my day clothes. I dressed quickly and was carefully and meticulously making my bed when I was stunned to hear radio music. An officer opened my cell door. 'Merry Christmas,' she said in a cheery voice. 'It's Christmas Day and you can all relax and enjoy the day.' It took several minutes for this information to sink in before, one by one, we poked our heads out of our doorways.

'Go on,' said the officer, 'you can wish each other a merry Christmas.' She turned and walked out of the cell block, leaving us on our own. Tentatively, we walked to the centre of the aisle looking at each other. Then we all hugged and cried and bounced around, holding hands and laughing. Glad to be free of the oppressive regime, we ran through the dark corridor of the cell block, outside to the summer sunshine. It had been so long since we'd been able to enjoy human contact and it felt wonderful. We were teenage girls who had just one day to become best friends, so we made the most of it. We sat in a group, talking over the top of each other in our excitement but still looking over our shoulders, just in case. Lillian filled us in on what had been happening back at Parramatta, and what news she had of 'the outside'. We told her how we had loved her strength in standing up to the officers on her arrival. We also told her how pretty her hair looked, short. In fact, we were all looking fresh-faced and healthy from the country air and exercise.

After breakfast in the dining room, we sat in the sunshine again, listening to music and talking — we couldn't stop. Then the Salvation Army arrived and gave a short Christmas service.

We sang Christmas carols with them, 'Silent Night' and 'Away in a Manger', and they left us presents of chocolates and their magazine, *The War Cry*. When they had gone, we sang a very loud rendition of 'Jingle Bells'.

We jumped about playing ball then put on more records and danced our Parramatta Jive, loudly singing along with the music. We could not stop laughing. It was our one day of celebration and joy for us and we weren't going to waste a minute of it. We squealed and cried as we opened presents from our families; the gifts were mostly sweets, chocolates and books. We ate the sweets and, at the end of the day, returned all the other presents to the officers, to be given back to us the day we left to return to Parramatta.

The officers organised a traditional Christmas lunch of turkey, ham and baked vegetables including Christmas pudding and custard for dessert. The servings were huge and no girl had a half meal. Some of the officers' children joined us for lunch too — they were nice kids. We played a rowdy game of tunnel ball with them after lunch, while Matron and the officers sat in the shade of the veranda, cheering us on. I looked over at the laughing, smiling strangers; it was like I had never seen these people before.

Exhausted, we fell into bed with full stomachs and almost-smiling faces. It was a memorable Christmas Day: the only day the officers showed us a little kindness.

NOT BEING ALLOWED to speak certainly gave me plenty of time to think, and I could think about whatever I wanted; they had no way of controlling my thoughts. Mentally, I took myself to calm places — to the beach, to the ocean — I was meditating without knowing what it was.

My singing dream hovered, an intangible vision. I sang inwardly. I always had a song in my head. It was my comfort and helped me cope with the loneliness. I'd picture myself on stage in a beautiful gown, holding a microphone, the audience cheering for me. My dream gave me hope and my thoughts were my pleasure.

But mostly, I cried, desperate for my mother. In the quiet darkness, I would try to picture her beautiful face, her blue eyes, and remember the scent of her signature perfume. I missed her terribly and didn't understand how she could move interstate and leave me to rot in this place. Didn't she care at all?

I had to get out of Hay. Some days, I was sure I was having a complete breakdown. I was crying more often and felt my sanity was being tested as my emotions seesawed between rage and despair. Almost out of control, they coiled in dark recesses of my body, wanting to explode but with nowhere to go. I often thought of walking up to those vicious officers and screaming in their face, 'You have no right to treat me this way!' Doing it would have made me feel good but another month in Hay would have broken me. The only way out was to do as they said. Behave. Be good. Be silent.

AS MYSTERIOUSLY AS WE WERE TAKEN from Parramatta to Hay, in the middle of the night, so we were returned. We had no way of knowing when our time was up. On a scorching January day, I was in the sewing room struggling with another canvas bag when I inadvertently hummed a little tune that was racing around in my head.

'Get up off that chair!' Miss screamed.

It took a moment before I realised she was speaking to me. I hurriedly put down my sewing and stamped to attention. 'Yes, Miss. Report back to you, Miss.'

'Give me ten laps,' she ordered. Oh no, anything but running today, I thought.

'Yes, Miss. Report back to you, Miss.' I marched to the door then ran around the sweltering yard with my elbows tucked into my waist, my hands as fists and my knees high, the blazing heat and glare from the path making me squint. After the third lap, the supervising office standing near Matron's office called out, 'Keep running towards Matron's office. She wants to see you.'

My mind spun. I couldn't possibly endure another trip to Isolation and another month on my time. Matron was sitting behind her desk when I marched in and stamped to attention in front of her, sweating and panting, my eyes directed to the floor.

'Sharyn, you have been here five months. You have now changed your attitude towards authority for the better, dropping your more provocative behavior, and have absorbed our training program to your benefit. I hope you have learned your lesson.' She shuffled some papers in front of her. 'It is now time for you to return to Parramatta. Sir will take you to the van and you will be driven to Narrandera, to meet the train and your escorts. Goodbye and good luck.'

That was it. I was dumbfounded. Five months of my life, wasted in that hellhole. It took a moment to regain my senses before I answered, 'Yes, Matron. Report back to you Matron.'

No time for goodbyes — to whom would I say them anyway? I was forbidden to speak, forbidden to look. I had no personal possessions to collect and I certainly didn't want to go near that hateful cell again.

The van rattled along the dusty country roads back to Narrandera, while I sweltered in the back, tossed around like a rag doll. The train trip back to Sydney was quiet, the officers were not armed and I had no handcuffs this time. When I wasn't admiring the scenery of the outside world, I read the book my mother had sent me for Christmas. It was Louisa May Alcott's *Little Women*.

HAY GIRLS RETURNED triumphant to Parramatta Girls' Home. It felt strange to have this hero-worship from the other girls and the attention was overwhelming after spending five months in nearly total silence and isolation. I found it difficult to unprogram myself, still unconsciously marching and stamping for the next few days, which scored me 'unprivileged' points because the Parramatta officers did not like it at all. My sense of self had been so successfully suppressed that I was lost and confused. They had finally crushed my spirit. My personality had changed; now, I just wanted to keep to myself, keep my head down, knuckle under and get out of there. Sandy was the only one of my Parramatta friends still there. My friend Rosie had left, and big Joyce, and Karen and even crazy Sammy — they were all gone. Deanna and Lillian were still in Hay.

There were many new girls, too, and a new hierarchy on the four in-girls' steps. Interestingly, now there was a permanent place for me on the top step, if I wanted it. Everyone thought I was tough to have survived Hay and I believe they were right. I doubt that many of those cruel officers could have survived what they put us teenage girls through.

In late March, my mother wrote telling me she had sent money for my plane fare to Townsville, so I guessed it wasn't long before I was to be released. She said they were all looking forward to seeing me but they hoped I had learned my lesson and would behave.

The day of my release still came as a surprise, since again I was given no warning. One morning after Muster, the superintendent told me to report to his office immediately and, just like that, it was over. Standing in front of him for what I was determined would be the last time, I heard, 'Sharyn, you have completed thirteen months training here and at the Institution for Girls at Hay. As you have now attained commendable status within this School, I have recommended you for discharge and, in view of the length of your committal sentence, originally set at six months, approval has been given. You will now be escorted to Sydney Airport and put on a flight to Townsville, where you will be placed in the custody of your mother. Goodbye and good luck.'

AFTER I WAS RELEASED, it was another eight years before Hay Girls Institution was eventually closed on June 30, 1974. In the thirteen years of operation, three hundred and sixty-six girls were transferred to Hay, one girl dying during transit.

By then, people were finally starting to believe the shocking stories of assault and abuse of Hay girls, as the *Sydney Morning Herald* stated on July 3, 1973: 'In May, the Superintendent of Hay was suspended, following allegations by five girls of unlawful assaults. He was allowed to resign rather than face a Public Service Board inquiry.'

Unfortunately for those girls still in Hay at the time, the serious nature of the allegations and suspension of the superintendent was not enough to close it down immediately. Those poor wretched girls had to endure another year of cruelty and deprivation until the department saw reason.

Simultaneously, Parramatta Girls' Home was also under investigation, as the same *Sydney Morning Herald* article makes clear. Like academic Peter Quinn, I feel the investigation's findings are too shocking to leave out:

> *In June, the Superintendent and Deputy at Parramatta were suspended from duty, pending an inquiry by the Public Service Board. The allegations sprang initially from a complaint by a relieving Deputy Superintendent, confirmed by statements from inmates and other staff. A preliminary investigation by a senior executive indicated a large number of girls had been systematically assaulted in a variety of ways, that unlawful segregation had been taking place, that a girl's jaw had been broken and there had also been sexual assaults.*

Finally, someone in authority had acknowledged the truth and taken action on it — something us girls had been fighting to convince them to do for twenty-five years! The results of the investigations have never been available and, I assume, no official charges were laid. Parramatta Girls' Home* closed in September 1974, three months after Hay.

---

*   To view more photos of Parramatta Girls' Home and Hay Institution for Girls, go to www.TheInconvenientChild.com and click on the 'Parramatta' and 'Hay Girls' headings.

CHAPTER NINE

Freedom

PAPERWORK WAS EXCHANGED at Admissions and I was handed my original clothes. I'd lost weight so they were loose and didn't fit me well, but it was better than wearing that ugly, shapeless uniform. From the back seat of a police car, my nose pressed to the window, I drank in the sights and sounds of freedom as I was driven to Sydney airport by two police officers. They put me on a TAA jet flight to Brisbane and then I changed planes for Townsville, this time to a smaller Fokker Friendship. I'd never been on a plane and the excitement and sudden independence was overwhelming. By the second flight I'd gained a bit of confidence but it didn't stop me from being air sick, which interrupted my flirting with a boy across the aisle.

My family greeted me at Townsville airport, including my cousins Jean and Charlie and their family, who were holidaying with my mother. I was sure my cousins were furious with me for running away that night but I hadn't wanted to return to the unhappiness of my mother's house. By contrast, their home was filled with love and laughter and it was such a wonderful place that I had never wanted to leave them. But they had forgiven me so I hugged them in appreciation of their unconditional love. Later, before their holiday ended and they returned to Sydney, Jean quietly took me aside and told me she desperately regretted her decision that night I'd asked to stay, wishing ever since that she had said 'yes'. If I ever needed them again, she told me, they would be there for me, no matter what.

My mother's welcome was restrained as usual. She had created a new life for herself, her husband and son, in a lovely sunny house in a quiet Townsville suburb. But I was overjoyed to see her, so we all started off well, with family outings, barbeques and lots of fun and laughter. Nothing could dampen my spirits. I was free, I was out — and there was no way I was going back!

After my cousins had returned to Sydney, I was accepted into nurses' training at Townsville General Hospital. I moved into the nurses' quarters and spent my two days and nights off each week staying with my mother. I had missed her dreadfully and tried to talk to her about what happened to me in Parramatta and particularly Hay, but she offered no sympathy and really didn't want to know, always interrupting the conversation with, 'Well, that's the past, look to the future.' She had the same answer when I asked about my father. She still refused to give me any information, particularly his name. My mother disliked any kind of confrontation and refused to admit or discuss my problems. She would never face them, not ever.

I became restless, unhappy and agitated but still I tried to act responsibly and live up to my mother's high expectations. My four-year-old brother was gorgeous and I loved him but my mother still didn't look at me or treat me with the same love and affection she showered on him, no matter what I did.

The reality of being locked in a prison cell was finally catching up with me. Then, although free, I'd gone straight to the rigid routine of hospital training and the discipline of supervising nursing sisters, meanwhile studying biology in a classroom setting — it was eventually too much to ask of myself. The fact I was free did not mean my problems were solved — in truth, they escalated. The little girl who had gone into institutions at five and come out at seventeen was deeply disturbed. For five months I struggled and didn't know why.

My mother was keen for me to meet a nice boy: a university student or a boy with a good job and a nice car. Unfortunately, the boy I met owned a Triumph motorbike, a leather jacket and flying boots. I thought he was very cool. My mother thought he was a lout. We rode dangerously fast on his fantastic bike, all around the town, and spent nights making out on the beach. My mother told me to 'get rid of him' when he picked me up one night, his noisy bike causing her embarrassment in the quiet little street. When I told Johnny, he picked me up in a taxi the next time and paid the driver at the next corner, where he had parked his bike.

The fact was, I couldn't do better than Johnny and, anyway, I felt safe in his company. He listened as I told him where I had been and what had happened, and he didn't pass judgment or expect anything from me. My mother was delusional if she thought some well dressed guy from university, on his way to becoming a lawyer or a doctor, was going to understand a black girl who had spent most of her life in institutions. Johnny may have been a bikie but his tough exterior hid a caring guy who was patient and kind. I was infatuated with him and flattered by his attentions, and it felt deliciously dangerous to be with him.

One evening about ten-thirty, I quietly let myself into my mother's house after being dropped off from the hospital by Johnny. As I tiptoed toward the kitchen from the front door, I looked up to see my mother standing at the top of the stairs, looking like the movie star she imagined herself to be, draped in her pink flowing peignoir.

'I thought I told you I do not want that filthy bikie boy and his bike here,' she said.

'I like him,' I said, trying not to be too defiant.

'I don't care what *you* like. I told you to get rid of him. This is my home. You are embarrassing your stepfather and me with your hoodlum boyfriend.' It was obvious she had been drinking as she weaved down the stairs, clutching the banister for support.

'He is a nice person,' I said, hoping she would see reason.

'I don't want to see him or his filthy motorbike ever again. You just get back to your studies at the hospital and make something decent of yourself. Do you hear me?'

'Yes,' I said, as she reached the bottom of the stairs and, swaying slightly, stepped over to face me.

'Your stepfather works very hard to pay for your education and how do you repay him? By hanging around with a filthy bikie and bringing him back to our home!' Her hand reached out and gripped my chin, her fingers digging in as she pulled my face close to hers.

Now her voice was raised and her flushed face was so close to mine, her sour whisky breath rushed at my face.

'Look at you, you're a slut! That's what you are — a tramp. No decent boy is ever going to want you. God, my life would have been so much better if I had never had you!'

As I recoiled with the shock of her words, she raised her hand to slap me. We stared at each other, frozen for a moment, her furious face a deep crimson. Then her hand, held high, came down hard. I picked up my overnight bag, turned on my heel and walked to the door, my cheek hot and stinging.

'See the monster *you* created? Well lady, I'm out the door!' My hand gripped the door handle, ready to yank it open.

'You go this time, girl, and you don't ever come back!' I didn't hesitate. I slammed the front door behind me and strode down the street.

When I had turned the corner, I sat in the gutter and sobbed. She had finally said it. She had never wanted me, let alone wanted to live with me. That's why I had been raised by nuns, and why, even when she knew they were mistreating me, her maternal instincts were not strong enough for her to have comforted me. I finally realised I was an embarrassment to her. She must have felt relief when I was sent to Parramatta; not because I might be rehabilitated and return a good girl. No, it was so that she would be free of me. Free to get on with her life of being a wife and mother. For four years I had watched her cuddle, play and fuss over my little brother, showing her love for him, but this was never how it was with me. I did not fit into her world and even if I was bad enough to be sent away, it was better than having to explain me. She couldn't answer my questions, let alone strangers' questions. The dream of living with the Princess Mummy was well and truly dead. It was time for me to find my own way.

I went back to my room at the hospital, packed a bag and, first thing the next morning, bought a one-way train ticket back to Sydney, taking two long and boring days and nights to get there. This time she did not report me missing.

KINGS CROSS HAD CHANGED A BIT in the eighteen months I had been away. More bars, restaurants and strip clubs had opened along Darlinghurst Road and in the side-streets, many of the old terraces now housed so-called 'massage parlours'.

I rejoined my group of runaway friends living and surviving on the streets. Surf City was still my favourite place to go to dance and listen to music. The Australian music scene was exciting with the emergence of new, Aussie bands and Surf City always featured the latest and the best. They were no longer re-doing versions of songs by popular British bands, these homegrown Australian bands were creating their own original sound and music style.

One balmy October evening, I was hanging around outside Surf City waiting for my friends and watching the passing parade of people wind their way down Darlinghurst Road. It was twilight, that time of day in the Cross when, as darkness descends, a dirty, drab and unattractive street gradually morphs into a vibrant, colourful and exotic place, crackling with excitement. Mesmerised, my daydream was interrupted by a voice swearing. I turned to see a sexy-looking young woman struggling to pick up a gown and a feather boa she had dropped, while desperately trying to hang on to the others she had clutched in her arms. Dressed in a mini-skirt, stiletto heels and in full make-up, her hair in a long blonde ponytail, she looked like a model. I rushed over and helped her pick up the outfit.

'Thanks, love,' she said. 'Come quick. I'm late for my show set up.'

We almost ran along the street, then up a walkway and a flight of rickety stairs and into a dressing room filled with chattering, almost-naked women.

'Be a love. Hang those there for me would you?' said my new friend, pointing to a rack of slinky and shimmering gowns. 'My name's Sheeba by the way. What's yours?'

'Sharyn.' I said, my eyes darting around the room while my senses drew in the heady fragrant cocktail of perfume, hairspray and make-up.

'Well thanks again, love, you are a lifesaver. Girls, this is Sharyn.'

'Hi Sharyn,' they chorused. A tall girl with straight black hair stood up and turned to face me. She was wearing nothing but stiletto heeled shoes and a red G-string. I wasn't quite sure where to look but she could see I was fascinated.

'Never been in a stripper's dressing room before, eh?' I shook my head then blurted out, 'You're all so beautiful!' There was a ripple of laughter and a couple of 'thanks love' responses.

'You're not so bad yourself. How old are you?' said the beauty with black hair, looking me up and down.

'Seventeen,' I said.

'Pity,' said black beauty.

'Want to hang around for a bit and help us get ready?' asked Sheeba.

I looked around at the small dressing room, the mirrors surrounded by lights, the benchtops covered in lipsticks, powder and brushes of all sizes, hairpieces and wigs, and the racks overflowing with sparkling and heavily beaded gowns. 'I'd *love* to,' I said.

I watched the girls skilfully applying their make-up, carefully gluing on long false eyelashes and teasing and combing the wigs into an assortment of styles. I helped where I could and watched as beautiful girls turned into magnificent creatures. Too soon, it was all over.

'Sorry, love, we have to go down for the show now. Thanks for your help. Come back any time,' said Sheeba.

I made my way back to Surf City and my friends, the sights and smells of the dressing room still teasingly palpable. What a glamorous life they must lead. One day . . . I thought.

SOMETHING I HAD WANTED TO DO for some time was to find Ellie and Dorrie. It wasn't difficult — I recognised the Womerah Avenue terrace house immediately, although it was a little shabby and smaller than I remembered. I knocked and Ellie was at home. She hugged and greeted me with so much screaming and tears, I thought she would frighten the neighbourhood. Very little had changed and as soon as I stepped inside, I became a small, adored and pampered child again as memories and emotions washed over me.

Over a home-cooked meal, Ellie was sad as she told me her mother Dorrie had died of cancer, several years earlier. That hurried goodbye hug fifteen years earlier was the last I'd ever have.

The ships were still coming in; not like the good old days but, every few months, she would throw on her most colourful frock and her best hat and head on down to the wharves. I laughed. Ellie was still up to her old tricks. She was still a fine-looking woman and had a man friend named Martin living with her. He seemed nice and smoked and drank as much as Ellie. We listened to their favourite jazz records, sipping whisky as we talked, then Martin stood and bowed and asked Ellie to dance. As the two of them shuffled around the floor I glanced up and was suddenly that child again, crouched at the top of the stairs watching the crowd laughing and dancing below. I remembered how it felt to lie in bed while a party was still in full swing downstairs, feeling secure as I drifted off to sleep to the sound of men's voices and women's laughter, the lush sounds of swing music and the pungent smell of tobacco wafting under my bedroom door.

Later in the evening Ellie said to me, 'You know baby, you should talk to your Mum about your father.'

'Oh Ellie, I try,' I said, my eyes filling with tears. 'She just gets upset and says he's dead.'

'Oh, dead! Your father isn't dead. What's that woman talking about?' Although hope sprang up in my heart, I didn't quite believe her, so I approached cautiously.

'Well, maybe he is. Maybe she is telling me the truth.'

'No way!' said Ellie.

'What do you mean?'

'Well, how would she know? Who's been in her life telling her he's dead? Nobody, that's who. If your father was dead, baby, I would know it before your mother so I'm telling you, he is not dead!'

'I hope you're right. You knew my father, didn't you Ellie?'

'Oh yes. He was a fine man then, good-looking too!' she laughed.

'Well, she won't even tell me his name. Do you know his name?'

'Baby, I can't. Your Mum needs to tell you that. Tell her you talked to me and I said it is time you knew about your father. If she doesn't tell you, I will, but promise me you will sit quietly with your mother and ask her first. All I know is, that man is not dead. Well, he wasn't last time I heard about him.'

'How long ago was that?'

Ellie thought for a minute. 'How old are you now?'

'Just eighteen.' We both fell about laughing.

We laughed a lot. Hers jolly, thick and crackling from too many cigarettes, filled the house just as I remembered. I loved her with all my heart that day. She and Dorrie would always be family to me because when I needed a home and love, they gave me the happiest one of my childhood; actually the only home. But I knew Ellie was still a loyal friend to my mother, just like her mother had been. I didn't tell her I had nowhere to stay; I just left and walked back up to Kings Cross. I was a troubled teenager in dire straits, drifting around with a head full of confusion and unachievable dreams, and absolutely no direction. I was also black, an oddity in a white society, and had no idea who I was.

I HAD AN OVERWHELMING DESIRE to be free, physically and mentally, and I was no longer bound by the restrictions of being underage. Jenny, an ex-Parramatta girl, had joined our street kids group. It turned out that she felt the same, so off we went, hitchhiking up and down the east coast of Australia. We hitched rides with truck drivers mostly and also had a rule we would only travel with one man or a male and female couple, in a car. We rented bed-sitter flats and, as there was an abundance of jobs for unskilled labour as cleaners, waitresses, babysitters and nannies, we had plenty of work. Whenever the mood took us, we packed up and hitched to another town, city or state. We had some funny and sometimes dangerous situations on the highways.

Hitching one day, we were both tired and hadn't been able to get a ride for hours. The next car to pull up carried two young men in their thirties. We were both so tired and they seemed harmless, so we broke our rule. Fifteen minutes later, sitting in the back listening to two creepy, beer-swilling, chain-smoking men telling us we had better 'hawk it or fork it,' we realised we were in trouble. Jenny pretended to be car-sick and as they slowed to pull over, we grabbed our bags, pushed the doors open and threw ourselves out of the moving car, landing badly on the road. Grazed and dazed, we stumbled blindly through the scrubby bush for miles, sure that they were behind us. We didn't break the rule again.

Free to do whatever we wanted, it was a fun lifestyle for a while. For the first time, I felt alive, young and free. But my deep-seated feelings of shame and low self-esteem, made me reckless. We lived in rooms, caravan parks and ritzy hotels. We were wined and dined by nice men and we explored Australia. Jenny and I got sick of each other's company after nine months and went our separate ways back in Sydney. Australia was a different place then. There was an air of innocence in the mid-sixties; it was a time when it was still fairly safe for young girls to hitchhike and most people were genuinely decent.

Back in Sydney, I met my future husband when I started waitressing in a restaurant. I hadn't lost sight of my dream of becoming a singer but I didn't know anyone with a band who could give me a start and I had no self-confidence. Anyway I wanted love, a family and a home of my own first.

PAUL CAME INTO MY LIFE one afternoon on my way to work. As I walked past his workshop, he wolf-whistled me. This went on for several afternoons until he finally stopped me and asked me out. Heavily tattooed, he was gentle and good-looking and his infectious laughter wrinkled his brown eyes in an appealing way. I liked him and felt an instant connection. He had been a wild boy in his youth and had spent time in a boys' detention centre — Mount Penang, a place just like Parramatta Girls' Home. Having the benefit of a supportive family, he'd been able to get his life back on track and had a job as a motor mechanic.

After our first date, Paul took me home to meet his family. The instant I met them I knew I had to marry him. I adored them, especially his mother, Maria. She adored me too, although I didn't get the same approval from his father, Frank, a conservative career soldier. He didn't like the idea of mixed-race relationships and kept saying, 'What about the children?'

Paul's parents lived in a palatial home with and an enormous fireplace and spectacular water views in the elite eastern suburb of Vaucluse. Over steaming plates of lovingly prepared food, I shared noisy family dinners with his parents, four sisters and a brother. As soon as Grace was said, everyone spoke over each other as the eight of them laughed, reminisced and made plans for the future and I desperately wanted to be part of the family. His mother Maria became the light of my life. Round and jovial, she embraced me as one of her children, nurtured me and showered me with the motherly love I so desperately craved. She was also a religious woman and many Sunday mornings I accompanied her to church, which created a special bond between us.

In January 1968, Paul and I moved in together into a tiny flat in Womerah Avenue near Ellie's house, becoming regular visitors. It was also the 'summer of love' in Australia, particularly in the Cross. Hippies had made King Cross their home from the mid-1960s with the spread from the United States of the hippie counter-culture and so-called sexual revolution. The Cross was the perfect breeding ground for the Hippies because it was always the first to embrace new and antiestablishment cultures. They evolved from a youth movement of young bohemians and Beatniks who originally moved into San Francisco's Haight-Ashbury district. There, they created their own communities, listened to psychedelic rock music, embraced the sexual revolution and used drugs to explore what they called 'alternative states of consciousness'. 'Peace and Love' was the theme of their 1967 summer of love in San Francisco where thousands of 'flower children' wearing flowers in their hair, handed out flowers and made peace signs to passers by, inspired by Scott McKenzie's hit 'San Francisco'. Now, six months on, the song was a hit in Australia and the same 'scene' was happening in Sydney's Kings Cross. Wandering home from local restaurants on balmy summer's evenings, Paul and I were often stopped by Aussie 'flower children' with long hair and colourful tie-dyed clothes. I enjoyed their music but not as much as I enjoyed the exciting black Motown artists who reignited my desire to become a singer. Actually, the only obstacle in our relationship was our arguments about me wanting to become a singer because Paul wanted me to stay home and just take care of him.

After about a year of feeling trapped and stifled, I was pushing a trolley around the supermarket and a thought hit me: this is forever. At twenty, 'forever' seemed like a long time. I abandoned the trolley, went home and called Tracey, a friend who had recently arrived back from New Zealand. She was planning a trip around Australia so, in a moment of impulse, I rang and told Paul I was leaving him and went to meet Tracey at Central Railway Station where we caught a train north to Brisbane. Staying in a boarding house, we heard about a barmaid job offering on-the-job training, in Goondiwindi, a small town not unlike Hay but in outback Queensland. We rang and were accepted. After a five-hour bumpy bus ride, we finally arrived.

The woman who owned the pub was horrified when she saw me. '*You* can't work behind the bar,' she said. 'We have an Aboriginal mission here and a ban on the local Aboriginal people drinking in the Hotel.'

'But I'm not Aboriginal,' I said.

'Doesn't matter. You cannot work in my bar!'

I refused to give in, so the sheriff was called to help sort out the problem. Eventually, the woman offered me a job housekeeping and caring for her children, which I accepted.

I moved in to her quarters above the hotel and Tracey shared a room downstairs with another barmaid. It was a big Queenslander type hotel: two storeys with a wide veranda all round, and a pretty rowdy crowd on the weekends. The town was a typical unsophisticated outback country town, hot and dusty. As Tracey and I walked down the main street, the residents didn't hide their curiosity and blatantly stared at me — in a way much more obvious than the way I was stared at in Sydney. There were still very few African-American-looking people in Australia at the time and fewer still who were wearing expensive clothes, trendy sandals and jewellery.

Each day began early, preparing breakfast for the boss' two little girls. I cut their lunches, organised school bags and uniforms, walked the girls to school, went grocery shopping on my way back, did a full day of housework — cleaning, washing, ironing, preparing the evening meal — and then collected the children from school, helped with their homework, served dinner, read to them, washed the dishes and, finally, finished about eleven. At the end of the week, this woman threw my pay packet at me. It contained just a few lousy dollars.

'Do you know who Abraham Lincoln was?' I asked.

'Yes, so what?'

'He abolished black slavery,' I said, as I walked past her to find Tracey, who was equally as horrified. She hadn't liked her position either, especially since she was caught sneaking icy cold beers out to the Aboriginal people sitting in the shade of the hotel on days of heatwave temperatures.

We packed up our bags and returned to Brisbane the same day and, from there, I rang Paul who was overjoyed to hear I was coming back to Sydney. We sorted out our problems and moved into a modern apartment near Bondi Beach. I settled into a happy life of domestic bliss, setting up and decorating our new home and spending my days cleaning and polishing and learning to cook, with Maria's help.

Paul and I went to see *Hair: The American Tribal Love-Rock Musical* a couple of months after it opened in the old Minerva Theatre in Orwell Street, Kings Cross. Although the musical's profanity, depiction of illegal drugs, free sex advocacy and full-cast nude scene caused heated comment and controversy, several of its songs became anthems of the anti-Vietnam War and Hippie peace movements. The musical broke new ground in musical theatre and nude was no longer considered lewd. But what was intriguing for me was that it was the first time I (and, probably, many other Australians buying tickets) had seen African-American singers and performers live on stage. I loved it!

Paul and I married at the end of the year in a lovely Paddington church, two weeks after my twenty-first birthday. It was an intimate affair, with family the only guests, and my mother having come down from Townsville. I'm sure she breathed a sigh of relief — I was now someone else's responsibility. I was also in the mid-stages of pregnancy.

On our first Christmas as a married couple, the family's traditional celebration of attending church, opening presents under their enormous tree and sharing a sumptuous Christmas feast, was an unexpected and exciting experience. Their generosity and warmth was overwhelming, making it a Christmas celebration I have never forgotten. As a result, Christmas Day and birthdays are occasions I celebrate with a passion.

I WAS OVERJOYED at the prospect of being a mother, of having my own baby to love and love me, unconditionally. I was also fortunate to have a smooth and trouble-free pregnancy. Four months after our wedding, I gave birth to our son Anthony in March, 1970. A perfect baby boy, he was born within thirty minutes of my arrival at the hospital. I gazed in wonder at my beautiful baby, at his fair hair, brown eyes and honey-coloured skin. I was deliriously happy. In the same church where we were married in, we christened him wearing Paul's family's forty-year-old christening gown of delicate lace, with Paul's brother and sister as godparents.

I made friends with some musicians who lived in our apartment building. They started to call in with their guitars and wrote a couple of songs they thought suited my voice. Excited, I told Paul but he didn't share my enthusiasm. One evening, the musicians invited a man from a record company to listen to us. He was impressed and talked about a recording contract. After they left, I was excitedly bouncing around the room when Paul turned to me and said, 'Get over it. Can't you see all these blokes want is to get into your pants? You're my wife. Forget the crap and get on with looking after me and the baby.'

Disillusioned, I honoured my husband's jealousy and again put aside my dreams of becoming a singer. It wasn't so hard — underneath, I believed I wasn't good enough anyway.

AFTER FEELING PAIN in her neck and throat area, Paul's mother saw the doctor and was diagnosed with cancer. She was just forty-eight years old. As her conditioned worsened, my father-in-law was regrettably away on business much of the time so the family asked me and Paul to move in to help out. It was my honour to do so.

Maria and I became even closer, after many long talks late into the night, when her pain was too intense for sleep. I learnt so much about life from this wonderful, dignified woman. When she was able, we drove to the shopping centre and went for walks in the sunshine. She adored playing with the baby, who also adored her. As the cancer took hold, she began to lose her memory, then forgot just about everyone except her baby grandson. She passed away a year after diagnosis, at age forty-nine. I was just as devastated as Paul and his sisters, brother and father.

Maria was an inspirational woman and a loving friend. She was the mother I craved but never had. She loved me, helped me and accepted me; no questions asked. Her honesty, courage and love for her family has influenced me all my life since. She would have been heartbroken to know her passing also signalled the end of my marriage to her son. I realise now that I married because I was desperate to belong to their family. The reality was that Paul and I had different ideals and each needed from the other what we couldn't give. And we were both too immature to make a life-long commitment. The relationship had lasted just over three years and our marriage a little more than a year.

My mother was sympathetic after my separation. I had nowhere to go so she agreed the baby and I could stay with them in Townsville, until I got on my feet. I packed us up and was on the train the next day. Lars suggested I return to college and complete the school exams I missed earlier in my teenage years, so my mother took care of Anthony while I went to school.

The happy-families situation didn't last long. I wasn't living up to my mother's high expectations, whether real or imagined, and within a few months we were arguing in front of my baby son and my little brother, who was by now about nine years old. Anyway, the family were preparing to move to Papua, New Guinea so the baby and I returned to Sydney. Apart from a couple of visits, Paul and Anthony hardly saw each other again.

BACK IN SYDNEY I moved in with my cousins Jean and Charlie, who made room in their home for me and the baby. One evening, a girlfriend and I were in a bar and while walking back to our table with two glasses of wine, I literally bumped into Philip. Apologising for spilling a drink on him, he smiled and I was smitten. All muscles and tatts, good-looking and a charming heartbreaker, he was a bricklayer at the time but was on the lookout for a get-rich-quick scheme. He was fit, strong and healthy with a killer smile and a great personality. Though he had a tough exterior, he was a gentle man and we had a good time together. It wasn't love — it was fun.

The day I realised I was pregnant, I'd just had a call to say he was in a motorbike accident and was in hospital. I went to visit him to tell him my news about the baby, expecting rejection. Instead, he was delighted.

'It's a lovely thing we're having a baby,' he said, breaking into a smile.

'I'm not happy at all. I don't know how I'm going to support two children. I already struggle to take care of Anthony.'

'Don't worry. You have me. I'll help you. I'll never let you down!' And he didn't.

IN THE EARLY DAYS of my unexpected pregnancy, my mother made it known she thought I was foolish to burden myself by bringing up two children alone. I had no idea how I was going to manage but I had to try. I was the only parent, so it was my responsibility to be the best I could be.

Still living with my cousins, I started a housekeeping job in a small hotel in the city. My pregnancy was beginning to show but I was young and energetic and determined to get enough money together for a house. I caught the bus all the way into the city each day, leaving Anthony in the care of a friend who had two little children the same age. This was a busy hotel with a staff of European cooks, waitresses and housekeepers who were mostly non-English speaking migrant workers. Each morning we set the breakfast tables for approximately forty guests, many of them American soldiers on R&R leave from their tour of duty in the Vietnam War. My job was to help serve breakfast, wash the dishes then clean ten rooms and bathrooms each day, for sixty dollars per week.

The boss was very sympathetic and gave me the job as long as I promised to be extremely careful of health. I was used to hard work and desperate to save every cent to put towards the first home of my own. Besides, the cleaning was simple: making beds, dusting furniture, wiping down the benches and cleaning the bathrooms. After scrubbing cement paths and paint off walls in Parramatta and Hay, this work was easy. The American soldiers were generous with tips. One in particular, a quiet man, was always concerned about me because I was 'in the family way.' We had long chats about his hometown of Maryland and his family.

When I was seven months' pregnant I found a small and cheerless apartment for an affordable rent of eighteen dollars per week, within walking distance of Bondi Beach. It did have three bedrooms so I planned to find someone to share it, and the rent. I chatted to the landlady and asked if she would consider holding it for me, until I saved enough to pay for it. She said she would make no promises, but would try.

At eight months' pregnant, the boss asked me to leave my job. I protested and begged him to let me stay for a few more weeks, just until I had enough money to get the apartment. 'Sharyn, I cannot keep you on any longer. It is against the law for me to employ you at this late stage in your pregnancy,' he said sympathetically, patting my hand.

By the end of the week it was time for me to go. My boss had arranged a morning tea in the staff room and my co-workers had knitted lovely gifts of baby clothes. Of course I cried. The boss gave me a much-appreciated bonus cheque then passed me an envelope from the gentle American. In it was a hand written note and five hundred dollars cash! It read: *Dear Sharyn, God bless you and your babies. Best wishes, Dr John Wilson.* I was overwhelmed by the generosity, kindness and thoughtfulness of these wonderful people.

I collected Anthony and went to the little apartment at Bondi Beach and handed over the deposit plus two months' rent, to my patient new landlady Mrs Abbot. The apartment was furnished with cheap furniture but I knew I could turn it into a warm and attractive home; plus, it was close to the beach, to the shops and a park for children. I was thrilled. Holding my son in my arms, I danced around our new abode.

I advertised in the local paper for a single mother with one child to share my flat. A long day became depressing when a dozen single mothers arrived in answer to the ad. Most of them had sad stories of depression, poverty and being chased by violent ex-partners. I wanted a happy home so none of the women were suitable. Then, at about eight o'clock that night, after I had tucked Anthony into bed and I lay soaking in the tub, there was a loud knocking. Wrapping myself in a towelling robe, I answered the door to find an apologetic curly-haired blonde, holding in her arms, a miniature version of herself. Her name was Jackie and her little daughter, Belinda. She talked nonstop as she pushed her way into the apartment; something about being a great cook but she never cleaned windows, and wasn't willing to pay more than a certain amount per week. This crazy woman was like a whirlwind but I laughed, knowing immediately that I had found my flatmate. She turned out to be a fabulous cook, a brilliant budgeter and my child loved her. And she became my newest best friend.

Two weeks later, Jackie and I left the two little ones with our motherly landlady and headed to Paddington Women's Hospital at two o'clock in the morning so that I could bring baby Patrick into the world. Another beautiful son, this gorgeous baby had dark curls, honey-coloured skin and the sweetest smile. It was June 1972 and I was twenty-three years old.

Jackie and I settled into a life of babies, toddlers and nappies, surviving on the Widow's Pension Class A (meaning that, although we weren't widows, we were 'women with dependent children'). It wasn't much and we struggled to make ends meet but we survived and were happy in my little flat.

CHAPTER TEN

Private Dancer

LATE IN 1972, Jackie and I decided to treat ourselves to a special Friday night out so we dressed in our evening best and left our motherly landlady Mrs Abbot babysitting the three children while we headed up to Kings Cross. Jackie had been there before but I thought it might be fun to show her the Cross through the eyes of an ex-street kid.

We stood outside Surf City, looking up at the huge *Drink Coca-Cola* sign flashing above the ever-changing time on the clock, at the top of William Street. Slowly, we walked along Darlinghurst Road, me pointing and talking flat out. 'There's the Pink Pussycat strip club and the Hasty Tasty is still there underneath it. Oh, and that's new.' And, 'I don't remember that. What was here?' All the while, memories came flooding back with the smells and sounds.

As we meandered along, the street became busier and filled with a remarkable assortment of people: a woman in an evening gown and dripping diamonds, clasping the arm of a dinner-suited man; long-haired hippies wearing fringed jackets and headbands and colourful beads, making a peace sign to anyone who noticed them; musicians carrying guitars and all dressed in what seemed an industry uniform of a white shirt and black pants; groups of American GIs swaggering along, eyeing the approaching Australian Naval servicemen in an age-old rivalry; wide-eyed couples from suburbia wearing slacks and cardigans; and groups of eager young men, nervously giggling and shoving each other towards the leggy prostitutes in mini-skirts and shorts, standing on alleyway corners giving the timid boys the 'come on'. I noticed people staring at me — with my chocolate-coloured skin and exotic appearance I was an oddity, even amongst this fascinating mix of humanity.

Now the spruikers were outside the strip clubs, competing furiously for patrons. These burley blokes, dressed in white shirts, bow ties and black pants, enticed the male passers-by up or down the dimly lit stairs into their club for the strip show. The men paid a small cover charge to see the show but, once inside, paid exorbitant prices for their drinks.

We could literally feel the pulse of the place. The street was illuminated by hundreds of neon signs, the brightness so intense you could almost hear the hiss of gas being forced through the coloured glass tubes as they flicked on and off.

We strolled till we reached the El Alamein fountain on the corner of Macleay Street and decided the music and aromas wafting from the Bourbon and Beefsteak Bar were too good to resist. Revived after a drink and a meal, we wandered back to the Persian Room because we liked the sound of the soul music drifting up to the pavement as we'd walked past. Making our way down the softly lit staircase, a waitress settled us at a table. We ordered drinks and a snack and started to groove to the music. (The liquor laws required food to be served with alcohol for a nightclub to retain their licence.) Looking around the room, I noticed a group of four stunning-looking girls enter, dressed sexily but elegantly, so I guessed they must be models. They caused a bit of a commotion as they made their way through the room to a table near ours, all the men swivelling their heads to get a better look. The girl with the long, swinging platinum ponytail looked familiar. They were chatting and laughing, tossing their hair, crossing their long legs and looking around the room when suddenly, the platinum blonde looked at me, cocked her head then smiled. I smiled back, so she walked over to our table.

'I know you — I'm sure I do. My name's Sheeba,' she said. Immediately I remembered. How could I forget that wonderful evening I'd spent in the Stripper's dressing room?

'Of course! Yes. I helped you dress for your show. I was a kid then but I sure remember you. I'm Sharyn and this is my friend, Jackie.'

'Come over and join us. We're between shows and having a snack on our break. We're from the Paradise Club next door.' Jackie and I joined them and spent the next hour laughing, talking and listening to their stories. The band was great with a handsome lead singer and three girls who looked like the Supremes but the whole room was watching *us*.

'We have to go back for our next show,' said Sheeba. 'Come in and watch and be our guests.' Excitedly, Jackie and I followed the girls through the nightclub and up the stairs, causing just as big a commotion as when they arrived.

Next door was the Paradise Club. The shopfront window was blacked out and completely covered in large black-and-white photos of all the girls in various costumes and stages of undress. A large neon sign shone above the entrance. Through the doorway was a barely illuminated stairway leading down into the club. The spruiker stopped his pitch to a group of young men because their attention was suddenly diverted to our approaching group.

'Evening ladies. Back for the show . . . and you've brought some pretty friends I see,' said the spruiker.

'Hi Ricky,' said Sheeba and, pointing to me, 'this is my friend Sharyn and Jackie. They're here to see the show.'

'Welcome pretty ladies! Be my guests. Watch your step on the stairs . . .' The group of young men needed no more convincing and eagerly followed us down into the club.

At the bottom of the stairs was a small foyer-lounge area with a couple of tables and chairs. The other girls disappeared but Sheeba took us over to an office on the right, where a well-dressed middle-aged couple were busy with tickets and paperwork.

'Hi Mr Ramone, these are my friends Sharyn and Jackie and they're my guests for the show.' Sheeba turned to us, 'This is Mr and Mrs Ramone. They are my bosses and they'll look after you.'

'Welcome ladies,' said Mr Ramone with a big smile, 'follow me and we'll find a nice table for you.' We followed him through into the club. I had a sense that Mrs Ramone watched me walk away, but she soon turned to fuss over the group of young men who had followed us in, collecting their admission money and distributing tickets. Mr Ramone seated us in one of the comfortable booths lining the back wall, giving us an excellent view of the room and the stage at the other end. I surveyed the room. From where we were sitting, it was three steps down into the main floor area of the club. The subdued lighting of the interior disguised the tawdry décor — after all, the focus of the room was the semi-circular stage. Coloured spotlights illuminated the closed black lurex curtain. To the left of us, at the back of the room, was a large desk from where the sound and lighting was operated. The music was loud and funky and a blue haze of cigarette smoke hung in the air, contributing to the stuffy atmosphere. Black vinyl-covered booths lined all three mirrored walls, which made the room seem larger than it was. The main floor space below was crammed with small tables and chairs, filled with men of all shapes, sizes and ages. There wasn't a spare seat in the place. Leggy, very well endowed waitresses, dressed in tight black mini-skirts, figure-strangling bustier tops and black fishnet stockings, tottered on three-inch high heels, squeezing between the tables with their trays of drinks held high to prevent any accidents. As they served the drinks to each table, they bent over showing an expanse of ample cleavage to the receiver and a quick flash of out-of-bounds to the customer at the table behind. They obviously relied on tips to supplement their pay packet. Their sexy walk and wiggling bottoms gave the men a taste of what was to come.

The lights went out, a bright spotlight hit the curtain and the spruiker from upstairs, now standing at the sound desk announced, 'Ladies and Gentlemen, welcome to the Paradise Club! Before we start the show, there are a few rules and regulations. No cameras and please be nice and quiet while the ladies are performing.' Wolf-whistles and cheers from the patrons interrupted his spiel. 'No reaching, no groping and definitely no getting up on the stage.' This prompted more whistles and bawdy comments. 'Settle down, settle down. Now, we have a great show for you. Please welcome our very own . . . Gypsy!'

Right on cue, the first few bars of 'Big Spender' belted out from the speakers, the curtains parted and there stood one of the girls I'd met earlier, her sleek dark hair and creamy skin luminescent in the spotlight. In a clinging, shimmering, floor-length red dress and long matching gloves, she slowly twisted and gyrated, emphasising the beats and rests in the music. Delicately, she nipped each gloved finger of one hand, pulling slightly to loosen it, then peeled the glove off, twirled it overhead then let it go, to land at the side of the stage. She repeated this seductive removal for the other glove. The crowd sat silent and mesmerised. Now the music changed to funky and sexy, the volume so high I could feel the bass thumping in my chest. Teasingly, Gypsy crossed her arms and reached up, undoing a tie on one shoulder then the other, all the while building the anticipation. Finally the garment slipped to the floor, revealing a skimpy bikini top of two tiny triangles of red lycra, straining to cover each ample breast, and a minute red G-string. The men at the close front tables whistled and called out but she ignored them, instead playing up to a table of men further back in the room. She stepped out of the dress and moved with the music, grinding her hips back and forth and slowly making her way to the front of the stage. Then she bent over, legs apart, wriggling her shoulders and breasts (which were now threatening to pop out of the red triangles) at the men at the front tables. This time, the whistles were mixed with cheers and calls for her to 'take it off'. She reached behind her back and, as she stood up, her tiny top dangled from her hand. She twirled it over her head and let it go, expertly making it land with the gloves. Standing in four-inch spike heels, she swayed and gyrated then blew a kiss from her scarlet-red lips with one hand and touched the side of her G-string with the other. It dropped to the floor and there she stood for the briefest moment — tall, curvaceous and stark-naked — before the stage went black. The room erupted. The audience clapped and cheered and Jackie and I whooped and cheered with them. Wow! The waitresses rushed around the room taking drink orders but concentrating on the men at front tables. Jackie and I ordered another drink too. Before we had a chance to catch our breath, the show continued.

'Ladies and Gentlemen . . . direct from Paris, France, please welcome young Nicolette!' announced Ricky.

From the side of the stage skipped Nicolette to '*Sous les Ponts de Paris*'. Dressed as Irma la Douce, she wore a tight red-and-white striped top, a black mini-skirt, black fishnet stockings and stilettos, a red scarf tied at her neck and a black beret atop her straight auburn hair. The piano accordion in the music set the scene perfectly. Her routine was not as raunchy as Gypsy's but she was cute and coy and the men loved her. Next was golden-haired Susie, dressed as a cheerleader in red, white and blue, and the American GIs went wild. The whistles and comments were particularly lewd for Princess Pleasure, a statuesque Amazon dressed from head to toe in skin-tight black leather, including over-the-knee black boots. Her pièce de résistance was her whip routine; as she removed items of clothing she used the whips as seduction props, stroking and caressing them, then turning them on the men at the front tables. Lightly whipping and teasing the men into a frenzy, she suddenly cracked the whip a number of times, snapping her arm left then right then left again. Jackie and I jumped in fright but the excited men yelled and applauded with delight. She was brilliant. Then came Trixie, in a sparkling full-length gown, a huge feather boa, long gloves and an enormous beehive hairstyle. She had a superb figure *for a man* — Trixie was the Paradise Club's drag queen. The show went for about an hour and a half and there were seven girls in all. Between each act, the waitresses scurried about taking and delivering drink orders. This was obviously thirst-making entertainment for the men!

Each girl's routine had a theme and began with appropriate music before changing to raunchy or rock music for the remainder of her strip. Some were fun and light-hearted, some were sexy and sensuous, and some were very raunchy and quite explicit, including the contortionist, but all the girls were absolutely gorgeous. The show's finale was my friend Sheeba. The front curtain was closed, creating an air of expectation.

'Ladies and Gentlemen, from the wilds of the jungle . . . heeeeere's Sheeba!' The speakers belted out the *boom — boom — boom-boom–ba-boom* of the wild and rhythmic jungle-drum intro of Sandy Nelson's 'Let there Be Drums'. The curtain opened and there stood Sheeba in a leopard-print bra and a layered, strategically-torn, leopard-print skirt and bare feet. Her long platinum hair was still tied tightly in a high-ponytail. But I'm sure Jackie and I were the only two who noticed what she was wearing: all the men in the room stared transfixed at Sheeba as she suggestively caressed a huge diamond python she had wrapped around her body! She swayed and danced with the snake, then placed it into a large, round, lidded basket and picked up two rustic-looking torches from a bucket. As she touched them to a cigarette lighter, they burst into flames then Sheeba rumba'd, kicked and gyrated in a spectacular fire-worshipping act before swallowing swords of fire. In-between swivelling her hips and gyrating with the flaming torches, she seductively removed the layers of her skirt then the remainder of her costume, leaving just a G-string when the lights went out. The crowd loved her and we were all still clapping and cheering after the curtain closed. Now that's a show, I thought.

Sheeba and Mrs Ramone joined us about ten minutes later. 'What did you think of the show ladies?' asked Mrs Ramone.

'It was wonderful!' I said, gushing over the two of them in my enthusiasm. 'The costumes and the music and the girls are so beautiful. Oh Sheeba, the snake and the fire!'

Mr Ramone appeared behind them, 'Great show, Sheeba. And you, Sweetheart,' he said, turning to me, 'how would you like to work here?' I was stunned.

'No! Ah no . . . No I couldn't . . . I wouldn't know how to do that!'

'Yes you would — it's not so hard,' said Sheeba enthusiastically.

Mrs Ramone jumped in, 'We have a teacher and all the girls will help you. And we pay good money.'

'Yes, Shaz go on!' said Jackie, wide-eyed.

Somehow I was talked into it, agreeing to turn up the next day for a rehearsal, and Sheeba, Jackie and I went for coffee across the road to talk some more. Out in the street, which even after midnight was still filled with people and fluorescents bright as day, Sheeba, in her skimpy mini-skirt, tight top and stilettos, created traffic chaos as she trotted across the road to the coffee shop, cars stopping and men wolf-whistling. Inside the café, we ordered cappuccinos and talked.

'You are going to take this job, aren't you?' she asked.

'I don't think so' I laughed, feeling shy and self-conscious.

'Why not?' she asked, looking serious.

'I can't take my clothes off in front of people!' I said.

'Honey, you're tall, you look great and you have a great figure. Be sensible! Make your money while you're young and don't worry about it. You have a couple of kids, don't you? How much do you earn now?'

'I'm on welfare — about forty dollars a week,' I said. She smiled, shaking her head.

'Well, you're about to make a *lot* more than that! Christmas is coming, think of your kids.'

'Lots of money?' I asked, bending under the pressure.

'Come on, take the job. I'll help you,' said Sheeba enthusiastically.

'And I'll look after the babies while you're working,' said Jackie.

'I can't believe I'm considering this but I could really do with the money,' I said, conceding defeat.

STRIPPING HAD FAST REPLACED BURLESQUE in the United States in the early 1960s and Australia soon followed the trend. By the mid-1960s, it was a popular art and, in Kings Cross, a number of strip clubs lined the so-called 'dirty half-mile' of Darlinghurst Road between William and Macleay streets. Patrons usually had to go down into basements or climb nondescript staircases to upper floors of the buildings, whose street frontage was reserved for legitimate cafés and restaurants. While the spruiker touted outside, the prospective patrons waiting at the entrance inside were given the once-over by the club's bouncer. If they were too drunk, too loud, or just looked like trouble, they were unceremoniously shown the exit. Those deemed acceptable were relieved of an entrance fee, seated and encouraged to drink nonstop at outrageous prices. The artistes offered the tantalising promise of something, with much teasing and flashing, so there obviously had to be rules. Stripping was seen as an art and the clubs aimed to keep it tasteful. Rules stipulated 'no touching' and any patron who couldn't contain himself or attempted to join the performer on stage would be brusquely shown the door. And the Vice Squad and detectives from Darlinghurst Police Station kept an eye on things.

It was now 1972 and Kings Cross had become red-light central and the hub of Sydney's organised crime, thanks to the arrival of thousands of American servicemen on R&R leave from the War in Vietnam. The first US Air Force plane-load had arrived in 1967 filled with war-weary GIs, their wallets bulging with money and a giant thirst for alcohol and sex. The excitement of hanging around American GIs and what their money could buy attracted Sydney's girls and the Kings Cross entrepreneurs wanted the servicemen's money. (This continued until 1974.) Unfortunately, they also brought with them a taste for heroin, marijuana and other pharmaceuticals including the by-now-popular drug LSD (also known as 'acid'). While notorious criminals rubbed shoulders with crooked cops, illegal gambling, prostitution and drugs flourished.

SUSIE THE DANCE TEACHER (who was also Susie the Cheerleader) met me at the club at noon for the next day's rehearsal. She was tall, supple and patient and kept telling me 'to think burlesque'. Her boyfriend Ricky was the club's spruiker, sound and lighting operator and janitor. While Susie was teaching me to gyrate and pole dance, he was busy wiping down tables, emptying rubbish bins and cleaning the place. Wearing my bikini, stiletto heels and little else, she had me doing bumps and grinds as I hugged each of the poles on either side of the stage. Swivelling my hips to 'Chicago', I could not grasp the art of striptease and I was hating it. In the middle of showing me how to drop my bra, Susie stopped.

'What's wrong?' she asked, trying not to show impatience. 'It's easy. All you do is unfasten it on the number one count, two to drop the first strap, three-count is the other strap and four it's gone.'

'No,' I said.

'Why not? It's not that hard to lose your bra. The next step is your G-string. Now that I can understand, but this is simple, so what's wrong?'

I pointed to Ricky who was now busy vacuuming the floor, oblivious to us.

'What?' asked Susie, swinging around.

'It's him! He's putting me off. I can't take my clothes off with him here!'

Incredulous, Susie looked at me then laughed and laughed. 'Honey, there's going to be a hundred like him here. Forget Ricky. He's seen all the girls naked and doesn't pay any attention any more, I promise! Just drop your clothes. Think about buying your little boys some great Christmas presents and don't worry. For God's sake, they're men! They are going to love you!'

I rehearsed all afternoon, repeating the moves over and over. 'All you have to do is be sexy. Think burlesque,' said Susie. 'Relax, enjoy it and you'll be terrific.'

By the evening of my first performance, I was so nervous I felt sick. I kept telling myself I was an idiot to even think of becoming a stripper but Susie had worked with me for three days and I had finally perfected my routine. She showed me how important it was for my gloves, dress and bra-top to land in the same spot near the back curtain. I had to know where they were because, as I ran from the stage in the blackout after my act, I had only a few seconds to collect them.

We had been shopping and bought me a white crochet dress, long and backless, to wear with elbow-length white gloves, silver stilettos, a white spangly bikini top and satin G-string. My stage make-up was smoky-black oriental cats' eyes with false eyelashes, deep-red lipstick and my most transforming feature: a wig of almost waist-length straight black hair. In the dressing room, the chatter and easy friendliness was reassuring and being part of a group of girls again was comforting. Stepping back from my make-up table, I admired myself in the long mirror. Was that me? The long straight hair and the contrast of the see-through, white crochet dress against my dark skin looked fantastic. I felt like a movie star. I was set to appear fourth from the top, following Susie the Cheerleader. By now I was so nervous, I wanted to throw up. I started pacing up and down, telling myself just to walk out the door. The girls got so sick of watching me that in the end someone passed me a joint of marijuana. I'd occasionally experimented with marijuana but that night I sucked on that joint like my life depended on it. Waiting in the wings, I could hear the rowdy crowd encouraging Susie. I was still undecided when, too late, my escape-window closed.

'Ladies and gentlemen, please welcome to the stage the newest star of the Paradise Club, direct from Chicago, USA, the beautiful and dusky, Georgia!'

As the first bars of 'Chicago' boomed through the club, the crowd cheered. I stood frozen in the wings, still drawing on the joint. One of the girls grabbed it from me and two others pushed me onto the stage. Blinded by the bright spotlight, I couldn't see the crowd of men but I could hear their chants and applause. Remembering my routine, I glided across to the right-hand pole like a professional stripper. As the effects of the joint kicked in, I bumped and shimmied like a trouper, expertly removing each long glove and landing them in the designated spot. With my back to the audience and looking over my shoulder as I dropped the first strap of my dress, I got the giggles. I could hear a group of young men in the front as I dropped the other strap. 'Take it off Georgia!' one called, his mate joining in, 'Yeah, get it off!'

As my dress slid to the floor, I remembered to kick it with my heel to the right, so it was close to the gloves for my rapid exit in the dark. Swivelling my hips, I turned around, wearing only the white spangly bikini top, the tiny white G-string and silver stilettos.

'Check out her tits, mate!' It sounded so funny I started to laugh, then couldn't stop as the marijuana took away all control. The audience started laughing with me, then clapping, stamping and cheering me on. I laughed my way through the rest of the routine: bump, two, three, four; turn, two, three, four. Easily dropping my bikini top to the floor, I laughed till tears were running down my cheeks. The audience was with me, the whole room laughing together as I danced around the stage like it belonged to me. I pretended to not be able to undo my G-string. The audience, my bosses behind the front desk and the girls backstage laughed and cheered. I was a laughing mess when I finally dropped my G-string and stood there for a couple of seconds, totally naked. The song finished and half the audience rose to their feet, cheering and whistling. What a funny night it was! My bosses were delighted and said I was the new sensation. I was so stoned but it got me through. It was the first and last time I ever worked stoned.

AS GEORGIA, THE EXOTIC DANCER I brought in more money than I had ever seen. Our lives improved immediately, so Jackie and I moved out of the tiny apartment and into a large furnished house beside the sea. Up to that point, the reality of having two small children to bring up on my own with no emotional, physical or financial support was frightening. I had felt like I was drowning just trying to survive. Jackie was a godsend but she also benefited from my new-found affluence. It suited her to look after the children at night and take charge of the housework. Her daughter had a happy and comfortable home and I gladly shared my prosperity on frequent shopping trips and family outings. It made me feel good to be able to indulge us all in new clothes and toys for the children. In fact, during the day I was no different from most mothers: I spent time with my beautiful boys and made sure they were bathed and fed each evening before I left for work, just after six. The only thing to suffer was Jackie's social life because I worked six nights a week. Could I have worked an office job? Maybe. I could type but I was not skilled and I couldn't face restaurant waitressing again — the hours were too long and hard for such little reward. And I still had no confidence. The shame of being a bad girl, drilled into me in Parramatta and Hay, plus the failure of my marriage, had done little to improve my feeling of self worth. A stripper in Kings Cross was probably as good as I was going to be and, to be honest, at the time when Mr Ramone offered me the job, I didn't think I was good enough to be even that.

AT THE PARADISE CLUB we performed a show each night from Tuesday to Thursday and two shows a night on Friday and Saturday, except during the winter months when the cold weather kept customers away and we performed only one show and all went home early; Sunday night was one show and Monday was my night off. The Paradise and the Pink Pussycat strip clubs were the most popular of those in Kings Cross, along with Les Girls, a revue with an all-male cast of female impersonators. It was exciting working in the Cross in 1972 and being one of the 'nightshifters', rather than an ogling visitor, gave me a sense of belonging. I didn't think too much about the morality of what I was actually doing. For me, it was a job and I was enjoying the adulation and attention from the men. Fortunately, my body had regained its shapely curves soon after Patrick's birth and, at the time, my dark skin was seen as unusual and exotic, which is what Mr Ramone had recognised the very first night. He knew he would have an edge on the other clubs, having (I believe) the only black stripper in the Cross.

Between shows on the weekend, just after ten o'clock, we had about an hour and a half free. We didn't socialise with the patrons — they could look but not touch — but we did socialise. There was a Las Vegas atmosphere out on the street because most of the other strippers had the same break time. It seemed everyone was in the middle of a party and we wanted to be part of it. Food aromas from the coffee shops and restaurants mixed with cigarette and cigar smoke and the fumes of cruising cars. Inside these hotted-up Holdens, rumbling along with no mufflers, were yokels from the suburbs leering at the women, trying to figure out if they were strippers, hookers, transvestites or good-looking girls from the suburbs. Five or six of us would appear from the Paradise Club entrance dressed in our sexiest best: mini-skirts, short shorts, or clinging dresses, with stockings and stiletto heels or thigh-high boots and our faces done in full make-up. Then the fun would begin! Sometimes we went next door to the Persian Room to listen to the funky music, but mostly we crossed Darlinghurst Road, picking our way through the bumper-to-bumper traffic, and headed for the Andronicus Coffee Shop for a snack and coffee. Laughing and chatting, our ponytails and long hair flying, we ignored the whistles, shouts and general commotion we caused. We carried only a change purse in our hand, no handbags. This was the custom. The working girls carried the same but they also had a key ring hanging from one finger.

The Hippie counterculture was by now in decline but their lasting legacy was the promotion and use of cannabis or marijuana and psychedelic drugs, supposedly to expand one's consciousness. Also, the use of psychotropic drugs especially the hallucinogen LSD.

The Hippie drug culture, combined with the American GIs' demand, fuelled the burgeoning drug culture in Kings Cross. Drugs became readily available and you didn't have to look hard to find them. Often, the air around the Cross was heavy with the pungent smell of marijuana drifting from music venue stairways and was quite openly smoked at private parties, where joints were passed around like cigarettes.

MONTHS PASSED and I began spending more time with the girls from the club, socialising with them on our days off. Others had children too, so we had family barbeques and children's birthday parties together. After work, we often partied next door at the Persian Room or other nightclubs in the Cross like the Bourbon and Beefsteak, the Rex Hotel and Surf City; some virtually never closed. It was exciting to watch the entertainers and made me yearn to be on a stage singing, instead of stripping.

With the arrival of the jet age in 1964, Australia had become a popular destination for the great names of American show business and the Silver Spade Room at the Chevron Hotel, in Macleay Street, was considered the pinnacle of venues. For the considerable sum of around twenty dollars, patrons dressed in their finest were entertained at the Dinner Show or the later Supper Show where A-list entertainers — Frank Sinatra, Shirley Bassey, Sammy Davis Jr, Dean Martin, Jerry Lewis and Freddie Paris to name a few — would perform alongside Sydney's best musicians. It was considered the swankiest hotel in Sydney. (I heard it was famous for having gold-plated toilet seats in the restrooms. But, in true Aussie fashion, these were 'souvenired' too often and had to be changed to ordinary seats.) The other glamorous entertainment venues at that time were Chequers Nightclub in Goulburn Street, the Cheetah Room and the Latin Quarter.

We were not allowed to drink at work during or between shows but when work was over, we partied. I didn't much like the taste of alcohol but I soon discovered, if I drank enough, it made me feel confident. It also helped me to forget; forget where I'd been and what had been done to me. And it dulled my feelings of self-hatred. I had enjoyed my introduction to marijuana so, when I arrived home after work, I'd often smoke a joint to relax while I listened to music. Initially, I only smoked and drank at night when my baby boys were asleep and, besides a slight hangover in the morning, I was able to function normally. Scotch and wine were my choice of alcohol. As Georgia, I was desirable, provocative, sexy and confident. But, at home, I was still damaged Sharyn. I told myself this was where I was meant to be, that it was my destiny. I raised my children like any other mum during the day but went to work at night in the Cross, as a stripper. Despite the paradox, life was quite good . . . for a while.

MY MOTHER AND LARS had moved from New Guinea down to Melbourne but she and I were not speaking, except for the nights I phoned her, stoned or in a drunken stupor, crying and begging. By now I had a store of resentments that continued to breed like fungus in a dark humid place. I'd call her at midnight, demanding to know my father's name. Obviously, this didn't do much for our relationship.

'Hello Mum, this is Sharyn. Do you love me?' I'd ask. Curtly she'd reply, 'Do you know what time it is? It's midnight.'

'Yeah, I know but just answer me honestly, do you think you really love me or did you just keep me because you thought you should?'

'Sharyn, I love you. It's late. I don't want to wake up your stepfather. He has to go to work in the morning.'

'Well, if you love me so much why won't you tell me about my father? Did he ever get to see me? Did he hold me?'

'Stop it Sharyn, you're being silly. I'm going to put down the phone now. It's very late. Goodnight.'

I'd listen to the click of the phone being hung up in my ear and feel the lump in my throat. When I'd finished with the tears, I'd pour myself another glass of wine. Sometimes, in defiance I rang back. All I heard was the sound of an engaged phone: the sound of a woman in denial who refused to answer any more questions from a lost daughter, in the middle of the night. I'd disturbed her peace, yet again. My mother never questioned me about my life working in Kings Cross, just as she hadn't when I was in institutions. She really did not want to know, so she never asked.

By the second year, I had started to see the Cross and my job at the Paradise Room for what they really were — illusions. My bosses were nice people and I was safe working in the club, Bill the bouncer always saw to that. He and all the club bouncers were big 'bruisers' of guys. I always felt they should have been nicknamed 'Moose' or something similar. They looked incongruous in their black dinner suits, white shirts and bow ties, their suit jacket sleeves stretched and wrinkling over bulging muscles. Some had shaved heads to make them look tough, which was unnecessary because their size and presence was enough to intimidate any sensible person. But they weren't there to control the sensible ones but the drunks who thought they could take them on after a skinful of liquor and drugs, or the guys we called the real desperates: those up-close, can't-get-enough, maybe-I-can-grab-a-feel men, who crowded the front-of-stage tables. But us girls knew how to handle them and were adept at dodging a grope. These men misguidedly believed their favourite girl stripped and gyrated just for them. The club was always packed, especially on weekend nights. The patrons were a real mix of masculinity. Businessmen dressed expensively in well-cut suits, spivvy guys in shiny silk suits, guys more casually dressed and obviously less affluent, and sailors and servicemen. They were old, middle-aged or young, but all were horny and there to see and fantasise about getting what none of them got at home. The music was loud and it always seemed as though the heating was turned up; the place was stifling hot and everyone inside it sweaty because cool and comfortable doesn't sell drinks.

I continued to make bad choices of unsuitable men. My self-esteem plummeted. I was confused and never felt I was doing a good enough job of life as I tried to create a home for my sons, so I sank into the world of drugs. Just about every day I was stoned — not yet addicted, just stoned. I often smoked marijuana with a funny girl named Lee who loved the music of Barry White. Marijuana and hash were my drugs of choice. Now I found myself in dark places with Sydney's more 'colourful' characters and dope started to consume my life.

I MET CRAIG when Belle, a new dancer from the club, and I decided to see a band playing at a hotel near my house one warm summer evening. Struggling to find a seat in the packed auditorium, two long-haired guys headed for the bar so Belle and I took their seats. When they returned they were gracious to give us not only their seats but also their drinks. We all laughed, watched the band together then headed to the beach for late night drinks and joints. I was very attracted to Craig but there was an age difference — he was nineteen and I was twenty-five. We decided age was just a number.

Craig was a gentle man, empathetic and a good listener. He was also a musician. Music was his life and he was a walking music encyclopaedia. An outstanding guitarist, he was in a band and lived locally. Now we spent nights after my show going to see the best bands in the country. He taught me how to truly listen to music, to identify complicated basslines almost obscured by a strong melody, to recognise a particular riff or appreciate a musician's dexterity and skill in a complicated lead guitar solo — like a sponge, I soaked it all up. Craig idolised Jimi Hendrix, imitated the style of Cream and Deep Purple and was inspired by most of the heavy rock bands of the early seventies, including their drug-taking philosophy. I preferred black soul and R&B.

It wasn't long before he took me home to meet his mother Gretel and I fell in love with another family. She was warm and homely and embraced me and my children without reservation. My boys loved her too. She'd cook them cakes and always had special treats waiting for them, so Gretel easily became their surrogate mother when Craig and I moved in together, close to her home. We began to live a rock 'n' roll lifestyle, staying up all night watching bands, smoking dope and, because my children were with Gretel, a lot of the time we slept until noon.

Our home had a large spare room that we turned into a studio for Craig's band to rehearse. We also attracted a new group of friends, some of whom I realise now were just hangers-on — like my postman, who delivered drugs with my mail. But a friend who was a police officer often sat listening to the music and sucking on a joint in full uniform, which was very unsettling.

My job and the money it brought home enabled us to buy plenty of grass, plus other drugs Craig was into. After watching him 'turn on' with the hallucinogen LSD, one night I asked for a taste — and I was hooked. After that, I wanted to drop tabs of this mind-bending acid and go tripping whenever I could. Somehow I always managed to be straight by the time I went to work but, when my show was over, the cycle often began again. I used drugs as a crutch — they dulled my insecurity and gave me false confidence. We associated with like-minded people who were mostly new friends and did not understand the depths of my despair and, anyway, few of us were straight long enough to get into deep and meaningful discussions on life.

My children loved Craig, the music and being around the musicians but, obviously, this party scene was not a good environment for them. I thought bathing, feeding and clothing my boys was enough to make me a good parent. Now I clearly see it was not. I was irresponsible and selfish. My drug-warped perception was that if we didn't do drugs in their presence and my boys were as happy as they looked, I was doing something right. Not true. My children were dear little boys but their home life was confusing and disrupted by people I didn't know well popping in and out and those I did know well being (usually) inebriated, stoned or both. The other children they associated with were our friends' children and their lives were pretty much the same. Thank God for Gretel. She loved my children, cared for them and, I realise now, gave them a home and a haven away from the anarchy of my life. I had created a situation a bit like Ellie and Dorrie's — a party house.

MY LIFE APPEARED GLAMOROUS but basically I was a stripper in the sex industry. By calling myself an exotic dancer, I fooled myself it was legitimate entertainment. Sure, it took nerve to walk onto that stage but there were no real skills involved and it wasn't something my kids could be proud of. There is a fine line between the glamour and the sleaze and, when you scratch the surface, self-destruction is right there with the sleaze.

One Saturday evening late in 1974, between shows and dressed in my sexy best, I went for a walk on my own to sort my thoughts and really think about the meaningless life I was living. I looked around. The glow of the neon disguised the dirt and filth I knew was there during the day. The stale smell of overcooked and reheated food turned my stomach and, as I watched a working girl on the opposite corner struggle for customers, I felt a sense of shared hopelessness.

Heading for the El Alamein fountain, where as a runaway street kid I had sat contemplating my life, I stopped opposite the Bourbon and Beefsteak. A stylishly dressed lady walked towards the entrance carrying a briefcase and an armful of paper sheets. Greeted warmly, she was then escorted up the steps by the doorman. I realised she was the guest singer entertainer that evening for the piano bar. Oh, how I longed to be her!

I knew the Bourbon and Beefsteak Bar and Restaurant had been opened by a Canadian whose idea it was to give it a home-away-from-home atmosphere for visiting American celebrities and servicemen. American flags and other memorabilia decorated the walls and it served good food and great cocktails, with a small band and a singer providing elegant entertainment each evening till two o'clock. It was one of the first places to have an all-night licence and closed at six in the morning for cleaning then re-opened for breakfast. The idea had paid off handsomely and he had acquired the neighbouring property as the business grew, expanding to include a dance floor and dance band in addition to the piano bar.

From where I stood on Darlinghurst Road, I could now hear the music and a female voice singing a Roberta Flack song. I yearned to go in and listen but I had run out of time and had to get back to the Paradise Club.

After the second show, I went next door to the Persian Room with a couple of the girls and began drinking heavily, trying to block out my misery. An hour or two plus a couple of joints later, the girls left to go home but I wanted to listen to the singer I had admired earlier. There was still time so I wandered up the road, purse in hand, heading for the Bourbon. Dazed and depressed, I tripped and stumbled a couple of times, blaming my high stiletto heels. Outside the Bourbon, the 2 am traffic was at its usual standstill so I lurched across the road towards the entrance, weaving between the cars. Overbalancing, I hit the front bumper of a hotted-up Torana and, to break my fall, brought my palm down with a thump on the bonnet. The angry driver leaned out his window and swore at me, his passenger mate joining in. I wasn't in the mood to be polite and yelled an obscenity back. Finishing with an obscene hand gesture, I staggered through the remaining cars to catcalls from other drivers.

As I reached the steps, the doorman (the embodiment of Moose) put out his arm and blocked my way. 'Not tonight, lady. Sorry.'

Swaying slightly I looked up at him, not understanding. 'Pardon? I want to go in to . . .'

'I said not tonight. Now move away please.' Uncomprehending, I opened my mouth to ask again when he said, this time menacingly, 'I don't want your kind in here tonight annoying the customers. Now move away. I won't tell you again.'

I was dressed in short, tight, sexy clothes, and was drunk and aggressive — who could blame him? Turning on my heel, I felt the prickle and heat of humiliation creep up the back of my neck and flood my cheeks. 'One day, *I'm* going to be the one he greets warmly and escorts in, to sing all night with the band,' I mumbled. 'Just watch me.'

But I couldn't do it as Georgia, the stripper from the Cross. 'Make the choice Sharyn,' I told myself. I knew I would never be anything else unless I did something about it — right then.

I RESIGNED FROM THE PARADISE CLUB and worked as a waitress a few nights a week at Chequers. Previously, it had been a glamorous nightclub where international artists Shirley Bassey and Sammy Davis Jr had performed with an orchestra and showgirls, but now it was the hottest rock venue in Sydney. My Chequers job not only paid well with tips but gave me and Craig the opportunity to see the best musicians and singers in Australia.

One night I was rushing around with trays of toasted sandwiches and drinks and, as I hurried past the backstage area, a roadie asked for a platter of sandwiches. I told him I would do a trade: if I could sing one song with the band, I would give him the food free.

Not long afterwards, the lead singer walked up to me. 'So, you want to sing with the band?' I nodded eagerly. He asked what song.

'Jeff Beck's, "Tonight I'll Be Staying Here with You",' I said. He thought my song choice was pretty cool.

I was used to a spotlight by now but this was something else. I could feel it when I stepped onto the stage. The band started, I took a breath and away I went. The sound from the guitar amps and drums behind me was deafening — so much so, I couldn't hear a note I was singing so I had to think the notes as I sang. I was tempted to put my finger to my ear, and I did once or twice, to check I was in tune. I hadn't realised what it would be like to feel physically surrounded and buffeted by sound! The adrenalin rush made my heart feel it was trying to jump out of my chest but I sang with everything I had in me. In a moment it was over. It wasn't as easy as I'd thought and I knew now that I had a long way to go before I could call myself a decent singer, but I'd just had a real taste of my dream.

Craig was proud of me and applauded enthusiastically but his drummer said it was 'sacrilegious' I should even attempt to walk on the same stage as one of Australia's best bands. He was not impressed with the 'would-be chick singer' trying to perform with his favourite band.

MY RESOLVE TO BETTER MY LIFE was thwarted by my love for Craig and my increased dependence on drugs to boost my feelings of self-worth. Unfortunately, my jobs were the enabler for his drug addiction. I continued to use drugs and spiralled deeper into the culture, smoking dope in addition to taking LSD which, due to the drug's pharmacological action, would then keep me up all night and half the next day. It wasn't until I had a really bad trip, during which I saw huge spiders and monsters and cried all night, that I stopped taking it altogether. (I have since discovered it increases blood pressure, heart rate and blood sugar and can cause convulsions, coma, heart or lung failure, or both, and ruptured blood vessels in the brain, in addition to long-lasting adverse neuropsychiatric effects like flashbacks, relatively long-lasting psychoses and severe depression or schizophrenia-like syndromes. I now shake my head in disbelief that I was so stupid, ignorant and indifferent to the value of my life. I say to anyone contemplating experimentation with any drug — don't do it! I am lucky to be alive.)

I tried to take care of my children but taking drugs had become my top priority and my children's needs were not always met. I thought banning anyone using drugs around them until they were asleep was OK but I see now how distorted my sense of reality was. At the time, this kept a few people away but it did not solve the problem and I didn't have the strength of character to ban myself from taking them.

Heroin entered our lives in 1975 when I was twenty-six and my sons were aged five and three. Craig was immediately under its spell and he and his friends became regular users. I was not interested — it frightened me. Also, I couldn't watch as people stuck a needle into their arm. It made me squirm. Instead, I'd prepare food and drinks for them in the kitchen but by the time I returned there would be drugged, glassy-eyed people nodding off to sleep in my lounge room. I watched Craig change from a laughing, gentle man, with dreams of playing guitar onstage, into a restless wreck always on the search for his next hit. He constantly asked me for money, which I gave him, and, when I didn't have it, he'd hock his guitar or records, or whatever, just long enough to get a hit. Within a few days, he would be back at the hockshop to retrieve his treasured goods.

Still, I was blind to his addiction — I didn't know anything about heroin. I'd look at his pimply sallow skin, his constant scratching and, when 'high', his blank stare, and try to have a conversation with him, which was impossible. Now, he lived in the moment with no plans for the future, except to find his next hit.

We started to argue often. I wanted him to stop using. Craig had little patience and was easily irritated. I was getting fed up with the drugs and all the people in and out of our house. The good times had gone.

'I'm worried for you, please stop,' I'd plead, and often I thought he saw reason.

'That's it. It's all over. No more. I'll stop right now,' he'd promise. For the rest of the day I'd flit around the house cleaning and cooking, feeling relieved and happy, until later that night when he hit up again. Many afternoons, I sat with Gretel at her kitchen table and cried, explaining that I loved Craig but I hated the drugs and didn't know how to stop him using. Feeling equally helpless, neither did she.

I'd wanted to try heroin but I was afraid. I considered myself a drug user, not a drug abuser and felt I was not yet addicted to anything, so I stayed away from smack. But I continued smoking dope, using speed and drinking heavily. With Craig in his trance-like state, I felt isolated. That was why I eventually tried it: to feel closer to Craig and see what all the fuss was about. He protested but I insisted. At the kitchen sink, Craig mixed the heroin and water in a spoon then heated it by holding a lit match under the spoon. Then he sucked the liquid into a syringe and tied a belt around my arm and injected the heroin into my vein. I staggered a little, felt the 'rush', closed my eyes and immediately understood how people become addicted to it. I will not lie — the feeling was euphoric. I finally got it. But this is the promise that enslaves you, as you try to achieve that elation again and again.

Heroin is destructive. It is also the greatest pain-killer on earth. It killed my pain, both physiological and psychological. Drugged, I felt at peace and extremely confident and excited by life. I believed I was the perfect mother and the ideal daughter. I'd make big plans but was too stoned to turn them into reality — the drugged state killed any spontaneity, joy and love, but I couldn't see it. As soon as I came down, the reality of who I was and what I had become was like a smack in the face. It was too painful, so all I looked forward to was my next hit. I wanted to feel the rush, the high and the confidence again. I was slowly being caught in its destructive, vice-like grip. Now I understood why Craig and his friends kept using heroin.

My life was all over the place and, in my drugged fog, I didn't know how to make it any better. I tried but plunged deeper into the sewer of my life.

I continued to call my mother, disturbing her at all hours of the day and night. I rambled and mumbled, begged and pleaded and tried her patience. When I wasn't high I felt depressed and confused and worried about my children. I was all they had and that wasn't much, in the condition I was in.

'Will you look after my boys if ever anything happens to me?' I asked my mother during a begging and pleading phone call one night.

'No Sharyn. I'm sorry but I won't,' was her reply. What a shocking admission. I was dumbfounded but at the time, too stoned to realise the significance of what she'd said.

It did make me angry enough to finally go and seek out Ellie to demand she tell me my father's identity. I had respected her wishes and not pressed her again for the information but now I had to know. It had been seven years since Paul and I had lived in Womerah Avenue. But, I was shocked to discover she had moved — gone — and nobody had any idea where to find her. I had missed my last opportunity.

LATE ONE EVENING, Craig, his drummer and I, had a hit in the kitchen after the kids went to bed. I immediately overdosed, collapsing unconscious on the floor. The guys ran me up and down the backyard, turning the hose on me to try to keep me awake. I slipped into a comatose state but still they ran me up and down, willing me to live. They thought I was dead but, eventually, I came around. They put me to bed and sat beside me most of the night, watching to make sure I was OK. I opened my eyes the next morning to find them fully dressed, sitting on the bed beside me.

'Lady, you want to thank God you're here today,' said Craig. 'Go in there and kiss your boys. You nearly died last night.'

I had risked dying in order to satisfy my craving. You would think that frightened me, hearing their story of how my heart actually stopped beating; but no, I was blind to the depths to which I'd sunk.

A few nights later, Craig did not come home for dinner. Actually, he had not been home all day. I had fed and bathed the boys, tucked them into bed and proceeded to pace the floor, drinking and chain-smoking cigarettes and getting angrier by the minute. I pounced, the moment he arrived home.

'Where have you been?' Agitated, I kept pacing.

'Over at Nick's,' he said casually.

'Doing what?' My agitation was growing.

'Having a hit. Why?'

'Were you now? What about me? Did you think I might like to be asked over? How could you be so selfish? You went to Nick's to have a hit and you didn't bother asking me? Well, f—k you!' I screamed, banging things around.

Marching through the house, I slammed the bedroom door and sat on the end of the bed, my whole body shaking with absolute fury. How dare he!

I started to cry. I reached over to the dressing table for a tissue and, as I did, I glimpsed myself in the mirror. The face looking back was pathetic. My eyes were red and puffy, my hair was a mess, my face was thin and my expression so sad. I looked wretched. Why was I so angry? Because I didn't get a hit of heroin? With perfect timing, my door squeaked open and two little faces peered around it.

'Are you alright Mummy?' a small voice asked.

There they stood in their little pyjamas, eyes wide and worried about *me*. I pulled them into the room, gathered them in my arms and wept into their clean-smelling hair. Deep, wracking sobs of disillusionment and disappointment over who I had become and the life I had been so close to giving them. They were not frightened by my distress: they were my beautiful sons. Finally all cried out, I took them both by the hand and walked into the living room where Craig sat strumming his guitar.

'This is stopping right now,' I said.

It had to end there and then, because I knew *that* had been my moment of becoming a heroin addict. I had tried to hide who I was with drugs and tried to be someone I wasn't, hoping people would like me. Although I had been using only a few weeks, if I did not end it now my emotional problems would make it too easy for me to sink forever into the black hole of heroin addiction. It was my beautiful sons who stopped me that night from becoming their junkie mother. If I had not stopped, I would surely have died. I was all my babies had and it was up to only me. I had to make a life we could all be proud of.

I packed up my children, took what money I had left and moved us to the sanity of the suburbs to start a new life, away from Craig, the drugs and Kings Cross.

CHAPTER ELEVEN

The Music in Me

MY SONS WERE NOW MY FIRST PRIORITY. It was early 1976 and my darling little boys had shocked me into facing reality so I settled down, committed to becoming their Mum and getting to know my children. I loved my boys with all my heart and my intention was to give them the best childhood I could.

I got a job in a coffee shop near the house I'd rented in the southwestern suburbs and Anthony started at the local school. Young families with children, similar in age to my two, filled the quiet suburban street and our next door neighbour was a real blessing — a kindly grandmother named Mrs Priest who had popped over to introduce herself with a gift of freshly baked cupcakes.

Soon after moving house, Anthony turned six and I wanted to throw him a birthday party. Carefully, he wrote a list of those he wanted to invite: his little brother, a couple of his school friends and his new playmates in our street. When I asked him what he wanted for his birthday, he replied, 'I want to see my Daddy.' Paul and I hadn't kept in touch but I knew where he lived, so I made contact and invited him to the party the following Saturday.

The day arrived and Anthony, Patrick and I excitedly decorated the house with balloons and streamers and set the table with a bright party cloth, party hats and whistles. An eager Mrs Priest helped me make fairy bread and chocolate crackles as we heated the sausage rolls and party pies in the oven. It wasn't long before my backyard was filled with laughing, shrieking children playing Pin the Tail on the Donkey and Pass the Parcel.

Paul's arrival was heart-wrenching. A beaming Anthony rushed over and clung to him and wouldn't let go of his father's hand for the duration of the party.

As everyone was leaving at the end of a great day, Paul promised to keep in touch with his son so Anthony went to bed with a big smile on his face. Paul did see him again — occasionally.

Each afternoon after work, I'd catch up on the day's washing and prepare dinner while the boys played in the backyard. They shared a bedroom, which made the evening routine a bit easier. I'd read them a bedtime story after their bath then sing them a little lullaby as they drifted off to sleep. It might sound like I'm painting a picture of domestic harmony but it didn't happen immediately. I battled to cope financially and emotionally but at least I was away from the destructive and dangerous drug scene that had begun to consume my life. I was anxious and restless, searching for an elusive something. I still sabotaged anything positive in my life, convinced I wasn't good enough or deserving of anything worthwhile.

I replaced the drugs with alcohol. At times I drank so much that I made a dreadful fool of myself in public, stumbling and often saying things I regretted later. I drank every evening after I'd put the boys to bed and most nights I blacked out; plus, I still smoked marijuana in an effort to dull my senses and my feelings of inadequacy. Also, I didn't know how to parent my boys and asking for advice would have contributed to my sense of failure. I was inconsistent with discipline and indulged the boys far too often, buying them everything they wanted, hoping to compensate for my lack of good parenting. Some days they fought constantly, chasing each other through the house and knocking over a favourite ornament or vase. I had little patience with this behaviour and would send them to their room. Often I yelled and screamed but I tried to be careful not to lose my temper with them. I would ground them after something they had done wrong — then forget about it, ten minutes later. Kids are smart. Mine could sense I was insecure and disorganised and they took advantage of my confusion, which created havoc. Even though they bickered and squabbled, they were fiercely loyal and protective of each other and quick to put up a united front against me or anyone else.

Music was the best salve for my pain. At night when the boys were asleep I played my favourite artists, usually Al Green or Dionne Warwick. I lit candles or sat in front of the fireplace, poured myself a Scotch or wine and imagined myself singing on stage. I needed to believe I could find work as a singer but my low self-esteem was always in the way, constantly questioning my talent. The voice in my head saying, 'Yes you can!' was drowned out by the louder voice saying, 'Forget it. You can't sing. Nobody is going to want to hear you sing, let alone pay you to do it.'

But life has a way of sending us to our destiny.

BY LATE 1976, coffee shop waitressing just wasn't paying the bills and Christmas was coming. Having missed out in my own childhood, I always decorated the house and a tree and spoiled the boys with lavish gifts and the full festive spread. I knew Anthony wanted a model plane kit and Patrick had been desperately hoping for a Green Machine, a green trike with big black wheels that was being advertised as the 'hottest ride in town'.

I found a new job as a teacher's aide at a special school for children with disabilities. It was within walking distance and operated during standard school hours, which suited me very well since I could walk home each day in time to meet Anthony's school bus and these hours weren't difficult for dear Mrs Priest, who babysat Patrick while I was at work.

The job also turned out to be very therapeutic and the perfect one for me. As I watched the day-to-day struggle of these inspirational children and the enormous amount of love and care the teachers and parents showered on them, I realised I had many blessings to be thankful for. Many of these remarkable children had been born with muscular dystrophy (a severe muscle wasting disease) or Down syndrome, and some had Autism. Many of the children were paraplegic or quadriplegic and others were living with brain damage, the result of accidents, yet all of them were joyful. The children loved music, so I had great fun singing songs as I wheeled them from their classrooms to the bathroom, or adjusted a calliper or took them to therapy with the physiotherapist.

It was the children's physiotherapist who commented on my singing. 'You have a lovely voice, Sharyn' she said. 'You should be singing all the time. Why aren't you a professional singer?'

'That would be nice, but it will never happen,' I said feeling a little embarrassed but ever hopeful.

'Why not?' she asked.

'Because I'm not good enough.'

'You don't know until you try,' said my colleague.

One morning she handed me a clipping from a newspaper, calling for auditions for a musical theatre show called *Let My People Come*. It sounded like a gospel show to me so, with permission from the principal, I made an appointment to audition the following week.

'Good. Now just have some faith in yourself and go for it. I know you'll do well,' said my encouraging work mate. I hugged her

I had no idea where to start so I went to Paling's music store in the city and purchased the printed sheet music of 'Ain't No Sunshine' from a revolving display rack. Excited, I rushed home and wrote out the lyrics and practised the song with my Bill Withers record.

When I arrived at the Balmain Bijou Theatre a few days later, there were literally hundreds of singers and dancers already there to audition. Filling out my audition form, I panicked when I had to list my musical experience. Surreptitiously I glanced over the shoulder of a girl sitting near me. She had a long list of dance groups and shows, so I wrote I had four years' experience singing in bands. No one needed to know I had been a waitress at Chequers when I sang a song with one of Australia's most popular bands.

Hours later, my name was called. I walked onto the stage in the dark theatre, passed my printed music page to the pianist and sang 'Ain't No Sunshine' — out of key! Even though I'd practised it over and over again, I sang it as I'd rehearsed it with the record and didn't listen to how the pianist was playing it. It must have sounded dreadful. A voice out in the darkness asked me to sing another song, so I belted out 'Johnny Be Good'. Unrehearsed and without sheet music, it actually felt better. Then the voice in the dark said, 'Thank you very much,' and that was that.

To my joy and amazement, I received a phone call from the casting director three weeks later, telling me my audition for a part in the chorus had been successful. He would send plane tickets and information about the meeting with the current cast, who were playing their final weeks in Melbourne, where our rehearsals for the Sydney show were to begin. I was incredulous, ecstatic and terrified all at once. My Lord! I was about to become a professional singer and in the theatre, no less. I had no idea what the show was about and I didn't care. I was far too excited and eager to jump into my new world.

Let My People Come was to open in August in a well-known Sydney theatre and I was thrilled to be in the cast. I hugged my children and told my friends and neighbours, the dry cleaner, the butcher, the people in the local delicatessen and anyone else who would listen. I was over the moon but, sadly, had to give notice at my job. The lovely children's physiotherapist hugged me and wished me luck in my new career.

Excitedly, I called my mother in Melbourne and explained I would be there, rehearsing for two weeks, and asked: could the children and I stay with her? I also asked if she would look after them while I was at rehearsal. She declined. Her reason? She had not been well of late and it was inconvenient.

Fair enough — I was too excited to let her dampen my spirits — but now I was in a real bind. The boys and I had stayed in contact with Gretel and she was upset that she was unable to help. Mrs Priest was away in the country, visiting relatives, and I couldn't ask the other families in the street to take responsibility for my sons while I was interstate for two weeks. But I also knew I could not let this opportunity of a real future for me and my children pass by.

As the time drew closer I became increasingly desperate. I had no other family support and had exhausted all avenues. Eventually, after making tentative enquiries, and with nowhere else to turn, I had to put my boys into the care of the Red Cross for the two weeks of the Melbourne rehearsal. Their children's respite home, near a

Sydney beach, seemed to be a good place but I was devastated. Was this history repeating itself? I had tried to prepare and reassure them but Anthony was only seven and little Patrick was just five, the same age I was when my mother had abandoned me to the nuns. Driving away was gut-wrenching. Did they feel abandoned? Was there a cruel supervisor waiting for one of my boys to step out of line before administering brutal punishment? I shuddered as demons from my past stirred. I had no choice and it broke my heart.

I stayed in a Melbourne hotel for the first two days with two other singers and a dancer who had auditioned in Sydney, a funny auburn-haired girl, a soprano who'd studied classical music for years, and a young male dancer. We were invited to the show on our first evening.

The theatre was packed and our excitement palpable as we sat proudly, tall in our special seats. The lights went down and the curtain came up on eighteen young and talented entertainers who sang the first song of the evening, with lyrics beginning '*Screw! Screw! Everybody loves to screw*'. I sat stunned as the cast proceeded to sing songs of love between straights and love between gays (both male and female) and songs of fornication and masturbation. We gradually sank down from our position of pride in our plush theatre seats. The final scene of the first half had the cast stripped totally naked, singing something about loving your body! Now, we were practically in the foetal position. I glanced at the looks of panic and horror on the faces of my would-be cast members and, of course, returned the same expression. Secretly, I couldn't help but laugh at the irony. Here I was, trying to leave behind Georgia the stripper from the Paradise Club, only to take my clothes off and be acceptably naked in legitimate theatre!

The second half was even more graphic. The audience loved it and yelled for more. After repeated curtain calls, we were taken backstage and introduced to the performers. A talented lot, many of them had previously been in *Hair*, *Jesus Christ Superstar* and *Godspell* and were, I felt, far too talented for this show. My auburn-haired friend and I managed to plaster a smile on our faces as we told the cast how wonderful they were — which was true, their voices were terrific and the musicians had been great — but I was unnerved by the explicitly sexual lyrics. For my friend and the other two, it was the dancing on stage totally naked that was perturbing. As we left to return to our hotel, we were reminded that our contracts were to be signed at ten o'clock the following morning.

We spent the rest of the night drinking bottles of wine, lamenting that this would probably not turn out to be a good career move, and how embarrassing it would be for our families. Finally, though, we talked each other into going ahead. The rest of the cast had come from great shows, we reasoned, and surely they wouldn't have agreed if it was going to be bad for their careers.

As it turned out, it was a wise move for me to stay in the show. We rehearsed every day and I learned so much from my fellow cast members. I learned to sing harmonies and was choreographed for the dance routines, which, as an untrained dancer, I found to be challenging but very exciting when it all came together. To be honest, I suspected I'd been given the chorus part fundamentally because of my skin colour: a rare occasion where it worked in my favour. This was the Australian version of a Broadway show representing people of races and colour and there were still only a couple of black artists in Australia, particularly of African-American descent. Realising this was my 'big break' and my chance to fulfil my dreams, I was determined to show them I could do it, and do it well. My audition had been woeful and would not normally have secured me the part, but the producers obviously saw potential and, I'm sure, were relieved when my singing and presentation improved during rehearsals.

We moved from the hotel to 'the mansion', an enormous house which had been rented as accommodation for the cast. My room was huge and even had a fireplace. It was a great place with fascinating people dropping in, wonderful parties and good times. Socially, we had a great time in Melbourne but my boys were always in my thoughts. Worried, I made several phone calls to the Red Cross home but was informed they had settled in well. I had to take their word for it.

LET MY PEOPLE COME, we learned from the director, first opened in a theatre on Bleecker Street in New York's Greenwich Village then on Broadway in 1974, where sexual freedom reigned for one hundred and six explicit performances. We had a lot to live up to! It turned out we would become part of a phenomenon: worldwide productions of the show would continue into the 1980s. Although it was subtitled 'A Sexual Musical', so you knew to expect a bit of 'naughtiness', the music and lyrics were actually extremely racy, even by today's standards. Basically, it was a musical revue about sex, including nudity and a lot of x-rated language, but the underlying message was one of humour, freedom and love, and about glorifying the beauty of the human form.

The Melbourne production received a standing ovation on its closing night. Despite the controversy created by church and morality groups, it had been a huge success in Melbourne, so now we headed back to Sydney with the other cast-members and crew for more rehearsals before the show opened there.

Landing in Sydney, I caught a taxi from the airport to home, dumped my luggage inside the front door, then jumped into my car and sped off to pick up my boys.

When they saw me they ran to me as fast as they could. The scene was just like those Sundays when I ran to greet my mother at the convent — except I hugged my children tightly and smothered them with kisses. It was so wonderful to hold my little boys again. I collected their bags and thanked the staff while the boys said their goodbyes to their new pals. They were full of stories as we drove home: Patrick had made some new friends and quite enjoyed his time but Anthony was glad to be out of the place. Nothing serious had occurred but, because he was taller than the other kids his age, the staff had expected him to do the same chores as the bigger boys.

The very next thing I did was rush off to be fitted for contact lenses. There was no way I would be caught onstage wearing ugly glasses — especially naked!

The Sydney rehearsals were exhausting: there were more songs to learn and the dance routines were difficult. Then it came time for the first dress rehearsal where we finally had to take our clothes off. The Melbourne cast had been doing it for nine months and thought nothing of it. In fact, I had noticed during our time there that many of them wandered around backstage during and after the performance, unselfconsciously in various states of undress. I watched how my cast members disrobed and I did the same; no sexy moves this time! I'm sure they were watching to see if we felt uncomfortable but I was determined to be professional and, honestly, it didn't faze me one bit. Still, the rehearsals and preparation were a challenge and incredibly exciting, especially with all the adverse press coverage the show was receiving.

Opening night at the Balmain Bijou Theatre there was a throng of media and protesters marching outside with banners declaring the show should be shut down. The censorship police were out in force, the result of church groups and wowsers doing radio and television interviews for weeks prior, about the disgusting content of the show, which of course encouraged more of the public to buy tickets. Opening night was sold out.

Our large girls' dressing room buzzed with excitement as the sweet fragrance from well-wishers' flowers mingled with greasepaint and nervous sweat. Because of the show's content, my children could not be there but my neighbourhood friends came, including Mrs Priest, as did two of my mother's sisters: my funny aunts Laura and Josephine. They laughed and loved the show and later came to the party and mingled with the celebrities. As my darling Aunt Laura hugged me she said, 'I told you your name would be up in lights. Now look at you!'

The production ran for about four months and I never missed a performance of the eight shows a week, revelling in my first professional singing job. Opening night, I was a bundle of nerves and adrenaline for the whole performance and just concentrated on getting through the show. As the first weeks progressed and the dance routines and songs became second nature, I gradually felt more confident and started to relax and enjoy myself. Onstage, the energy and enthusiasm radiating from my cast members was palpable and hearing my voice amongst theirs, contributing to harmonies and the overall sound, was exhilarating. Then there was the audience applause. This was where I had wanted to be for so long, what I had dreamed of, and now it was a reality.

Let My People Come certainly didn't turn out to be a highpoint or highlight of my career but it was the beginning, the break I had yearned for — and for that, I will always be grateful. It taught me professional discipline, professional etiquette and that if an opportunity presents itself, you've got to grab it with both hands and give it all you've got. You never know where it will take you. By the way, I never again took my clothes off onstage. I'd been there, done that.

AT THE END OF 1977 when the show finished its successful run, another opportunity arose for me to continue in my new-found career as a singer. I was out with friends at a suburban club one evening where, after much cajoling on my friends' part, I sang a couple of songs with the band. The musicians liked what they heard and at the end of the night, invited me to join their band Vegas because their female singer was leaving to go into a theatre show. It seemed almost serendipitous.

We rehearsed a couple of times and they gave me two weeks to learn about thirty songs, then on the second Saturday night there I was, the new female singer of the covers band Vegas, in the same club. Our venues were smart hotels, yacht clubs, ski resorts and the local clubs, dances and function centres. We played every Friday and Saturday night, Sunday afternoons and, often, mid-week. We also played corporate functions, balls and weddings. I dressed in trendy wide-leg pants and looked the part with my 1970s afro hairdo. I was becoming a proficient singer, my tone and range improving with the constant work. We didn't have roadies so we all carried the amps, big speaker boxes, instruments, drums and microphones. It was hard work being in a band. Arriving early, we'd lug in and set up our equipment, freshen up then play for the function and, when it was over, pack it all up again and cart it back to the cars then drive home, usually the last to leave the venue. Just part of the process of paying our dues.

The money I earned singing with Vegas was reasonable, but it was not enough to support two growing boys in school who were now eight and six. I always splashed out on their birthdays and Christmases, regardless of my financial situation. And now there were all the extra-curricular activities. Both boys had been playing soccer for a few years but Patrick excelled, his team winning the competition year after year. Anthony was an excellent swimmer and was selected to join a squad, meaning coaching and 5 am training sessions with clusters of other shivering parents sharing a thermos of coffee to keep warm.

My boys loved music, as well as sports, but I wanted to instil an appreciation of live performance so I took them to as many live shows as I could. Under a giant marquee at Wentworth Park, my boys clapped and squealed with delight at the larger-than-life *Disney On Parade* characters. There wasn't a spare seat as excited children screamed and parents smiled indulgently. As the cast were taking their final bows, I turned to little Patrick but he was gone! Disappeared! My heart leapt in panic. I grabbed Anthony's arm and dragged him protesting down the shaky temporary seating structure and rushed over to the security guards who were preparing for the crowd to exit the packed Big Top. Hysterically, I garbled that my little five-year-old was missing and tried to give them a description. They sprang into action. After what seemed an eternity, a burly guard marched over holding up a struggling Patrick.

'Got him,' he said handing him over. I couldn't help myself. I shrieked at him, releasing my pent up panic. 'Where were you? How could you run off like that?'

'I wanted to say hello to Goofy,' he said. As his big brown eyes welled with tears, how could I stay angry?

The one thing I had learned to do well during my long years in institutions was cleaning — it was second nature to me and I was very good. I had mentioned to some of the other mothers while helping in the school canteen, that I was looking for house cleaning work and it wasn't long before each week was full. This suited me perfectly because I cleaned people's houses while the boys were at school and my hours were flexible. The nights I sang, I had plenty of time to cook and settle them down before the babysitter arrived, or my children went for sleepovers at their friend's homes while I worked. In return, I took my babysitters' children out to the movies or the football, or would keep them at my home for the afternoon, to give their parents a break. I was blessed to be surrounded by so much kindness. I was a single mother with no family support and finding reliable and trustworthy babysitters was my biggest challenge. My mother had not been there for me when I was a child and was also not available to my children. She never looked after them, babysat or offered to help. I have hundreds of happy photos of her with her grandsons; however, those occasions were interstate visits, Christmas Day or particular outings. I sometimes wonder if my mother purposely distanced herself, choosing to live in cities as far away from me as possible. Our relationship was amiable and our phone calls generally cordial, until I'd make the mistake of asking about my father. I just couldn't let it go — I needed to know who I was.

One evening our band was booked to play at the Chevron, a ritzy Sydney Hotel. We entertained the dignitaries at a prestigious function to welcome the Australian and American ambassadors to Sydney. During the dinner break, I stared in disbelief as I saw the black servicemen, resplendent in their uniforms, having to wait at the back of the line for their smorgasbord meal. I was so upset that the boys in the band had to stop me walking out the door. I had never seen such blatant racism. I marched over and spoke to the servicemen about it and they just shrugged their shoulders saying, 'That's how it is, Ma'am.'

'Not in my country!' I said indignantly. The truth was: it *was* in my country and it had been happening to me all my life. I had been segregated in my own family because of the colour of my skin. And it wasn't easy for my sons either.

Anthony stomped in one afternoon after banging the front door, while I was having a catch-up chat with Gretel on the phone. He was visibly upset so I quickly said goodbye and went to see what the matter was.

'What is it?' I asked concerned, trying to put my arm around him.

'Nothing,' he said, hanging his head as he tried to shrug me off. I persisted and finally got it out of him. 'Why do you have to look the way you do? I wish you looked like all the other mothers!' he sniffed, still unable to look at me.

'What do you mean?' As I held him close I was afraid I understood only too well.

It turned out he was being bullied at school because I looked different with my dark skin and afro hair. He had been defending me against the name-calling not only because I was his mother but because he felt he was the 'man' in the family. I held my courageous seven-year-old tighter so he couldn't see my tears, and my proud but breaking heart.

With perfect timing, Alex Haley's *Roots*, the award-winning six-part historical epic, was shown on television. Night after night my sons and I sat up and watched our history. *Roots* chronicles Haley's search to find his origins and the progress of his own family through many generations, from the kidnapping of an African warrior ancestor Kunta Kinte by American slave traders, to eventual post-Civil War freedom. After watching this brilliant but horrifying story, I said to my sons, 'That is your history. That is why we are black. Be proud of who you are.' And they were. Soon, I overheard Anthony confidently telling his friends, 'I am Australian and I am part black American and I'm proud of it.'

'Yeah, I'm proud too,' said little Patrick, echoing his big brother.

As the 1970s came to an end, I'd learned my craft in the band, staying with them for two years. The musicians were excellent and professional and we became firm friends. As they were family men, over the years we'd often get together socially with their wives and children for barbeques and parties. But, as a new decade began, it seemed time for me to move on.

I WAS AMBITIOUS and gaining confidence in my singing ability but I realised that to advance my career I would need to be represented by an agent. I had been given great advice by a leading agent who specialised in country singers and entertainers. She was kind and very helpful but we had different ideas as to where my career was headed.

As fate would have it, I had the opportunity to introduce myself to Lynn Rogers, an entertainer I idolised and a legend in Australian cabaret. Imagine my excitement when she offered to tutor me! My mentor was a highly successful international performer who had starred at the London Palladium and Victoria Palace Theatre, the New York Latin Quarter and Las Vegas Stardust and I was honoured to be her pupil. She arranged for me to perform in an upcoming industry Showcase of Talent for agents and managers, so we started work right away. She gave me instruction on how to walk onto a stage, how to take a microphone from the stand, the correct order of fast and slow songs to create an interesting show, the style of dress to wear, hair and make-up techniques and how to talk and engage an audience.

Lynn surprised me with a gift of a glorious yellow crocheted full-length gown to wear for my performance. Cut low at the front and almost backless, the gown had huge bell sleeves — very 1970s — and between the crochet spaces and the lining were shiny disks that sparkled under lights. The colour accentuated my dark skin and the slim-fitting style clung to my curves and emphasised my height — I looked a knockout. I named the dress 'Big Bird' and she was my favourite stage gown for many years.

On the evening of my Showcase performance I was so nervous and excited that the butterflies in my chest kept catching my breath. This was my second major career opportunity and I was going to give it everything I had. It went so well that immediately after my performance I was approached by a kindly gentleman who signed me on the spot and became my agent. Not only did he take ten percent of everything I earned, he also changed my name to Sharyn Crystal because he thought it sounded more theatrical. He had no idea why I was laughing when I told him I thought the name sounded more like a stripper's!

He put me straight into a trio band performing three times a week in the lounge area of a large suburban RSL Club. We played laid back, easy-listening songs in the early part of the evening, moving on to pop and dance music later. It was always a nice surprise to see women doing the Parramatta Jive on the dance floor in front of me. Of course, I recognised the Parra Jive immediately; it was such a distinct dance style and only ex-Parra Girls were proficient in the steps. Even if I didn't know the women I'd say hello and have a drink and a chat with them during my break.

To improve my musical knowledge and expand my repertoire, I studied the technique of great singers — Ella Fitzgerald, Mahalia Jackson, Aretha Franklin, Lena Horne and Sarah Vaughan. Whatever it took, I wanted to know it all.

THIS WAS A GREAT TIME in Australia for cabaret and variety performers in the Clubs. These clubs were mostly RSL (Returned Services League), Rugby League (football) and golf, and lawn bowling clubs, which were scattered through Sydney suburbs and country towns all over New South Wales.

These clubs are such an integral part of NSW social culture that I feel it's important to provide a bit of background. In fact, clubs have been a part of NSW communities since early colonial times. Initially, they were for Australia's wealthy menfolk, who had imported the British model of the gentlemen's club where important men could go to do business, and to drink together socially. Over the next one hundred and fifty years, the atmosphere of the clubs grew more relaxed by degrees until, by the mid-1950s, gaming was introduced — namely poker machines. Gaming profits gave clubs the means to offer competitive prices for drinks and the funds to build or renovate premises. Now scattered through Sydney suburbs and country towns, and fitted out in the latest fashions in décor (often, lots of chrome, wood veneer and garish carpeting) clubs also attracted a new clientele: women. Soon, the local club was wholeheartedly embraced. A fair notch above the Aussie pub in terms of sophistication, it was the new place to socialise in the community or treat 'the lady wife' to a night out.

From the 1970s, the Australian live entertainment industry was the big winner. Offering patrons entertainment kept them on the premises longer, so many clubs started adding showrooms and auditoriums with a full-size stage, sound and lighting, and seating (for up to one thousand people in larger auditoriums). Australian cabaret and variety performers entertained in glittering shows backed by a six- or eight-piece orchestra and often supported by the club's resident dancers. The clubs had created professional venues and opportunities for Australian singers, comedians, magicians and jugglers to perform to enthralled patrons, bringing live entertainment to the suburbs. I was part of additional entertainment offered in comfortable lounge areas, where duo or trio bands added to the ambience and appeal of a night out at a local club.

While legendary artists Shirley Bassey, Frank Sinatra and Sammy Davis Jr were still headlining at the Silver Spade and concert halls, the large club auditoriums also presented popular international artists like Billy Eckstine, Johnny Ray and Gene Pitney backed by an orchestra and Las Vegas-style showgirls. During my breaks with the lounge band, I would stand at the back of the club's auditorium and watch the Australian and overseas entertainers. These were fabulous shows and I enjoyed them as much as everyone else did. As the girl singer in the band in the lounge, though, I was quite content. My elderly agent Ted Quigg had other ideas. He felt I needed to ditch the band and become a solo cabaret performer. One evening he took me into the auditorium to see a very talented female performer. After the show he said, 'You can do that.' I looked at him as if he were insane.

'No I can't. I'm happy with my little band,' I said. Still he persisted and, eventually, I agreed.

He put me into a club show called Australia's All Star Coloured Show —not quite politically correct now. Appearing with popular Aboriginal performer Jimmy Little, his brother Freddy and American instrumentalist Carl Bariteau, I was billed as 'a sensational new singing star' under my new name Sharyn Crystal. It was thrilling to be onstage with these seasoned performers and for the first time, I also had my own solo spot in a show. I bought a couple of shimmery evening gowns to wear onstage and as we performed in different club auditoriums most Saturday nights, my confidence grew and my stage presentation became more polished. I was learning the art of 'one out' performance.

I WAS STILL CLEANING during the week to supplement my singing income and, the year before, had taken a permanent position as housekeeper and personal assistant to the Barretts, a well-to-do family in the area. The hours were nine to five from Monday to Friday, and occasionally on weekends (if I was not singing) to help with social functions held in their magnificent waterfront home. They were a lovely couple with two sons similar in age to mine. Unbelievably, I stayed in the position for twenty years, on and off. Eventually they became very close friends and my boys and I were accepted as part of their loving family.

Juggling my singing, cleaning, children and mothering made for a hectic life. My sons were happy and doing well at school, Patrick in particular. From his first day he happily waved goodbye and ran into school, leaving me tearful at the gate. Thankfully, over the years my parenting skills had improved, although I was still drinking heavily but not when I was working. I used alcohol to relax on my days off and when I arrived home at night after a gig. I still occasionally smoked marijuana — not all my childhood and adolescent demons had been exorcised. The one thing missing in my sons' lives was a father. My ex-husband showed little interest in his son and my youngest son's father visited only occasionally. Several romantic relationships had floundered and fallen apart, sabotaged by my fears and insecurities.

My mother's attitude toward me had changed dramatically since I'd found a career in music but our relationship still ran hot and cold. Sometimes the children and I visited her and Lars in Melbourne, staying in the two-storey home my stepfather had designed and built. It was modern and spacious with my mother's touch of elegance: Italian-tiled bathrooms, a fashionable colour scheme and soft comfy sofas in the living rooms. My brother was now a teenager, and an excellent ice hockey player, and lived downstairs in his own apartment. Those visits were pleasant and gave my children a chance to spend time with their grandparents and young uncle. Looking back, though, I realise I was never once introduced to any of their friends, neighbours or business colleagues. I'm sure they had a social life — my mother enjoyed entertaining — but no one was invited over while I was there, so, in a way, I was still being hidden.

I felt sure she was proud of me as a singer and, with my stepfather and other family members, came to see my shows whenever she visited Sydney. However, I was always careful *never* to call her 'Mother' in public as this would upset her and turn her to ice.

I also needed her to be proud of me as a mother and when she commented that it must be hard to raise two boys on my own, I told her how much I loved them and that someone had to do it and I was all they had.

I never seemed to get ahead financially and as a consequence the boys and I moved a few times when rents were increased. As a single mother, I had applied for assistance to the NSW Housing Commission, a government agency that supplied public housing assistance for single parents at a reduced rent but I was still waiting to be accommodated. My mother was often generous, buying me jewellery she thought would look nice on stage, or pricey new clothes, and nice gifts for the boys, but she had never offered any financial support, though she knew I struggled. I remember once asking her for five hundred dollars when the going got really tough. She lent it to me but I had to repay every cent. The unexpected gifts I received in the mail rarely compensated for the time during my childhood that we had spent apart and nothing could make up for her unwillingness to talk about my heritage and answer questions about my father.

In the winter of 1980, my Mother, Lars and my brother came to stay. The boys adored their young uncle and he was terrific with them. I rearranged the rooms and scrubbed and polished the house until it shone, which was no easy task in the old house but I wanted everything to be perfect for her.

We had enjoyed a lovely day, including watching the boys play soccer and that evening, I lit a roaring fire and cooked a special roast dinner. Then Lars played board games with the three boys while Mum and I tackled the washing up. After the kids went to bed, Lars and I played chess while my mother relaxed, she and I with a couple of glasses of Scotch; hers neat and mine with Coke. Lars went to bed so Mum and I settled down with another glass of Scotch and listened to Ella Fitzgerald as we chatted, laughed and drank.

When I felt the mood was comfortable, I gently broached the subject.

'I know you don't want to talk about it but could I ask you a question about my father?'

'Well, if you must. What is it, Sharyn?' she said irritably.

'Could you tell me something about him?'

'I've told you many times, he's dead. He came to Australia . . .'

'Yeah, yeah, I know that story. But how do you know he's dead? Who told you?' I could see she was becoming agitated so I put another log on the fire and poured us both another drink, giving her a chance to calm down. The new log crackled and popped in the flames.

'I don't remember. I just know that I went down to see the next ship that came in and I asked the boys where he was and none of them knew.' She took a gulp of Scotch. 'One of them must have told me. I don't remember,' she said dismissively. I pushed on.

'Well, then he could still be alive. What was his name? What did he look like?' She was tearful now, dabbing her eyes with her lace handkerchief, which she kept up her sleeve.

'Please tell me more,' I pleaded, leaning towards her. She pulled away, grabbing her glass.

'There's nothing to tell. I loved him and he deserted me. He told me he was coming back to take me to America, like what happened with Rosa. I thought he was coming back but he deserted me and he deserted you.'

'So he knew about me?' Suddenly I was excited.

'He deserted me and you!' Her hysteria was rising, as was her voice. 'Why do you want to know about a man who left us? He left me!' She was crying noisily and I worried that her loud voice would wake the children but I couldn't stop.

'What was his name? Please tell me, what was his name?'

'Stop it,' she shrieked. With that, Lars came hurrying into the room.

'What's going on here? Have you upset your mother again?' he asked angrily.

'Oh Lars,' she bleated as she rushed over, leaning in to him, in tears and trembling. 'She's upset me again. She's doing it again.' He shot me a furious look and led my now hysterical mother into the bedroom and locked the door.

I pondered what she'd said. Could it be that because he had deserted her, she punished him by deserting me and locking me up all those years of my childhood? Did she feel it also gave her the right to deny me his name? I had suffered for the sins of my father. As I sat staring into the fire, Ella with perfect timing, sang 'God Bless the Child'.

Early the next morning, my cousins arrived unexpectedly and my mother, supported by Lars, shuffled to the car. They refused to stay with me again.

As always, I backed off with the questions about my father. Even as an adult, I was still seeking her love and approval and worrying that she would cut me off if I displeased her. Consequently, I was often moody and irritable and frustrated with life.

Anthony was now ten and had shot up, growing head and shoulders above his friends. Not only was it embarrassing for him, being so tall and skinny, but he was being teased about his height at school. So I took the boys to see the Harlem Globetrotters, the incredible basketball team from the USA, when they came on one of their visits to Australia. They all stood between six and seven feet tall. Somehow, I also arranged for the boys to meet them after the game. As they made a fuss of Anthony, telling him how great it was to be tall, and that girls loved tall boys and how special he was, I could see his attitude change. My young man felt ten feet tall after that inspirational meeting and strutted around with his new 'black' walk chanting proudly, 'I'm tall and I'm black.' He joined our local basketball team and hung a poster in his room of his hero, Kareem Abdul-Jabbar, the famous black basketball star. Patrick was into all sports — you name it, he loved it — and was a walking sports historian.

IN ADDITION TO the All Star Coloured Show, I was still gigging frequently with the RSL club trio band, but to keep me in constant work my agent also booked me to sing with a cocktail-lounge pianist in some of the finer up-market hotels dotted around Sydney's harbourside. This was reliable work and pay for a couple of years. These were what I call 'lovely gigs' — subdued lighting, swish décor and expensively dressed couples sipping cocktails served by attentive waiters — an appreciative audience. I enjoyed wearing stylish gowns, seated on a stool at the grand piano with my pianist dressed in a dinner suit. We played all the standard songs including 'The Lady is a Tramp' and 'Misty'. Sinatra tunes were popular and anything ever recorded by Cleo Laine, Ella Fitzgerald and Randy Crawford.

I also loved singing in the elegant restaurants and piano bars in Oxford Street — the centre of entertainment for Sydney's gay community. A couple of pubs had been completely transformed into sophisticated places of entertainment: nightspots where the décor may have seemed a little over-the-top because it always included plenty of pizzazz.

With an eye for elegance, the chic restaurants always included crisp white tablecloths, sparkling silver and efficient, gorgeous waiters. And the facilities! Although it may have originally been a broom cupboard or a storeroom, depending on the venue, the entertainer's dressing room was always fully decorated and fitted out with mirrors, special lighting, hanging racks and often included extra touches like a small vase of flowers, tissues and hand towels. They'd thought of everything and I always felt very special. And I always frocked up. I wore glittering and sequined evening gowns, sparkling jewellery and high heels.

The gay men and smattering of women were great fun, great looking, stylish and fashion-conscious. I had a special repertoire of songs just for those nights and my audiences were encouraging, very appreciative and effusive, 'Ooh, love your jewels, love your frock and *loved* that song darling.' And I loved being there.

Singing with the trio band one evening in 1981, while glancing around the room I noticed two handsome black men sitting at a table, watching me intently. Imagine my surprise and anxiety when I realised one of them was the legendary Freddie Paris! In my break they invited me to join them. Freddie, by then a resident in Australia for some time, had just performed in the auditorium and introduced me to Clayton Davis who was in his show: Freddie Paris and Black Magic. For me, it was the start of a special professional friendship with Freddie. Over the next ten years he mentored me, giving me confidence in my ability and my colour. Freddie had grown up in the Deep South, in New Orleans, during the racial discrimination of the thirties and forties but had spent much of his professional career based in San Francisco. With this wisdom, he encouraged me to be proud of my heritage and who I was and many times, we discussed our African-American roots and how difficult it had been for me growing up in Australia, with no one to relate to or talk to about it.

In early 1982, I joined another club production show called Caribbean Carnival with Freddie's friend, trumpeter Clayton Davis. The show was great fun with bright colourful costumes. I sang calypso songs and 'Rum and Coca-Cola' while dancing around the stage like a black Carmen Miranda in a headdress, complete with mountains of tropical fruit. There were still very few black performers so the show was different and popular with the club bookers.

I chose to leave when I was offered a long contract to star in the production show at a theatre restaurant in Sydney. Beachcomber Island was a popular Polynesian-themed restaurant in Drummoyne. The room was decorated island-style with palm trees and tropical flowers growing on vines, a swimming pool onstage and a volcano behind it, which actually erupted each evening during one of the dance routines. Not falling in the pool was the main challenge and every now and then someone lost their footing. Waitresses wearing bikinis and sarongs delivered to the patrons an array of fluorescent drinks and platters of questionably themed 'tropical' food: the menu listed a selection of fruity rice and salad dishes in addition to barbequed meats. The show followed with limbo dancers, a reggae band, musical numbers and Hawaiian dancers. The audience joined in the limbo and everyone had a great time. In addition to the cast musical numbers, I had my own spot in the show.

My children loved coming to work with me. My family of various cousins came and even my mother went under the limbo stick. After two years, towards the end of 1984, my run in the theatre restaurant came to a close.

My agent had been pushing me to start my solo cabaret career for almost four years now and, finally feeling confident in my ability, I agreed. I had paid my dues, so to speak, and I was ready for my own 'one out' cabaret show. My agent rang to say he'd booked me into a Saturday night cancellation spot at an RSL club in two weeks' time — there was no turning back now!

I went to a musical arranger and bought twenty standard charts. A basic musical arrangement or chart for a song consists of eight pieces: parts for piano, guitar, bass guitar, drums, trumpet, tenor saxophone and trombone. I can't read music so I sat while the arranger patiently explained each one and taught me how to converse with my future club musicians and 'read the charts'. I believe this is unique to Australia. In other countries the artist would have a rehearsal with the band or orchestra before performing a show but in most Sydney clubs, a time is allotted for a brief 'talk through' of the charts with the band, about an hour before the show. It shows the calibre of the musicians and the artists to be able to do this. Some entertainers and most club production shows employ their own musical director (or MD) who is often a piano player. This MD converses with the band in these cases and plays and semi-conducts them through the show. I had bought charts previously, for songs I sang in the production shows, but we had used a musical director so this was quite daunting for me. I went home with my twenty new charts and a rehearsal cassette of the songs with just the instrumental backing and spent the next two weeks perfecting the songs. I also bought another new long sparkling dress, evening shoes and jewellery.

My housekeeping job and singing covered our cost of living but my singing career expenses were also high. In addition to car running costs, meeting the need for a selection of glamorous evening gowns did not come cheap — not to mention publicity photos and my agent's percentage from each job. The biggest outlay, though, was the music charts. Stock arrangements basically bought off the shelf, with everyone having exactly the same chart, can range from thirty to fifty dollars each. Custom arrangements written specifically for you can cost hundreds, and sometimes thousands, of dollars each. Every time you want to add a new song to your show, you buy another arrangement.

Nervous and excited, on the Saturday night I arrived at the club two hours before my start time. I wanted plenty of time to prepare! Backstage, I was shown to a small dressing room. It was nothing fancy — just a large mirror surrounded by some Hollywood-style lights on the wall, a benchtop in front of it, a chair and a clothing rack. I unpacked my gown, make-up and charts. The silence was unsettling. There was no chatter and banter and shared anticipation of the coming show. There was just me.

I paced up and down for a while, anxiously going over the songs and the 'order of show' in my head then, too soon, the band was ready for the 'talk through'. Smiling and trying to look relaxed, I handed out my charts, already collated for each instrument in song order. I talked through the songs, discussing tempo, key changes, things to look out for (like a beat rest), and which songs were segued (play the following song without a pause) and which I would talk between. Back in the dressing room I changed, touched up my make-up and stood back and looked at myself in the mirror. My dream of singing on stage in a shimmering gown had helped me survive the most traumatic times in my childhood and, tonight, I was finally here. Just me, performing my own show.

I stood in the wings, took a deep breath and said a prayer as the compere chatted to the audience, then announced, 'Ladies and Gentlemen, please welcome a new singing sensation, Sharyn Crystal!'

The audience applauded and the band played the introduction for my first song, a happy up-tempo number. As I stepped from behind the curtain and walked to the centre of the stage, the white spotlight hit me. A voice in my head said, 'You've done this plenty of times before, the stage is home to you, the difference is it's just you on your own. Show them what you can do!' I took the microphone from its stand and belted out the first song. The audience applauded: they loved it.

The rest of the show was a triumph for me. I chatted to the audience between songs, sang soulful ballads and up-beat dance numbers and, each time, the audience showed their appreciation. I felt wonderful as my black hair shone, my long, white sequined gown shimmered in the bright light and my diamante earrings sparkled against my dark skin. As I took my final bow to the applauding audience I thought, 'I have done it! These people love me and I'm not the worthless nothing I was told I was, all those years.'

CHAPTER TWELVE

Love and Other Cruises

THE COMMITTMENT and energy I had put into my career was starting to pay off in success and recognition. Now I had the time to yearn for other things. I longed to be in love. I daydreamed of a little house with a white picket fence and a *Cosby Show* lifestyle. How nice it would be to have a man around the house, especially as my teenage sons were becoming a handful, giving cheek and backchatting me. They were fifteen and thirteen and Anthony now stood taller than six feet, six and wore size 12 shoes. Plus they were both permanently hungry, costing a small fortune in food bills. They also had a taste for designer labels, mostly Nike and Billabong, so I encouraged them to get part-time jobs. Anthony had had a paper run as a small boy, and had washed the neighbours' cars, knocking on their doors with a bucket and cloth in hand. Now he worked at McDonald's after school but Patrick wasn't interested — every spare moment, he played sport.

The Department of Housing had finally found us accommodation and we settled into a comfortable three-bedroom apartment near the beach, and just thirty minutes from the city. No more moving! Over the years, I had collected an assortment of furniture and I enjoyed choosing new bright cushions and a rug to give the place a more homely feel and I bought new curtains for the living room and my bedroom. I loved plants and couldn't pass a nursery without bringing home a new fern or potted flower to nurture. Although it was obviously smaller than a house and had no yard, the boys loved the flat, especially their bedrooms. As teenagers do, they went surfing, listened to music, had their friends over and both were doing well in high school.

As long as I didn't hassle her about my father, even my mother and I seemed to be getting on. I always sent a card, a gift, and had flowers delivered to her, on Mother's Day and her birthday, and I had really splashed out the year before on her sixtieth birthday. At the time, Lars had thrown her a surprise birthday party and some of my Sydney cousins had flown down for the event but I was not aware of this. I had not been invited. My mother, Lars and my brother visited each Christmas Day, arriving laden with gifts for us all, but always chose to stay with my cousins.

I had joined entertainment industry associations and made a point of going to their social functions. Meeting other entertainers was important and many were becoming good friends. Bookings were increasing for my solo cabaret show and four nights a week I sang at the Rex Hotel piano bar in Macleay Street, where the patronage were the Cross nightshift people: mostly entertainers, dancers, club owners, spruikers and bar staff who called in to unwind with a drink on their way home because the piano bar stayed open later than most clubs. Sitting on a high stool next to the grand piano, I sang what I called 'three in the morning music': laid back bluesy ballads and romantic love songs.

My favourite gigs were the Mandarin Club and Taxi Club, two trendy nightclub-cum-bars in the city. Here I fronted their resident bands of highly accomplished musicians, many of whom were recording session players during the day. I always took my charts but, mostly, these talented musicians knew just about any song I wanted to sing. I loved these nightclub gigs. It was a pleasure singing with such professional musicians and, often, visiting musos and international artists would join us onstage, then the room would really rock. The patrons were all ages, well dressed and there for a good time and the atmosphere was electric, but they were also late nights. We didn't start playing till ten and finished after two in the morning.

One night at the Taxi Club, I was halfway through a song, my eyes sweeping the room, when I felt my heart stop for a beat or two. A man — a man I recognised immediately — was standing off to one side, staring at me. His presence unnerved me. At the end of the set I made my way through the crowd to the bar but I never took my eyes from him. I needed to know where he was. As I picked up my drink, I felt sick — he was heading my way.

'Hello, pretty lady. I was hoping to buy you that drink.'

My skin crawled as a rush of adrenalin shot through my body, the drink threatening to slip from my trembling fingers. My mouth had gone dry but I managed to squeak, 'Thanks but you're too late.' Taking a deep breath I fought to regain my composure.

'Maybe I can buy you the next one,' he said as his eyes travelled up and down my body. 'I like listening to you sing but I like looking at you more,' he leered.

I was adept at handling this type of behaviour from men and usually excused myself politely but this one was different. Sarcastically I said, 'Do you now?'

Not put off by my derision, he added quickly, 'I'd like to get to know you. Would you —'

'Oh but I already know *you*,' I interrupted. 'Don't you remember me?' He cocked his head to one side in a question, a smirk on his face.

'It was quite a few years ago,' I said. 'In a stable.' I paused. 'You called me Midnight.'

I watched as a look of recognition passed across his face, then it seemed to drain of all colour. Leaning in towards him I hissed, 'Shame on you!'

He stepped back abruptly, bumping the people behind him. I stood my ground, not breaking my stare and willing my eyes to burn a hole into his soul. Then I turned my back on him and with dignity, made my way to the stage, but my drink was empty by the time I got there. I now ignored my enemy and made him invisible just like Lillian had advised me to do, all those years ago on the Covered Way in Parramatta. Another demon faced and exorcised.

MANY OF MY ENTERTAINER FRIENDS were cruising. I was not and wanted to, desperately. I dreamed of the day a cruise ship company would invite me to sing on a magnificent ship, cruising to America. How wonderful that would be! But it seemed only the best entertainers were offered cruises. Towards the end of 1985, I was bemoaning this fact to an entertainer friend who was a regular cruiser. The following week she invited me to a party and introduced me to the entertainment bookings manager for P&O. I told him how much I would love to sing on ships and had never had the opportunity, so he gave me his card and asked me to call him on Monday. When I did, he booked me as the guest entertainer for the Christmas and New Year cruise to Fiji, Vanuatu and Noumea on the beautiful *Oriana*. I explained I couldn't leave my two teenage sons at Christmas so he invited me to take them too, all expenses paid plus a generous remuneration.

As they were keen surfers, I had promised the boys a beachside holiday in Queensland.

'I've got some bad news guys,' I said as they came through the door after school. 'The trip to the Gold Coast is cancelled.'

'Oh Mum,' they groaned in unison. 'Please, can we go?' asked Patrick putting on his best pleading expression.

'No. But the good news is, we're cruising on the *Oriana* instead!' They were delighted.

Preparation for the cruise was exciting. We needed passports and shopped for new clothes to wear on board. I spent days preparing my music, ensuring I had the right mix of material for the audience and the ship's orchestra.

SS *ORIANA* WAS THE LARGEST and last passenger ocean liner built in England in 1960 and she was a legend in Australian waters. Surely everyone had cruised on Oriana. A contemporary of P&O's *Canberra*, she was the last survivor of the famous Orient Line ships that sailed the England-to-Australia route — by ship is a very dignified way to travel, I've always thought. She was big — nearly forty-two thousand tonnes — and in 1973 she became a full-time cruise ship carrying nearly two and a half thousand passengers and crew. By

1982, she was so popular P&O based her in Sydney, solely for South Pacific cruising. Other shipping lines had also entered the Australian cruising market; Russian, Italian, Greek and a Chinese company were all vying for the increasingly popular cruise dollar.

By the mid-1980s, the *Oriana* had become a victim of her own success. P&O had announced she would be withdrawn from service so I felt lucky I'd been booked for a cruise before she was retired. She just couldn't compete with the discounted fares on smaller ships. One of these was the popular *Fairstar*, which had been a major player for some time in the Australian cruise market.

Walking on board *Oriana* on December 23, 1985 I was amazed at her size. Her long wooden decks seemed to stretch forever and beautiful timbers lined her corridors and public rooms. She smelled of oil and polish with a hint of salt, reminding me of a well-loved vintage artefact: slightly shabby but lovingly buffed to perfection. She truly was a grand ship.

We were greeted by the cruise director, in the main reception area. While we chatted, I noticed a large board titled 'Entertainment' and there near the top was my ten-by-eight-inch publicity photo, underneath my name in big letters. I tried to act cool but my boys spotted it and rushed over to have a closer look. We were shown to our cabin, which was unexpectedly large, then the crew surprised the boys with their own cabin next to mine, much to their excitement. We unpacked and hurried up to the Promenade Deck. Standing at the railing I watched my boys grinning with pleasure as they threw streamers to the crowd on the dock below. I could hear a band playing the 'Jamaican Farewell', the music wafting from the deck above. As the ship slowly pulled away from Circular Quay and sailed past the Sydney Opera House, I wondered if life could be any better.

The cabaret and show rooms were impressive and entertainers were backed by a skilled orchestra and Las Vegas-style showgirls. Many of the cruise staff, dancers and performers were British, as was the captain and several officers. Nightly they sat at a table close to the stage and cheered the shows. I made certain my gowns were exquisite — people expect to see entertainers in beautiful sequinned dresses, sparkling jewels and high heels.

A Christmas cruise is filled with families, so my choice of songs had to include something for older audiences as well as mums, dads, the teenagers and the children, and not forgetting the thirty-year-olds looking for romance. A substantial song repertoire is essential for on board entertainers. Plus, you need to talk to people from different walks of life; not just the audience but those working on board who came from the four corners of the globe. The crew members not working on show nights were able to watch it on closed circuit television in the crew bars and cabin quarters, so it was often a good thing to keep them in mind as well. Most were thousands of miles from their home, working seven days a week for months at a time and grateful for the work since jobs paying enough to support the family were virtually non-existent in their own countries.

My shows were a success, I was very happy with my performances and every one enjoyed them. The only challenge was not staggering on the rolling stage! Aware I was on constant show and assessment, I was flattered when passengers often stopped to chat to me or pass on a compliment and signing autographs was a thrilling new experience. The first time, I glanced behind me to see who they were asking. I'd never expected it to be me! The Stern Gallery was the large disco room with a resident rock band playing each night from ten till two in the morning. The social scene on board was great and I often met up with passengers and the cruise staff in the Stern Gallery at the end of their long day and night.

The boys made new friends, participated in the on board activities and together we explored the tropical ports, bargaining in the markets for mementos. It was a Christmas and New Year to remember.

It became official: *Oriana* would end her cruise duties three months later on March 27, 1986. I couldn't be more astonished and delighted when I was asked to be a guest entertainer for her farewell voyage. The afternoon of her departure, bands played and the wharf was waist-deep in streamers as thousands of people and the media came to say goodbye. It was an emotional departure with passengers crying openly as the tugs pulled her away from Circular Quay. As she sailed down Sydney Harbour for the last time, a huge flotilla of small craft churned the water, jockeying for position between the police boats and tugs.

It was a fun cruise, yet also nostalgic and emotional. There were colourful and poignant ceremonies to mark her last voyage, in which tropical flowers were scattered across the water as island dancers and singers farewelled *Oriana* in every port. The tributes left most of us on board in tears but then the party would begin again. During our days at sea, *Oriana*'s artworks, furniture and bric-a-brac was auctioned to the passengers, with much excitable bidding, but the item everyone was waiting for, the ship's bell, was presented to the Captain instead.

On a bright sunny morning of March 27, *Oriana* returned to Sydney, ceremonially flying the Orient Line house flag for the last time as she sailed majestically through Sydney Heads. A fleet of small craft escorted *Oriana* up the harbour and under the Harbour Bridge led by a fire-fighting tug shooting torrents of water into the air from her fire hoses. Then she slowly docked at the Pyrmont Passenger Terminal. A sad day, it was the end of an era in Australian cruising.

SO MUCH FOR CRUISING! Now I had no ship, so I continued with my solo cabaret show in the registered clubs and my piano bar and nightclub gigs. I so wanted to be offered a cruise on the Sitmar Line's TSS *Fairstar*, the most successful ship cruising out of Sydney. I'd heard June Evans was the woman you needed to impress. She booked *Fairstar* and seemed to be the doyen of the cruise entertainment booking industry.

Frustrated after months of waiting, one day I marched into her office and explained to the young man sitting at the desk that I was the last entertainer on *Oriana* — I thought someone would have rung me to offer me work on *Fairstar*! Across the room, a high-backed swivel chair spun around and there sat a middle-aged, self-assured woman peering over the top of her glasses at me. Oh dear — it was June herself.

'Sharyn Crystal?' she asked with a wry smile. I nodded, a little embarrassed. She slid the chair a few feet to a desk, then beckoned me over to sit opposite and turned a giant, open leather-bound book towards me. 'Pick a cruise,' she said. I glanced down and pointed.

Then she turned the page. 'How about this one? And this one? What about this date?' Five cruises later, 'Do you want to confirm them?' she asked. I nodded enthusiastically. 'Welcome to *Fairstar*,' she said, now with a warm smile.

For the next eleven years I would sing my way around Asia and the Pacific numerous times each year cruising on *Fairstar*, until she was finally taken out of service in 1997. She was a wonderful ship and I am honoured to be part of the *Fairstar* family.

LIFE WAS GOOD. I'd just about given up on finding love but I was singing in clubs, cruising, my boys were happy and I was making ends meet. I still cleaned but now I also looked after the business of my new agents, a husband and wife team who were also entertainers. They had an attic office in their spacious home and, when they went overseas or on cruises, my children and I would house-sit their home and I'd keep an eye on their office. They taught me the basics of their business, which I found incredibly interesting. Eventually they offered me part-time work as an agent's assistant and I thrived on it. I loved working behind the scenes of the entertainment industry and I found I was also good at it.

Then, in late 1987, the husband was hospitalised with a life-threatening illness and was unable to run the agency. Some of his entertainers moved on temporarily to other agents but I couldn't waste time looking for a new one so I applied for a barmaid job at a local hotel which was also a popular music venue for bands. I thought a job where I had no idea what I was doing might at least be a good opportunity to gain a few skills.

By four each afternoon, the place was packed with thirsty tradesman and workers lining up for a cold beer. Three girls were flat out pulling beers in the rush and I was slow as could be. The men were so patient, waiting while I filled glass after glass with froth! Embarrassed, all I could do was smile and say, 'Sorry, love.

I'll get it this time.' It took a couple of days but finally I got the hang of it.

One afternoon I looked up to see Charles Bronson waiting patiently and smiling at me. Of course it wasn't *the* Charles Bronson but gosh, he sure looked like him. I blushed and took his order. After that, each afternoon I smiled at him and he smiled back.

I decided he was married because he'd arrive around four and leave about twenty minutes later. When I mentioned this to my barmaid friend Vivien she explained he was a local regular and wasn't married.

'Then you'd think by now he would have asked me out, huh?' I said.

'Well, have you told him you fancy him?'

'No way. *He* should make the first move,' I said. Viv laughed.

Apparently, while we were chatting, the man's drinking buddy overheard our conversation. That afternoon before he left, Charles Bronson came over to me and said in his best Croc-Dundee voice, 'So do ya wanna go out for tea?'

'Tea? You mean for dinner,' I said in my best posh voice.

He looked me straight in the eye. 'Make up your mind, Sweetheart. Do ya wanna go out for tea or don't ya?' Of course I said yes.

Allan and I went out for dinner at a local Italian restaurant and had such a good time that I invited him to an industry gala event, which he also enjoyed. As the weeks progressed, so did our romance. We couldn't have been more opposite — but then you know what they say about opposites.

He was a tradesman, a plumber who started work in the early hours of the morning, worked hard all day and went to bed early. I was the nocturnal singer who came home around the time he was leaving for work. But we were crazy about each other and had both found love so the next step was to live together and combine our families.

One evening, just before he moved in, I asked him to take me for a drive to the beach. We parked overlooking the surf and talked, while red-legged seagulls squealed and squabbled around the car.

'You know I love you very much,' I said, turning in my seat to look at him. 'I want us to live together but, before we do, there are things I need to tell you.' He opened his mouth to protest but I went on, 'I need you to listen and if at the end, you decide you don't want to continue with me, then I understand but I have to be honest with you.' I turned back to stare at the ocean. 'Some things I'm very ashamed of but you need to know them and better I tell you now, than someone else does.'

My lovely man sat and listened as I told him the story of my life. I told him about my mother and, through tears of shame and humiliation, I told him about the orphanage and the institutions. I told him I had worked as a Kings Cross stripper and about the drugs and that I still smoked marijuana occasionally and continued to drink every day. As I talked I kept glancing at him nervously, trying to gauge his reaction. Finally, I said, 'Well, that's it. I'm not just a singer. I've done lots of things I'm ashamed of and whatever happens now, I understand.'

Allan looked at me. 'Is that it?'

I nodded, dabbing my eyes with the soggy tissue. He leaned over and lifted my chin so we were looking into each other's eyes.

'I love you and I will love you for the rest of my life. You are a beautiful lady,' he said as he put his arm around me, hugging me close. Relieved, I laughed. 'So let's go home. I'm dying for a cold beer,' he said.

My teenage sons were now seventeen and fifteen and Allan had four-year-old twins — a boy and girl he adored who came to stay every other weekend and in the school holidays. After a slight furniture reshuffle and the addition of 'blokey' things in the garage, it was a happy family atmosphere, with our children getting on well and Allan and I enjoying our new life together. He was a positive influence for my boys too, coming into their lives at a time when an authoritative role model was needed. At times, he had them helping with the sanding and polishing of wooden tables and shelves he'd made. A fit outdoors person, Allan also introduced us to the pleasures of fishing.

ANTHONY KEPT GROWING and now stood an astonishing six feet, ten inches tall. One afternoon during a game of basketball, he collapsed and was rushed to the children's hospital where a brusque specialist finally diagnosed an illness called Marfan syndrome. In his abrupt bedside manner, this insensitive and tactless doctor told my shocked son he had a genetic disease that can attack the joints, heart, lungs and eyes and that there was no cure for it. Still trying to grasp the enormity of the situation, I heard the doctor say then that it was hereditary: either Anthony's father or I had passed it on to him and one of our parents would probably have it also. Finally, he told Anthony not to smoke cigarettes, not to have children and that, if he took care of himself, he might live to be about forty. We were both devastated.

I asked my ex-husband and my mother. Neither knew anything about it. Now I really had to find out about my father but my mother still refused to talk. In desperation I became more insistent, creating scenes and arguments, even pleading, but she would not budge. She'd just hang up, repeating the phrase I had heard countless times before, 'I am going to put down the phone now.' In the end, she refused to speak to me, full stop.

My darling son was mortified at his prognosis. To make matters worse, he was crushed when told he could no longer play his beloved basketball so he went into total denial. He just wanted to get on with his life without acknowledging he had Marfan's. I immersed myself in information about it so I could be aware of what to expect.

During this time, I happened to see a television interview with a woman whose daughter had Marfan syndrome. I immediately telephoned the station. I requested they pass on my contact details to the woman, who called me back. She had started a Marfan syndrome support group and I joined her committee. I needed to learn everything I could about this mystery illness.

I discovered that Marfan syndrome is an inheritable or genetic disorder of the connective tissue. (Think of this tissue as a type of 'glue' that helps support all the organs, blood vessels, bones, joints and muscles.) In Marfan syndrome, this glue is weaker than normal and because of this the workings of the heart, blood vessels, bones, tendons, cartilage, eyes, nervous system, skin and lungs can be affected. Just like Anthony, people with Marfan's are often tall and thin with long limbs (often their arm span is greater than their height) and may have slender, tapering fingers. The most serious potential complication would be for Anthony to develop defects of his heart's valves and aorta.

Having checked my mother's side, and my ex-husbands, I now needed information about my father. By now, I'd gleaned enough to know that it was caused by mutations in the FBN1 gene. All humans have a pair of the FBN1 genes that can carry the Marfan trait. But, because it is a dominant trait, people who have inherited only one affected FBN1 gene, from either parent, will have Marfan's. Anyone with Marfan's has a fifty per cent chance of passing it on to their children, which is why the doctor had told Anthony not to have children. But Marfan syndrome affects different people in different ways; some have only mild symptoms, while others are more severely affected, requiring medication and operations. In most cases, the symptoms progress as the person ages; many people with Marfan's can live on into their seventies, just like the rest of the population.

I WAS EVEN MORE DETERMINED to discover my father's identity but first I had to get my mother to speak to me again.

I continued to send her long newsy letters about the children and their achievements at school and in sport. I sent her photos and continued to send Christmas cards and lovely presents and flowers on special days. I loved her and, at this point, was prepared to do anything to heal the wounds. Eventually she relented.

'Look to the future, Sharyn,' she said. 'I have made a new life for myself and I am happy with your stepfather. I don't want to talk about the past. Your father is dead and the past is dead and gone.'

Well, she knew about her past but I didn't have one. I could see she wasn't going to budge so I tried to help Anthony using the information I had. She kept the answer secret and even though I still didn't know my father's name, I had to leave it alone.

CHAPTER THIRTEEN

Fire, Triumph and Ice

OUR HOUSE BURNED DOWN IN 1988. Not a house exactly, but our lovely three-bedroom apartment and almost everything was gone.

Having a day off work, my eldest son Anthony had decided to go surfing. As he pulled his surfboard from the top of his wardrobe, a foam mattress stored for visiting friends fell on top of his bed. It was winter, his electric blanket was left turned on and must have shorted through the day because, when my younger son Patrick came home after school, he smelled smoke in the overly hot apartment. Anxiously checking the house, he rushed into his brother's room to see a small fire had started on the bed. His immediate reaction was to quickly grab the foam mattress and run with it to the balcony. As he opened the door, the draught of fresh air hit the mattress and it exploded into flames which leapt to the curtains. In the seconds it took for him to throw the mattress onto the balcony, the flames had spread to the carpet then the velvet sofa. Frantically, Patrick tried to beat out the advancing fire but within seconds, our apartment was well alight.

As fate would have it, at that moment Anthony appeared, back from the beach. While yelling at Patrick to get out and warn the neighbours and call the fire brigade, he quickly looked around and thought 'What can I save?' Charging through the burning apartment, he opened the hallway closet where I stored my musical arrangements. As the fire raged around him, he threw armful after armful of charts into mine and Allan's bedroom then slammed the door and ran for his life as the fire engine arrived.

At work in an agent's office, I received a frantic call from my children to come home because our house was on fire. In a panic, I drove the thirty minutes home with my heart racing but feeling relieved and thankful my sons were alright. I was met with a scene from a disaster movie: police cars, fire engines, fire fighters, yellow crime scene tape and hundreds of onlookers. I could see police detectives questioning my boys as I frantically pushed my way through the crowd. At the front, I was held back by a fireman.

'Sorry lady, you can't go there.'

'It's my place and they're my children,' I said bursting into tears, so he let me go. As I hugged my boys, I stared in horror at the top of the three-storey apartment block and the smouldering black portion that was our home.

Allan, the boys and I had lost everything we owned except for the contents of the bedroom which, thanks to Anthony, included my wardrobe of stage outfits and, most importantly, my hundreds of musical arrangements worth thousands of dollars. My smart-thinking son had saved my career: I could never have replaced all those expensive charts. The firemen, however, were not impressed with my son's heroics. He didn't realise it at the time but Anthony had put himself in grave danger and risked his life to save my music.

It became a routine investigation after the police ascertained it had been a terrible accident. Apparently, the weight of the mattress on the electric blanket, left on high and not securely fitted straight and flat on the bed, had caused it to malfunction. The apartment, locked up all day with the windows tightly shut, had kept the fire contained, hot and smouldering, but when oxygen then fresh air from the balcony hit the mattress, it exploded into flames, quickly becoming an aggressive fire.

Patrick had run downstairs knocking on doors and screaming 'fire!' to the neighbours, who called the brigade, before everyone fled. Luckily the fire station was just a few minutes away and they were able to control the blaze and stop it spreading through the building. As gallant as Anthony was, he could have lost his life. The firemen told us that, on discovering a smouldering mattress like that, the best thing would have been to shut all the doors to contain the fire, including the bedroom door, call the fire department and run. The resulting damage would have been a lot less.

By now, Allan had arrived so the firemen escorted us all up to our charred black hole. It was strange and eerie to walk into the dripping, blackened remains of my home. I'll never forget the acrid stench, the puddles of water and mounds of muck that were once our prized possessions. I opened my scorched bedroom door and starred in disbelief at the room — everything was untouched, as I had left it that morning. The exception was the floor, strewn wall-to-wall with layers of musical arrangements. Amazing what a closed door can do in an inferno!

'Sorry about the mess Mum but I thought, what can I save? I looked at the photos and CDs and records but it had to be your music,' said Anthony, putting his arm around my shoulders.

'I'm sorry Mum,' said Patrick. 'I didn't know what else to do.'

'Oh Patrick it's not your fault. It's nobody's fault,' I said wanting to reassure him.

'It's OK mate,' said Allan. 'We'll survive. As long as you're both OK.'

I started to cry again as shock and realisation of how close my sons had come to serious injury or death, sank in. Shaking my head in disbelief at the mounds of charts, it suddenly dawned on me: I had a gig in a few hours. My lovely neighbour, thankful her home hadn't burned down too, let me phone my mentor Lynn Rogers to say I couldn't do the gig that night because my house had just burned down. Then the Salvation Army arrived to offer help and shelter, which was a great comfort. We were able to stay with Allan's parents for a few days but, for the second time in my life, I thanked God for the Salvos.

The day after the fire, we returned to salvage what we could. My neighbour took us to her apartment where one of the children in the building handed me the contents of her piggy bank. Her kindness brought tears to my eyes. (I later bought a painting of a clown with that money, which hangs in my home today.) Then my neighbour opened her door to a courier, who passed me an envelope. Inside was thousands of dollars from the entertainment industry! Apparently, after my garbled phone call, Lynn Rogers had immediately phoned the industry associations to tell them what had happened.

We were not insured and had to start again with electricals, furniture and even the basics. The Australian entertainment industry also rallied and overwhelmed us with gifts of new clothes, blankets and homewares. We felt humbled by the generosity of these wonderful, kind people to whom we're still so thankful. The Department of Housing moved us to temporary accommodation while our apartment was repaired and refurbished. Allan and I worked hard in our jobs to get our lives back on track and, thanks to Anthony, I was able to sing in the clubs and on ships to help us recover financially from the disaster.

Three months later, we returned to our refurbished apartment and a warm welcome from our neighbours. My elderly neighbour had looked into the black hole one day and rescued one of my badly singed indoor plants. She had nursed it back to life and presented it to me looking strong and healthy — a true gift of love.

My boys suffered guilt for quite a while after the fire, in hindsight thinking of things they could have done. I told them that life throws us lessons to learn and that they should be proud because, without their quick thinking, the whole building could have burned down or lives lost, as many of my neighbours were home that day.

MY MOTHER AND LARS had now moved from Melbourne to retire on the NSW Central Coast, an hour or so north of Sydney by car. No matter how much I tried to deny it, in my heart she was my Princess Mummy and I still craved her love and acceptance and needed to keep her near me. Had I never again asked her to discuss the circumstances of my birth, we probably could have carried on living happily ever after.

In April 1989, I was booked as one of the guest entertainers on *Fairstar*'s three-week, Far Eastern Cruise. My sons were busy doing other things. Anthony was now living with his girlfriend and working as a computer graphics artist and Patrick was in his last and important year in high school. I asked Allan to go but he said it was better he stay home with Patrick, plus he was very busy at work.

I called my mother. As she had not been cruising before, she agreed a cruise from Sydney to Bali, then on to Singapore to fly home, would be a wonderful trip to do together. I was overjoyed. The next weeks were filled with excited phone calls as she told me about her purchases of evening clothes for the formal nights and outfits to wear to dinner, days by the pool and touring around tropical Bali. As we laughed and eagerly planned our wardrobes, I revelled in the renewed closeness of our relationship.

By now, after about twelve cruises as a guest entertainer, *Fairstar* was like my home-away-from-home. As we boarded we were greeted warmly by the cruise director and with lots of hugs from the cruise staff. Of course I introduced my mother as 'Grace', *never* as my mother. Our cabin was perfect for the two of us and as we entered, we laughed as we chose which of the single beds, drawers and closet space we'd use. Flowers were delivered to our cabin from my darling Allan and my mother placed them beside two bottles of French fragrance on our dressing table between the beds. We'd made a pact to buy more at duty free prices from the perfumery in the ship's shopping arcade.

After unpacking, I gave my mother a tour of the ship, trying to dodge the hundreds of lost-looking passengers searching the corridors and stairways for their cabins. I proudly showed her the show room where I would perform, the nightclub, the hairdressing salon and gymnasium, then led her out to the pool deck where we sat at the bar and ordered champagne, giggling like teenagers. I relaxed, enjoying the glow from the champagne and the pleasure of the moment. For most of my life I had dreamed of spending time like this with my Princess Mummy and now it was even better than I could have imagined; the two of us excited and chatting, enjoying a new-found closeness.

As the afternoon wore on and passengers appeared on deck looking for a vantage point for departure, I was recognised and greeted enthusiastically by returning passengers who had seen me perform on previous cruises. Secretly, I was thrilled to receive such admiration in front of my mother.

'Sharyn darling, I'm so delighted it's you who'll be performing for us on this cruise,' came a loud, yet cultured voice from behind us. Turning, I recognised Margaret, a much travelled and elegant woman and a regular *Fairstar* passenger whom I had come to know. I took the opportunity to introduce them. 'Grace, this is Margaret, a *Fairstar* regular. Margaret, this is Grace.' This was the usual introduction for those outside the family. Having my mother here every day, I'd need to be careful not to slip up, to make sure to call her 'Grace', even in my head.

Over the following days, my mother — *Grace* — and Margaret became pals, dashing off for cocktails in the afternoons and meeting in the casino later in the evenings. I was busy with rehearsals and preparation for my shows, so I was pleased that Grace had found a companion in Margaret.

The second night at sea was the formal Captain's Cocktail party. Ladies dressed in evening gowns and men in a suit or tuxedo and were introduced and photographed with the captain and his officers. After dinner was the Gala Welcome where all passengers were introduced to the cruise staff and guest entertainers, dancers, comedians, DJs and orchestras, bands and children's entertainers. As a guest entertainer, I performed three songs and, though only a short introduction, it was an important spot since it served to entice the passengers to come to my full show later the following week. I was scheduled to perform on one of the at-sea nights, between leaving Bali and our arrival in Singapore.

My fellow entertainer for the cruise was Liz Layton, a good friend who was full of life and laughter and was an energetic performer along the lines of Ethel Merman and Sophie Tucker. We'd become close over the years and she was probably the only person on board who knew that Grace was really my mother. Grace and I cheered loudly through Liz's show as her music touched our hearts. Though Australian and white, Liz had at one time been married to a black American and was the perfect person to be on this cruise with us. She understood only too well the issues between me and Grace and was sympathetic to both of us. We were having fun together until one lunchtime when Grace snapped at Liz as we were walking from our deck lounges to the poolside buffet. Laughing, Liz had commented, after I said I was not wearing sunscreen, 'Oh, just because you're black doesn't mean your skin doesn't burn.'

Grace quickly interjected. 'Sharyn is not black, she is coloured.'

'Grace,' said Liz, 'she really is black.' Grace stopped and turned, the bright sunlight accentuating her blonde hair and creamy skin. 'No, she is not black. Her skin is brown. She is a coloured woman. It sounds so much nicer than black.' Liz looked at Grace over the top of her large sunglasses and said, ever so gently, 'Well Grace, in some parts of the world it is actually an insult to call a person of colour "coloured". The word "black" is much more acceptable.'

In an impatient gesture, Grace removed her sunglasses and leaned towards Liz. 'Well, I think it is rude. Sharyn is coloured.'

Liz and I looked at each other and raised our eyebrows.

'So what do you prefer to be called, Shaz?' asked Liz.

'Well they say black is beautiful so I am staying right there, sister.' As Liz and I laughed, Grace flounced off to the buffet ahead of us. All this talk about colour made her feel very uncomfortable.

THE EVENING OF MY CABARET SHOW, Margaret and Grace made sure they were at the head of the line to get the best seats in the show room. Nervously, I peeked through the curtain from backstage to see a full house and Grace and Margaret in the front, chatting amiably. I had dressed carefully in a long white bugle-beaded gown, silver high heels and a white Billie Holiday flower in my hair. My mother had not seen my show for quite some time so I wanted to make this one memorable. Waiting while the dancers opened the show, I finished my show prayer (which basically consisted of 'please Lord, make these people love my show because if they don't there is every chance they may throw me overboard'). Over the drum roll I heard the cruise director's announcement, 'Ladies and Gentlemen, please welcome the delightful Sharyn Crystal.'

I walked onto the stage and into the bright spotlight to thunderous applause and sang the first bars of my opening song. (I always feel this song gets a little lost on an audience because by the time they have looked at the frock, the shoes, the jewellery, the hair and make-up then listened, it's almost over.) I sang a gentle ballad for the second song then I chatted and told short anecdotes about myself and different cruises. I tried to make it a personal show, helping the audience to relax like friends at a lovely party. I sang songs they knew so they could sing along with me as well as popular songs they could clap to. They laughed at my jokes, of which very few were funny but, still, I could do no wrong. Every song worked for me, the *Fairstar* orchestra of exceptional musicians backing me were faultless, and the show was perfect. I looked around the faces of people from all over Australia and New Zealand. Sipping cocktails, they looked elegant in their gowns and tuxedos and I could tell from their enthusiastic expressions that they were loving every minute of my fifty-minute show. Finally, I ended with my rendition of 'Somewhere Over the Rainbow', a song close to my heart as I, like Dorothy, have always had big dreams. The instant it finished, this very special clapping and cheering audience, rose as one and gave me a standing ovation. I felt exhilarated, humbled and grateful. I glanced towards Margaret (who was standing and cheering, clapping her hands above her head) then towards my mother who was beaming and applauding. I was suddenly aware of how far I had come. Oh, where was that lost little girl? She was standing centrestage on a beautiful ship in the middle of the ocean, accepting accolades from an admiring audience. I felt very proud of myself. 'Thank you Lord,' I whispered.

I took my bows and graciously thanked my audience. I almost wanted to hug each one of them because they didn't know how special this evening was for me. My mother was amongst them. As I took my final bow, the cruise director joined me on stage and announced excitedly into the microphone, 'Ladies and gentleman, what a wonderful show! The fabulous Sharyn Crystal.'

I raced back to our cabin to change from my gown to a cocktail dress. I was joyous, the smile never leaving my face. I touched up my make-up and hair, grabbed a small handbag and headed back to the bar to join my friends and Grace for after-show drinks. I floated through the rest of the evening, overwhelmed as passengers and crew congratulated me on my performance.

WHEN ALL ELSE FAILS, I pray. As a child, my Catholic religion was about 'the fear of burning in Hell for all eternity' kind of Catholicism. As an adult, I had held on to my belief in God but tossed away the fear. I am very spiritual and prayer has never failed me. So it was a strange day, the day I turned on God. It had begun so simply.

The morning after my show, Grace and I dined in the restaurant for breakfast. I actually had a hangover. Not a bad one, but we had drunk too much champagne the night before so we both needed a good breakfast. It helped. Arranging to meet Grace back in our cabin, I dashed to the show room to collect my music charts. On my way from the backstage area, more smiling faces greeted me with congratulations on my show. As I hurried along the outside deck, I could feel the warmth of the sun on my shoulders. I stopped for a moment and leant against the railing, inhaling the salty breeze from the ocean shimmering to the horizon. It was truly a beautiful day.

I turned to go and there was Margaret hurrying toward me, dressed in crisp linen and a sunhat. 'Oh darling, your show was wonderful last night,' she enthused, hugging me. 'First class. And your gown — just exquisite! Wonderful, darling.' Then she lowered her voice, 'Oh, I hope you don't mind but Grace told me your secret.'

'My secret?' I asked, smiling. Margaret pulled me closer to her, 'Yes, Grace told me last night. And I promised not to tell.' She glanced around then whispered, 'I know Grace is really your Mother. She asked me to keep it a secret and begged me not to tell the other passengers and I won't. Your secret's safe with me.' Then she stepped back and chortled, 'Well I must be off. Have a lovely day, darling.' And with that, she bustled away.

I swear I felt my heart split in two.

I stood, unable to move, for who knows how long — time had stopped. Then I walked slowly in a stupor, to the back of the ship. I remember staring at the horizon line, my mind too numb to process anything. Then the scene blurred to a hazy mess as my eyes brimmed and the pain kicked in. I couldn't believe it. Fourteen hundred people on board this beautiful ship loved me openly but the one person I wanted to didn't. She didn't love me enough to own me. I was still my mother's God damned secret! Her shame astonished me. I felt violated and abandoned again. Alone, I slumped on a bench and let the humiliation and misery pour out of me.

Then I got angry. Bloody angry. I stood, grabbed the railing and looked into the heavens. I felt I was staring right into God's eyes. From the core of my being I roared, 'Enough! It's out of your hands. I don't want your help anymore. I want nothing from you. I will deal with this myself.'

I had never experienced rage like it. It was so strange — like my soul was driven to save itself. I knew what I had to do. I was so furious that, had I run into anybody, my professional image would have been shattered in a moment. Yet, strangely enough, I did not. I don't remember passing or seeing anyone. I was on a mission. Down, down, down countless stairs I headed, into the bowels of the ship to the crew bar. One of my favourite Italian bartenders was cleaning the bar and greeted me with a warm smile. I asked him for a bottle of my mother's favourite Scotch whiskey. I hurried on back through the ship and didn't stop until I was outside the cabin. I took a deep breath and opened the door.

Grace was pottering about inside, her beautiful face breaking into a smile as I entered. 'Hello, little star. Did you get your music?'

Keeping my composure, I managed to match her radiant smile. 'Yes I did and look what else I got?' I opened the bag. 'Your favourite.' She smiled knowingly as I placed the Scotch on the dressing table. 'So after tonight's show, let's come back here and have a few quiet ones together. A bit of an early night.'

'That sounds great,' she said. 'I am writing myself a note that when we get to Singapore, I am going to buy you some big sparkling earrings. I noticed last night you need a large pair to go with that lovely gown.'

THE CRUISE STAFF put on a fun show that night, including a performance of their signature musical-comedy sketch, 'Upon the Sea'. Margaret, Grace, Liz and I applauded and cheered then, immediately it was over, Grace and I made our apologies and headed to our cabin for our girls' night in. On the way, I detoured past one of the bars to collect a jug of ice and a jug of Coke. Grace insisted her Scotch be served neat but I liked to add ice and Coke because I didn't particularly like the taste of alcohol, just what it did to me. We sat on opposite sides of the cabin, she on her bed and me on mine. I poured and handed her one of what was to be several glasses of neat Scotch.

'Cheers,' I said.

'Skol,' laughed my mother, who was enjoying this illicit soirée (my stepfather frowned on her drinking). We laughed as we talked about all her favourite subjects: hair, make-up, jewellery, clothes, shoes and finally, after a couple of hours of drinking, we talked about men.

'So,' I said, refilling her empty glass, 'you and Lars have been married for a long time now.'

'Yes, twenty-seven years. Nearly thirty years. It is a long time, isn't it?'

'Sure is. You love him a lot, don't you?'

'Yes, he's a wonderful man.' She'd begun to slur her words.

'My little brother and Lars look so alike, don't they?'

'Yes, it's funny, isn't it?' I didn't know what was funny or unusual about it and, at that point in time, I didn't care. I felt guilty deliberately pushing her but I refilled our glasses, spilling Coke on the dressing table in the process. Scotch sloshed out of her glass as she picked it up. We were both quite drunk now.

'Is the reason you can't talk about my father, because I look like him?' Sucking in her breath through clenched teeth, she straightened up and looked me in the face, her nostrils flaring.

'There you go again. Why, oh why do you have to spoil everything and upset me? You *always* spoil everything, Sharyn.'

Tonight your 'woe is me' whine is not going to work, I thought.

'Yes, I do, don't I? But is it true? Do I look like him? Do you see him every time you look at me?'

'I don't want to talk about this,' she said huffily.

'Yes, you do. I want you to tell me my father's name.'

'No. It's none of your business.'

'Well, I'm making it my business. Now you tell me right here and right now.'

She slammed down her drink, more Scotch sloshing from the glass. 'Do not speak to me like that Sharyn. I am your mother!'

Her words stung my cheeks. My Mother? I was incensed. This woman had never mothered me a day in my life! I felt like shaking her. I was fast running out of scotch and patience.

'Forget that you are my mother. Forget it! Let's just be two women on a ship somewhere in the middle of the ocean. There's no one here, just you and me. Lady, if I have to get up and lock that cabin door to keep you here for the rest of this cruise, I will.' I could feel my anger rising and my pulse quickening. I had to calm down if I was to get what I wanted. I took a breath and continued, rationally. 'I have a right to know my father's name. My children have the right to know their heritage. My son has a terminal illness, possibly inherited from my father. My grandchildren and all future generations have the right to know their heritage. I am the only black person in a totally white family. I am forty years old and I need to know who I am. Don't you understand that? You are the only one who knows this information. If you die before me, you'll take that with you. You *must* tell me his name. I don't want to know your business, just his name.' I was crying, pleading — the little girl in me desperate to know: who is my father?

I held my breath. The silence in the cabin was deafening. I call it a holy silence. Very softly, she said, 'Thaddeus Killens.'

I fell forward off the bed, onto my knees.

'What did you say?' She stepped over my crouched body and swayed into the bathroom, quietly closing the door behind her.

'Thaddeus Killens, Thaddeus Killens,' I repeated over and over, willing myself not to forget it, in my drunken state. Frantically, I began searching for pen and paper. I remembered signing autographs earlier in the evening, so I quickly emptied the contents of my handbag onto the carpet and found a pen and a scrap of paper.

'How do you spell that?' I said, mostly to myself, as my mother came out of the bathroom dressed in her nightie, stepped over me again, pulled back the bed covers and lay down in bed. I scrambled to my feet, clutching my precious scrap of paper to my heart.

'Is there anything I can do for you?' I asked.

'Yes. Turn off the light,' she said, icily.

I STEPPED OUT of the cabin and leant against the closed door, still clutching my scrap of paper. Thaddeus Killens. My Lord! I knew it was real. My mother could not have made that one up.

What now? I had to tell Liz. I tried to walk sedately down the long corridor but between the swaying of the ship and my inebriated state, I ricocheted off the walls. In the end I gave up and ran all the way to her cabin, pounding on her door, oblivious of the time.

'Who is it?' she growled sleepily.

'Lizzie, it's me. Quickly, open the door.' It flew open.

'Are you alright love?' she asked. I stood there, drunk and clutching my piece of paper with a stupid grin on my face.

'Thaddeus Killens,' I said. She knew immediately.

'Oh my God! Your father's name.' She pulled me into the cabin. 'You're drunk! God, how's Grace?'

'Worse! Lizzie, I've got my father's name,' I said, waiving the scrap of paper.

'Oh your life won't be worth living tomorrow, my girl.' We hugged and we cried.

'Quickly, get dressed. We're going out to celebrate,' I said.

'Are you mad? It's after midnight.' But of course we did. We bought a bottle of champagne, an ice bucket and two glasses and headed to a bench at the back of the top deck. Sitting on our seat, quietly watching the ship's wake sparkle in the moonlight, we made a toast.

'To you, my friend,' said Liz.

'Thank you.' I looked to the heavens and realised I had stood in exactly the same place earlier in the day. Then I had cursed the Lord. Now I thanked Him. 'Thank you Lord, for all you do. I couldn't have done it without you.' I felt at peace, as though everything I had ever wanted had been granted. Now I couldn't wait to get off the ship and find my father.

THE ICE-PRINCESS MUMMY barely spoke to me for the remainder of the cruise. We were polite but she was cold. I didn't mind. I was just surprised how easily she had remembered my father's name after forty years. How cruel not to tell me earlier in my life! All those distressing midnight phone calls with me crying and begging her to tell me something about myself. What was this woman thinking? Did she have no compassion for me? Well, the truth was: she did not. She had known my father's name all those years but would not tell me. What had happened to this woman, to make her so cold towards me? I was her only daughter yet she preferred to see me suffer, rather than comfort, nurture or simply be kind to me.

Still, I was elated. I could not stop smiling. I had what I had waited for, all my life. Now I could search for my father and find out who I was. I desperately looked forward to knowing this man.

The ship finally docked in Singapore. Mother and I checked into a smart hotel, she thawed a little and we enjoyed ourselves touring around. The following day we flew home to Australia. Together, we pushed our baggage trolleys through the doors from Customs and there were Allan and Lars waiting to greet us.

Smiling sweetly, my mother's parting words were, 'Never again.'

That was fine with me.

CHAPTER FOURTEEN

Ray Charles, BB King and Bourbon

THE SEARCH for my father began. I knew he was a serviceman but I didn't know in which service, so I sent letters to the US Department of Navy, Army and Air Force. Most took months to reply and when they did, all required more information, specifically a Social Security number. All I had was his name. I was fired up with enthusiasm but the response was so slow. It was an agonising time.

Was I crazy? Probably. It was late 1989 and there was no such thing as email, no Internet and definitely no Google. Here I was, trying to find a man after forty years, on the other side of the world in the USA, amongst a population of two hundred and fifty million people. One man — and all I had was his name. It seemed impossible.

I wrote to the US Consul General in Sydney and received a similar reply but with a page attached suggesting different organisations in the United States who may be able to help, including the US Coast Guard, the American Red Cross, US Consulate General Australian offices and practical solutions like US local newspapers and police authorities. Of course, all these depended on me having a date of birth, last known address and of course, a Social Security number. But one small paragraph in the letter gave me hope. It suggested the Sydney US Consulate General's office had some telephone books and 'these are available for your perusal'. I rushed into their city office and spent hours copying all the US Killens' phone numbers I could find. Allan and I stayed awake for a couple of nights because of the time difference and telephoned everyone on the list. It was quite funny really. I had some bizarre conversations with Killens people who were fascinated that I was calling from Australia, searching for a missing relative. I was touched that so many offered to be my family, but each call was a dead end. I drank a few bottles of wine in the process and made new friends; but none could help.

During this time I had an unexpected call from Lars, asking could he stay overnight as our apartment was close to the airport and he was meeting a relative from overseas on an early flight. I was delighted and cooked a special meal and prepared the table with a fresh linen tablecloth and candles. After dinner, we chatted amiably.

'Well, that's it for me,' said Allan after a while, glancing at the wall clock and standing up. 'I've got my usual five o'clock start. Night Lars, I'll wake you before I go.' He bent down and gave me a quick kiss. 'Night, love.'

I poured Lars a cup of tea and myself another glass of wine, then lit a cigarette and sat down. He looked at me, 'For a singer you smoke too much,' he said.

'Yes, you're right. I'll give it up one day.'

'You drink far too much, too.'

I frowned in annoyance. 'Do you know the life I've had? It's a wonder I'm not hitting up smack and selling myself on a street corner somewhere.' I held up my wine glass, twirling the stem in my fingers. 'Why do you think I drink? Maybe it's because I've been rejected by my mother and family all my life. When you married my mother, I thought I could finally belong but you never told your family I existed, did you?' The room was silent except for the humming of the fridge.

'No, I did not,' he replied, softly.

'Why not? Why didn't you tell your family about me?' Lars hesitated then looked me in the eyes.

'Because, at the time you were getting into trouble.'

'What trouble? I was a teenager! You didn't have to tell them anything. All you had to say was that the woman you had married had a thirteen-year-old daughter.' Silence again. I pressed on. 'I knew that and it hurt me deeply. And do you know what made it worse? You didn't send them a photo of me *and* I know why.' I waited for my inference to register.

He averted his eyes and stared into his cup. Familiar tentacles of shame crawled up my back. Then anger stirred.

'You know, at birth my mother handed me to strangers and when I was five, she abandoned me in the supposed care of nuns who bashed me. Then, when I was teenager being tortured in a detention centre, she abandoned me again when you two moved interstate. All I ever wanted was to be loved by her but she kept locking me away. Even at forty, no matter what I do or achieve, she still won't own me. Will I always be her secret?' Lars continued to stare into his cup. Why wouldn't he look at me?

Fighting back angry tears, I gulped down my glass of wine. Anger felt so much better than shame. And with that anger came a feeling of entitlement. 'So don't tell me that I smoke and drink too much. Besides, this is *my* home and I will do what I want. And yes, I *will* find my father. Watch me.'

I left the room and in the bathroom splashed cold water on my face. When I returned, he was still sitting at the table.

'So what if you find this father of yours? Then what?' he asked, challenging me to justify the anguish he felt I had caused my mother with my persistence.

'I don't know yet. But I need to find out who I am and where I belong.'

There was never any doubt: I had to look for my father. Although I knew Lars was angry I was searching for my father, I thought his anger on this subject hypocritical and confusing. Whether I found my father or not wasn't the issue. I just had to try.

MY SINGING CAREER was thriving. No one was more surprised than me, each time an agent phoned to book me to entertain in a club auditorium. Excited and grateful for the opportunity to perform, often backstage I could hear the audience rushing for their favourite seats when the auditorium doors opened. Some liked to be close to the front while others preferred to sit in the dark, towards the back.

Walking onstage to the first song's introduction and dressed in a glittering stage outfit, I was always astonished when the audience applauded. How amazing: I hadn't done anything, just walked across the stage, yet they would be applauding. What a perfect career for the child who just wanted to be loved, feeling all that love flooding across the footlights!

Over the ten years I had been singing in the clubs, many audiences knew me and my children well because I frequently told stories of family achievements or some amusing anecdote, to create the relaxed friendly atmosphere I preferred for my shows. Often I was greeted at the club's entrance by the patrons saying, 'It's so lovely to see you back again — we're looking forward to your show today. How's the family?' I'd ask them in return, since I knew many of them by name. Usually, entertainers did a club circuit, appearing once or twice a year in each club.

One particular club I performed in more than twice a year was Marrickville RSL, a very popular club with a large auditorium in the multicultural suburb of the same name. It had been one of the better entertainment venues in Sydney, featuring big shows with orchestras and showgirls and still managed to keep the entertainment program going but with smaller bands and fewer dancers. The club's management invited me to be their guest to draw the raffle for their staff awards function. I was delighted to.

On the day, I enjoyed the ambiance of the awards ceremony lunch with the board of directors and a room full of regular club patrons. Feeling relaxed and enjoying the proceedings, my interest was piqued when the secretary-manager announced, 'We have a surprise award today. It gives me great pleasure to announce that the 1989 Entertainer of the Year Award, goes to Sharyn Crystal!' I was flabbergasted. I looked around thinking a mistake had been made but the audience was on its feet, clapping and cheering. Shaking my head, I made my way to the stage. My mind racing, I humbly accepted the award, an attractive plaque featuring a golden treble clef. It was a surprise and an unexpected honour. Driving home to tell Allan, I couldn't help but think, though I may not have found my father, I had found my true vocation.

Obviously, Allan was very proud of my achievement. He had always been my most ardent supporter, coming to my shows when he could, but he was also my best critic.

'It doesn't surprise me that you won, Shaz,' he said. 'You are a lovely singer but you are an excellent entertainer. Audiences love you.'

MY BUSINESS CAREER was also thriving. Part-time work in various agents' offices had paid off and I was now working for one of Sydney's largest agents, Peter Brendle. I had worked for his company only a few months when I was offered the position of Assistant Publicist for the upcoming Ray Charles and BB King Australian tour with the Philip Morris Superband. I remember the evening my boss Peter and his assistant Carolynne offered me the job. I was astonished. Me, the street kid with dreams of becoming a singer, was to take care of the legendary Ray Charles and BB King! I had absolutely no idea what to do — but I knew I could do it.

For this tour, the Superband included Aussie trumpeter James Morrison and was to be fronted by Ray Charles and BB King. The huge schedule for the Australian leg had to be handled with precision and my job was to liaise with all media regarding publicity.

Ray Charles' manager in Los Angeles, Joe Adams, notified us that Ray was happy to be interviewed but only at the first press conference in Perth, Western Australia. Ray wanted to come to Australia to play his music and meet the fans and had decided one interview was enough. Meanwhile, I was being inundated with calls from journalists and television stations wanting to interview Ray. BB King had already toured Australia with U2, but he graciously offered to sit in for interviews that Ray couldn't do — trouble was: everyone wanted to interview BB as well. This was certainly my baptism by fire.

Allan was feeling a bit neglected after eating too many lonely TV dinners because I was still at the office each evening till very late. I promised him I'd leave at five the next day and cook him a special meal. He was pleased.

Heading for the door at five o'clock, the phone rang. In exasperation, I picked it up and found myself talking to a music teacher in Queensland who taught at a school some miles from Brisbane. He was desperate for tickets for the sold-out Brisbane show, for himself and his ten blind music students aged five to fifteen. I knew it was impossible but I took down his details and said I'd do what I could.

That night in bed I tossed and turned next to Allan, worrying about ten blind children learning to play musical instruments. They would be the perfect audience for Ray, BB King and the Superband. Eventually, I got out of bed, dressed and headed for the office in the middle of night, typed a fax and sent it to Ray's manager Joe in Los Angeles, who immediately faxed back, 'Do whatever you've got to do to get those children to the concert and arrange for them to meet Ray.' And so it was done.

The day before the tour began, Carolynne and I congratulated ourselves on how organised we were for the entertainers, orchestra and entourage who'd arrive the following day. We had triple-checked and ticked every minute detail, ensuring nothing was left to chance. Nothing was, and we felt very proud of ourselves.

The following morning, we arrived at the office early, ready for our exciting day. Limousines and coaches had been arranged to transport the contingency of stars, musicians, entourage and show personnel from the airport to their luxury five-star hotel in the city. As I prepared our first hot coffee of the day, Carolynne checked the answer machine for messages. A deep American voice said, 'Good morning, this is Ray Charles' valet, Vernon Troupe. We have changed hotels. We are now at the Hilton.' Carolynne and I looked at each other and screamed in horror.

'The Hilton? What are they doing there? What are they doing in Sydney?' She quickly found the Hilton's phone number and dialled, then requested Mr Troupe's room. (We knew never to ask for Mr Charles' room. Everything went through Vernon Troupe.) Carolynne's phone conversation was a series of one-syllable words. 'Oh . . . Oh, no . . . No, of course . . . Oh dear,' and lots of yes's — then she put down the phone looking decidedly pale.

'Quickly, turn everything off. We have to go to the Hilton,' she said, grabbing our coats.

'What happened?' I asked, switching off lights and locking the office door. She filled me in, as we hurried to my car.

'Seems our superstar and his valet arrived a day early. When they checked into the hotel last night, Ray was hungry so Vernon ordered a club sandwich from room service. A young bellboy took it upon himself to deliver the food straight to Ray's room, instead of Vernon's.' I gasped, immediately realising the implications. 'Ray was irritated to find a stranger at his door but he also couldn't get his room telephone to work, and since the bellboy was there anyway, Ray asked him to check his phone.' We'd reached my car and as we jumped in, I wondered how could this have happened? I thought we'd covered every possibility. Carolynne took a moment to settle herself in the car then she continued.

'Well, it seems the bellboy looked around and discovered the bathroom phone was off the hook. In a chastising voice, he said to Ray, 'Here's the problem. Can't you see the phone is off the hook in here?'

'Oh my Lord,' I gasped. 'Did he *really* say that?'

'Ray was incensed and didn't feel safe in that hotel anymore so they immediately packed up, checked out and caught a taxi, downtown to the Hilton.'

There goes my new job. It was fun while it lasted, I thought, as I drove frantically through the early morning peak traffic towards the Hilton Hotel.

Nervously, we approached Vernon's hotel room door, wondering what the reception would be. Graciously, he invited us in and as we tentatively sat down, he explained that on all tours, he notifies hotel staff around the world in advance that he and Ray are to have adjoining rooms and no one is ever to knock on Ray's door. They must liaise with him on all matters. Carolynne and I already knew that and had briefed the hotel accordingly. We apologised profusely for the breakdown in communication on the other hotel's behalf. Obviously there wasn't much we could say to defend the ignorance of their staff. We were horrified.

We all decided it was better for Ray and Vernon to remain at the Hilton. Ray had stayed there before, they knew him well and it suited everyone's needs.

After the fiasco of losing Ray Charles, Carolynne and I spent the rest of the morning making certain there were no more disasters. Back at the first hotel, while we double-checked all was perfect in BB King's room and the other rooms were in order (the hotel's management were extremely apologetic), our tour manager and his assistant met everyone at the airport. The hotel check-in procedure went smoothly, though I did find it difficult to keep my professional composure as I greeted some of the world's finest musicians; all seventeen were wonderful gentlemen. And of course, there was the man himself, BB King.

BB King is the King of the Blues, a true gentleman and a delight to work with. Escorting him in limousines to TV and radio stations for interviews, I felt privileged as he charmed me with stories of his life. Always immaculately dressed in a silk suit and tie, with matching pocket handkerchief, he toured the world three hundred days of the year. He was gracious and had a warm greeting for everyone, from cleaners and receptionists to television and radio hosts. I watched as he greeted his fans openly, never refusing an autograph, photograph or a simple chat and he often distributed his famous guitar picks as souvenirs.

Happily, the rest of the tour went without a hitch. One of my favourite musicians on the tour was the delightful Harry 'Sweets' Edison who greeted me each morning with a big smile. An extraordinary trumpet player, he had played for thirteen years with Count Basie and performed with Billie Holiday, Frank Sinatra and Ella Fitzgerald. Walking through the hotel lobby one morning, I noticed 'Sweets' sitting in a corner, reading the newspaper. He happened to look up and, seeing me, dipped his hat and said, 'Good morning, young lady. How are you on this fine day?' Imagine that! Harry was one of the most famous and respected musicians of his day, a member of all the pioneer orchestras. Ellie and Dorrie had played his music constantly throughout my childhood, so I pulled up a nearby chair and we had chat — just small talk about the weather and the tour, but it made me feel fantastic.

THE NIGHT OF THE BRISBANE CONCERT, a small bus chauffeured the Queensland music teacher, ten excited blind students and their parents to the Brisbane Entertainment Centre, where they were immediately escorted to Ray Charles' private dressing room. During their conversation, the children discovered Ray also used the same type of braille computer so a lively discussion followed.

'Yeah, you do that, and dot 3, and then press enter,' said one of the children eagerly.

'Wow, is that so? Then what do you do?' asked Ray grinning, enjoying himself. The children all started talking at once.

'You press dot 6 and —' said one child but before he could finish, another chimed in, 'But that's only if you've done the echo bit first.'

Ray was whooping with delight. Interruptions of, 'Ten minutes to showtime, Mr Charles,' went ignored as Ray encouraged the children. 'Then what do I do?' And the children kept telling him more until, reluctantly, Ray could stay no longer. The children and their entourage were shown to their special seating and enjoyed the best concert they had ever heard.

One of the world's great superstars of music, Ray always greeted me with a lovely smile and a kind word and often had me laughing out loud, as I shared his fun sense of humour. I have special memories of walking arm in arm with this legendary man, as we chuckled about something funny that had happened to him.

On the day of his departure from Australia, I was sitting next to him chatting on as I do, when he said, 'Hey Sharyn, you did a fine job. Thanks so much. But man, you know the part I loved the best? Meeting those little children. You know Stevie Wonder and me, we got the same computer. Well, Stevie's real good on his, so I rang him up and I said, "Stevie, put on your computer man," and he did, and I said to Stevie to do this and that and press enter. Well Stevie, who's excellent on his, screamed out, "Hey, Ray how did you learn to do that?"' Ray threw back his head and laughed and so did I. He had loved it.

The following year the Superband returned to Australia, this time starring BB King and the superb Dianne Reeves. This tour was equally successful and gave me a chance to renew my friendship with BB and form a close association with Dianne. BB greeted me warmly, enquiring about my family and, to my astonishment, asking after my sons by name.

Dianne Reeves was great fun, and exquisite in dress and beauty, but it was her rich voice that left a lasting impression. A first-class entertainer, Grammy Award-winner and a truly lovely woman, she spent many hours talking with me about personal things, which I cherished. It felt surreal, gliding through Sydney in the back of limousines, chatting and laughing with these charming and supremely talented people.

ONE LATE SUMMER'S EVENING in 1992, I was enjoying a rare quiet moment in front of the telly, when the phone rang. A woman's friendly voice said, 'Hi Sharyn, we haven't met but my name is Joy. I have a regular gig I can't do for the next four weeks and I'm wondering if you would fill in for me?'

'Oh, thank you, Joy, for thinking of me. Tell me about it,' I said as I opened my diary and hunted for a pen.

'It's an easy gig. You'll be working with a terrific quartet, some of the best musos in town. You do three sets a night, from ten till two. They're a fun crowd and it's decent money.' Quickly scanning my diary pages, I could see I had plenty of bookings but I always welcomed more work.

'Sounds great, where is it?'

'The Bourbon and Beefsteak bar in Kings Cross.' Oh, my Lord! Who thought that phone call would ever come? 'Sorry about the short notice but can you start this Friday?' she asked.

'Yes that's fine,' I said evenly. Keeping my composure, I wrote down the details, thanked her and hung up. Me! Singing at the Bourbon and Beefsteak! It was my dream come true. I thanked God. I knew He always listened; just, sometimes, He took his own sweet time answering my prayers.

During the next few days I rehearsed my songs over and over and I drove myself nuts, trying on an assortment of outfits to wear to the gig and onstage.

On Friday night, right in the middle of my old stamping ground, I stood nervously across the road looking at the Bourbon and Beefsteak. Eighteen years later and the street was still packed with people. Little had changed, yet everything had changed. The noisy street atmosphere still crackled with anticipation, the rose-coloured glow of neon still fooled the eye and the food aromas were appealing but only to the hungry. The working girls were busy but not dressed as elegantly as in the old days, now wearing shorts and tight jeans. As I walked towards the entrance carrying my music case and stage outfit, who should be standing there but my old friend the doorman! Oh no, he's going to turn me away, I thought. I felt sick with shame as I remembered our previous encounter. But he approached me smiling.

'Good evening, Ma'am. Can I carry your case for you?'

'Thank you,' I managed to stammer and handed it over. Taking my music case in one hand, he took my elbow and escorted me up the couple of steps and inside the entrance. A distinguished gentleman approached, smiling with his arm extended to shake my hand. 'Good evening, Sharyn. Bernie Haughton. I believe you will be entertaining us while Joy is away.'

'Yes Sir,' I said eagerly. I was delighted to finally meet him. After establishing the Bourbon around twenty-five years earlier, he was now a celebrated Kings Cross identity.

'Call me Bernie. We're pretty relaxed here.'

Memories flooded back as I picked my way past the length of the busy bar with its hundreds of postcards and memorabilia pinned to the wall behind and sparkling stemmed glasses hanging from racks overhead. I clicked across the dance floor in my heels and, stepping onto the small platform stage, introduced myself to the musicians then I glanced around the already bustling dining area. The décor hadn't changed. The familiar red carpet, the black vinyl booths and banquette seating along the side wall, the small tables draped in red cloths and crammed close to squeeze in as many diners as possible on small timber chairs, and the Americana posters and flags — it was all still the same. That night, as I sang to a packed dance floor of happy partying people, I considered the irony. I had returned to Kings Cross again, but this time not as a troubled street kid or a drugged stripper but triumphant, as a respected and admired entertainer. I said a quiet prayer and thanked God for my life. How blessed I was and how happy to have fulfilled my dream.

Bernie was a terrific boss and, indeed, a gentleman: warm, generous and much admired. It was a sad day when he passed away in 2002.

My friend the doorman always treated me with courtesy and respect. I have no idea if he recognised me or remembered that shameful scene all those years ago. If he did, he never let on and I certainly never mentioned it.

The Bourbon was a sensational place to work. I loved singing there and over the years, it became a regular gig for me. The booking was usually three or four nights a week for a month or two straight. By midnight it would be packed to capacity with guys and girls lining the bar, flirting and eyeing each other in the hope of finding romance while busy white-aproned waiters delivered overfilled plates to tables of hungry after-theatre, after-movie and after-party diners. The place would be jumping, the dance floor crammed with revellers and the atmosphere thick with cigarette smoke, food aromas and that sweet smell of hard liquor.

Often, visiting overseas celebrities and musicians joined us onstage for a jam and then the noisy crowd would really go wild.

Particularly exciting were the times American naval ships visited Sydney harbour, especially the massive aircraft carrier USS *Enterprise*. Just like the old days, thousands of white-uniformed American sailors now hit the streets of Kings Cross and partied. And just like the old days, the rivalry persisted. If a scuffle broke out, which it often did, the dinner-suited bouncers would speedily grab the offenders by the scuff of the neck and quickly but politely show them the door. It gave me an insight into how it must have been for my mother, her friend Rosa and Ellie and Dorrie in their time, when the Americans brought their fun to town.

CHAPTER FIFTEEN

The Search

I HAD BEEN SEARCHING for my father on and off, for three years now and was no closer to finding him. Each time Allan and I thought of a new possibility, I would excitedly write to the US, only to suffer an emotional roller coaster ride as my hopes were dashed. Every reply was the same: more information please. These dead ends left me frustrated and disillusioned but I consoled myself with the fact that I finally had a name: the name of my father and a name for myself — my roots.

Other than the disappointment of my fruitless search, life was wonderful. Anthony and his girlfriend had blessed us with a granddaughter and Patrick was training in the hospitality industry. I was proud my sons had grown into responsible young men. Allan's twelve-year-old 'twinnies' were thriving and he and I were happy and content.

My relationship with my mother was amiable and pleasant. After finally getting her to reveal my father's name, I had no reason to quarrel with her anymore (though I often wanted to challenge her and ask just how a mother could tell her desperate child that her father was dead and deny her his name for forty years).

One night, after too much wine, I was lamenting my situation with my close girlfriend Lindsay, who knew my story well. We were discussing the theory that in denying my father's existence, my mother had emotionally detached herself and denied my existence, except for the times I had forced her to face the reality of my presence. Even in my inebriated state, it was a revelation. I thought back and pictured my mother — always immaculately groomed and smiling sweetly, arms laden with gifts or flowers — and saw there was little genuine warmth behind her façade. In that moment, I realised she would never embrace me as her daughter.

AT A VARIETY PERFORMANCE in a large club one afternoon, I was sharing the backstage dressing room with Little Pattie. Over the years as a performer, I had met her many times at industry and social functions and had come to know her well but as Patricia Amphlett, her real name. As we were dressing ready for the show, we laughed and chatted, catching up on news. I stopped and turned to look at her. Her trademark blonde bob framed her face, animated now as she recounted a story about singing at a charity event for disadvantaged children.

'Trish, sit down for a minute. I've got something I want to tell you,' I said. No one in the industry knew my background — that was *my* secret that I had kept hidden. But suddenly I felt the time was right. I took a deep breath.

'In 1965 you received some letters from a lonely, confused girl in Parramatta Girls' Home.' She looked at me quizzically. I rushed on before my courage deserted me. I told her what a big fan I had been as a fourteen-year-old and how I had copied her. Then about dancing to 'Stompin' at Maroubra' under the Covered Way in Parramatta, and me writing to her and how much her letters had meant to an abandoned, lonely young girl who'd been locked up because she couldn't fit in. I had felt invisible to the outside world, ashamed and dehumanised but her letters had helped me to realise I mattered — that someone important cared. By the time I had finished we were both crying. Then we hugged and laughed and had to do our stage make-up all over again! Trish has always kept my secret.

I CONTINUED TO WORK for agents and kept up my cleaning job during the day and performed my cabaret show in the clubs, my band gigs at the Bourbon and cruised the Pacific regularly each year, entertaining on *Fairstar*.

'Would you like to do a cruise to South Africa and England?' asked June Evans, flipping the pages of her large leather-bound book.

'Are you kidding?' Is it any wonder I loved this woman! Her belief in me was uplifting. She booked me to perform on the *Achille Lauro*'s five-week voyage back to Southampton, ending the ship's summer cruising season in Australia.

From Sydney we sailed to Fremantle, then across the vast Indian Ocean to tropical Mauritius. A few days later, we sailed down the east coast of South Africa and into Durban's port. The evening prior, all passengers and crew were given a briefing on what to expect regarding apartheid and racial discrimination in South Africa. Obviously, I found this subject particularly interesting and important.

It was May 1992 and just a few weeks earlier, after two years of slowly dismantling the Apartheid system, and Nelson Mandela's release, President FW de Klerk's ruling party had held a whites-only referendum seeking approval of the reform process. The result was a large victory for the 'yes' side. Still, the entertainers on board decided to meet at nine o'clock the following morning and travel as a group to go sightseeing, just in case.

I slept in. At ten o'clock, I stood at the gangway, blinking into the bright sunshine, wondering whether or not to go by myself. The alternative was a day alone on an empty ship, so I said a quick prayer, took a deep breath and stepped onto South African soil. Headed towards Durban town and the shopping centre at first I hurried, feeling a little uneasy, but the cloudless blue African sky and the warmth of the sun calmed my nerves. I slowed to a leisurely stroll and took in the sights. Walking past a lush park, I noticed a large crowd of people gathering some distance away so, taking a detour through the gardens, I went to see what interested them. Joining the crowd, I saw they were gathered around a rotunda, expectantly watching musicians tuning instruments. I had been inspired by Paul Simon's *Graceland* album, on which he'd used African rhythms and musicians, and I was eager to hear some real African music. I soaked up the party atmosphere, looking around at the colourful clothes worn by some of the women, their kaftan type dresses and headscarves reminding me of Ellie. No one took particular interest in me as I waited with the crowd and, suddenly, I understood why. Everyone was black. For the first time in my life, I was surrounded by black people. I didn't stand out — everyone looked like me! Laughing out loud and talking to myself, I rummaged through my bag and pulled out my camera. I turned to the people beside me, who were by now noticing the woman causing a minor commotion. I thrust my camera at them, babbling excitedly, 'Please, take a photo of me with you all. I can't believe this. This is wonderful!' Someone clicked off some photos as I stood, my arms around my new friends, beaming. Oh dear. Now I *was* standing out in the crowd — not because I was different in colour but because I was acting crazy and talking with a funny accent! With that, the band started playing. It was a Wilson Pickett song! I stayed for a while, listening to Motown songs played by black South African musicians, then wandered on into town. Recorded on my camera for posterity though, was the day I was, finally, *not* different.

I ran into some passengers who invited me to join them for lunch. As we took our seats in a curry house, I realised everyone was black except for my companions. This day was becoming an enlightening experience for me. I was captivated by the beautiful faces of the African women, so much so that I asked the two girls at the next table if they were models, only to find that they worked in the local chemist shop

I wandered along the Golden Mile, the wide stretch of golden sand and deep blue surf reminding me of Australia. On the Promenade I ordered a coffee from one of the many outdoor cafes and sat enjoying the carnival atmosphere. I watched and smiled as young school children filed off a school bus two-by-two, holding hands. Then I realised: the first off the bus were white, then, the black children from the back lined up. This was the first time all day I'd noticed any real discrimination. I looked for more indications and saw a shop sign saying: *we can refuse permission of entry to anyone, at our own discretion*. South Africa was on the way to integration but it would be another two years before the first democratic elections were held, allowing people of all races to vote.

After Durban, the majority of the ship's passengers were white South Africans, plus a few remaining Aussies going through to Southampton. On board were a lovely black South African couple in their seventies, who invited me to join them for lunch. They explained a great deal about South African politics, including the fact they had just been issued with passports. They had raised and educated three children who were now very successful in business and had celebrated their parents' milestone of acquiring passports by shouting them the cruise on the *Achille Lauro*. After seventy years, these lovely people were finally able to leave South Africa for a holiday.

Sailing into Cape Town, I made arrangements to spend the day sightseeing with the ship's band singer and her guitarist husband. On a cable car ride to the top of Table Mountain, when the two women we were chatting to discovered we were from the ship, they offered to give us a personal guided tour of Cape Town. We set off along the coastal road to see places of interest. Driving past sandy beaches of pounding surf, it was as if we were driving in Australia, except for the families of baboons bickering and fighting along the side of the road. We stopped the car and got out, and stood buffeted by a stiff salty breeze as our friends pointed to a small island in the distance. It was Robben Island, a former leper colony and the prison home of Nelson Mandela for twenty-seven years. As the women told us what they knew of the shocking conditions the prisoners had to suffer at this isolated place, I shuddered as visions of Hay suddenly surfaced. I quickly pushed the painful memories back into their hidden, deep recess.

After Cape Town, the next port was St Helena then the final port before Southampton would be the island of Madeira, Portugal, which I was looking forward to visiting. *Achille Lauro* was a lovely ship and I enjoyed the time on board between ports.

Sitting in the ship's movie theatre one morning, I couldn't believe my eyes at the story unfolding on the screen before me. It was about the dreadful hijacking of this lovely ship. In Egyptian waters, in October, 1985, she was hijacked by four men carrying machine guns. They were from the Palestine Liberation Front and they took control of the ship for two days, murdering a disabled American passenger during the negotiations. The hostages were finally released after the hijackers negotiated an escape plan; but the hijackers were eventually caught, tried and convicted. In 1990, a made-for-television movie named *Voyage of Terror: The Achille Lauro Affair* was released, starring Burt Lancaster and Eva Marie Saint.

As I sat in the dark, it was frightening to watch terrorists with machine guns rampaging through the dining room and show rooms where I performed. I asked one of the Italian security guards if showing the movie was a good idea, as I felt some passengers might find it unsettling and it was probably not a good PR move. He laughed and didn't understand my concern. 'We are honoured a movie has been made about our ship and Burt Lancaster is a famous actor. It is a movie triumph,' he replied. What could I say?

Arriving in Southampton, I was greeted by close ex-Sydney friends who took me to their lovely home in Kent. I stayed with them for a week, exploring the countryside and visiting London on exciting day trips.

It was a wonderful way to see the world but more importantly, I arrived home in Australia with a new sense of who I was.

WORKING IN HIS BUSINESS as a plumber in The Rocks area of Sydney, Allan noticed a plaque on a small heritage building. Amongst other things listed was 'Maritime Archives' so he wrote down the address. That night as I prepared dinner and Allan poured himself a beer, he told me of his discovery.

'You know, it might be a long shot, love, but this could be a good place to continue searching for your father.' I spun around, a half-peeled potato in my hand.

'What do you mean?' I asked, not quite comprehending what he meant but excited at the prospect.

'Well, think about it. If you counted back nine months from the day you were born, you might find the name of the ship your father was on.' Alan was looking at me expectantly.

'Oh my Lord. Of course! So what's that — February? So if I try to find out what ships came into Sydney Harbour in January and February in 1948, my father's name should be on a list somewhere.

You're brilliant!' I said, tossing the potato in the sink and rushing over to give him a hug.

The next morning I called the number and after a lengthy explanation, I was told to come to another building in the city the following Wednesday at nine o'clock. Apparently the records I wanted had to be sent in from the National Archives repository. I had been searching for my father for six years now and was no closer to finding him, so anything was worth a try.

I arrived at the offices early on a blustery winter's morning, filled with anticipation of what lay ahead. I completed a form and explained again at length that I was looking for the crew list of American ships that had visited Sydney Harbour in January and February of 1948. Ushered into what appeared to be a library or reading room, I waited in the environment of serious readers: that hushed, reverent silence and slightly musty smell of old books filled with even older words. The first leather-bound volume was delivered by a librarian and placed on the table in front of me. It was huge — almost two feet long, wider than a foot and about two inches thick. I said a small prayer as I placed one hand flat on the deep green leather cover and ran my fingers along its burgundy spine. I opened the tome, revealing flimsy pale-green pages that had faded to pale-yellow at the edges from exposure to light. Each lined page had nine typewritten columns. The information on each ship was quite comprehensive. It gave the ship's name, the port of registry, the date and place of voyage commencement and the name of the ship's agents, then a complete list of the crew with six columns of personal details listed for each member. After half an hour I had worked my way through only a few ships and realised that, to find the information I craved, this was not going to be a quick records check. I may have felt a bit discouraged but I was not without hope.

All day the staff delivered the big green volumes containing the details of every ship that had sailed into Sydney Harbour in those first few months of 1948; ships from every country in the world including Chinese, Danish, Russian, English and American ships. As thousands of names passed through my hands, it seemed an almost impossible task, even though I skipped all ships except American. But I didn't stop — I was on a mission.

Fatigued, in the early afternoon I took a break and stretched my legs, taking a short walk along busy Kent Street to clear my head, then went back to the task. I prayed a lot that day, particularly each time the librarian delivered another volume with a sympathetic smile.

'Come on Lord, come through for me, please,' I'd whisper.

By late afternoon I was exhausted and my arms ached from carefully lifting the flimsy pages of the giant books, which hinged along the top. The offices were preparing to close so I thought I would finish the current volume, go home and come back again the next day. The next page was another American ship, the *F. Southall Farrar.* Port of Registry: Brunswick, Georgia. It had commenced its voyage from Longview, Washington State, on November 12, 1947. I ran my finger down the crew list of thirty-five names. Stiffly, I lifted the page of the big volume looking for the remaining crewmembers.

There it was! The first name at the top of the page: Thaddeus Killens!

The world ceased to turn.

I was suspended in time for what seemed an eternity. The sound of screaming brought me back to reality; then I realised it was me. I was jumping, crying, laughing and shouting all at once. 'I've found him!' I yelled. 'My father's name and my father's ship! It's here! Thank you God, thank you.' Office staff and other researchers came rushing from all directions, my sudden outburst concerning some but those who knew why I was there were smiling.

'It's my father's name. I haven't met him yet, but I will now!' I was ecstatic.

I disrupted the peace in the reading room that afternoon but nobody seemed to mind as they gathered around my table, anxious to see what I had found. The staff took the volume and carefully photocopied the pages for me. I hugged several of them then ran out into the street towards my car with my father's name, for the second time, pressed to my heart. I couldn't wait to get home to my Allan.

We celebrated with champagne that night as we studied the information, spread out on the kitchen table. Thaddeus Killens was twenty-four years old the day he had joined his ship in Everett, Washington State, on March 25, 1947. Thaddeus was US-born and one of only two African-Americans, or 'Negro' as it listed under 'Race' in the crew documentation. The other was a Robert S. Hunter, thirty-eight, who had also joined the ship in Everett, Washington. Under the heading 'Capacity in which Engaged', my father was listed as 'M/M': a Messman. I realised my father was in the Merchant Marine and not an enlisted serviceman as I had always assumed. The *F. Southall Farrar* had arrived in Sydney in early February and departed Australian waters from Fremantle, Western Australia on March 3, 1948. I tried to imagine my father, travelling the world as a young and handsome twenty-four-year-old in the Merchant Navy. I contemplated our connection with the sea and my love of ships and cruising.

Now I wanted to know everything about his ship so, the following day, I drove in to the city to the Maritime Museum and spoke to the librarian. She searched their records for information and photocopied details and photos of the *F. Southall Farrar* under construction in the Brunswick, Georgia, shipyards.

It turned out that the *F. Southall Farrar* was a Liberty ship, built and launched in July 1944. At the time she entered Sydney in 1948, she carried a crew of thirty-seven and was owned by the United States War Shipping Administration and United States Maritime Commission. Somehow all these details mattered to me; after all, this was all I knew about my father.

So what was a Liberty ship? The librarian then photocopied this information for me and grateful, I headed home. Relaxing with a cup of tea, I laid out all the information. It explained that Liberty ships were cargo ships, built in the US during World War II, and were cheap and quick to build. Eighteen American shipyards built more than seventeen hundred Liberties between 1941 and 1945, the largest number of ships produced to a single design. Apparently, after the war, many Liberty ships survived far longer than their originally designed lifespan of five years, including my father's ship, which was decommissioned and scrapped in Beaumont Texas in 1966. That was about the time I was released from Parramatta and Hay.

Officially classed 'EC2' (Emergency Cargo Size 2), these ships were also called the 'workhorses of the deep' and designed to carry about ten thousand tons of cargo but in wartime conditions often carried much more, being loaded to their Plimsoll lines and then having deck cargo added. It seems the term 'Liberty-size cargo' for ten thousand tons, is still sometimes used in the shipping business today. During the war, President Roosevelt had nicknamed them the 'ugly ducklings' but he and many military leaders had praised the role of the US Merchant Marine who crewed these ships, as the 'Fourth Arm of Defence'. The Merchant Marine Corps was responsible for putting the US armies and their equipment on enemy territory and maintaining them there. After the war when my father sailed into Sydney, the Liberty ships were still transporting homeward bound occupational troops from the Pacific campaign back to the United States and moving other goods around the world.

I DIDN'T KNOW what to do next with all the information I had. I could guess the year of my father's birth but had no actual date and I still didn't have that all-important Social Security number which the US Government departments required. The Internet, a fledgling entity I'd heard of, was not on my list of resources (plus, I had no idea how it worked, nor did I know anyone who had it connected). For months, excitedly I told everyone and anyone who would listen that I had found my father's ship and what I knew of him. I daydreamed of our first telephone conversation and, more so, of our first meeting. What would I say? What would he say? I wondered what he looked like and how he might react. I felt sure he would be proud of me and all that I had achieved.

Patrick had met a lovely girl and had finally settled down and now he as well as Anthony had given me grandchildren. My relationship with my mother was still amiable. I called her often and invited her on outings and she and Lars joined us for family lunches with the boys, their partners and babies. However, I chose *not* to tell her of my thrilling discovery. I saw no point.

In November, I ran into a friend who I hadn't seen for a while and told her my exciting news. In the 1970s, she had given birth to a daughter by an African-American serviceman who had come to Australia on R&R leave during the Vietnam War days. Unbeknown to me, her daughter, now grown-up, had decided to find her father and had used a private detective agency in the USA. Why hadn't I thought of that?

Immediately, I phoned the number she gave me for the agency in Texas and spoke at length to a kindly and sympathetic man, telling him my story and what I knew of my father. He made no promises but he felt sure he would have success. A few days later, on December 5, 1995, I received a letter from him confirming our conversation. He'd also enclosed the Investigative Agreement for my signature plus other forms and questionnaires to be filled out with as much information as I knew, both researched and told as hearsay. I completed the paperwork, included a cheque in US dollars and sent it back express. Then I waited.

It was a wonderful Christmas that year, filled with joy and the anticipation: my search was almost over. I would finally be the daughter of a man I'd waited forty-seven years to find.

I was invited to sing at Sydney's premier Carols by Candlelight concert at Darling Harbour, on December 23. As a warm December breeze fluttered candles held by the audience of twenty thousand, I felt sure I was glowing with a visible aura as I stood on the stage, singing one of my favourite Christmas carols. I gazed at the illuminated faces of mothers and fathers holding their children, families content in their completeness. I felt sure that in a few weeks I too would feel complete.

In early January, an entertainer friend moving to Queensland offered Allan and me his house to rent while he was gone and we jumped at the opportunity. We liked our little apartment but the prospect of a three-bedroom house in a neighbouring suburb, with a garden and outdoor entertaining area, was too good to pass up. I notified the Department of Housing and thanked them for their support over the previous years. We felt that, as we were now financially secure, it was time for us to move on and make our home available for another family. The department were surprised but appreciative of our attitude.

Two days before moving, standing amongst the chaos of half-packed boxes and clutter, I opened a just-delivered letter from the detective agency, dated January 9. My heart skipped a beat as I read:

Dear Sharyn,

I believe I have found your father but I do not have enough information to verify if he is the right one. I am trying to get the information now. I will let you know.

I jumped and screamed and cried, big happy tears rolling down my face. I read the rest of the letter. He required more US dollars before the information could be released so I rushed to the bank and sent the money by express. I waited again, this time certain in the knowledge I had found my father.

The move was effortless, due mainly to my euphoria. Nothing could dampen my spirits and enthusiasm. I unpacked and decorated our new home with care, preoccupied with thoughts of showing my father my life in Australia and of the family reunion that, one day, may take place there.

Ten days later, I read another letter from the detective:

Dear Sharyn,

I believe I have found your father. Unfortunately, he is deceased. He died in October of 1981, in California. I am trying to get his death certificate for you.

'No, no, no. Please God. No . . .' I howled, the sudden lump in my throat strangling my voice and my heart pounding from the adrenalin. The letter went on to say:

There is another search you can do and that is a background search on him. Hopefully we can find out if he was married, had children, who would be related to you, and other information that would be of interest to you. Let me know if you want me to do this. I wish he had been alive.

My legs buckled beneath me. I sat, shocked and bewildered, staring at the letter in my hand. Then I wept. Deep grieving sobs of loss and defeat, of longing and disappointment and the injustice of wasted years of unnecessary lies and deception.

Eventually, I composed myself enough to pick up the phone and dial. When the familiar voice of my mother answered, I said quietly and evenly, 'I really do not want to talk today but I have just received a letter and I believe you should hear it.' I read her the letter.

'Oh, he died in 1981? I thought . . .'

There was nothing to be said as far as I was concerned so I interrupted with *her* favourite line, 'I am going to put down the phone now.' And I did.

I walked, letter in hand, to the stereo and put on my favourite Nat King Cole record. I have no idea why that was my choice of music but it seemed right and comforting. At four o'clock when Allan walked in the door, he was met with the sight of me, keening and wretchedly miserable, sitting in the middle of the living room floor surrounded by soggy tissues, as Nat King Cole sang 'Unforgettable' very loudly, for the umpteenth time.

'Hey, love, what's wrong?' he asked.

I passed him the letter. He looked at me sadly then went to the refrigerator and poured himself a beer and me a chardonnay.

'Well, this is really sad,' he said, blinking back tears as he sat down beside me and put his arms around me. 'But you know, like the letter said, we can keep searching. You might have sisters or brothers.'

'No,' I said, shaking my head. I felt beaten. 'I can't do this anymore. I've thought about it all afternoon. I've spent a lifetime getting to this point but now it's over. I have got to get over this thing, once and for all. Besides, if my father did have family, they might not want me turning up on their doorstep.'

I put out my hand and Allan passed me the letter. I glanced at the last paragraph again and then said, more to myself, 'No, I can't. This was between me and my father. And now it's over.'

CHAPTER SIXTEEN

Divine Intervention

I MOURNED the death of my father. The intensity of my grief took me by surprise in a way. I had never known this man yet he was a part of me, and I of him. I had longed to meet him all my life — now it would never be. I tried to make sense of my shattered hopes and dreams. What was I doing and where was I in October 1981? And what had I accomplished? I knew that, by then, I had really turned my life around and was achieving my ambition of being a singer and I was the mother of two wonderful young boys — his grandchildren. Would he have been proud of me? Then I remembered it was also during this time I had met my mentor and friend Freddie Paris, a contemporary of my father, although a little younger. Had God sent Freddie to reassure me, at a time I needed encouragement and confidence in my birthright because my father was out of my reach forever?

I emotionally detached myself from my mother, not running after her any more and no longer imploring her to love me. *I* never stopped loving *her* but I was through with begging and trying to be the perfect daughter. It took a while for her to comprehend the shift in our relationship. My mother finally had her way. My father was dead.

Allan was wonderful. Always supportive and sympathetic in my grief, he was not about to give up so easily. Sipping a glass of wine in the evenings, I'd often talk about what might have been and he'd gently say, 'This is no reason to stop searching. You might have sisters or brothers. A family. Wouldn't you like to know what your father looked like? Maybe they would send you a photo.' Eventually

I agreed — he was right of course. I *was* longing to see a photo of my father. I had pictured him so often in my 'meeting my father' fantasy and knew it would be wonderful to really see him.

I sent another letter to the detective agency, requesting one final search for children or the wife of Thaddeus Killens. I received a reply with all my father's details, including that vital social security number and the date of his birth, the names of his mother and father, his last known address in Compton, Los Angeles and the name of the cemetery in Compton where he was buried. There was also a note saying that all his records had been passed on to his wife Doris, who had unfortunately died the year following. All records had since been misplaced so they had no way of knowing if there were any children. During the next few months I wrote a couple of letters to his last known address, asking if they knew the Killens family and, if not, would they pass my letter on to someone who may know them. I had no reply.

I had no idea where Compton was, although the name sounded vaguely familiar. In an effort to know everything I could about my father, I drove into the city again, this time to the State Library in Macquarie Street to see what I could find out about the suburb.

At the library, I discovered Compton was in South Los Angeles County and had become a city in 1889, evolving into an all-white, affluent area through the early 1900s. When the dismantling of segregation began in the mid-1950s, many African-Americans influenced by Compton's close proximity to Watts (a predominately black neighbourhood) had moved into the area, turning it into a much sought-after neighbourhood for the black middle class of Los Angeles. I gathered from some photographs that signs of Compton's past affluence were evident in the relatively spacious and attractive family homes that lined certain suburban streets.

So my father had lived in a nice middle-class area.

Reading on, I was surprised to find that several issues had then contributed to Compton's decline. In the early 1960s many whites started to flee the area, a trend apparently spurred on by the Watts Riots in 1965, which prompted a large number of Compton's middle-class black residents to leave, too. It seems this exodus left behind a community of lower-income residents with needs for public services, which put a strain on the city's budget. I paused to digest this information and look at more accompanying photographs.

Turning the page, I learned that crime, beforehand mainly gang-related (between the Crips and the Bloods), had become significantly worse in the late 1980s with the introduction of crack cocaine. (Thank goodness I'd given up drugs before that came along.) I realised my father had by that time died so, maybe, his family had moved on.

Finally, I read that the richer residents of the neighbourhood started to leave, faced with the worsening safety problems, and that after the 1992 riots in the South Central Los Angeles area (where street gangs used the riot as an opportunity to settle scores with each other) many more African-Americans moved out.

That was why the name was familiar — I remembered the media coverage of those terrible riots. Had my father's family been affected by that?

Meanwhile, Latino families had moved into Compton and were becoming the largest ethnic group in the city. But many people still thought of Compton as a primarily black community. All the way home I couldn't help thinking how different Sydney was from what I'd just read about Los Angeles.

Over a Friday beer after work, Allan was discussing the outcome of my search with David, one of his close mates. David mentioned that their mutual friend Barry Conroy was going to Los Angeles for a few weeks' holiday with his American wife and family and suggested that maybe he could visit the grave and take some photos of it for me. We organised a lunch the following Saturday with Barry and Gail.

Over lunch, we talked about my long and emotional search for my father and its heartbreaking outcome. They listened and then read through the documentation I had received from the private detective in Texas.

Barry and Gail exchanged glances. 'You know we're going to Los Angeles in a few weeks?' I nodded eagerly. 'Well, if you trust me with this paperwork, I'll see what I can find out while we're there,' said Barry.

'Really? That would be wonderful,' I said, grinning and blinking back tears. Pointing to the paperwork, I said, 'Here it says my father is buried in Compton, Los Angeles. If it's at all possible, I would really appreciate it if you went to the cemetery. Maybe there's a headstone with the names of his wife and children. I really would like to ask them for a photo of my father.'

'Leave it with me. Oh, do you have a photo of you, just in case? I can't make any promises, but you never know . . .' Even as he said it, I could see Barry did not hold out much hope. Neither did I.

Arriving in San Francisco a few weeks later in July, the Conroys spent time with Gail's family before moving on to visit friends in Los Angeles. With only a couple of days' holiday remaining in LA, Barry arranged a family-free visit to Compton to photograph Thaddeus Killens' grave. Barry had lived and worked in Los Angeles for six years, about ten years prior so driving around using only the help of a street directory didn't faze him and he knew he'd find the place he was meeting his previous employer for lunch, afterwards.

Barry told me later that, setting off early on that California summer's morning, he could tell the day was going to be hot and dry as usual, so he'd thought an early start was a good idea. He'd been aware of Compton's reputation of being a so-called 'bad neighbourhood' but, driving through the main streets of the suburb, apart from a general run-down appearance and graffiti-lined walls, he didn't see much evidence of the tension and gang wars often portrayed on television — just people on their way to work.

As Barry turned from Compton Boulevard into the long and circular driveway of Angeles Abbey Cemetery and Memorial Park, he passed a row of white-stucco box-like crypts with low-pitched roofs which lined the entranceway's left and right boundaries. He parked his car to the side of the larger of two slightly world-weary, Spanish Mission-style buildings, guessing it would be the administration office. Behind them stretched acres of lawns and trees, creating a green and tranquil sanctuary in the middle of noisy suburban Compton. He calculated that the cemetery must cover almost five city blocks. As he walked to the front door he felt confident he'd have some solid information by the end of the day's proceedings.

Inside, he requested information and the burial site of Thaddeus Killens and a helpful clerk opened a large register, ran his finger down the list of names then wrote the directions to Thaddeus' gravesite, on a small receipt paper. He also wrote the name and address of the funeral home that had conducted Thaddeus' funeral. Handing over a grid map of the cemetery, the clerk told Barry he'd have to walk through the burial grounds to Section 440, twenty-one rows from the fence. 'Thaddeus Killens and Doris Killens are space number one, to the right of Henry James Baty.'

Barry thanked him and headed off across the lawn cemetery in the direction of Section 440. It was still fairly early but he told me he could already feel the day heating up. Sprinklers were pumping spray in wide arcs to revive the thirsty lawns and the fragrance of roses, mingled with freshly mown lawn, had lifted his spirits. Counting twenty-one rows from the fence, he reached the gravesite at space number one but the plaque read *Henry James Baty* and the plot beside it was unadorned. Confused, he had consulted the grid map, checked the section number and paced out the spaces again. Barry said this was frustrating because it had definitely been marked as the last resting place of Thaddeus Killens and his wife Doris. He wasn't looking forward to coming back to me empty-handed.

Two gravediggers were working nearby, so Barry checked his directions with them. They assured him he was in the right place but they were all confused by the incorrect name, so they traipsed back to the office. Half an hour later the error was sorted out after much discussion and checking of records. Back at space number one, the gravediggers removed Henry Baty's gravestone and placed it one space to the left. Looking down at the unmarked plot, Barry said a few respectful words on my behalf, took a couple of photos then asked for directions to Adams Funeral Home and Thaddeus' last known address of Arbutus Street, Compton.

Once Barry had explained the reason for his visit and the hope they may have information on the next of kin of Thaddeus and

Doris, the funeral home were sympathetic but unable to help so he'd made his way on, to Arbutus Street.

Driving through the suburban streets, Barry might've compared the area to his home beachside suburb of North Cronulla in Sydney with its golden sandy beaches, pounding deep-blue surf, neat three-storey apartment blocks nearer the beach and large substantial homes in the tree lined streets behind. And hills! The terrain was so flat in Compton, and there were modest bungalows as far as he could see. Most would have looked neat but almost all had heavy iron bars on the windows and doors and either high metal fences or brick walls, some defaced by graffiti. Granted, it was the middle of summer but, to Barry, everything seemed so dry and dusty. The kerbside grass strips were brittle and brown as were the lawns, and the plants in front gardens had looked thirsty. The trees dotted along the streets offered only slight respite from the sun. Occasionally, he'd spot an oasis of a house with lush lawns, healthy green bushes and colour from flowering plants in the front garden. The last known address of Thaddeus Killens was one of these oases, in Arbutus Street.

Barry had parked opposite the house and checked the number. It was a single-storey bungalow with a small porch over a centre entrance and a barred window at each end, both decorated with white shutters. When he was relating this part of the story to me, he had shown me a photo he'd taken. In it, a large scarlet-flowering bougainvillea wrapped around an end post of the porch, looking almost out of control with its long canes climbing the roof. A row of rose bushes in full bloom grew against the front walls and there were neat flowerbeds of bright petunias marking the side boundaries of the lush green lawn.

Although the street was deserted, Barry said he felt quite out of place and uneasy so, after hurriedly stepping out of the car, he fired off a quick photo of the house then drove off, relieved to be heading towards more familiar territory.

About a mile down the highway he stopped. He told me it wasn't deliberate but something made him pull the car over to the kerb. I have called it 'divine intervention'. He said his conscience and his reason began a tug-of-war in his head. 'You can't come all this way and go back to Australia with only a few photos. What if Sharyn asks if the people living in the house knew Thaddeus or his family? What are you going to tell her? You have to go back,' said his conscience.

'I can't go back,' reason had said. 'I'm too conspicuous. I'm asking for trouble, knocking on doors unannounced, in the middle of a black community. Think of Gail and the kids and just keep going.'

'Don't be ridiculous. Go back to the house. If you don't go back now, Sharyn will never know about her father. You're so close. Just knock on the door and see what you can find out.'

His conscience had won. So he'd turned the car around and headed back to Arbutus Street.

From what Barry's told me, when he pulled up outside the house for the second time, he felt even more unnerved but he got out, walked up the path and knocked on the door. A Latino woman peered through the crack of the slightly opened doorway. Her English wasn't good but she understood enough to tell him she didn't know the Killens and yes, she had received some letters from Australia but, not knowing what to do, had thrown them away. Maybe the lady a couple of houses down might know the family because she'd lived there a long time. Thanking her, Barry had hesitated then walked back along the path and turned right, down the street. He said he felt sure he was being watched — he could feel it.

The deserted street was baking in the summer sun and by the time he reached the intended house, his shirt was clinging to his back. It looked like nobody was home but he walked up the path anyway and rang the front door bell; and besides, the shady porch was a relief from the heat. A petite elderly black woman answered, opening the door half way but leaving the barred screen door closed and locked.

He introduced himself. 'Hello, my name is Barry. I'm from Australia and I am trying to find the family of Mr Killens who used to live up the road.'

'Whatcha wan', Mista?' the woman asked suspiciously, keeping her hands firmly behind her back.

'I have a friend in Australia who believes she is Mr Killens' daughter. I am looking for his family. She'd like to make contact with them,' said Barry, wary as to what she may be holding behind her back.

'Mr Killens bin dead for years. The family moved away.'

'Yes, I have just come from the cemetery.'

'What's your name?'

'Barry, Ma'am. I live in Sydney, Australia.' He had explained the situation again, holding out the picture of me. 'This is Sharyn. Would you please take this photo and here is my telephone number at my hotel here in Los Angeles and this is my card, with my phone number in Australia.' As she unlocked and opened the screen door a couple of inches, Barry had been relieved to see there was nothing in her hands. He passed the information through the crack. The woman turned the photo over, examining it.

'As I said, family moved away long time now. Had three daughters and a son you know.'

'No I didn't. Do you know where I can find them?' Barry knew I'd be excited to hear I had family.

'Don't know where they went but I can ask a bit. Someone might know. A daughter in Australia you say? Well I never.'

'Thank you Ma'am. Can I ask your name?'

'Rose Harrington. Now, God bless you and good day.' And with that, she had closed the door.

As Barry tells it, he'd turned to leave, reluctant to step out of the shade. Squinting in the glare, he retraced his steps down the path. There was still no movement in the street but he knew that eyes were following his movements with suspicion from behind curtained windows, no doubt wondering what this white man wanted with their neighbours. Thinking how different Australia was, with its mostly assimilated multi-racial suburbs, Barry had felt saddened by this feeling of danger and of being an intruder. The only difference between him and these people of Compton was his skin-colour. He didn't feel apprehensive anymore, just alienated: a trespasser.

Barry decided to look on the bright side: he'd found out Sharyn had a family. Three sisters and a brother! What would I say to that, he wondered. He had made his way to his lunch appointment, now very late, and by eleven-thirty the next morning he had managed to find Thaddeus' death and marriage certificates, plus the birth certificates of his four children, at the Compton City Clerk's office. His spirits were high. During the next couple of days, armed with the Los Angeles phone directory and a fledgling Internet, Barry had called as many Killens households as he could find with the matching initials, but had no luck.

Barry and his family had arrived home in Australia on a Monday morning and by that afternoon he was at his office. After three weeks away, obviously he had mountains of work to sift through so he put all thoughts of my search aside, to get stuck in. He intended to pay us a visit on Friday evening, with his good news. He was keen to show me the photos of my father's grave and former home and surprise me with the names of possible sisters and a brother.

Then Gail had rung, late on Friday afternoon. Barry knew something was wrong. Gail was sniffling, her voice breaking as she said, 'Barry, you've found Sharyn's family in America! I've just been speaking to her sister!'

I DIDN'T KNOW my life was about to change forever when Barry rang our doorbell at six-thirty on the evening of Friday August 9, 1996. Allan and I were just sitting down to a Chinese takeaway meal and *A Current Affair* news program on television.

'I'll get it,' said Allan, as I put the covers back on the food. Almost immediately, Barry appeared at the lounge room doorway, followed by Allan.

'Hi, welcome back. How was your trip?' I said, giving Barry a hug. We stood for a moment as he looked from me to Allan, then back to me, a look on his face I couldn't read.

'Sharyn, go to the telephone and call this number,' he said, reaching into his pocket and holding out a piece of paper with a number on it.

'Why?'

'Because there's a lady waiting to speak with you in Los Angeles,' said Barry, his voice cracking.

'Who?' I asked, beginning to pick up his vibe.

'Sharyn, she's your sister.'

'My sister? I have a sister?' I squealed, jumping up and down elated, not quite believing what I was hearing.

'No, you have three sisters and a brother!' said Barry, grinning widely. Clearly he'd been busting to tell me.

'Oh my Lord!' I said, as my hand flew to my heart, trying to calm its wild beating. 'Oh my Lord!'

'Call the number,' said Allan excitedly.

'Well, what do I say? I can't just say, "Hi, I'm your long-lost sister. Your father had a relationship with my mother." I mean, what will I say?'

'Just call!' yelled Allan and Barry in unison.

It was one in the morning in Los Angeles, California, but I swear that phone only rang twice. A smooth, mellow American voice answered, 'Hello?'

'Hello, this is Sharyn calling from Australia,' I squeaked.

'Hi Sharyn. I'm your sister, Debra. How wonderful! I spoke to Barry's wife Gail today. This is so amazing!'

It was the softest, most beautiful voice I had ever heard and I was a goner. I cried, she cried, Allan and Barry cried. It was a magical, wonderful moment and worth everything I had ever lived through, to hear that beautiful voice on the phone say, 'I'm your sister!' Then she said,

'Welcome to our family,' and I knew she meant it. 'You know you have two other sisters and a brother?'

'Yes, I mean no. I mean . . . what are their names, Debra?' I garbled excitedly.

'There's Donna and Sandra and Thaddeus. We call him "Junior".'

'You mean I have a brother called Thaddeus?' I was amazed. 'How old are you all?' When Debra told me, I realised I was the firstborn. I was the oldest sister. 'When did your parents marry?'

'In 1951,' said Debra.

So my father had been a single man when he met my mother. 'When were you born?' I asked.

'In 1954,' said the beautiful voice. 'And you?'

'November 2, 1948,' I said.

'Guess what, Sharyn?' said Debra, each time her accent pronouncing my name as 'Sheryn', which sounded strange but nice.

'What?'

'I am no longer the oldest,' and we laughed.

'No you're not. I am now your older sister girl, so look out!'

We cried and laughed for an hour or longer — I don't know — time was lost. She was so thrilled to meet me on the phone and I didn't want to wake up from the wonderful dream. Eventually, we said our goodnights after swapping phone numbers and promised to call each other in the next couple of days.

Cold Chinese take-away never tasted so good! Allan and Barry had eaten and been sitting in the living room having a few beers, while I spoke on the phone. I was like a kid at Christmas. I couldn't sit still, jumping up and down as I told them the conversation from the beginning, including how Debra had found me.

Apparently, Mrs Harrington had looked at my photo and thought to herself, 'I can't believe that Mr Killens has a daughter in Sydney, Australia. I've known this family more than forty years and they were good neighbours and good, church-going people. And Doris, she sang in the church choir.'

The way Debra told it, Mrs Harrington rummaged through a drawer, and found an address book with a forwarding address and telephone number for the family. She had dialled the number but a recorded message told her it had been disconnected. She'd been wondering what to do when a knock at the front door had disturbed her thoughts. The neighbourhood had been curious to know who the white man was and what he had wanted. Was he from the IRS? Was he coming back? Many in the street who had known the Killens had showed their surprise when she showed them the photo.

According to Debra, Mrs Harrington had told everyone she ran into, 'I never knew that Mr Killens had another daughter, and in

Sydney Australia, no less.' Apparently, long fingers of gossip had spread through the fascinated community till finally they touched the ears of a concerned young woman. So she too knocked on Mrs Harrington's door. 'Mrs Harrington, what's this I'm hearing that you're telling people Mr Killens has a daughter in Australia?' the woman had asked. She had good reason to make it her business: Tyra was a friend of Debra's.

'That's the God's honest truth — here,' Mrs Harrington had said, evidently handing the woman my photograph.

'So, the white man says this woman in the photograph is Mr Killens' daughter?'

'Sure 'nuff, that's what he bin sayin',' Mrs Harrington had confirmed, and then gone on to tell her the full story of Barry's visit.

According to Debra, Tyra had run down the street and straight to the telephone. But for days she tried with no answer. Finally, on the third day, the phone was answered.

'Hello?'

'Deb, this is Tyra.'

'Hi honey, how ya doin'?'

'Deb, I gotta ask you a question, but ya gotta be sittin' down when I ask ya.' Deb said the question had been a surprise: 'Deb, did you know your daddy has a daughter in Sydney, Australia?'

'Get outa here!' Deb had screamed, astonished.

Excitedly, Tyra had related everything she knew about the white man in Compton visiting Mrs Harrington's house, about going to get the news from Mrs Harrington herself, and seeing the photo. Then she had read out the telephone numbers.

'Good Lord!' Deb had said as she put down the phone. She told me she sat for a minute, her mind racing. Then she picked up the phone and dialled a number. As soon as it answered, she blurted out, 'Donna, guess what? Daddy has a daughter living in Sydney, Australia!' Donna had been shocked and asked how she knew this. Excited, Debra had related everything Tyra had told her until an equally excited Donna had told her to call the numbers. But first, Debra had made two more phone calls and had the same conversation, with similarly excited reactions. Then she called the hotel number in LA, only to be told the Conroy family had left and returned to Australia.

She said she had wondered what to do next. She had no idea how to call Australia. In fact, she didn't really know where Australia was. She'd heard of it — it was famous for kangaroos hopping around or something like that. She said she had also wondered: what in the world had her father been doing there anyway? Eventually, she had called the operator and asked for assistance to dial the number in Australia not knowing what to expect 'But,' she'd said, 'I knew a miracle had happened.'

Allan poured me another glass of wine then Barry handed me the photos and information and told us his story of finding my father's grave and the house. Barry had worked so hard and gone out of his way, running all over Los Angeles for me. And he was so patient with my questions about every detail of his adventure; by the end, I felt like I'd been there with him. I hugged and thanked him a thousand times but thanks would never be enough. How could I repay such kindness and generosity of spirit? He was Allan's mate — a man I hardly knew — yet he'd sacrificed time with his family for me, and changed my life forever. The bond of mateship is strong, but I had no words to describe the bond I felt with him — of gratitude. I was so ecstatic that, after Barry left and we'd gone to bed, I simply could not sleep. It felt like my blood was fizzing in my veins.

The following day, I walked around elated with a permanent grin on my face. I phoned my boys who were as delighted and excited as I was. I called everyone I knew and recounted the events — nothing would shut me up.

Then the telephone rang and a sexy, smooth low voice with an American accent said, 'Hi, Big Sister. This is your baby sister, Donna.'

That was all she had to say, to start up another torrent of tears. She cried. I cried. We laughed and spent two hours on the phone chatting like long-lost sisters, which is exactly what we were. My other new sister Sandra arrived at Donna's house while we were still on the phone, so we also spoke for a while. They were all so warm and wonderful and welcoming, and as thrilled as I was that we'd found each other.

I felt a special empathy with Donna that day. I was deeply touched as she recounted stories of our father, his work and his life in the services. I told her about my mother and about my life with Allan, our children and grandchildren. It was a very profound conversation. We ended with a promise to find a telephone company offering the cheapest international calls, so we could speak as often as possible.

After saying goodbye to Donna, I joined Allan in the garden. He'd been preparing it for spring and took a break and poured us a drink. Sitting in the weak winter sunshine, I recounted the conversation. He shared my excitement and, when I had finished, went back to his gardening. I sat a little longer, enjoying my reverie. As I picked up the glasses and walked away, he called, 'You know that lounge suite we've been saving for?'

'Yes?' I answered.

'Well, what would you prefer? A new lounge, or a trip to America to meet your new family?'

I screamed, dropped the glasses on the lawn and ran to him, my arms outstretched. Laughing and crying, I hugged him and silently thanked the Lord for sending me this compassionate, caring man.

'Hey, that was supposed to make you happy, not make you cry!' he said, laughing.

'You are wonderful. I love you so much.'

'Go book your ticket,' he said with a smile.

And that's just what I did. I booked a return ticket from Sydney to Los Angeles, leaving November 6. Then I called my sisters to tell them I was coming over.

THE FIRST PHOTO OF MY FATHER arrived in the mail the following week. The young man staring back at me was dressed in a United States Army uniform, complete with hat and insignia and looked to be in his late twenties. He had met my mother when he was twenty-four years old, so the photo would have been taken a few years later.

There he was. I stared at his face, examining each detail in the black-and-white photo. His eyes were large, dark and warm and his lips were full and perfectly formed, with the hint of a smile showing at the corners of his mouth and a subtle moustache, dusting his top lip. His nose was broad and strong and his skin, smooth and very dark. His uniform was immaculate, the embossed gold buttons shining and the embroidery of his chevrons (or corps badge) and rank insignia of Staff Sergeant, with its three stripes and one rocker, satin-smooth and flawless. On his head was his service dress cap, the shadow from its hard peak just touching one eyebrow and the large embossed eagle on his cap's badge resplendent in its detail.

My father was the most handsome man I'd ever seen. I drank in the image of him. He was magnificent. He looked a proud man, respectful and firm in resolve, yet gentle. I knew this man — he didn't look at all unfamiliar. He looked like the person I had imagined all my life. It was a strange sensation but I could feel love swelling in my heart.

I had found my father at last — my roots. It was at this point, I realised the enormity of what we had done in finding him. It was indeed a miracle; one that had taken a lifetime to happen. I felt all-powerful! Ecstatic! A wave of rapturous emotions washed over me before, without warning, they turned to deep sadness. I realised I would never meet this beautiful person. I would never hold his hand, touch his face, hug him, buy him a gift or have him walk me down the aisle. He was already gone. He had been here and had lived his life, and was gone. Numbed, I sat staring into space. Then the grief tears came again.

Hours later, all cried out, I started to get angry. As my resentment grew, so did my fury. What gave my mother the right to deny me knowing my father? When I had been a child maybe she had the right to make the choice for me — but once I'd become an adult it was also my choice, not hers alone. What about our pleasant heart-to-heart talks? Couldn't she have told me then? Then I recalled the desperation of my midnight phone calls, the heartache of begging my mother to 'please, just tell me my father's name' and the way she would put down the phone, totally dismissive of me. All those years of begging, cajoling and pleading with her, 'Who is my father?'

And with bitterness I remembered how easily she had said his name when she *did* finally tell me. She had *never* forgotten it. She'd *always* known it. So why did she keep me waiting forty years? It was such a cruel thing to do. What did she get out of it; what was her motive? Was it to have power over me? She didn't need it — I had always loved her unconditionally. But what kind of love had this mother given me?

Anger raged inside me, scorching and intense.

The result of her spitefulness was that father and daughter were never to meet. The man had died before she'd given either of us the choice, or the opportunity to know each other. Was this what she'd always intended?

Picking up my father's photograph, I traced the outline of his face with my finger. Maybe it was an illusion but I was sure I could see understanding and recognition in his eyes.

All my life I had never, ever doubted that he was a good man. I'd always carried this feeling with me, maybe to contradict my mother's secrecy, her rejection and my low self-esteem.

Placing his photo on the table, I walked out into the garden and the chill of a gloomy afternoon. Seesawing emotions of love, resentment and rejection were confusing and ruining the joy of seeing my father's face for the first time. I managed to shake them off but animosity towards my mother stayed with me like the taste of a bitter pill.

I got down on my knees on the prickly lawn. I beat my fists into the ground, trying to let go of all the anger and sadness. I was really weeping now. Then, I prayed out loud, 'Please God, in this hour of wonderfulness, don't let me be bitter. Please help me stop this rage in my heart.' It seems improbable I know, but a ray of sunshine poked its way through a cloud. God always gives me what I pray for — I just have to know where to look for it.

I walked back inside, splashed my face with water, made myself a cup of tea and picked up Debra's letter, ready to read her news.

Out fell another photo. It was of four young African-Americans at a party, laughing and with their arms around each other's shoulders. Smiling, I turned it over to read the inscription: *Dearest Big Sis, this is your family. We are Debra, Sandra, Donna and Thaddeus.*

My heart leapt with joy.

CHAPTER SEVENTEEN

Telling Australia

MY AMERICAN FAMILY were beautiful. And I mean *really* beautiful. The girls in the photo were dressed in the latest fashions with great figures and perfect hair and make up. My sisters looked just like the black models I'd seen in fashion magazines! And Thaddeus Jr — he was the image of our handsome father. My family. I said the words over and over to myself. Well, I may never know my father but my gorgeous sisters and brother would tell me everything I wanted to know and we had the rest of our lives to do just that. I went to the phone and dialled Los Angeles. Debra answered.

'Hello?'

'Hi beautiful sister,' I said. 'I've just received the photos. Thank you so much. They're wonderful.'

I was so grateful for those following magic days. I prayed often, thanking God for his blessings and for answering my prayers. I had never really known a mother's nurturing, a home with a loving family or a normal childhood. Why? Because of the colour of my skin.

So I had created my own loving family. I had my two precious boys, my Allan and his twins and now our grandchildren. But finding my roots and American siblings had been one of the best things to happen to me and I was going to enjoy every second with them. I couldn't wait to actually meet them and find out everything denied me. So far I had created a good life. Now it was going to be even better.

I proudly showed anyone and everyone the photos of my father and family. Allan and I attended an entertainment industry gala ball, where I proudly passed around my photos, telling anyone who didn't already know the circumstances of the search for my father. They were fascinated. That night, my friends and peers pushed me to contact the media with my story, as they felt it was so intriguing and inspiring. Although I was desperate to tell the world of my new-found family, I wasn't sure the world would find it that interesting if they didn't know me.

As fate would have it, a few days later I received a phone call at home from the producer of a popular daytime talk and entertainment show, wanting to book the owner of our rented house for a television appearance. I explained my friend had moved to Queensland temporarily and gave his new phone number so he wouldn't miss the booking. After I'd put down the phone, it took me a few moments to realise that maybe God had sent me another opportunity and I'd almost missed it! I sat down with a cup of tea and thought about it. Should I call the producer back? Maybe my friends were right — maybe my story was interesting. I dialled the number and boldly asked if he'd be interested in my story. After a lengthy explanation, he booked me to appear on the national television show to tell Australia how I had found my American family. We also arranged for my then production show group Sisters Incorporated, to close the segment singing 'We are Family'.

I phoned Debra, explaining that I was in the entertainment industry and there was a possibility of interest in our story. Would she or the family mind if I appeared on television and told our story to the Australian media? She assured me there was no problem and I should go ahead — tell the world. I thought: why not? I was ready to shout it from the rooftops anyway.

THINGS HAPPENED QUICKLY after that, and the following Monday, which happened to be our Labour Day public holiday, I sat trying to look relaxed in a comfortable chair, opposite smart blonde Kerri-Anne Kennerley on the set of her show.

Midday with Kerri-Anne was a nationally syndicated, ninety-minute lunchtime variety television show on Channel Nine, featuring interviews with Australian and international celebrities, musical

Let My People Come days, 1977

The band singer: weddings, parties,
anything, 1978 to 1981

During the years of production
shows: 1981 to 1984. I am now
Sharyn Crystal.

Me, resplendent in Big Bird, late 1980s. I've even added feathers!

Ray Charles with my tall son Anthony and me, 1990

BB King and me on the Phillip Morris Superband Tour, 1991

My home-away-from-home: the lovely *Fairstar*, circa 1991

Me with the love of my life: my Allan

Thaddeus Killens

Sandra, Thaddeus Jr, Debra and me in New York, 1996.
Donna and me (inset).

With Ellen and Richard Killens in North Carolina

The inimitable Aunt Decie and me in Fairmont,
North Carolina, 2001

After church, with Aunt Decie and Albert, standing
beside his shining Cadillac Seville, 2001

Sharyn Crystal: Entertainer (PHOTOGRAPH BY GEOFF DAUTH)

performances and comedy spots. Taped in front of a live audience and hosted by popular media personality Kerri-Anne Kennerley, five days a week her audience was charmed by her enthusiastic interviewing style and fascinating guests. I was overjoyed and honoured by the opportunity I'd been given to tell my story.

I had asked her please not to mention my mother's name or ask too many personal questions about her, since it would embarrass her, and Kerri-Anne had graciously agreed.

As she introduced me to her audience, I couldn't help wondering if this was such a good idea after all.

'A guest who phoned us has suddenly discovered she has three sisters and a brother living in Los Angeles that she didn't know anything about. Please welcome singer, Sharyn Crystal,' said Kerri-Anne.

Over the audience applause, Kerri-Anne continued. 'Welcome, Sharyn. We'd like to explore your story today. Let's go back to five years ago. You are with your mother on a cruise . . .' Carefully and very briefly, I touched on the circumstances of my birth, never knowing about my father and finally being told my father's name. As I talked my mind ran ahead, trying to make sure everything I said was put delicately.

Kerri-Anne began her probing questions: what had I been told as a child? Why had I not lived with my mother till age twelve? Careful in my explanation, I gave my wicked grandmother a lot more understanding and compassion than she'd ever given me. Then I said I'd been sent to a boarding school where I'd spent my childhood, till I ran away at age twelve. Oh dear, this was proving more difficult than I thought. Was my mother watching this?

'You had contact with your mother through that whole time?' asked Kerri-Anne. Respectful of my mother, and as usual wanting her approval, I painted the rosy picture I'd always wanted to believe was true: 'All the time. My mother used to come every Sunday and take me out and we had some lovely days together but I never went to her home. It was just a very, very hard time for my mum . . . but I needed to be with her.' My mind was racing now. Am I saying this the right way? Will she approve? I know I'm being careful but am I being careful enough? What on earth is she going to say!

Kerri-Anne's next question was a doozey. 'When you arrived at twelve, to your mother who was living with her mother . . . what was life like for you?' Oh no. How was I going to answer this? I licked my lips and ploughed on, painting a picture of my grandmother with the edges very blurred and dancing around her bigotry. Then came the big question from Kerri-Anne, 'What sort of acknowledgement did you have from within the family at twelve, going to live [there] through those teenage years?' To buy myself some time, I babbled about having wonderful cousins.

'But how were you explained?' asked Kerri-Anne. Think, think, think . . . I'll tell half of it but be careful, I said to myself.

'Um, I was explained to my immediate family as "our little friend from America". Um, to visitors . . . I wasn't there, I mean, I was. I just wasn't introduced to visitors at all.' No mention of being locked away or being adopted. I felt I had let my nasty grandmother off extremely lightly. I even said she'd never been cruel — how much more respectful to my mother could I be? I sat with a fixed grin, trying to cover the panic in my brain.

'So . . . you were told that your father was dead. When finally you learned his name, what did you do?' asked Kerri-Anne. Finally — safe ground. I could answer this and the next questions happily and enthusiastically. I explained my search through the archives, the joy of finding my father's name then getting the awful news he'd passed away. On a small monitor at my feet, I glimpsed a couple of photos of my father, which I'd given to the producer, so I started to relax. Kerri-Anne mentioned that I had found sisters and a brother in Los Angeles and I briefly told the story of Barry's discovery, really warming to the interview now.

Glancing at the monitor again, there was a photo of my cherished family, smiling. I talked about my first phone call with Debra and how wonderful and accepting they were of me.

'And you're planning on visiting?' asked Kerri-Anne.

'Yes, I'm going in November. I'm going to meet them in November,' I said, feeling excited just talking about it.

'Well Sharyn, you're going to stay with us because you're going to sing for us . . . Sisters Incorporated is the name of the group so . . . we'll take a short break . . . and we'll come back . . . stay with us,' said Kerri-Anne, looking into the camera.

As the camera pulled back to audience applause, Kerri-Anne leaned forward and told me I was doing fine. Her assistant came over for a brief chat with her, so I took the opportunity to look around at the audience. Most were smiling at me while some chatted quietly to each other. I'm doing OK, I thought to myself. *Surely* I haven't said anything to upset anyone. In the next instant, Kerri-Anne was back on camera.

'. . . We're talking to singer Sharyn Crystal about a family she never knew she had . . . it is an incredible story.' Turning to me, Kerri-Anne asked, 'What sort of pressure did you have growing up with a black heritage in a family who made it very difficult, [not] acknowledging that you were one of their own?' She'd lulled me into a false sense of security, so I wasn't ready for this one. My mouth went dry and I could have killed for a glass of water but, instead, I took a deep breath and ploughed on.

'They didn't really make it difficult but they didn't want to talk about it and so, I just felt that I needed them to talk about it.' How much more diplomatic could I be? Again, I thought: who knew this was going to be so difficult?

'Because you grew up with a blond-haired, blue-eyed . . . stepbrother and a mother and a father.' I babbled something about my beautiful brother, then, collected my thoughts enough to say, 'At times it was really, really hard but nobody was talking about it and I really needed to know who I was.'

Just as I was thinking I didn't want to be there anymore, Kerri-Anne repeated some of the earlier details about my father and about finding my American family, 'You found his family back in Los Angeles . . . and I know you're going off to visit them, which must be pretty exciting, after many telephone calls.'

'Oh, the happiest time of my life is right now, yes it's great.'

'Well, we just want to surprise you a little bit today . . .' As soon as she'd said the word 'surprise', I thought: oh dear, what's coming?

'because on the line from Los Angeles we have your sisters Debra, Sandra, Donna and your brother Junior,' Kerri-Anne finished, pointing to a large screen to my left.

There in living colour, were my sisters and brother, plus Debra's daughters Kristina and Je'Don, all sitting in a row on chairs in a studio in Los Angeles and smiling back at me! I couldn't speak — emotions rushed like a wave, up through my body and stuck in my throat, strangling my voice.

'Oh wow. Oh. Oh wow . . .' was all I could say, soaking in the sight of them, while the studio audience went crazy.

'Ladies and gentleman in Los Angeles, please formally through the satellite . . . meet your sister Sharyn. Hi and welcome,' said Kerri-Anne as the audience applauded and oohed and aahed.

'Hi Sharyn, we love you Sharyn. Hi sister,' they all said together in that special way they pronounced my name — Sheryn. I loved it.

'Oh look. Oh I love you too. Look at you. You are so beautiful. Oh look . . .' I said, not quite sure if I was breathing and not quite believing what I was seeing.

'Because you've only in fact, communicated through photographs and telephone calls, is that right Debra?' asked Kerri-Anne

'Oh yes, all the time . . .' said beautiful auburn-haired Debra, her creamy chocolate skin almost translucent under the studio lights. '. . . Can you hear me?'

'Yes, I can hear you and you look beautiful,' I said, watching Debra give a little sniff and wipe away a tear.

'Now Debra, tell me how you reacted when you first found out that you had a half-sister in Australia.'

'I couldn't eat and I couldn't sleep all night long. I was so shocked and I was so happy. I couldn't wait to talk to her and, after talking to her, there was such a connection. It was unbelievable. You know . . . sometimes once you find a person its like, where do you go from here but talking to her, there was just a bind right away and I love her so much . . .' The camera came in close on Debra's face. Her big eyes were welling with tears and all I could think was just how truly beautiful she was. 'And you know, we tell each other we're going to grow old together,' she said.

'Yes we are, yes we are Debra . . . This is wonderful,' I said, no longer able to hold back the tears myself. 'Why didn't you tell me? We were only talking on the phone a few days ago. Donna, wait till I get you,' I said, including Donna in the conversation. We all laughed.

'Donna,' said Kerri-Anne, 'did you ever have any knowledge of any other family member? Did your father ever say anything to you?'

'No he did not but it's so funny . . . I was telling Sharyn, Friday, that, you know, I always wanted another sister. I always wanted a big family . . . I'm so happy. I've always loved her but yet I just met her . . .'

As the camera closed in on gorgeous Donna showing her wavy black hair cascading over her shoulders, an assistant rushed in offering me a tissue. Gratefully, I grabbed it and wiped my eyes but I could see on the monitor the producer had quickly switched back to me, so all of Australia saw me blubbering.

'This is so wonderful. Oh, this is so beautiful,' was all I could manage to say, still wiping away tears. I'm not often lost for words but this time I was absolutely thrown. Then Kerri-Anne asked if my family could appreciate how difficult my life had been, in my never-ending search for my identity.

The camera panned across to my stunning sister Sandra, dressed in a red dress, her hair black pulled in high bun on her head, accentuating her huge almond eyes. 'It had to be hard for her but I'm so glad we found each other and we can make up for all that lost time, Sis. I love you and can't wait to see you.'

'Oh this is beautiful. You're all so beautiful,' I said *again*. I couldn't believe what was happening and rather than try to think of clever things to say, I just let my heart do all the talking.

'Girls, you sadly lost your father in 1981. What do you think his reaction would be today and to when you meet?' said Kerri-Anne directing the question to my family.

'I think he would be very happy . . . very proud because we're a very close family,' said Sandra. But another deep, sincere voice kept saying, 'Very proud. Very proud.' It was my gorgeous brother Thaddeus Jr, standing quietly in the row behind my three sisters.

'She would have been accepted without a doubt,' said Debra immediately.

'Oh no problem whatsoever. She would have never had to go through what she went through,' said Sandra.

'We loved her instantly,' said Debra.

'My dad has always loved his children . . .' said Donna. I shook my head in wonder at the love and total acceptance of me, by this close and loving family. By this time, I could tell my eye make-up was running down my face but I didn't care. I was with my family.

Kerri-Anne had one more question for them and this time, she directed it to Thaddeus.

'Now Junior, tell me how many children in your family? . . . how many brothers and sisters are there?'

'Three sisters, well four sisters now and me. I'm the only boy, the baby of the family,' said my brother. My heart sang as I was unconditionally enfolded into this wonderful family.

'Well family in Los Angeles, as you may know, Sharyn is an excellent singer. Have you ever seen her perform before?' asked Kerri-Anne.

'No,' chorused my family, all eagerly grinning. Kerri-Anne said, light-heartedly, 'Well Sharyn . . . dry those tears . . . if you make your way over . . . we are doing an international audition for the family . . .'

I walked across the studio as if in a dream and joined my group, already standing in front of the Geoff Harvey Orchestra, ready to sing 'We Are Family' to my family, and to Australia. The orchestra, consisting of some of Australia's most accomplished musicians, played the introduction and, as I sang those joyful first few lines, it couldn't have been more heartfelt. I sang the song to them, constantly watching them on the big screen. There they were — my family: my brother and sisters and my nieces, who had now joined them on camera. As the song finished to enthusiastic audience applause and clapping and cheering from my family, Kerri-Anne announced, 'Sisters Incorporated in Sydney and sisters and brother incorporated in Los Angeles; Debra, Donna, Sandra and Junior, what do you think of your sister?'

'Amazing. Wonderful. Beautiful. Awesome. You go girl. You just work it honey,' they said, talking over each other. Kerri-Anne wrapped up the show and it was over.

But not for me. The producer kept the satellite link open and we were able to talk for a while longer. They told me how the show's producer had contacted them all, days before, and sworn them to secrecy; how limousines had been arranged to ferry my family to a Hollywood studio for the crossover segment on the show and the excitement of finding the television crew had make-up and hair specialists on hand for them. A sumptuous buffet of food and drinks had also been laid on, smorgasbord style. My new family were treated like royalty and again sworn to secrecy. I was the only one who had no idea of any of it. It was incredible.

BY THE TIME I ARRIVED HOME around four, Allan had been fielding phone calls nonstop from friends and family and our answer machine had run out of tape, full of messages of love and congratulations. Being a public holiday, it seemed everyone had stayed home on that unusually cold and overcast October day and watched television. The celebration continued into the evening as our home filled with friends and neighbours, the laughter and chatter interrupted by popping champagne corks. By six o'clock, my home fax machine had spewed reams of congratulations pages onto the floor. Amongst them were enquiries from people all over Australia, looking for their American fathers and wanting to know how to go about it and the name of the private detective I'd used. Apparently, the television station had been inundated with phone calls after my segment and the producers had passed on the enquirer's phone numbers for me to follow-up. When I wasn't talking to family and friends, I started calling some of these people to answer their questions. Interestingly, they were all looking for white fathers in America.

By mid-evening, in all the excitement and phone calls I realised I hadn't heard from my mother so, eagerly, I called her.

'Did you see it? Did you see me? Did you see the family?' I asked excitedly. As soon as she started speaking I recognised the ice in her voice.

'Hah. She's asking, did I see it?' she said sarcastically to me but, mostly, to someone else in the room; I assumed it was my stepfather.

'Are you OK?' I asked concerned.

'How dare you tell my life on television! How dare you tell the world about my past,' she spat venomously.

'*Your* past?' I was incredulous. 'It's *my* past too. I hardly discussed you at all and, under the circumstances, I think you can be thankful that was all I said. I thought I'd been very gentle with you and your vindictive mother. It's *my* life and I now have a past I can talk about. I'm sorry you didn't enjoy the show and . . .'

'I'm hanging up the phone now Sharyn,' said my mother. The phone clicked in my ear. Well, this time I really didn't care. I had found love and acceptance in my father's family and if my mother didn't like it, it was her problem. I thought her attitude was very unkind. Was I being insensitive? No! She could never be happy for me, no matter what I did. In her eyes I should accept whatever she dished out. Her problem was: I hadn't always behaved the way she had wanted me to. I had been fighting back since I was a girl, trying to survive and find some meaning to the hideous life she had forced upon me. Well, those days were now well and truly over. I'd never intended to be disrespectful to her and I never was. No one had ever known my mother's true identity. I had always kept her secret from the world, just as she kept me secret. The only difference was that mine came from a place of love and respect— something my mother had never shown because of the colour of my skin.

MY FRIEND JENIFER GREEN and I were talking on the phone a couple of days later about the *Midday* segment and finding my family. Raised in Australia, Jenifer found fame in the US as an actress in movies and well-known television shows, and was an exceptionally talented entertainer, appearing at the Desert Inn in Las Vegas and television variety shows including *The Merv Griffin Show, The*

Tonight Show and Bob Hope's specials. Dividing her time between America and Australia, she kept in close contact with her friends in the US when she was home. Jenifer was very excited for me and suggested I send a fax explaining my story, to her friend John-Michael Howson in Hollywood, which I did.

John-Michael is a well-known, flamboyant Australian media personality and at the time, was living in Los Angeles. He was Australia's number one Hollywood reporter, often the first with breaking news or the latest gossip on Hollywood's A-list celebrities for Australian television and radio shows.

John-Michael telephoned from his home in Hollywood late the following evening. 'Absolutely love the story. Tell me more,' he said, so I repeated an abridged version of my life. 'I'm going to New York next week and I'd like to pass it around and see if we get any nibbles. What do you think?'

'Wonderful,' I said, a bit overwhelmed by all the attention. After a couple of days, I didn't hear anything so I forgot about it and started preparing for my upcoming cruise on *Fairstar*, plus my trip to meet my family in Los Angeles on November 6.

I was cleaning the house on a Saturday morning when the telephone rang.

'Hello?'

'Sharyn, this is Gordon Elliott in New York,' said a deep, well-modulated man's voice.

'Yeah, right. And I'm Whitney Houston,' I said flippantly, sure someone was playing games.

He laughed. 'No, it really *is* Gordon Elliott,' said the voice.

'Really?' I asked, still sceptical.

'Yes, Sharyn. I want you to come to New York and tell your story on my show,' he said. 'Would you do that?' I stifled a scream of delight. New York! Did he say New York?

'Oh gosh,' I said, my mind racing.

'I think it's a terrific story. Will you come over?'

'Yes, yes I'd love to,' I said, regaining my composure.

'That's great. My producer will be in touch to sort out the details.'

'Oh dear,' I said, suddenly in a panic. 'I'm booked to sing on a cruise from October 21 till early November. Will that be a problem? I can come after that. Well, I was anyway. I'm flying to Los Angeles to finally meet my family.'

'It shouldn't be a problem. I look forward to meeting you.'

'Me too. Thank you so much,' I said, putting down the phone and not quite believing the conversation had happened. I danced around the house. New York! *The Gordon Elliott Show!* Oh my Lord!

I certainly knew who Gordon Elliott was. He had been a radio personality then a television presenter in Australia, before moving to the US in the late eighties as a reporter and producer on *A Current Affair*, then *Hard Copy* and had also hosted *To Tell the Truth*. Moving to CBS for *This Morning*, he now hosted his own one-hour talk show, *The Gordon Elliott Show*, with a viewing audience of around twenty million people. And I was going to tell them my story!

First I called Allan at work then I called Debra in LA.

'OK, you guys. I've just had a call from Gordon Elliott in New York, asking me to fly there and be on his television show. Are you all in on this? Is he planning some kind of reunion show or something where they surprise the guest by having the long-lost relatives jump out of closet?' Debra roared laughing.

'Honey, there is no way in the world I am going to New York. No way. I couldn't get that time off anyway. I'm much too busy in my job. I'll speak for the rest of the family and say to you that I don't think any of them are going to New York either. And you know that Donna won't even get on a plane, so I can assure you she won't be doing anything like that. You just head on over there and have a wonderful time and we'll see you when you arrive back in LA.'

My sons were very excited that I was flying off to New York. They were still great fans of the American basketball super heroes and anything labelled with an American sports brand. Allan thought it was terrific and knew it had always been my ambition. New York was a city I'd always yearned to visit but had never expected to actually see.

I was booked to entertain on *Fairstar*, leaving on October 21 and returning November 1, then due to fly to Los Angeles or New York on November 6. I was still waiting for confirmation from Gordon Elliott's producer. October flew by with lots of phone calls to my sisters as we planned all the fun we would have together in Los Angeles, plus I had plenty of singing engagements to keep me occupied and focused. I changed the format of my floor show to incorporate a brief story of my search for my father, my devastation at his passing then my joy at finding my family. I'd then sing two Nat King Cole numbers, 'Around the World I Searched for You' and 'Unforgettable' as a tribute to my father. This segment was deeply moving for me and, judging by their reaction, also my audiences. After each show I was amazed how many of them told me they had seen the *Midday* segment.

I ARRIVED ON BOARD *Fairstar* expecting a fun cruise filled with days spent in anticipation of my trip to the US. I didn't expect it to also be a nostalgic and emotional cruise. It was announced that *Fairstar* was being decommissioned in late January so, after thirty years, she only had three months remaining to cruise the South Pacific. It was time for her retirement and, I realised, it would be my last cruise on my lovely home-away-from-home.

My shows were a success and I was having a wonderful time with all my regular cruising staff mates, reminiscing about old times on *Fairstar* and talking about my trip to the US. One afternoon I was paged to the purser's office for a phone call. In 1996, ship-to-shore phone calls were still rare, as they were extremely expensive and fairly difficult to conduct. It was the *Gordon Elliott Show* producer Susan Horowitz, calling from New York. Amazingly, we chatted for around an hour on the crackling line as she delved for details she needed of my life, my search and finding my father. Then she broke the news that sent me into a panic. I had to fly out to New York on November 3, almost immediately on my return to Sydney. I would have only thirty-six hours to re-pack and organise myself for my month-long stay in America!

'But I'm booked on the sixth to LA. How am I going to change everything?' I asked, in a helpless panic.

'Don't worry Sharyn. Everything has been arranged. We've been talking with Allan and he's changed your LA flight date and he has your New York tickets and accommodation information,' said Susan reassuringly. Could my life get any better?

Later at the poolside bar on the open deck, I was chatting with Heather, one of the cruise staff, who over my years of cruising had become a close friend.

'Have you ever been to New York in winter?' she asked. Sitting in tropical heat of around one hundred degrees, I hadn't really thought about the weather or temperature in New York.

'Oh, I see what you mean. It'll be freezing won't it?' I realised I wasn't at all prepared.

'Don't worry. I've got just the thing for you,' she said. After dinner, down in her cabin she handed me her deliciously warm, full-length, black cashmere coat. 'Take that to New York and make sure you and that coat have a great time,' she said, giving me a hug.

Towards the end of the cruise, Heather organised a gathering for me, to celebrate my birthday and as a farewell for my trip to meet my American family. My *Fairstar* friends showered me with gifts, including a tiny silver *Fairstar* ship on a silver chain. Heather presented me with a gold brooch in the shape of a tiny guardian angel. Overcome with emotion and love for my *Fairstar* family, I burst into tears. It's funny how close you become to those you work with over many years. Some I might never see again, a handful I would keep in touch with occasionally and just a couple, such as gorgeous Heather, would remain my closest friends.

Arriving home, it was panic stations. I called my sons and all the family to let them know of my early departure. My mother was cordial and wished me a nice trip. We hadn't spoken since her reaction to the *Midday* show but she knew I was going to LA to meet my family. She didn't know, however, about the *Gordon Elliott Show* and, frankly, I didn't care what she thought anymore.

I had been looking forward to a party to celebrate my birthday and this momentous trip but it was not to be. My cousins, Patrick, one of my granddaughters and of course my darling Allan gathered at the airport to say goodbye. Full of good spirits, laughter and tears, I managed to hug them all before disappearing alone, into the Customs area and onward to my incredible adventure.

REALISATION AND EXCITEMENT KICKED IN somewhere over the International Date Line and the endless blue of the Pacific Ocean. I was *really* going to America. I couldn't remember a time in my life when I hadn't yearned to go but I never expected it would happen. In my career as an entertainer, I was always excited when my agent offered me singing engagements on board cruise ships sailing around the Pacific or to Asia and England. But many of my fellow entertainers were working on the American ships and this opportunity had eluded me. Now I was flying to America, on my way to see my American family. How thrilling!

I ordered champagne. The flight attendant asked about my trip. I told him I was going to appear on national television in New York, then fly to Los Angeles to meet my new American family. He listened then quickly excused himself, only to return a few minutes later. Handing me an elegant champagne glass, he filled it with Dom Perignon.

'That's a reason to celebrate with the best champagne,' he said. 'Enjoy. I'll be back to top it up in a little while.' How fabulous!

The flight arrived in Los Angeles, late morning. My Dom-Perignon flight attendant gave me a hug and wished me luck. Feeling as though I'd been awake all night, and disoriented after the thirteen-hour flight, I wandered through the terminal and the business of clearing Customs and Immigration. I had to transfer to United Airlines for my New York flight, so I walked out the front of the airport building and joined the line for the shuttle bus. Looking across the road, it took me a moment to comprehend: I was staring at the hotel where my father had once worked as a chef. My sisters had told me he had been one of the first black chefs in America, in that exact hotel. I shook my head in disbelief as I realised I was finally in my father's hometown. It felt very odd, yet very spiritual.

Waiting patiently in the balmy weather for the shuttle bus, I was startled to hear my name called. A family of Australians rushed over to me.

'We saw you on the *Midday* show with Kerri-Anne. Bet you've come to meet your family in LA,' they said excitedly. As my puzzled fellow bus queue passengers looked on, the family hugged me and said how much they had loved the segment, then went on their way. As I marvelled at the power of television, little did I know what God had planned for me.

The mid-afternoon flight to New York seemed endless, taking another five hours before landing at JFK just after midnight, New York time. Still excited but now jet-lagged and confused, I followed the other passengers through the terminal to the baggage carousel and waited patiently for my luggage. Glancing around, I noticed a couple of neatly dressed men in uniform, complete with caps, holding signs. It took a moment to realise the most smartly dressed chauffer was holding a sign with *my* name on it. Wow! I suddenly felt very important. I walked over and introduced myself.

'Good evening, Ma'am. My name is Joe and I am your driver. I will take you to your hotel but first, let's collect your bag,' said Joe, pointing back to the luggage circling on the carousel. An icy blast of frozen rain cleared some of the fuzz in my head as we stepped through the doors of JFK airport.

'This way Ma'am,' said Joe, leading me in the direction of the longest and sleekest stretch limousine I'd ever seen. Joe put my luggage into the trunk after making sure I was comfortable. How nice this was happening to me! I had arranged many for other people but to be greeted with a chauffeur-driven stretch limo in New York was really something. Joe gave me a running commentary as we sped along the freeway, passing through the borough of Queens with its cute suburban houses, many already decked in festive Christmas lights. I was amazed at the amount of traffic on the roads, even at this time of the morning.

'We're just crossing the East River, Ma'am, and this is the Queensboro or 59th Street Bridge,' said Joe. The massive steel girders of the long bridge seemed to form a tunnel as we passed beneath them. And there it was, on my left! The famous Manhattan skyline of black skyscrapers silhouetted against the blue-black night sky, the thousands of tiny lights in windows twinkling up and down the buildings. My body tingled with a rush of adrenalin. I am finally here in the city of my dreams! As I settled back into the luxurious leather seat, wearing my friend Heather's very soft and warm cashmere coat, I watched Manhattan envelope us and softly sang 'If My Friends could See Me Now'.

CHAPTER EIGHTEEN

Telling America

THE LIMOUSINE PULLED UP outside an elegant Manhattan hotel at 569 Lexington Avenue. The smiling uniformed doorman stepped forward and opened my door.

'Welcome to Loews, Ma'am,' he said, helping me from the car. Joe handed my luggage to a bellboy, who placed my bag on a shiny trolley and wheeled it into the spacious lobby. I felt melancholy for some reason as I said goodbye to Joe, the only person I knew in New York City.

Opposite the front desk area was a restaurant and circular bar. Even at this late hour, smartly dressed people sat eating and drinking, as a cocktail pianist played a familiar song.

After checking in, I was handed over to a confident young man who escorted me and my luggage up to my room on the fourteenth floor. I tipped him ten US dollars, not knowing if it was enough or not.

The room was elegantly furnished and had a view of the busy New York street and buildings. There in the middle of the table was a huge basket of fruit, a gaily-wrapped bottle of champagne and a vase of beautiful flowers. The card read: *Welcome to New York. We will be in touch very soon. Love, Gordon.* I burst into tears. What is wrong with me, I thought? I sat forlornly on the edge of the bed then reached for the telephone and dialled Sydney. When Allan answered I blubbered, full of self-pity.

'Oh Allan, I'm so glad you're there. I'm so sorry. I should never have done this trip. I am insane. It's one-thirty in the morning in

New York and I'm all alone. I'll probably be murdered. They kill people here, you know!'

Poor Allan sympathised with me but laughing, said 'I think you have jet lag, love. Why not just climb into bed and have a good sleep. You'll feel better in the morning.' As usual, he was the voice of reason.

Agreeing and assuring him I loved him dearly, I put down the phone and looked around the room. I switched on the television and picked up the menu and rang room service, ordering a bowl of vegetable soup and a chilled bottle of champagne to celebrate my first night in America. Waiting for the food to be delivered, I played around with the remote control on the television set — one hundred channels! Good heavens! We only had five in Sydney.

A waiter arrived with my food laid out on a trolley, complete with white linen cloth, serviettes and flowers. There was a huge bowl of delicious steaming-hot soup, freshly baked warm rolls and champagne on ice, in a silver bucket. I sat in front of the television enjoying the soup and champagne, feeling like a kid on Christmas Day. There was so much to see: music channels, talk shows, sport and the latest movies nonstop — twenty-four hours a day. How marvellous!

I ran a bath to pamper myself, using all the tiny gift bottles, and lay in the luxurious bubbles, thinking about sleeping. A lightbulb in my brain snapped on. Am I nuts? I'm finally in New York City and it's open for fun, twenty-four hours a day. If I don't have a great time here, my friends will never forgive me!

With that, I leapt out of the bath and looked at the bedside clock. It said *02:30* — time to party. I applied make-up, did my hair and slipped into the proverbial little black cocktail dress and high heels, grabbed a handbag and headed for the lift. It's marvellous what lipstick and mascara can do.

Down in the foyer, I walked over to the still-busy bar and pulled up a stool next to a group of young people. As the barman leaned toward me I said, 'I'll have whatever they are drinking.' The people beside me turned and smiled. Extending my hand, I said, 'Hi, I'm Sharyn. I'm from Australia.' Perfect opening line. Within seconds we were deep in conversation. They all wanted to know about Australia and I, in return, wanted to know everything about them. We had a great time and I stayed until dawn, on my first day in wonderful New York. At 6 am we said our goodbyes, exchanging business cards. I went back to my room and passed out until noon.

THE HOTEL CONCIERGE marked Bloomingdales, Saks Fifth Ave, Rockefeller Centre, Radio City Music Hall and Times Square on a map and off I set, dressed in a smart suit, high heels and, of course, Heather's coat. Stepping out onto busy Lexington Avenue, my breath steaming in the chilly air, I stopped for a moment to take in the smells, sights and sounds. Yellow taxis darted in and out of the almost stationary traffic on the five-lane avenue, their horns honking in frustration. Sleek cars with well-dressed drivers, waited impatiently at the red light as New Yorkers, rugged up against the cold in business suits, and tourists, casually dressed in jeans and runners, crossed the busy 51st Street intersection en masse. Tall, wall-to-wall buildings created a roofless tunnel up and down Lexington, the sombre colours of the buildings broken by the brightly lit displays in the street-level shop windows. I'd walked about half a block, soaking in the thrill of the city, when I realised my smart suit and high heels were totally impractical for my afternoon of exploring. I rushed back to my room and quickly pulled on a pair of jeans and runners, like the other tourists.

I walked and walked, absorbing the hustle and bustle of the city almost by osmosis and taking mental pictures of the places I'd read about or seen in movies. Exploring Saks Fifth Avenue, I bought a couple of mementos then crossed Fifth and wandered down a narrow tree-lined plaza between two buildings, only to find myself at the edge of the huge sunken Rockefeller Plaza ice rink, surrounded by towering skyscrapers. The majestic gilded statue of Prometheus glowed in the chilly afternoon sunlight as ice skaters almost two stories below me, raced and twirled and fell in a heap, laughing.

Am I *really* here, I thought to myself?

Another block and I was outside Radio City Music Hall staring at posters for the upcoming Christmas Spectacular and photos of the famous Rockettes in their distinctive costumes. Another couple of blocks and I was finally standing on Broadway! I stood in Times Square, looking up at the huge screens, their neons glowing brightly in the now gloomy late afternoon light. I couldn't believe how easily I'd walked around and how friendly everyone seemed. New York was everything I'd hoped it would be.

I arrived back at the hotel around six to find a note from Susan, the *Gordon Elliot Show* producer, inviting me for dinner with her assistant Julie, at eight o'clock. As I chatted easily with the two very delightful women, they filled me in on the show procedure and what to expect the following day. A limousine would take me to JFK for my flight to LA after the taping of the show, which would be in front of a live audience but would not go to air nationally till the following week.

PACKED AND READY TO GO at ten o'clock the next morning, the limousine arrived to take me to the television studio at the CBS Broadcast Centre on West 57th Street. Pulling up outside what appeared to be a theatre, I was ushered through the hundreds of people already lined up, waiting to go inside. As I was shown into my well-appointed dressing room, the door was shut behind me. I shrugged at their security measures then helped myself to the steaming pot of coffee and the cookies laid out invitingly on the table.

An assistant escorted me to hair and make-up, the doors closed after I entered each room, including the bathroom. Somebody walked me there and locked the door behind me. Now I was impressed — they certainly looked after the welfare of their guests.

Back in my dressing room, my hair and make up done, Gordon Elliott came in to meet me before the show. Dressed in a suit and tie, he was very tall and very nice and told me how much he was looking forward to the show. We chatted for a few moments, I thanked him for my wonderful trip to New York, and then he left, closing the door behind him.

I paced the floor, suddenly feeling impatient to get started. I was excited to be on the show but I was more excited about my afternoon flight to Los Angeles after the show. I knew all my family would be there to welcome me and I couldn't wait. Never once had I had second thoughts about the outcome of my search or worried my new family may reject me. There was a bond and empathy we had all felt right from our first phone calls and I loved how they had embraced their big sister immediately. My thoughts were abruptly interrupted by an assistant.

I was led from my dressing room to backstage of the *Gordon Elliott Show* set and instructed to stand behind closed double doors and wait. Suddenly, music blared and I could hear the audience cheering and clapping; obviously Gordon had walked onto the set. I had appeared on shows in Australia but nothing had prepared me for the enormity of being on television in the US, knowing I would be watched by over twenty million people. It was astonishing and so exciting. I could hear Gordon introducing the show.

'I love stories like the one you're going to hear today . . .' said Gordon, 'as you know this woman's story, you keep on saying to yourself, if this is true it's going to make a magnificent book or a movie but it develops even as we talk today so I want to bring her out and begin telling you her life. Ladies and gentlemen, please welcome Sharyn Crystal. Sharyn, come on out!'

The doors opened and I stepped onto the set to thunderous audience applause. As Gordon, in shirtsleeves, strode over to me, all I could think was: wow, look at his wild spotted braces! He kissed my cheek and, taking my hand, led me to two comfy armchairs placed in the centre of what looked to me like a large comfortable living room. Suddenly I felt nervous, and still jet-lagged from my exhausting adventure, but somehow he made me feel very special. As we settled into the chairs, Gordon began, 'Now, Sharyn's story begins in my homeland of Australia and it was a love story. It began as a love story didn't it Sharyn?' Here we go again I thought.

'It *was* a love story. My father was an American serviceman and my mother, a blue-eyed blonde Australian and they met when my father's ship was in Sydney in 1948.' I continued to talk about their meeting, my father's ship leaving and my mother discovering she was pregnant. Gordon and I then discussed the stigma of being born illegitimate and black into a white Australian society and Gordon explained the complexities of the White Australia Policy, for the benefit of his American audience, '. . . so you can understand the atmosphere that,' turning to me, 'when you were born, black babies were not part of anything that anyone wanted anything to do with,' said Gordon. 'So this is the world you entered with a white mother . . . continue telling the story.'

Be careful how you say this, I thought, but I explained my grandmother's bigotry and my mother's difficulty, remaining completely respectful to both of them as I had been on Australian television.

'What was the worst thing she said about you?' asked Gordon.

'"You are the worst thing that ever happened to my daughter. Somebody should have drowned you at birth."' Over a collective gasp from the audience, I continued, '. . . my grandmother was just bitter and twisted and just could never deal with it.' There — I'd said it and I didn't care.

Gordon and I then talked about my very early childhood years and the joy of living with Ellie and Dorrie. I told Gordon and the audience about meeting the ships and the parties, the music and the love that enveloped me during that time. Gordon had swivelled sideways in his chair, leaning towards me as we talked about acceptance and the wonderful home Ellie and Dorrie had given me.

Now we discussed my mother's visits and my adoration of her. 'Then you get taken one day,' said Gordon, in a comforting gesture, placing his hand over mine. 'She comes to the house and decides to take you out of there.' I explained the circumstances.

Remembering and talking about that day, without warning my throat swelled and ached with backed up tears, choking my voice. I was suddenly there, feeling the pain of being ripped from Ellie and Dorrie yet torn by my love for my Princess Mummy. Finally I managed to say, 'It was really, really sad for me and it was really, really sad for my . . .' I couldn't go on.

Gordon, still holding my hand, asked in a sympathetic voice, 'It was sad because — why Sharyn?' Now I was losing it. My throat still ached. I didn't want to cry but I knew it was inevitable. 'It was the only home I'd known and it was a good house, you know.' Lost in my emotions, I wasn't really aware of where I was. It felt like I was just talking with a close sympathetic friend. Gordon handed me a tissue because he could see my eyes brimming. 'Where you went next wasn't good?' he asked.

With tears rolling down my face, we talked about my devastation at being sent to the convent and the appalling abuse and beatings I was subjected to because of my bed-wetting, then about running away and life with my grandmother and mother. I may have been upset but, strangely, I felt more relaxed here in America, maybe because my mother and Australian family were not likely to see the interview, and judge me even more.

Eventually Gordon switched to me finding out my father's name, the details of my search, finding I had an American family and my excitement at flying to LA after the show, to meet them. Gordon asked my father's name and I said proudly, 'Thaddeus Killens'.

'We took the liberty of sending a crew to the home of Thaddeus Killens . . . they wanted to talk about your father . . . let me just point you to one of our monitors and here are some of your brothers and sisters, half-brother and sisters talking about your dad.' I looked at the beautiful images of Debra, Donna and Thaddeus Jr on the large screen as they spoke openly about a wonderful father who was loving, supportive and caring, the shots of their faces intercut with photos of my father I had never seen. My chest ached with love and longing for them all.

Gordon then cut to a commercial break, saying the show would return with more tapes and messages after the break. As Gordon and I chatted briefly, I noticed many people in the audience wiping away tears. These people are crying for me, I thought, feeling a little overwhelmed. As the show was being taped and not live, almost immediately Gordon re-introduced the segment. 'We're talking with Sharyn Crystal . . .'

Gordon recapped my story and pointed to the screen again, to another videotape of my family. Debra, Donna and Thaddeus spoke of genuine love and immediate acceptance of me by my father, had he known of my existence. How he would have enveloped me into their family and they wanted to make up for that loss. I couldn't speak. I thought my heart would burst and break at the same time.

'You're going from here to Los Angeles. You're going to meet them for the first time. You've obviously had phone calls . . . please indulge us, I want to bring one caller to air. Hello, are you there?' said Gordon. 'You are Sharyn's sister Donna is that correct?'

'Good morning Sharyn, good morning Gordon,' said Donna's voice, wafting through the studio. The now-smiling audience applauded. Oh wow! This was almost too much — what Gordon and his crew had done for me with the wonderful tapes and now Donna on the phone! Gordon thoughtfully grabbed a couple more tissues and put them in my hand as Donna said how much she loved me and couldn't wait to see me. Then she talked about our father, about the wonderful man he was. Of how she likened him to a Bill Cosby type character, spending quality time with his children even though he worked two jobs, sixteen hours a day, to support them and look after them; he always had time for them all.

'Donna, I want you to stay there but I know you have your brother and sisters on the phone . . . can you put them on? I'd just like to get the family together here on the phone,' said Gordon. 'Are you there? Hello?' Looking into the audience I laughed. I can't believe this I thought, shaking my head in disbelief, waiting to hear their voices. Instead, it was a sound technician's voice, 'Gordon, we seem to be having a problem with that.'

'Oh, OK. Do you want to take a break or do you want to send someone out?' said Gordon. Oh no, a technical hitch, I thought. Well, I guess I'll be in LA soon enough.

'No, let me send somebody out,' said the voice.

Gordon jumped up and marched across the studio, mumbling to himself, as I sat taking the brief moment to collect my thoughts after the emotional videotapes. He opened a door, closed it, then, calling for the audio guy, he started back across the studio towards the door I'd entered which was over behind me. There were a few soft laughs from the audience but, on the whole, we all waited patiently. I felt a bit embarrassed for Gordon and his team, that he was having technical problems on national television. He ran the last few meters to the door and opened it, talking to himself, it seemed. Behind me, he took a male-voiced person by the hand and pulled him into the studio, at the same time saying, 'Thaddeus. Sandra. Debra.' Stunned, I swivelled around and couldn't believe my eyes. Oh my Lord, there they were!

The audience went absolutely wild, jumping to their feet, clapping, cheering and crying. Thaddeus was the first across the studio into my arms, then Sandra and Debra. We held each other in a joint hug, all sobbing then breaking apart to finally look at each other's faces. It was one of the most emotionally charged moments of my life, next to the birth of my two sons and seeing my father's photo for the first time. Nothing would ever again come close. I was finally holding my family, my flesh and blood.

'Oh this is so beautiful . . . what have you done, Gordon Elliot?' was all I could manage to say, crying as Gordon directed us to the extra chairs which had magically appeared. Gordon himself, was moist-eyed and obviously genuinely moved by our story. We tried to sit down but kept hugging each other, not wanting to let go. Still applauding, the audience cried and laughed with us. Eventually, Gordon managed to settle us in our seats.

'Do you know there's something really bitter sweet about this?' said Gordon, on his haunches to my right and holding my hand, 'The perfect family you could have had, was there but you never knew.'

My sisters almost both spoke at once. 'Yeah, but we're here now,' said Sandra.

'We want to make up for lost time,' said Debra, as the smiling audience applauded again. We all chatted and laughed, overwhelmed by the enormity of the moment.

'All I can say is, how blessed am I? This is beautiful,' I said, looking for a fresh tissue.

'For the first time in her life, Sharyn Crystal is holding hands with her sisters and her brother after spending her existence up until this point trying to find her family,' said Gordon.

The rest of the show sped by as we talked about our families and I gushed about my mother saying she was beautiful, kind and generous to a fault. Why? Maybe I was hoping this time she would approve if she saw the show. My sisters and brother talked about finding they had an older sister and how they had instantly loved me. It didn't seem real but it was.

'What does it mean when this kind of thing happens to a family? Can you let us in this window for you?' asked Gordon, directing the question to me.

'For me? This is Heaven . . . I've waited a lifetime to find this beautiful family and, for me, I've been living in limbo in Australia. All my family in Australia are blue-eyed blonds . . . but now I can find out about me and who I am,' I said from my heart. More chatting and laughing with Gordon and the mood shifted from emotion and poignancy to delight and celebration. After almost thirty minutes, our segment was over.

We crowded into the Green Room after the show, still laughing and all talking at once as champagne was poured. But the surprises weren't over. Gordon had arranged a belated birthday cake for me, accompanied by an American cousin, Lesley, who lived in New York and who had also been in the audience. Apparently, her grandfather and my father had been brothers. It was a magical experience, holding my sisters' and brother's hands. We couldn't let go, hugging and kissing and loving every minute of it. We all gratefully thanked Gordon and his team; then we were on our way.

A quick photo shoot outside the studios in front of yet another stretch limousine assigned to take us to the airport and we drove away. As we finished off our bottle of champagne laughing and chatting, we luxuriated in the soft leather seats and expansive interior, feeling very special.

'Hey Sis, are you a superstar in Australia?' asked Thaddeus.

'No,' I laughed. 'Why?'

'Man, they must love you Down Under. I ain't never been in no limousines and I ain't never been on a plane before, let alone two, and *two* international television shows. Man, this is so cool!'

'Well, little brother, I'm not a superstar. It's just that the whole world loves our story,' I said.

Sandra filled me in how firstly, the *Midday* show people had sent limousines to take them all to Hollywood for the satellite cross and how the *Gordon Elliott Show* had arranged to interview and videotape them for the show. Then they sent more limousines to pick them up and whisk them off for their flight to New York, then on to stay in a fabulous hotel before being taken to the studio that morning. It was an exciting time for my new family and Thaddeus in particular was really enjoying himself: as he had said on the show, 'Man, it's cool to have another sister!'

The late-afternoon flight back to LA was wonderful. Seated together, we talked excitedly about everything and our miracle of finding each other, becoming a little boisterous as once again, the flight attendant refilled our glasses with champagne. The surrounding passengers couldn't help but overhear our conversation and were intrigued so we told them our story. They loved it. About an hour out of LA we hit rough weather. As the plane bounced and shuddered, Debra became quite nervous.

'I hope this baby ain't gonna crash. This is why Donna won't fly and wouldn't come with us,' she said, trembling.

'Come on Deb, do you think God held hands with our father to put us all together like this for it all to end with the plane falling out of the sky? I hardly think so,' I said confidently. 'Sister, we're going to grow old together'.*

LOS ANGELES WAS HOT compared to New York, even though it was around ten at night when we landed. Debra had left her car at the airport so we piled in to her shiny Jaguar, a very fine car with interior wood panelling and the rich smell of leather.

By the time we arrived at Donna's apartment on Crenshaw Boulevard it was late. Still, it seemed the whole neighbourhood

---

* To watch the *Midday with Kerri-Anne* television segment, go to www.TheInconvenientChild-Midday.com and to see the *Gordon Elliott Show* segment, go to www.TheInconvenientChild-Gordon.com

had come out to welcome us. My petite youngest sister rushed over and nearly bowled me over with her embrace, her mischievous dimpled smile and big brown eyes alive with excitement. I adored her instantly. I was then introduced to Debra's daughters, my nieces Kristina and Je'Don, both aged in their early twenties, and Sandra's young daughter Jessica. Too excited to sleep, Kristina's baby daughter Alicia was there, as well as a few neighbours, including the motherly Mrs D from the apartment downstairs and Betty and her daughter Cheryl from the apartment across the way. It had to be around two before everyone left, leaving Donna and I to clean up.

I already knew a lot about my remarkable sister from our phone calls when she'd told me stories of our father but this night was very special for both of us. We sat down quietly with a cool drink each; mine alcoholic and Donna's just juice. (A non-drinker, I was soon to discover she was very anti-drugs and alcohol and anything mind-altering. Amazingly, she can have the best time on a dance floor and be stone cold sober.) We bonded immediately over another in-depth talk about our father. She pointed to her parents' wedding photo on her mantelpiece in the living room. 'Your mother and my father, I mean our father, look wonderful together,' I said.

'You know, Big Sister, we call our father "Daddy". All of Daddy's children call him that. He would love it if you called him "Daddy" and so would we.' That was it. I was off again, crying like a baby.

The following morning, Donna, an accountant, had to go to work so she was dressed and headed out the door by seven.

'Now Big Sis, do *not* go out there until I come home. This is LA, not Sydney. I promise you I'll take you out for a tour when I get home around five o'clock, OK? But, here is a spare key, anyway, and my work number. Call me at anytime but do not use that key until I come home.'

An hour later, standing on the balcony of Donna's apartment overlooking Crenshaw Boulevard and cradling a hot coffee, I looked into my father's world — Los Angeles South Central. Across the road lay the Crenshaw Mall, a huge shopping complex and what seemed like thousands of cars and people, walking along the street. Slowly, I realised every single one of them was black. Stay indoors?

No way. This was my father's territory and I was the original little black street kid from a totally white country. How was I going to feel fear here? I showered, dressed in my most comfortable jeans and t-shirt and was out the door so fast.

Crenshaw Boulevard was really something. I checked out the cars as they drove past. Every driver and the occupants were African-American. Well, who is to say what their heritage was — all I know is, everyone was black. Wandering through the mall I was surrounded by hundreds of black people and none of them were staring at me. Not one! I looked just like everybody else. Only once before, in Durban, had I experienced this. But somehow this was different: a wonderful feeling of belonging. I felt very comfortable here — a feeling of kin, of being exactly where I should be. For the first time in my life I was living in an all-black community and it felt wonderful — like I had finally found home.

The stores were bright and glowing with multi-coloured Christmas lights and decorations and full of tastes and sights I'd never seen before. I wandered through a toyshop filled with an array of black dolls and even black Barbie dolls and every picture book was filled with stories of black children and black families. The Nike gear and sneakers were selling for only fifty dollars. Back home I'd have to pay up to two hundred and beyond for such shoes. There were real American hamburgers and hot dogs and, instead of hearing boring muzak, I grooved along to Wilson Picket and Marvin Gaye. Intending to pick up a few grocery items in a supermarket, and overwhelmed by the sheer choice of products, I asked a little old black woman where I could find the tomato sauce.

'Where you from, child?' she asked, hearing my accent.

'Australia, Ma'am,' I said.

'Well, Crocodile Dundee!' she shouted, laughing.

I thought she was wonderful. I told her the whole story of my stay in America and she loved it, hugging me and promising to watch the show when it went to air in America the following Tuesday. I wondered if Paul Hogan knew he was such a hero in downtown Crenshaw Boulevard. I felt very proud.

All my sisters called me several times through the day. Donna was not happy I'd gone out on my own but, true to her word, we met my sisters later for dinner in a nearby restaurant and bar.

THE GORDON ELLIOTT SHOW went to air nationally at 2 pm Los Angeles time on Tuesday, November 12. My family didn't go to work that day but instead congregated at Donna's apartment for lunch, to watch the program together. Gathered around the television set, we chatted and laughed in nervous anticipation as the showtime arrived. None of us could really remember much of what had happened at the time, due mainly to excitement and our overwhelming emotions. The show started and as the story of my early childhood and difficulties unfolded, one by one, my sisters wept quietly. During the commercial break, we all hugged and cried. They were horrified at what I had been through in my childhood and my quest for love and family acceptance. I hadn't realised they didn't really know my full story and, on both shows, had not seen my interview segments before their appearance. I'd told them bits during all our phone calls but of course we'd talked mainly about them and my father, a bit about my mother and mostly my current life.

We all screamed with delight as Gordon opened the door and we were united on national television, clapping and cheering and crying with the audience. As we drank champagne and replayed the segment, commenting and laughing and pointing at ourselves, I thanked God again for giving me this wonderful loving family. The rest of the day and evening was a celebration with friends and neighbours stopping by and the segment played over and over again.

Once the show had aired, unbelievable things began to happen. Apparently, the station was bombarded with calls from people who had loved the show. The power of television never ceases to amaze me; however, this response was incredible. It was understandable the Aussie family I had bumped into at LA airport should remember me: Sydney only had five television channels and I'm only one of a handful of black people in the public eye in Australia. American television, on the other hand, had literally hundreds of channels and dozens of talk shows dominating daytime television, with black Americans and a multitude of nationalities appearing every day. (I'd watched quite a few since my arrival and the truth was: I just loved US television). Many people had amazing stories to tell but, honestly, once the show was over I could recall the story but would never have recognised the face.

My brother Thaddeus wanted to take me to Universal Studios but first we had to hire a car for him to drive. There was no way I was driving in a strange country, on the wrong side of the road and the wrong side of the car!

Thad loved the white sporty car I'd chosen and turning up the 'doof-doof' music, we headed off to Universal Studios. Cruising along the freeway listening to some hip-hop station with my wonderful brother sitting relaxed behind the wheel, I was wondering how far Universal Studios was from my sister's house when I saw mountains. 'Are they mountains?' I squealed.

'Oops,' he said sheepishly, sitting up straighter in the jazzy car, 'I must have missed that exit on the freeway.' Are you kidding me, little brother? He just loved the terrific little car and had decided the two of us would go for a very long drive. I laughed and laughed.

Eventually we arrived at Universal and had a great day seeing the movie sets and rides.

'What else do you want to do?' asked Thad.

'I would love to go to Hollywood,' I said.

'OK, let's go.' We walked for ages trying to find the car park. Lost, we decided to ask directions in a souvenir shop. As we walked in, there was Whoopi Goldberg. My brother jumped around. 'Hey, I know who you are,' he said.

I took one look at the person who was the image of Whoopi and, though I have yet to meet her, I just knew this person was much too tall. Rather than spoil my brother's fun, I headed towards the teenage blonde behind the counter, to ask directions to the car park. She took one look at me and flipped out.

'Oh my God! I know who *you* are!' she screamed, racing around the counter to me. 'You're the lady on television from Australia.' Then she turned to Thaddeus and threw her arms around him, giving him a big hug. 'And you are her brother. Oh my God, I just loved that show! It was great,' she said, now turning to hug me. 'My Mom loved it too. Wait till I tell her.' Now she was crying and laughing — it was wonderful. 'Whoopi' joined in the fun, wanting to know the story. Ten minutes later we left two very excited people and with the right directions, found the car park.

'Wow!' said Thad. 'Whoever thought that would happen?' He was feeling so proud and so was I.

'Do you know, little brother, I think God likes us,' I said, smiling.

Stopping on the way at a Taco Bell for food, I explained I'd never eaten Taco Bell so he should order for me at the speaker.

'Good morning, may I take your order please?' said the distorted voice of a woman. As Thad began ordering, I leaned over and said, 'Oh, don't forget the serviettes.'

My brother doubled up, laughing. 'Soyviettes? What is that? A type of sauce?' he asked, pronouncing it 'saas' which started me laughing. We couldn't stop and giggles then came through the speaker box, our laughter infectious. I tried desperately to think of another name.

'Napkins,' I said.

'Oh, napkins! Napkins,' said my brother to the speaker box. 'My sister comes from Australia. She wants napkins!' It was hysterical but it was one of those times when you really had to be there to appreciate it, I think.

Hollywood was fun but nothing like I imagined. The Walk of Fame reminded me of Kings Cross in Sydney — just one long strip of road and a footpath covered with stars and movie stars' names on them. In a bar we had a drink and watched Shaquille O'Neill playing basketball on television then we took photos up and down Hollywood Boulevard. I was very excited.

Donna and I had made plans to have a quiet, early dinner before we met Debra and Sandra at a nightclub. The restaurant was down in South Central, a truly fine seafood place. I was a cigarette smoker in those days. The restaurant had a smoking lounge but did not sell cigarettes. I told Donna that on the way in I had noticed a liquor store across the road.

'No, Big Sis, you can't go walking alone out there. This is America not Sydney. You can't go out there.'

After much protesting, I assured her I'd let the doorman know where I was going and would ask him to keep his eyes on me as I crossed the road. I was not worried as the doorman looked exactly like Mike Tyson. No one was going to mess with that man. He promised to watch me as I headed across the road but to be safe, I put on my street smarts, carefully checking out everything around me. After all, I was the black street kid from Kings Cross — not that my family knew that yet. The street was deserted and my eyes were wide open. I could understand my sister's concerns; even in Australia I knew the reputation of parts of South Central but I also knew I had Daddy walking by my side. I felt very safe in this community and felt no fear; these were my people.

Two young black women walked out of the liquor store carrying bottles of alcohol. I kept my eyes ahead as we strolled by each other. All of a sudden, one of them did a double-take.

'Jesus, I know who you are,' she said, her sudden exclamation making me jump slightly. 'You're the lady on television. Oh, my God!' Instantly, she was hugging me and right up close in my face. 'I bet I know what you're doing. I bet you're having dinner over there at Ma Belles with the sister who didn't go to meet up with you in New York.'

I couldn't believe this conversation was happening. She went on and on, telling me she and her momma, her sister and her cousin had loved the show and cried buckets of tears. She told me I was so blessed and I agreed with her. After many more hugs, these two caring women wished me luck and went on their way. I bought the cigarettes in the liquor store and returned to the restaurant to be greeted by the doorman.

'Ma'am, I was keepin' an eye out for ya. It seemed fine. You OK?'

I assured him I was feeling fine and headed back to tell the tale to my little sister.

Later that evening, we celebrated in grand style in a Los Angeles nightclub, the likes I have never seen before. The night was MC'd by a well-known actor and comedian, Renaldo Rey. Unbelievably, *he* had also seen the show and relayed my story to the hundreds of people in the nightclub, then invited my sisters and me onto the stage where we were given a standing ovation and free drinks all night long! By this time, I had been introduced to Long Island Tea, a very potent drink.

I met so many people that evening, including Renaldo, who told me he'd spent a lot of time in Sydney and had loved it. As I watched the patrons dancing to some of the best R&B I'd ever heard in my life, played by an LA band that should have been winning Grammy Awards, I began to notice how different to me, these black people were. Watching the way they moved and greeted each other, their dress style and general demeanour, I realised how white I was — not black at all! Wasn't this ironic? I would have to get my sisters to show me how to be black! And the first lesson was how to dance.

I love to dance but my sisters *really* knew how to dance. Their sense of rhythm was amazing, like they had moves between the moves. I was mesmerized as they all performed a dance called the Electric Slide, a very cool and funky version of the Nutbush or Bus Stop. (I found out later it was created by American dancer Ric Silver and originally called 'the Electric'.) Eventually they pulled me, protesting, into the middle of at least a hundred people and showed me the moves. At first I had two left feet but, given time, I was grooving with the best of them.

WE ARRIVED HOME at four in the morning and by nine, we were dressed for Church. The West Angeles Church of God in Christ on Crenshaw Boulevard is the local church for many of America's famous African-Americans, including Stevie Wonder and Denzel Washington who are often seen attending with their wives and children. But nothing could have prepared me for the next hour of my life.

On arrival, hundreds of people were queued up dressed in their Sunday best, the women in hats and very stylish dresses and men in suits and ties. Little girls flounced in cute dresses and patent-leather shoes, their hair braided with ribbons, and young boys wore little suits. The building was very modern and featured a marble entranceway, over which sat a tall cross surrounded by a colourful mosaic. Inside the vast auditorium, a band of musicians and a huge choir of some of the most harmonious voices ever assembled sat resplendent in white robes in front of six towering modern stained glass windows. In a recess on the wall over the altar hung the biggest gold cross I had ever seen. The Preacher, Reverend Charles Blake, performed an inspiring service, appropriately about family.

I loved Gospel Church. It far outweighed anything I had ever seen or heard before. The congregation called out and answered the preacher and sang and danced with joy and love. I stood beside my sisters and my brother, my cheeks wet with tears of gratitude to God for putting me in this space. Toward the end of the service, the Reverend Blake asked us all to close our eyes. 'If anyone has not asked God for forgiveness for something they are so ashamed of they have never told anyone, please raise your hand.'

Awash with shame, memories rushed back of the desperate child, kneeling and drinking the 'toilet water'. Then I remembered my life of alcohol and drugs and the day I had almost become a junkie mother. I thought of the decadence and wild nights in Kings Cross, of promiscuity, intolerance, impatience, anger and hurtful remarks. I slowly put my hand in the air. The preacher invited those with raised hands to join him at the altar. As I stepped past the loving grasp of my sisters and walked towards the altar, I was accompanied by about thirty people. Some I guessed were only eight, nine and ten years old. Are you kidding, I thought. What could you ever have done wrong?

We were led into an anti room and joined by two more preachers, who asked us to again close our eyes and focus completely on whatever it was we needed forgiven. I took myself to those places of shame. The preacher prayed and, miraculously, I felt a powerful sensation like a wind rush through my body. Almost as if God had breathed a cool, cleansing breath through me. It was astonishing.

The preacher asked us to open our eyes and as he said another prayer, people began crying and weeping softly. The door opened and the first person I saw was Donna. I walked into her arms and as she hugged me I quietly whispered, 'Thank you, God.'

On our way home, Donna called into a service station convenience store to buy grocery items for the traditional after-church breakfast Daddy used to cook. She said it was time I tried Daddy's favourite: bacon, grits and juice. Waiting in the car, I noticed a woman filling her car and staring at me. Unexpectedly, she stopped and began running toward me, calling out and waving her arms around. Something terrible must be happening I thought, feeling panic as I looked around to the back of the car. Suddenly the woman was beside me, gesturing for me to get out.

'I knew it was you! I knew it was! You're the lady from Australia. Hallelujah! God bless you. Your story is a miracle!' she said, her hands on my shoulders, then hugging me. Still feeling a little shaken, I hugged her back, thinking: I can't believe all this attention. From the store, Donna had seen what was happening and had rushed over. When she realised it was another fan, she smiled. 'People just love our story!' she said, shaking her head in wonder.

That afternoon, Donna and I had been mucking around as we tried on clothes in a Nieman Marcus department store. We were dancing around in hats and odd shoes and just loving being sisters, behaving and giggling like a couple of kids. An elegantly dressed woman approached us and in a soft voice said, 'I saw you two on television. I am so happy for you.' Standing there blushing in our crazy clothes, we thanked her and grinned. As we walked away, Donna said behind her hand, 'Wouldn't you have thought we could have been looking our glamorous best?'

It didn't stop. People made a fuss of us; we were recognised all over California, even on a trip to Magic Mountain with my sister Sandra and her daughter Jessica.

DONNA ORGANISED an elegant cocktail party to celebrate my arrival and invited the family and many of her friends to meet me. Her apartment overflowed with very cool-looking African-American people: women in a style of clothing and hairdos I'd never seen before and sleek, sensational-looking men. I had never experienced a party like it. At one stage, we gathered around and watched the *Gordon Elliott Show* video. The room hushed as I told my story then erupted with the television audience when my family walked through the door. Amongst the crowd were comedians, lanky basketball stars, Donna's boss plus members of the Los Angeles Police Department, who gave me a badge and made me an honorary member of the LAPD. Everyone was so excited the Killens clan had come together in this miracle.

CHAPTER NINETEEN

We Are Family

MY PRECIOUS SISTERS appeared similar in personality although their individuality became apparent as I spent time with them. Donna, for instance, is the cutest, tiniest and smartest of us all. She is very cool and hip but she is also spiritual, and it's she who taught me about my 'roots'.

A few days after the cocktail party, Donna and I drove to a small community museum called Museum In Black, where she introduced me to its owner. As she chatted to him I looked around at the African tribal masks and carvings, drums and jewellery. There were also fascinating items of clothing, photographs, albums and household objects filling every spare bit of space, symbolising African American culture over the decades. A bookcase was devoted to books on black celebrities and leaders and I was intrigued by the placards celebrating the names of black inventors and claims of their creations — such as a traffic signal, the dustpan, the rolling pin, a refrigerated railroad car and a type of pencil sharpener.

Then Donna led me through a beaded curtain into a smallish room and it was here I saw the reality of black slavery and the fight for civil rights. Lining a wall were mounted drawings of slave ships and scenes depicting unimaginable cruelty and degradation on board. I stared in astonishment at diagrams of racks on a slave ship's lower deck, showing the placement of hundreds of wretched souls, crammed shoulder to shoulder. There were other drawings on the wall of capture, shipment and the suffering endured in every day life on plantations; there were photos of slaves, of injuries inflicted by whipping, posters advertising the arrival of slave shipments and a copy of a hand written receipt for the sale of a slave. Donna stood quietly beside me as I tried to understand what I was seeing. I thought I knew about slavery, after all I had seen *Roots*, but confronted with this I realised my Australian education was sadly lacking and I knew nothing.

We moved on to the display covering racial violence, which had sickening graphic photos of lynchings; black people hanging from ropes tied to tree branches with crowds of white people looking on, including women and children! There were burning crosses, the Ku Klux Klan and a mass grave of bodies. I starred in shock, struggling to comprehend these unimaginable images of brutality.

Donna took my arm and silently led me to the next section on segregation and the status of African-Americans as 'non-persons' and their fight for Civil Rights. Slowly following the exhibits along the walls, I read the segregation memorabilia and signs like COLORED SERVED IN REAR, *Colored Waiting Room* and *Drinking Fountain* with an arrow to *White* and an arrow to *Black*. There were ads for minstrel shows and product packets with derogatory names like Sambo and Brown Beauty tobacco and Black Boy and shelves of black dolls and ornaments in all sizes, particularly of 'Aunt Jemima' and 'Mammy'. There were photos and information on Rosa Parkes and the Montgomery Bus Boycott, the Little Rock Nine, the Greensboro Sit-ins, the Freedom Riders and of course, Dr Martin Luther King and the March on Washington for Jobs and Freedom, then the Selma to Montgomery Marches which I remembered seeing on television in my early teens. Donna stood beside me, reverently pointing to items and explaining the circumstances and their significance.

Feeling shaken at the insanity and cruelty on the walls, I turned my attention to the glass-topped display cases and chests in the centre of the room. Some stone rings the size of small donuts intrigued me, until I read they were hung on slave's bodies in clusters of fifty or more, to impede escape. I couldn't bring myself to imagine what the stains marking some of them were. There were chains used for slave transportation and weights used for drowning slaves. I stared in confusion at a number of different sized half-discs that looked as though they clamped together but I couldn't figure out their use.

Then I felt sick as I realised they were transportation shackles and the tiniest sizes were used for babies and little children. I could take no more. I ran through the beaded doorway, through the shop front and out into the car park, my hand covering my mouth and tears streaming down my face.

Donna appeared beside me and put her arm around my shoulder. 'It's a disgraceful chapter in America's history but it needs to be shown. To be seen,' she said. 'We will never understand the cruelty and the reasons but this is your heritage — who you are. Be proud of that and rejoice in what we have achieved through unimaginable hardship.'

At home we read books and watched films on African-American culture and society. Donna talked to me about the history of black America, discussing Malcolm X and the black American music scene. This little bundle of female strength with a passionate sense of solidarity often had me enthralled with her knowledge of our history and her black pride.

I MOVED TO DEBRA'S after a week with Donna and we had a wonderful sisters' bonding time. Debra loves to shop and enjoys the finer things of life: smart cars, beautiful homes, expensive jewellery — and did I mention stylish clothes which, incidentally, are also her business. This was real 'girlfriend time'. She took me to fine restaurants with her girlfriends who, like her, were all dressed in the latest fashions and drove sleek sports cars. Tall and beautiful, Debra's elegance is reflected in the way she chooses to live. Her home was filled with fine furniture and paintings, tastefully decorated with Deb's unique style. As the firstborn, Debra was Daddy's little girl, very loved and very close to Daddy. He spoiled her and she has expected every other man to follow suit.

As I've already mentioned, Debra drove a late model Jaguar at the time and together we went to see the first home Daddy bought for the family in Watts, then to his last family home in Compton, the place my friend Barry had photographed and visited with Mrs Harrington.

From the little I'd learned of Watts, I knew it was a predominately black neighbourhood and was the scene of race riots in August 1965. I also remembered reading that in 1992, South Central Los Angeles, including Watts, was the scene of the Rodney King race riots. Debra explained how the riots had started, that Rodney King, an African-American had been brutally beaten by four white police officers during an arrest. The police officers were charged and after a lengthy trial they were acquitted. Evidently, the apparent injustice sparked the riots, then arsonists burned down supermarkets, restaurants, drug stores and mini-malls causing a billion dollars in damages and fifty-three people died. Debra had read that many of the crimes were gang-motivated or perpetrated with snipers firing at police as they tried to control the situation until the army and marines eventually restored order after six days.

Oh dear, what were we thinking? Here we were, my sister Debra driving me through Watts in her sparkling blue Jag to show me Daddy's first home. We arrived at a two-storey vacant building, the once-pristine white-stucco walls now grubby and smeared and the painted porch canopy, steps and window trim a grimy blue grey. We couldn't go inside but took photos of each of us sitting on the stoop at to the front door. Staring at the house, I felt close to Daddy, knowing this was the first home he had bought for the family. Debra pointed out the different rooms and reminisced briefly then, seemingly nervous, headed back to the car.

'Are you OK?' I asked.

'Sure, it's just that this is still not a safe place and nobody feels totally safe in Watts,' she said apologetically, as she turned the key in the ignition.

The car refused to start. She tried again and again.

'Oh no, we just *can't* break down in Watts!' said Debra, panic rising in her voice.

I noticed two men next door, working on their car in the driveway. As I started to get out of the car, Debra tried to grab my arm but missed.

'Sister, this is not Sydney. This is Watts'.

I called over to the young men that our car wouldn't start and would they mind helping us. As they approached us, Debra hurriedly locked her door but they turned out to be very helpful. Looking under the hood, they diagnosed a flat battery and finding jumper leads, got us started. No problem. Relieved, we thanked them and drove off.

Pulling up at the kerb outside Daddy's last known address, I thought of my friend Barry from Cronulla and smiled imagining him, a white boy, in Compton.

The Latino woman Barry had spoken to was not at home but I recognised the house from Barry's photo. The garden had died back for winter but there were still a few crimson flowers on the untamed bougainvillea. Debra talked about family occasions and events as memories came flooding back to her. As I listened I gazed at the house. This house and street had been my strongest lead in my search and I couldn't quite believe I was actually here. Before walking down the street, we took a couple of photos of us standing on the path in the front garden.

Then I had the pleasure of meeting the delightful and wickedly funny Mrs Harrington. She greeted us warmly and invited us into her neat home for coffee. Petite with mischievous eyes, and colourfully dressed, I felt an instant connection with this remarkable woman who had played such a significant part in finding my family. We laughed as she told us the details of Barry's visit; how she thought he might be from the IRS or an encyclopaedia salesman but, whoever he was, there was no way he was getting past her screen door! It was so special to meet her and I thanked her profusely for following through with Barry's request to find my family.

Driving home feeling nostalgic and chatting quietly, Deb became concerned as the Jag started playing up again. Sure enough, on the freeway the engine spluttered and died. With horns honking and drivers shouting obscenities as they tried to manoeuvre around us, Deb managed to coast the car into the far lane before it stopped dead.

'Fancy breaking down in a new Jaguar on the famous Los Angeles Freeway,' I said, being no help at all and giggling. Understandably, Debra was distressed because we really needed to get off the road.

Answering our prayers, a dishevelled-looking man appeared out of nowhere. Deb put the car in neutral and he pushed us off the freeway and onto the verge. Looking around, I couldn't see a car anywhere so I was intrigued as to where he had come from. Asking him, he pointed up the hill from the freeway, to some trees.

'I live up there,' he said. I was confused because I couldn't see a house. We gave him a few dollars and thanked him for helping us, then he disappeared as quickly as he had appeared. As we waited for help, Debra explained about the homeless people in Los Angeles. This courteous and homeless man had saved us from potential serious injury.

Fortunately, it wasn't too long before a tow truck arrived and took us and the car, back to Debra's house. I think Debra was quite relieved her task of taking me to see the old family homes in Watts and Compton was over. She was happy living in her fashionable townhouse in suburban Los Angeles with all its mod cons and luxuries.

THE DRIVE TO SANDRA'S a week later, took around an hour and a half. Sandra and her young daughter lived in Lancaster, a city in the Antelope Valley about one hundred and twenty kilometres north and slightly west of Los Angeles. As she sped along the freeway I was fascinated as the scenery gradually changed from urban Los Angeles sprawl to semi-arid terrain then, eventually, to what looked to me to be desert! It might have been early winter but the weather was hot and very dry and I was glad when we arrived at Sandra's modern Spanish-style home. She explained their homes are built to compensate for the massive temperature shifts, particularly during summer when the daytime temperature is around ninety-eight degrees and drops up to thirty degrees at night.

Sandra is the middle sister with movie star looks and a slim figure who favours her mother Doris in appearance. She is softly spoken, sensitive in nature and is the voice of reason, often the peacemaker in the family. She is maternal, loves children and is a wonderful cook, inheriting Daddy's special talent.

While Sandra went to work as a dental assistant and young Jessica was at school, I kept myself busy doing housework. After all, this was the suburbs with no mega-mall to explore across the road. I cleaned and polished, washed clothes and put them in the dryer and cooked a couple of evening meals for us all.

'Oh my, look at the house. Sharyn, it's beautiful,' said Sandra admiring my handiwork, the first evening. 'Oh and the kitchen looks far too good to cook. Let's get take-out.'

'Yes please,' said Jessica jumping up and down.

'What would you like? Do you eat buffalo wings, Sharyn?' asked Sandra. 'Do you have those in Australia?' I looked at her like she was mad.

'Oh no, I don't eat buffalos,' I said, a little indignantly.

'Oh, OK then, how about we get some pizza?'

'Sounds great,' I said, relieved I wouldn't have to struggle, gnawing on some poor, tough and stringy buffalo.

Sandra is also fun-loving with a little girl's giggle and when we visited the Magic Mountain amusement park, I realised she had no fear of those big rides. In fact she and Jessica went on the fastest, wildest, most gut-wrenching rides in the park while I stood calmly and gratefully at the bottom, watching. No, thank you!

On the third day, Donna phoned. 'Honey, I am getting you back to Crenshaw Boulevard as quickly as possible. That's enough time in that desert country.'

Returning to Donna's apartment I was greeted by her neighbour, Betty. 'Honey, I was so worried about you out there in the desert. You know they got rattlesnakes there by the hundreds? My sister's girlfriend put her hand inside her clothes dryer and nearly died when she found a big rattlesnake!' she said, her eyes huge with concern. I was so glad Betty hadn't told me *before* I went to Lancaster.

That night Donna came home with take out for dinner. 'I bought some buffalo wings — have you tried them?' she said, placing a box on the kitchen counter top. What is it with these things, I thought, so I gingerly lifted the lid. Inside were marinated chicken wings — did I feel foolish! 'Its chook! I thought it was . . .' I said, cringing and too embarrassed to say the word.

'Thought it was what?' said Donna, with a knowing smile. 'And what is chook?'

'Chicken! That's what we call chickens — chooks!' We laughed till the tears ran down our cheeks.

DONNA IS THE SMARTEST of us all, as I've already mentioned. An accountant by trade, she's a career girl with her own apartment, a snappy red sports car and is on first name basis with half of Hollywoods' rappers, music and movie industry people. Everyone loves our girl. She's very hip, knowing exactly the right show to see and where to buy the latest fashion or best CDs. She was Daddy's girl, as opposed to Debra being Daddy's little girl. Even though Donna is the baby sister, she is the strongest of us all, very independent, highly educated, sassy and wise beyond her years.

Relaxing in Donna's lounge room one evening, Donna, Debra and I were having a sisterly heart to heart talk. I felt so secure in our relationship I now had the courage to ask a question that had been intriguing me. 'Why were you all so accepting of me, loving me immediately with no questions asked?' I had to know.

'The only time we ever heard our parents argue was late at night when they were in bed,' said Donna. 'We would hear Mommy say, "Thaddeus, I don't know why you didn't just get yourself a white woman. You like them so much."' I was a bit surprised at this revelation but it seemed to make sense.

'Well, perhaps my timing was right to find you now and not when Daddy was alive because my arrival might very well have upset your mother.'

'Hell no,' said Debra, 'Mommy would have loved you too. She would have welcomed you with open arms. She would have loved all of Daddy's children.' Debra smiled at me, misty-eyed. 'I remember when Daddy used to talk about his time in the Korean War. He said he wanted to adopt one of those little babies and Mommy said she would have loved it. If Daddy had known about you he would have looked after you and taken care of you, just like he always did with us. Daddy loved children and he would have loved you too, Sharyn.' Our eyes filled with tears, as they always did when we talked about our father.

'He was a good man,' said Donna. 'Not the kind of man to abandon his children. Daddy would never have done that.' No wonder I loved this family.

I learned my father was the youngest of twelve children, born and raised in North Carolina. My sisters and brother were the only members of this huge extended family living in California; the rest remained mostly in North Carolina. We talked about various cousins they were quite close to but I was especially excited to hear one of Daddy's sisters was still very much alive and spritely, aged seventy-seven. Aunt Decie was the third youngest and only remaining child of my father's generation. We called her and my sisters introduced me over the phone. As we chatted I felt an affinity with her and promised to call her often, when I arrived home in Australia. We also phoned their cousin Richard and his wife Ellen (Richard is the son of my father's oldest brother). We had a wonderful conversation and really hit it off. I knew I would be calling them often too and I knew they would really hit it off with Allan.

THE WHOLE FAMILY, including my sisters' children and grandchildren, came together to celebrate Thanksgiving on November 28. Having grown up in Australia, I had never celebrated this holiday and knew little of its significance. I was sad my time with my beloved family was quickly coming to an end and with only a few days remaining, it was a wonderful and memorable opportunity for us all to be together. Sandra arrived the evening before, laden with food. She and I stayed up most of the night watching movies while the turkey cooked, in preparation for the sumptuous Thanksgiving dinner the next day. She prepared an amazing array of food, with tastes and smells to delight any Aussie: turkey with dressing and giblet gravy, mashed potatoes, yams, green beans, macaroni and cheese and corn bread. Dessert was chocolate cake and strawberry cake.

During the afternoon, I was standing at the kitchen sink washing dishes when my brother Thaddeus walked up behind me laughing.

'What's so funny?' I asked, dripping suds as I turned around.

'Man, you are definitely your father's daughter! You and daddy have the same skinny, knock kneed legs,' he said, hollering with laughter. Delighted he could see a family resemblance, I wasn't completely sure it was a flattering compliment!

For a little girl who always craved affection, I am blessed to have found such a demonstrative family. My sisters and brother are so affectionate, always hugging me and each other and I loved how often, spontaneously, we would fall into each other arms laughing at a joke or a funny story.

Later that afternoon Donna and I were having one of our sisterly hugs when she took my face in her hands and smiling, stared at my face. It was then I realised she had a dimple in the middle of her right cheek: an unusual dimple. I also have the same dimple and had searched other people's faces for it, all my life.

'Oh Donna, we both have my dimple!' I screamed in delight. We rushed over to the wall mirror, standing side-by-side and peering to have a closer look.

'Yes,' she said laughing, 'and so did daddy!' What a special inheritance I thought, grinning.

In the afterglow of our splendid meal and feeling mellow with the effect of wine and champagne, my sisters, brother and I talked about Daddy. They told me all they could remember of him, particularly how much he loved Christmas — that he would stay up all Christmas Eve preparing the special Christmas breakfast table and putting lights on the tree, so when the children woke on Christmas morning it was truly a festive and beautiful day. He would then reset the table and cook and bake all day, as people called in to drink eggnog and share Christmas cheer. Being a chef by trade, he didn't particularly like to come home and cook but at Christmas he revelled in preparing the turkey, ham and all the vegetables and the cakes and puddings. For them, he was the greatest Santa Claus.

I was hungry for every scrap of information about him and I could picture it so clearly as they told me how Daddy loved to relax, listening to Nat King Cole music as he smoked his pipe, sitting in his rocking chair with his children sitting on the floor around him. How he'd talk about the army, about his time in the service in Korea and camaraderie with the other troops, and how he was a proud and decorated soldier.

He had adored his wife, his children, his grandchildren and friends. He was a gentle and softly spoken man with a wonderful sense of humour. He was also sociable and loved to entertain, enjoyed gardening and worked hard in three jobs to provide a good life for the family.

My brother and sisters told me how Doris had loved Daddy so much that when he passed away on October 20, 1981, she died a year later on October 21, 1982. They were both only in their fifties and much too young to go. Daddy was also a heavy cigarette smoker, even after being diagnosed with lung cancer, though it was heart problems that had caused his death. They thought Doris had probably died of a broken heart.

SAYING GOODBYE AT the airport after spending a month with my precious and new-found family was extremely difficult for us all. We didn't know how long it would be until we were all together again but we now had a bond that would last forever. Crying and hugging each one in turn, I felt my handsome brother push a letter into my hand as he whispered that it was for me to read during the flight.

Watching Los Angeles fade into the distance as the plane climbed into the clouds, I was lost in my thoughts, remembering as many details as I could of the last unbelievable month. Then I remembered the letter. Thaddeus is a gentle young soul who often gets drowned out by his noisy sisters. He is fun, yet deep and gentle at the same time, a lovely man who is the image of our father. I had asked him about special stories he had, so he wrote me a letter. I unfolded my brother's gift from my handbag.

Hey Sister Killens,

I think I may have been seven or eight years of age when I began to go to work with Dad. You see, Dad worked three jobs to support all of us. It was one of the highlights in my life with him. The reason being, more time was spent with him at those times. Our father was the father to have, even though our time was short. He was a man of love and care and understanding. He would take me to one of his jobs and show me what it was that he does. He was a supervisor of two restaurants and a building maintenance worker among others. The building maintenance job I liked the best because he had more time to show me things. He taught me how to tell the time on one of those big school clocks. I remember he would give me a dime or a quarter for every one I got right. That was cool! After work, we would go wherever I wanted to go to eat. There was a hot dog stand on the way home. That was my favourite place to eat with Dad. I miss him. On his days off when he wasn't resting, he and I would do the yard work, like cut the grass, trim trees, plant the garden of vegetables, carrots, corn and lettuces. While we worked, I would ask him questions about all I could think of. He would answer all he could and tell me it was good to ask questions. He encouraged me to stay at school. I didn't know about evil in the world because Dad never let me see it. He just loved me. Growing up in an all female family was cool, but Dad was like me in a big form. We did guy stuff, we talked guy stuff. He was my father and I his son, and that meant a lot to me. He was also my best friend and I miss him still. I loved him so much that when he got sick and passed away, I didn't know who I was mad at the most, my dad for dying, or God. Either way, there was too much I didn't understand and wanted to know. I didn't know who I was anymore. You see before, I was Little Thaddeus, Big Thaddeus' son. I felt no one could identify with what I was dealing with. I no longer had a dad. I had a mom and sisters and I didn't do the things girls do, so my life of change began. I am going to stop here for now and I am happy and sad. Happy that you are in my life and I haven't talked about Dad for a long time, and sad because I miss him so. Jesus loves you and so do I.

Your brother, Thaddeus

Gazing out over the blue Pacific far below, I felt so sad to be leaving my sisters and brother yet excited to be going home to my darling Allan and my Australian family. Could I be more blessed? I quietly thanked God for my perfect life.

CHAPTER TWENTY

The Lost Daughter, Found

MY NEW YEAR'S RESOLUTION FOR 1997 was to visit my American family once a year and to have them visit Australia in turn. The previous year had been life changing for me in its outcome and one of the most significant in my life. It had also been highly charged emotionally, confusing, confronting and very disruptive.

Allan and I settled back into our routine, very happy in our friend's home, enjoying the garden and entertaining friends and our extended family. My sons were now twenty-seven and twenty-five, both with partners and children of their own, and Allan's twins were happy teenagers.

I dreamed of bringing the two families together but, first, we had to save and pay life's bills. I sang regularly in the Sydney clubs and continued cruising on different ships, now *Fairstar* had been retired. My housekeeping work for the Barrett family in their waterfront home continued, sporadically. I had a job with them whenever I was available, which was very generous considering this arrangement had been ongoing for seventeen years. I also freelanced around various theatrical and booking agencies but I don't know how I would have survived if it were not for my rock, Allan. He continued to be a hardworking tradesman. Punctual and reliable, he produced great work and never took a day off. He is fantastic!

I called my sisters and brother regularly, our conversations sometimes lasting hours. I often spoke with Aunt Decie over the phone; her youthful voice, no nonsense attitude and alert mind belied her years. My cousins Richard and Ellen become great phone friends as did Richard's sister Pocahontas and her husband Robert.

345

My mother showed little interest in my American family, which I suppose was understandable. Over the next few years our relationship continued to be reserved at worst and, at times, very pleasant as I had no interest in her past anymore. She and Lars were happy and content in retirement on the Central Coast, close to her nieces and nephews, the children of her sisters. Quite often I would drive up from Sydney to visit her for enjoyable lunches and, occasionally, Allan and sometimes Patrick and his family would join me, particularly around Christmas, for happy family get-togethers. But she had a way of lulling me into a false sense of security.

After a pleasant lunch one afternoon, I was telling her about an industry function I had attended recently where I had sat amongst a few very well known female entertainers, who I considered close friends. As usual I was trying to impress her, recounting the conversation and how I had held and played with one friend's very young baby.

'If these people knew who you really are, what you have been, they wouldn't want to know you, you know,' she said spitefully. I flashed a forced smile and changed the subject, her words still stinging my cheeks and familiar shame crawling through my body. Would I ever not feel this way?

IN MAY 1998, I was offered full-time work in one of Sydney's busiest agencies. The timing was perfect and I was delighted. I revelled in the interesting work and my days were busy and productive. Leading up to the office were about twenty stairs and, most days, I bounded up them two at a time, ready to start the day. I was paid well and often given bonuses which, of course, I'd put towards my family reunion dream. But then, wouldn't you know it, a bill would come in or an emergency, taking all our savings. That's life I suppose.

One morning as I walked from my car to the bottom of the office stairs, I had to stop as I was short of breath. I looked up the staircase, not sure I could make it. It took a few minutes to climb and I was gasping for breath by the top. I promised myself to get fit.

Late that night, in a panic because I couldn't breathe, I woke Allan. He rushed me to emergency where, after many tests, doctors diagnosed a leaking mitral valve in my heart requiring urgent replacement. I was amazed: I'd hardly been sick a day in my life. During the health history check, I was asked if anyone in my family had a history of heart problems. Without thinking I answered 'no', then thought I should mention Anthony was diagnosed with Marfan syndrome when he was seventeen. Had I ever been checked? I said no, so the doctor performed a points test right there and then. He discovered I had all the symptoms: a high palate, double-jointed limbs and fingers, was reasonably tall for my age, my arm span was greater than my height and I had a heart murmur. I knew it was hereditary and did not miss a generation but because I'd always been so healthy, it never occurred to me I had severe problems. Had I inherited this from my father and had passed it on to my son? If so, how ironic. The father I had spent a lifetime searching for and had never met, had left me a legacy: a heart needing care.

It's important to mention, even though Anthony and I have Marfan's, there was never any proof of Daddy having it. Although he died of heart failure, he also had lung cancer and had continued to smoke after his diagnosis. My sister said they all have a heart murmur but have never had the points test done, so it's only my belief that Daddy had Marfan syndrome.

I quietly asked the doctor if, with all the drugs I had taken, cigarettes I had smoked, and the drinking, this had contributed to my heart illness. I knew that lifestyle had consequences. I'd lost friends. Some had overdosed, some had died as the result of long-term health problems from the drugs and others had died, I believe, while procuring the drugs. Years after we'd hung out smoking marijuana together, Lee was the victim of a drug deal gone wrong; dead in a New York street. Heroin. She was just twenty-five. My beautiful Paradise Club friend Sheeba's ambition had been yearning to dance with the French Folies-Bergère. Finally, she went to Paris to follow her dream. I'd enjoyed her letters from Europe telling me how great her life was. As much as she loved Paris, and as stunning as she was, she was addicted to speed, which she used daily to keep her weight down. In the end, she was murdered, found dead in

Europe, the result of a drug related incident. Obviously I'd been lucky, and sensible, to get out when I did.

The doctor assured me drugs hadn't played a part in my condition as I was destined to have these problems regardless of my lifestyle and, in fact, my lungs were clear and my general health was excellent.

On June 7, 1999, I had major heart surgery.

In the days preceding the surgery, Allan — displaying bravado but extremely concerned — came to the hospital every day after work and during the day on weekends. The entertainment industry rallied as it always does, inundating my room with flowers, telephone calls and visits.

The day before my surgery, a friend was visiting, sitting by my hospital bed when a doctor came in to explain the procedure. I asked my friend if she would stay, which she did, holding my hand as the young surgeon explained I would be sedated with a heavy anaesthetic and, while I was asleep, the doctors would open my chest and tubes would be inserted into my heart in preparation for bypass on a heart-lung machine. Once this was done, my heart would be stopped and my aorta clamped, the machine keeping me alive while the surgeon opened my heart and replaced my damaged mitral valve. Once the new mechanical valve was tested and working, my heart would be stitched closed and the aorta clamp removed. As my heart regained strength, I would be weaned off the heart-lung machine then my chest closed. I'd spend a few days in intensive care, depending on the success of the surgery. Now all I had to do was sign a piece of paper, basically promising not to sue if anything went wrong.

I felt sick as fear, disguised as adrenalin, raced through my body while my brain struggled to comprehend the enormity of the situation. I had no choice, so I took the proffered pen and obediently nodded and shakily signed the paper. As soon as the doctor walked away, my friend and I burst into tears, bravely assuring each other everything was going to be fine.

The following morning as I was wheeled into surgery, I knew many people were saying prayers for me. Their prayers were answered and everything was fine.

Sandy, my blonde friend and protector from Parramatta Girls' Home insisted she move in and care for me on my return home. We had stayed in contact on and off over the years and she had followed my singing career in the clubs. I was very weak, struggling to do anything. Sandy rose early each day to bring me a cup of tea and toast, then helped me to shower, to dress and to get to the bathroom. She'd make me comfortable on the sofa with magazines as she vacuumed under every piece of furniture in my home. We institution girls never forget how to clean and she swept and mopped, scrubbed and polished then prepared the evening meal for us all. I never wanted to let her go. She was amazing and my home shone. All Sandy asked in return was to sit in the garden with her cigarettes and enjoy a couple of beers with Allan when he came home after work. Sandy was a good friend and a caring companion when I needed it most.

One month later I was back at my desk in the office. Not able to drive for months, I travelled to and from work on two buses, making the trip hours instead of minutes long. Work was too busy for me to be running around Sydney for medical check-ups so I arranged for a nurse to come to the office once a week, to take blood for tests.

After the success of finding my father and his family, I believed anything was possible. For years, Allan and I had dreamed of owning our own home and getting off the rental merry-go-round. In June 2000, we realised our dream. We'd finally saved enough to put a deposit on a little three-bedroom house, not in expensive Sydney but one and a half hours drive north on the Central Coast and just around the corner from my son Patrick and his family. We would have to commute each day to Sydney for work but we felt the time and distance involved was only a small inconvenience.

On moving day, I unpacked for what I hoped was the last time and watched as Allan stepped out a space in the good-sized garden, where he intended to build an aviary to pursue his interest in bird breeding. Over the next few weeks we began to transform the house into our home. I did my usual spruce up of hanging new curtains and buying bright cushions but this time, I also added smart new bed linen. Allan started on the aviary and created new garden beds in readiness for spring planting. I was fifty-one, had good health again, loving families in Australia and America and now, my own home. Life was wonderful!

ONE MONTH AFTER MOVING and a year after returning to work, I couldn't make it up the stairs again. The mitral valve replacement was supposed to make my heart stronger and give me a long and more energised life. Unfortunately, I had now developed three holes in my heart, which required more surgery. This time, however, the original surgeon refused to operate, saying it was too risky as he could not guarantee success but he could sustain me with medication. Shocked at my diagnosis, I considered the irony. My heart finally felt whole and was brimming with love now that I had found my family but physically it was disintegrating, filled with holes.

I realised I couldn't continue the pace of my life, including the stress and physical demands of my busy job. I needed to concentrate on my health and treat my heart with care. So, reluctantly, I resigned from my much-loved job.

I sought a second opinion. I researched my condition, telephoning doctors and surgeons and asking questions. Eventually, at St Vincent's Hospital in Sydney, I attracted the attention of a renowned heart surgeon. He was known for his work on the hearts of tiny babies and, fortunately, he was most interested in my case.

My second surgery took place a year after diagnosis on July 12, 2001, and was again successful. Knowing what to expect this time didn't make it any less frightening. My convalescence was long, painful and frustrating. My doctors asked me not to return to work, but to take it easy and allow myself to heal completely. It had been years since I'd last had a break — really taken time off. Gradually, as my health improved, I was able to spend time with my friends, particularly from the entertainment industry. We enjoyed long and happy lunches, laughing and crying over old times. It was during this time my close friend Heather from *Fairstar*, was diagnosed with cancer. When she was well enough she joined us, until the awful day her doctors told her they could do no more. It was heartbreaking.

Through her sister on the phone, I was able to tell my beautiful friend how much I loved her, ten minutes before she passed away that December. I miss her immensely but believe she is with me every day, as one of my guardian angels.

ON SEPTEMBER 11, 2001 the world watched in horror as terrorists flew planes into the New York Trade Centre buildings. Immediately I called my family in Los Angeles and North Carolina, then my cousins in New York to make certain every one was alright. I also phoned Aunt Decie. She was quiet that morning. She said she had been talking with God.

The following week I received a call from my now good friends and cousins, Richard and his wife Ellen in North Carolina. I listened in disbelief as they invited me and Allan, as their guests, to fly to North Carolina to stay with them and celebrate a family reunion on Thanksgiving in November, me as their special guest of honour. They would introduce me to as many members of the Killens family as they could put together in one place.

'Oh my Lord, how extraordinary! Are you serious?' I asked, not quite sure I had heard correctly.

'Of course. You're very important to us you know. And we'd like Allan to come too, if he can. Let us know and we'll make the arrangements.' I was overwhelmed by their generosity and unquestioned acceptance into their huge family. The timing was uncanny as it would be five years almost to the day since I first flew to New York and met my sisters and brother. By the time Allan arrived home from work I was so excited I could hardly speak. Unfortunately, Allan couldn't take the time off work but he encouraged me to go alone.

'This is your special time. Go meet your family, Shaz,' he said smiling.

My wonderful, generous man wanted so much for me to finally find out who I was. No one had ever loved me like Allan and I knew no one ever would. For him, Australia is the best country on earth and he looked forward to the day my American family could come here to visit us. Until then, he was happy to leave the travelling to me.

With clearance from my doctors, I flew out of Sydney on Sunday October 28, 2001, just six weeks after the 9/11 tragedy. Many friends cautioned me about travelling across America at that time but I had no fear. No terrorist was going to stop me from seeing my family. I knew this was meant to be: my trip of a lifetime.

THE INTIMIDATING PRESENCE of uniformed men brandishing large automatic weapons inside the Los Angeles terminal couldn't dampen my excitement at seeing Debra, waiting to greet me at the barrier. We both squealed with delight, hugging and talking at once. The rest of my family were waiting expectantly at Donna's and the moment I walked through the door, the previous five years melted away. We spent nine glorious days in LA catching up. We explored Disneyland with my nieces Alicia and Jessica, and Debra's daughters Je'Don and Kristina, now sophisticated young women, very generously took all of us to lunch at a swish waterfront restaurant in Marina del Rey.

On Tuesday 7 November, I flew to Raleigh in North Carolina. I was so excited to finally meet my cousins Richard and Ellen that once the plane door opened I almost ran along the sky-bridge to the arrival lounge. We all recognised each other immediately. Richard, a fine-looking fit man, was smartly casual in a polo shirt and chinos and looking nowhere near his early seventies and Ellen's classic elegance hid her bubbly, outgoing personality. We hugged and kissed and I cried. Settled comfortably in the back of their car, I chatted nonstop, hardly drawing breath all the way to Goldsboro until we pulled into the driveway of a palatial home. I stopped mid-sentence. It was Tara! Honestly, the house in front of me could have been from *Gone with the Wind*. Ellen settled me into my downstairs guest quarters (an exquisitely furnished bedroom with a large ensuite bathroom). My brother Thaddeus was to join me closer to Thanksgiving and his room was upstairs, near the den and overlooking the swimming pool. I felt very special in this magnificent home being showered with generous Southern hospitality and tender loving family care.

Over the next two weeks leading up to the Thanksgiving reunion, Richard and Ellen's home was a hive of activity with gardeners, swimming pool attendants and endless deliveries of flowers, food and crates of liquor. Everything was cleaned and polished until the already magnificent home looked positively glorious. I volunteered to shine all the silver — *that* I could do well. Sitting at the massive table in their formal dining room, I rubbed and polished, holding up each item to admire my handiwork. In a daydream, I found myself transported back to Womerah Avenue as if preparing for a ship's arrival. Then memories of Ellie and Dorrie came flooding back, catching me by surprise, which concerned Ellen when she found me sniffling at my reflection in a large silver tray.

As the weeks sped by, our friendship deepened as Ellen and Richard enfolded me into the family. Ellen's style and refinement was reflected in the furnishings and ambience of the house but it was her personality which filled the home. One afternoon, I followed the sound of classical piano music wafting from the music room to find Ellen sitting at their grand piano, skilfully playing a lovely piece I didn't recognise. I tiptoed in and watched, her salt and pepper hair falling forward around her brown face as she studied the keys in the soft afternoon light. But she saw me and stopped, throwing her head back in her now familiar laugh, like the crackle of a fire.

I was drawn to her warmth and Richard's generosity of spirit. Dr Richard Killens was the son of Thomas, my father's eldest brother and was the man I imagined my father would have been.

Four days before Thanksgiving, Richard and Ellen's daughter Ronda arrived from her home in Atlanta with her cute little boy, Zachary and the festivities began. The actual Thanksgiving reunion was to be held in the function room of a Goldsboro Hotel on Thursday, where accommodation rooms had been booked for the many relatives flying in from as far away as Cleveland, Ohio, and New York, but this house was going to be the hub.

ON TUESDAY MORNING, Ellen and I drove over to Fairmont, to take the matriarch of the Killens family to lunch. Aunt Decie was the last surviving of my father's sisters and brothers and today, we would finally meet. Pulling up outside a neat clapboard house on Pine Street, there, waiting on her front porch, was Aunt Decie: a solid, smartly dressed woman looking nowhere near her eighty-four years. This was not a woman to be trifled with! As I rushed over, I was struck by her strong resemblance to my father. She held out her arms to me, a warm smile on her face and a mischievous look in her eyes, behind gold-rimmed spectacles.

'Oh Aunt Decie. I can't believe it. I'm finally here. I was frightened we would never meet,' I said, trying not to knock her over in my enthusiasm.

'Oh child. I always knew we would. I've told you, you are blessed, a miracle.'

Half an hour later we arrived at her favourite restaurant, Fullers BBQ, in Lumberton. A long low green-roofed building, inside it was large and airy with sets of tables and chairs filling the main dining area and historical prints and memorabilia around the walls. But food, and mountains of it, was what Fullers was all about. It was already busy and a little noisy with the hum of voices and clatter of plates and cutlery.

Aunt Decie went straight to the buffet, filling her plate with fried chicken while I stared in amazement at the long lit bain maries of food and delicacies I'd never seen before. Ellen rattled off the names as she pointed to some of the dishes: chitlins, fried chicken gizzards and livers, liver pudding; the different beans and pea dishes including limas, broad, navy and black-eyed peas; and collard and mustard greens. Then there was corn, mashed potatoes, okra, fried cabbage, boiled cabbage and candied yams. Amongst the usual fried dishes like chicken, there were fried oysters, fried catfish and home-made pork cracklins. Ellen said the johnny cakes were a must to try. They were crispy-fried circles of cornmeal that you topped with a little molasses, which was provided on the table. I settled for food I recognised!

Aunt Decie wasn't just special, she was unique. Great fun, smart, wise and didn't suffer fools, she readily showed impatience if you irritated her. But she loved me instantly and kept telling me so. Our conversation eventually led to her life and my father's family.

Knowing my father had been the youngest of twelve children, I asked her, 'Aunt Decie, what was the order of birth of your brothers and sisters?' She looked at me, licking her lips as she finished her chicken.

'Well child, there was Lannie. She was the firstborn. Lannie Magnolia and then came Thomas Demascus.'

'You know their full names?' I asked excitedly. She nodded with a sly grin.

'Oh, my Lord! I need a pen,' I said, rummaging through my bag for a pen and paper.

'Honey,' she said peering over her glasses. 'You go find me some peach cobbler pie and I'll tell you anything you want to know.' I jumped up and headed for the dessert bar. Staring at the array of pies and cakes, I realised I had no idea which was peach cobbler. A man standing next to me was helping himself to a generous portion of banana pudding.

'Excuse me sir, which one is peach cobbler pie?' I asked. He turned, laughing.

'Hey, you're an Aussie. You're from Australia. I love Australia. Just came back from that Great Barrier Reef and Sydney.'

'Yes, yes I am. How wonderful. Is this peach cobbler pie?' I asked, pointing and trying not to appear rude but I was in a hurry. He chatted on, filling a plate for me with peach cobbler pie. I thanked him and hurried back to the table, borrowing a pen from a waitress on the way.

Aunt Decie reeled off the names of her eleven brothers and sisters like it was yesterday.

'Well, as I said, Lannie Magnolia came first. Then the first son, Thomas Demascus, then a girl Velia Blanch. Next came Floy and her name was Floy Fenall Shefonia Emmadela. Another son, Ompson Othera then next was Katie Susan — now she was named Susan after our mother — your grandmother.' Aunt Decie paused for a moment to give me a chance to catch up, and for her to sneak a quick mouthful of peach cobbler. 'Now, next was Lucy Levenia and she was named after our grandmother Lucy, that's your great grandmother. Then came Annie Nevada but we called her Nevada not Annie. Next was another boy Thornie Clariton then me, Decie Omega, then my sister Crecie Avegga and last, your father Thaddeus Avon.' She took a deep breath and let out a long sigh. I wrote as quickly as I could but stumbled over the difficult and unusual names, so I checked the spelling with her.

Ellen winked at me as I put down the pen. Looking over the list, I was stunned. I glanced at Aunt Decie but she was quietly devouring her peach cobbler pie. How did she remember the details of all of those brothers and sisters? With misty eyes, I leaned over and kissed her. She hugged me then asked for another piece of peach pie. Ellen and I cracked up laughing.

As we set off back to Fairmont along Highway 41, I was preoccupied gazing out the window at the late-autumn rural landscape of trees still ablaze with fiery colours and fallow fields, prepared for the long winter ahead. Aunt Decie, sitting tall in the passenger's seat of Ellen's car, suddenly pointed and said, 'Turn left at the next road.' We drove a few miles along a quiet country road. The countryside was fairly flat but it interested me that many fields were separated by rows and stands of trees. 'Stop here,' she said, pointing to the side of the narrow road. Ellen pulled over and turned off the car engine.

'Child, see that house over there?' Aunt Decie pointed to the ruins of a tumble-down timber cottage, standing alone and derelict in the middle of an empty field. A few remaining sheets of iron roofing, rusted to a deep brown, leaned where they had fallen, inside the L of two remaining timber-plank walls, bleached and weathered to a soft grey. The remnants of what appeared to have been a veranda stood against one wall, the rickety structure defying gravity and seemingly unsupported. A tall crumbling chimney stood isolated, defining the other end of the cottage. 'Yes, Aunt Decie,' I answered.

'That's where your father was born. That's where *all* of us children were born and raised and they're the fields our family worked,' she said. Staring at the ramshackle remains in the soft afternoon light, I cried softly in the back seat as Aunt Decie in an unwavering voice, told me the story of my father. The story of my roots.

IN 1845, ALEXANDER KILLENS, like his father, was born a slave on a plantation in the Deep South, in the State of South Carolina. He was my great grandfather.

With the end of the Civil War and the abolition of slavery in 1865, the plantation owners were left with no work force. Alexander, by then aged twenty, his father and brothers lacked capital, like many other freedmen, so they became tenants and sharecrop farmers. Working a portion of land on the white-owned plantation in return for a share of the harvest, the family hoped one day to save enough to buy the land from the owner. Having few possessions and not owning the land or the essential tools and draft animals, they also had to barter with the planter and local merchants for these essential items and repay the rental from their meagre profits, earning barely enough for the large family to survive. I can only imagine how hard life must have been for them back then.

By late 1878, Alexander, aged thirty, and his young wife Lucy, aged twenty-one, already had three young children. In search of a better life and to escape growing racial unrest and disenfranchisement, they migrated north and finally settled in Thompson Township, a sparsely populated rural area in Robeson County, North Carolina, where a plantation owner leased Alexander a parcel of his land which included a one-room timber cabin. June 1879 saw the birth of my grandfather Jefferson, child number four of what would be seven surviving children of eleven.

As the children grew, they would join their father to work the land, but it was not productive enough to support the growing family and, in the mid-1890s, some of Jefferson's older brothers were forced to leave home to work in Robeson County's logging industry to supplement the family's income. They also collected pine tree sap used for distilling into turpentine. It was gruelling, strenuous and dirty work.

A few years later, Alexander moved the household to another sharecrop lease in White House Township, a few miles south of Union City (later renamed Fairmont). Close by lived the Arnett family. In 1898, eighteen-year-old Jefferson married sixteen-year-old Susan Arnett (my grandmother) and they leased a sharecrop in neighbouring Orrum Township the following year. By then, Susan was pregnant with their first child, daughter Lannie, so it was fortunate that a modest three-room timber cottage, with a well for water, came with the land. This was the now-tumble-down ruins Aunt Decie had taken me to see.

Susan gave birth to another eleven children over the next twenty-three years. After Lannie, came Thomas (October 1901); two girls Velia and Floy (though Floy did not survive childhood); another boy, Ompson in 1907; then three more daughters named Katie, Lucy and Nevada had all arrived by 1913. They were followed by another son, Thornie (September 1914) and then Decie — who gave me this precious information — came along in February 1917. After her came Crecie, in August 1918, and finally the last child, my father Thaddeus, born in July 1923. I had wondered most of my life who my father was and I remember feeling overwhelmed as I stared at those ruins in the field, realising my father had been born right there.

According to Aunt Decie, the elder Killens children worked the farm with their daddy while Susan took care of the cottage and the little ones. At the end of each harvest season, Jefferson would negotiate a price for his crop, repay his loan to the plantation owner then the growing family would have to survive on the remainder until the next harvest. They saved enough to own a milking cow, a necessity, then, to ensure strong and healthy children.

By 1917 when Decie was born, land values had plummeted in the state of Mississippi as the boll weevil decimated the cotton industry and was spreading rapidly east, across the Southern States. But my astute grandfather Jefferson had already switched to tobacco, for which North Carolina was becoming a leading producer.

Susan worked tirelessly bringing up her brood. She grew vegetables for the family in a plot by the house and planted an assortment of fruit trees, simmering the produce in a big kettle over the fire to make preserves for the winter, then boiling down the pulp for jelly or jams. She still had to buy the staples of brown and white sugar, flour, salt, coffee beans, vanilla beans, cream of tartar and of course medicine: castor oil, liniment, snake oil and iodine. Occasionally she could stretch the family budget to include a yard or two of calico for making shirts and dresses, settling the bill at the store once the crop was in and sold. She made, darned and mended their clothes and kept the crowded house neat and clean.

But the winters were long and cold and it would have been difficult to stretch the money and food over those months, when nothing grew in the frozen ground.

Jefferson and Susan knew an education meant a better life and opportunities for their children, so for the few months a year it was open (between the harvesting and planting seasons, like most rural schools) the Killens children walked the few miles to the local one-room schoolhouse for 'coloured' children, where they learned reading and writing. The walk was tough, particularly in sleet and freezing rain during the winter months but Susan insisted.

When Aunt Decie told me how each evening the family gathered around the fire or the table in their common room, it was like I was there with them. By oil lamp and candle light, the children would read aloud from the Bible while Jefferson smoked his pipe and Susan did her mending or made intricately stitched patchwork quilts.

'The Lord was very important to our mother,' Aunt Decie had said. 'She instilled religion into us children and constantly talked about Him. We had to say our prayers on our knees each night at bedtime and we read scriptures from the Bible at breakfast.'

On Sundays, Susan made sure the whole family never missed attending the local Baptist Church to thank the Lord for his blessings, then, they would gather at home for Sunday dinner after church. Obviously, this is where Daddy's special Sunday breakfast tradition came from. In prosperous seasons, Susan's table was piled high with an assortment of the family's favourite food, the children and their parents packed tightly around the table, which Jefferson extended periodically to accommodate the new additions.

The family felt the impact of World War I, as Jefferson, aged thirty-eight, had his number come out in the Draft draw of early October 1918. Susan was left with ten surviving children and a farm to run, in the middle of a Spanish flu epidemic sweeping Robeson County. Jefferson returned in mid-1920 and Thaddeus was born in 1923, then the family experienced loss when Velia died in 1924, aged just twenty-one. By then, Lannie and Thomas had married and moved on.

Thaddeus the baby was too young to work the fields but, as soon as he was old enough, he was at his mother's side helping with the cooking. Decie remembered he was a quiet, well-behaved boy. Reluctantly, he helped with the farming as he grew older but he was far more enthusiastic in the kitchen. Sometimes I imagine him in the fields with Jefferson. It must have been backbreaking work for the children; those summer days hot and steamy, the heat sapping their strength. I can picture them trudging back to the cottage in the setting sun, salty sweat rings marking their clothes and their bodies aching.

By the time Grandfather Jefferson died suddenly in 1929, aged in his late forties, there were eight children still at home plus four grandchildren, Flonnie, Mildred, Evander and Dorothy. Katie had brought them back home with her the year before when her husband Rufus had died from pneumonia.

But Susan didn't give up, not even when the Great Depression hit. Through their love and her determination, Susan and the children managed to keep the farm going, even with diminished demand and crop prices plummeting up to sixty percent.

As the Depression worsened, Decie said, 'Our mother tried growing different crops including potatoes and greens as well as tobacco,' and kept just enough for the hungry family, preserving and drying produce to see them through the barren winter months. I'm sure she thanked the Lord they had each other and at least, had shelter and almost sufficient food, unlike millions of others.

Aunt Decie remembered summer afternoons when Susan would sit in the cool of the gallery (or open porch) as she snapped beans or shelled peas for supper, into a wide-mouthed bowl placed between her knees. She'd watch the children play and squabble as Katie's younger ones tried to keep up with eight-year-old Thaddeus, my father. Katie was the eldest daughter living at home and no doubt Susan relied on her for comfort and support. Katie was fortunate to have secured a job at the Fairmont tobacco warehouse in 1929 and the additional income she provided helped the large family survive.

But during the cold winter of 1932 to 1933, Katie got sick. Hard work, difficult conditions and poor nutrition led to Katie contracting pulmonary tuberculosis in December. By May she was dead. Katie was only twenty-five years old.

According to Aunt Decie, 'Susan loved the Lord but she was not sure why He was testing her so.' Can you imagine! Susan, still grieving for her beloved Jefferson and now another of her precious daughters was gone too. Her small cottage must have been bursting at the seams with ten hungry children and grandchildren and it was her responsibility to feed and clothe them all.

In 1934, seventeen-year-old Decie married, giving Susan one less mouth to feed but leaving a void of company and help. But life would become harder still for Susan. Now Lucy had contracted tuberculosis and in April 1935 she also died, aged just twenty-four.

It seems the long winter of 1935 was almost Susan's undoing. Too proud to ask for help and with no additional income, she had tried everything. The story goes that often she went hungry, dividing her food portion between the youngest children. She had patched and darned their clothes till it seemed only the patches held the garments together and she used what little fuel she had only for cooking, so the cottage was constantly cold and the winter chill easily penetrated the children's thin, underfed bodies.

The Killens family were well known in the small community and Susan's strength of character and resilience no doubt admired, so the family's plight did not go unnoticed. Unexpectedly, that December, salvation was given and very gratefully received.

I can picture Susan, holding herself tall and proud as she walked into the local newspaper office and asked to speak to the editor — because later, I discovered this notice had appeared in Lumberton's local paper *The Robesonian* (on Thursday, January 2, 1936) entitled 'Grateful':

*To the Editor of the Robesonian. Susan Killens, colored, wishes
to send thanks to Mr. M. A. Power of Fairmont, high school,
white, and Miss Emley Pulley, daughter of Mr. and Mrs. Robert
Pulley of Fairmont, and all the other students for their loyalty and
kind donation for Christmas. Susan Killens and grandchildren do
heartily thank you all for your beautifully decorated half-bushel
basket full of all sorts and all different kinds of fruits and candies
and we thank you for our shoes and clothes and toys and jars of
fruits. May God bless you all, for God loveth a cheerful giver.*
SUSAN KILLENS, *Colored, Fairmont,* N. C.

It must have been Susan's lowest point, yet from what I now
know of her, she would have been resolute — determined.

THORNIE REMAINED ON THE FARM as head of the family and protector,
refusing to marry or leave, and helped Susan through the Depression
years. No doubt he knew a family of five women and girls and the
two young boys, Thaddeus and Evander, would have been an easy
target for drifters and opportunity seekers.

Although the American economy had been slowly recovering
since 1935, in 1937 it took a sudden and unexpected downturn and
within twelve months unemployment had quickly risen to almost
twelve million. President Roosevelt's agricultural policy had been to
try to decrease agricultural production, to increase prices. However,
when production was discouraged, the tenant and sharecrop farmers
like my father's family suffered most by not being able to ship enough
to market to pay rents.

In early January 1938, the unthinkable happened. My grandmother
Susan fell ill. Over the following six weeks her health continued
to deteriorate until finally, on a cold and bleak afternoon in late
February, her tired body could fight no more and she died. Her
boundless love and sheer strength of character and resilience had
seen the family through their challenging life and death struggles
right up to the day, at just fifty-six, she could no longer go on. How
could I not be in awe of this woman — my grandmother? I am so

proud to be descended from her and my father and blessed, their genes make up half of who I am.

Thaddeus in particular, was hit hard by his mother's passing. He was only five when he lost his father, so for most of his young life his mother had been his sole parent. Aunt Decie told me that, at fifteen, he was growing into a fine-looking young man. With Susan's encouragement, he had done well at school in the hope of making something of himself. But he was too young to leave and life must continue on the farm, without their beloved matriarch. Thornie met and married Emma Thompson but did not move away. Instead, Emma moved to the farm and the two ran it together and looked after the remaining children.

THADDEUS' FAVOURITE DAY had always been Sunday. Each Sunday he put on his Sunday best clothes and with the family, attended the Fairmont First Baptist Church. He was proud and careful with his appearance, which has also been confirmed by my sisters. It seems that, back then, he liked his shoes to stay shiny and dust free and would give them a final rub on the back of each leg, just before he stepped into church. Everybody dressed up for church and enjoyed the opportunity it gave the families for social contact in the small community. Over the sixty years the family had lived in the area, Fairmont had evolved from a sleepy settlement into a bustling little town.

After church, seventeen-year-old Thaddeus liked to linger and gaze at the pictures of ships on advertising posters in the drugstore and general store windows. He had made up his mind he was going to travel. Apparently, sometimes self-assured 'coloured' girls in the small community vied for his attention but he would never allow himself to become completely distracted from his dream of seeing the world.

With the outbreak of war in Europe in 1939, America, though not at war, supported her allies with ships and weaponry, creating millions of jobs and consequently ending the Depression. Life on the farm became busy as demand for agricultural products increased. When America declared war on December 8, 1941, after Pearl

Harbour was attacked, Thaddeus and his remaining brothers were given occupational exemption from the Draft because of labour shortages in agriculture. Although the economy was booming, the huge demand for goods outstripped supply so, in early 1942, rationing was introduced. According to Aunt Decie, suddenly everyday items like butter, sugar, tea, coffee, meat and lard became luxuries, and essentials like firewood, coal and gasoline were almost impossible to get.

Thaddeus considered joining the large numbers of young men migrating from poor Southern farms, north to the munitions centres; but farming was all he knew and their crops and produce were needed for the war effort.

With the Surrender in the Pacific, the war officially ended in late 1945. A family meeting was called to discuss their future. Some wanted to stay on the farm and others, wanted to go and seek their fortunes.

Twenty-one-year-old Thaddeus wanted more than farm life. He had seen a recruitment poster in the post office in Fairmont. It read:

ENROLL

AMERICAN
MERCHANT
MARINE

Special Training
deck department, engineering, radio, steward, cooks etc.

Sign up to-day!
U.S. Maritime Service,
321 Chestnut Street, Philadelphia, PA

No doubt, that's what had caught his eye — cooks. There was no point signing up with the American Navy. He knew it was difficult as the forces still had a policy of racial restriction and segregation. But the Merchant Marine had a more lenient policy and had integrated crews on their Liberty ships.

I'm sure it was a big decision to leave the only home he'd ever known but with his siblings' blessings, he bought a bus ticket north, to Philadelphia. He signed up at the recruitment office on Chestnut Street and, after passing his medical, was shipped to the massive Sheepshead Bay Training Station in Brooklyn, New York. He did six weeks' basic training as an apprentice seaman, learning rules and regulations. He would also have learned to prepare for emergencies like the seriousness of fire at sea, how to swim under burning oil, how to use lifeboats, gasmasks, rescue equipment and basic gunnery skills. After passing induction, he was transferred for three weeks of practical duty aboard one of the Maritime Service Training Ships, operating on Long Island Sound and Chesapeake Bay. It was here, in addition to general deck duties training, he would have commenced training as a messman: a good plan to work his way up to cooks' and bakers' school.

At the end of World War II, Japan was occupied by the Allied Powers, led by the United States with contributions from Australia, among other countries. Thaddeus' first ship in 1946 was the USS *Marine Phoenix*, a Liberty ship transporting occupation troops and supplies from Seattle, Washington to Japan. She then loaded homeward-bound equipment and veterans of the Pacific campaigns and returned them to the United States of America. In early 1947, Thaddeus was transferred to the *F. Southall Farrar*, another Liberty ship and, by late that year, he'd sailed back and forth across the Pacific, delivering supplies and equipment to various ports in Japan.

Life as a messman is not easy and couldn't have been more different to life on the farm. He would have been kept busy as coffee man, assistant cook, pantry man, waiter, dishwasher, bedroom steward, and porter. He would also have been in charge of maintenance of the officers' quarters and mess-rooms. What would his brothers and sisters have said if they'd have seen him dressed and pressed, looking smart in his all white sailor's uniform of bell-bottomed pants, white shirt with broad sailor's collar, indigo tie and round white hat with its stand up brim perched on his head? I'm sure he often wondered.

On November 12, 1947 the *F. Southall Farrar* again departed Longview, Washington, bound for Japan; but this time, instead of heading straight back to the United States, she sailed south in late December, transporting goods to Sydney Australia. Twenty-five-year-old Thaddeus was one of only two listed 'Negro' crewmen on board. The other, Robert Hunter, was older (at thirty-eight) and the more senior rank of Steward but the two men were shipmates. Robert would have been at sea for some years and known the Pacific well. Thaddeus was looking forward to visiting Sydney, there's no doubt — especially after Robert would have told him of a fun party house run by two black women just for the 'coloured' boys. In the Kings Cross district, *that* was where the prettiest white girls in Sydney could be found . . .

I WOKE ON THANKSGIVING MORNING and lay for a while in the big comfortable bed, thinking about Aunt Decie and the story she had told me of my grandmother Susan, my father and the family. Richard and I had also spent time the previous evening, talking about what *he* knew of the family and of his father Thomas.

I got out of bed and went to the window. I looked out over the garden to the wooded area of tall pines and flamboyant autumn-hued maples marking the garden boundary. I couldn't get Susan out of my mind: her pride, courage and determination in the difficult era in which she had lived, the implications of her colour and how she had never given in.

My favourite story goes that, one spring afternoon in early April 1930, a white man carrying a large leather-bound book arrived at Susan's farm. He was from the government, there to fill out the 1930 US Federal Census on each of the thirteen members of the household. Susan had to recall the information for each child, including her grandchildren, as he wrote in the columns of personal details including their sex, colour and race, age at last birthday, and status: single or married and age at first marriage. He also asked if she could read or write. Susan firmly answered 'yes' for herself. He then asked if her children attended school and if they, too, could read and write. With pride Susan answered 'yes' to those last three questions, a pride this man would never understand. Just look what they had achieved: in spite of hardship, a loving family had prospered; they were educated and now had more opportunities as each generation added to the achievements and freedoms of the family. After all, her children were only one generation removed from slavery.

Apparently, even through the Depression, she had tried to keep up the tradition of the family Sunday dinner after church. During summer months when produce from her garden and fruit from her trees was plentiful, often her older children and their families would squeeze around the table and rowdy, laughter filled afternoons would follow. Richard had told me that at other times, she also had additional grandchildren living with her for months at a time due to illness or work circumstances with their parents, including himself and Pocahontas, two of Thomas' children. Her door was always open and the small cottage seemed to stretch to accommodate everyone.

This extraordinary and courageous woman had lovingly raised and educated eleven children (Floy hadn't survived) and numerous grandchildren and despite almost-constant adversity, it was obvious to me, she had been the glue which kept the fabric of the family together. I was sure it was Susan's strength of character and spirit I had inherited. And it was her resilience that had helped me survive.

Then I remembered the Museum In Black, which Donna had taken me to five years earlier in LA. I remembered what she had said in the car park, as I'd wept at the appalling inhumane images I had seen inside: *We will never understand the cruelty and the reasons but this is your heritage — who you are. Be proud of that and rejoice in what we have achieved through unimaginable hardship.* Now I really understood what she meant. And I *was* proud, extremely proud to be a child of this incredible black family.

Aunt Decie and her son Albert were the first to arrive for breakfast at Ellen and Richard's, arriving in style in Albert's lovingly polished, sleek dark-green '95 Cadillac Seville. My brother had arrived from LA the day before. I helped Ellen and Ronda produce a sumptuous breakfast of freshly squeezed juice, a variety of cereals and toast, eggs and bacon with hash browns and steaming freshly brewed coffee, all served in the elegant dining room at the long polished mahogany table.

Aunt Decie finished her breakfast and beckoned me to follow her to the quiet music room.

'Child, I have to give a speech today. If I talk, will you write it down for me?' she asked. I was honoured to be the one she had chosen. When we emerged a good hour later, the house was abuzz with a crowd of relatives who had arrived for brunch, including Ompson's children, their grown children and grandchildren; Richard's sister Pocahontas and Robert and their children and Richard's brother, Lester. Not only I, but my brother, was meeting cousins for the first time. After warmly greeting Poci and Robert, I joined the others around the garden overlooking the pool area where we sipped on iced tea and ate delicate finger food prepared by Ronda and Ellen. A fleet of cars lined the driveway, ready to take us all to the other waiting relatives at the function centre.

The function room was gaily decorated with overhead balloons and white linen tablecloths and on a low stage at one end, was a keyboard and microphone plus a large screen. Once everyone had arrived and was seated at the long tables, it was time for Aunt Decie's speech.

The image of Southern style, she was a flamboyant but immaculate dresser; that day, Aunt Decie was in a golden-brown dress with matching jacket, pearly coloured shoes and handbag and gold jewellery, her black hair pulled back from her brown, relatively unlined face. She stood on the stage, a microphone in one hand, her written speech steady in the other, and her gold-rimmed glasses, perched on the end of her nose. At eighty-four, she was remarkable. The room hushed.

'I am the third youngest child of Jefferson and Susan Killens,' she began. After what she had told me the day before, no wonder I could hear the pride in her voice. 'My father passed away when I was a small girl, leaving my mother Susan to raise all us children on her own. Life was hard. Before school and sometimes instead of school, us children worked the land, planting vegetables and growing tobacco and cotton. The older ones like Thomas would work in the town and send money back for the family.' As Aunt Decie spoke of her life as a young girl, I could have heard a pin drop in the reverent silence.

'Susan was always talking to us about the Lord. She would always say she is reapin' the harvest for the seeds she's sowed.' I glanced around the room as the stillness was broken with murmurs of 'Amen' from the rapt audience. Aunt Decie explained that through Susan's teachings, she became deeply religious with a strong faith, always believing that 'God is good'.

'I was a good-time party girl,' said Decie with a wicked grin. I burst out laughing along with the rest of the room as the mood changed and the audience responded. Decie had married young and had four sons. Unfortunately the marriage broke down, her husband having custody of their boys. The only way she could keep her children with her was to earn money, so Decie headed out of Fairmont to New York City where she worked as a lady lift operator in the massive Church Street Station Post Office. She lived frugally, saving every cent. Eventually she had enough and caught the bus to Fairmont, collected her sons and took them back to New York. A few years later, Decie and the boys returned to Fairmont where she had lived out her life, although at times when money was tight again, Decie caught the bus back to New York to earn more.

Because of racial segregation, black citizens were confined to the back seats of the bus. One trip from Fairmont, Aunt Decie told the assembled family, she had been standing for a good part of the journey, with the black men, because the bus was full. When she returned to the bus after a rest stop, she found one seat left in the whites only section, so she gratefully sat to rest her tired legs. A white man got on and demanded Decie stand up and give him her seat. Exhausted, she could stand no longer. The white driver knew Decie had been standing and noticed what was going on. As they were now out of the South, he demanded the white man stand and leave Decie to sit in the seat. 'That was real unusual in those times,' she said, with my older cousins nodding their heads in agreement. As

Ellen and Richard returned a knowing smile from across the table, again I thought how different my life in Australia had been.

When Decie grew older, Albert, her eldest son, moved to a house a few minutes from his mother to be close and care for her. She prided herself on the fact that she was now in her eighties and, though she disliked doctors and hospitals, was as strong as an ox because she took a daily dose of castor oil and did push-ups every day. To prove her point she proceeded to put down the microphone and do ten push-ups. Her speech had been quite lengthy yet everyone, including the children, had listened attentively — but as soon as she started the push-ups, the room erupted with whoops and cheers, the Killens family delighted. Thad and I jumped to our feet with the rest of our family, clapping and grinning as Albert helped her from the little stage.

A blessing was said and lunch was served from a long buffet of thanksgiving turkey, pork, ham, vegetables and corn bread with various desserts including fruit pies and Decie's favourite, peach cobbler pie.

Richard moved around the room with the microphone as each of the eighty guests introduced themselves and told of their relationship to the twelve children of Susan and Jefferson. I listened as children of Ompson, Decie and Thomas introduced themselves, then their children and their grandchildren. There was Albert and Bird, two of Decie's four sons; Richard, Pocahontas, Deloise and Lester, four of Thomas' nine children; and Robert, one of Ompson's three children. When Robert said his sister Lorraine from New York could not make it, I realised the young cousin at the *Gordon Elliott Show* was Ompson's granddaughter. Now it was time for Thaddeus' children to introduce themselves.

'Hi,' I said. 'I am the newest member of the Killens family'.

'No you're not — she is,' said a voice from the back of the room as a relative held up a tiny baby girl. We all laughed as I handed the mic to Thad and headed in the baby's direction to meet my newest cousin, while my brother introduced himself. To simplify my story, Richard and Ellen had arranged to run a videotape of my appearance and family reunion on the *Gordon Elliott Show*.

Everyone loved it. When it was over, many rushed over in tears to hug us and warmly welcome me to the family. Seeing my sisters' faces on the screen made me miss them even more and wish they could have been there to share it with Thad and me.

Ompson's grandson played the piano and a group of Ompson's great granddaughters — from teenagers to little girls — sang gospel songs, their black braided hair swinging as they clapped in time with the music. All afternoon Thad and I met our family and talked and sang more songs and said prayers. Bursting with pride, I looked around the room at my eighty gospel-singing cousins, descendants of 'the twelve': grandparents, parents, teenagers, children and babies. It was a real pinch-me moment. I imagined Susan proudly looking down. She hadn't seen all her children grow and prosper before she died, but here were *their* descendants. And my father. I was sure I could feel his presence. Twenty years earlier my stepfather Lars had asked me, 'So what if you find this father of yours?' Well, I thought, 'Lars — this is so what!'

The younger set stayed late into the evening, dancing to the disco. Ellen and I returned home and acted as chief babysitters while Richard and several of the men cousins sat around the living room, indulging in whiskey and beer and talking football and long-lost relatives. Three of the teenage boys returned early and sat with us. They were lovely with their corn-rowed hair and baggy jeans; very modern black boys with lovely manners. When Ellen and I had finally tucked the last of the exhausted children into bed she said, 'Sharyn, Honey, would you care for a glass of wine?'

'Cousin Ellen, I thought you would never ask,' I said, exhausted and exhilarated. As we clinked glasses, she winked at me.

'Welcome to your family,' she said. I hugged her. What a Thanksgiving — in the true meaning of the tradition! Words could not express my gratitude to Richard and Ellen for putting together this wonderful day so I could meet all my family at once. They had gone to considerable trouble and expense to make it a memorable event and I felt truly blessed.

MY STAY WAS NEARING AN END. Two days later on the Saturday
morning, Ellen drove me over to Fairmont to stay with Pocahontas
and Robert, for the weekend. I also felt privileged to have been
invited to accompany Aunt Decie to church on Sunday morning. I
was to return to Ellen and Richard's on Monday then fly back to
Australia on Wednesday.

This time, driving into Fairmont I looked at the historic town
through different eyes. I now understood the significance of the
area to the family, having first settled there over one hundred
years before.

Pocahontas and Robert had raised seven children and lived in
an elegant rambling, single-storey home surrounded by a beautiful
garden. Inside, the warm and homely atmosphere of the house
was reflected in the décor of comfy floral sofas with a mix of
plaid and floral window treatments and furnishings. Traditional
timber panelling lined some walls with wallpaper on others. The
centrepiece of my bedroom was a huge four-poster bed, crowned
with a billowing white mosquito net. Poci went to prepare lunch
and left me to unpack my weekend bag. I placed a few things
on the antique dresser, carefully moving aside the silver-framed
photos, and then wandered over to the window. Though it was
nearly winter and the large trees had lost a good number of leaves,
the garden still looked lush with neatly trimmed shrubs bordering
smooth green lawns. The smell of freshly brewed coffee was too
strong to resist, so I followed my nose though the house to the
kitchen where Poci and her daughter Jean, who lived next door,
were preparing southern fried chicken. Robert came in from the
garden and over lunch, in answer to my questions about the house,
they told me their story.

They had been a couple since they were quite young: Poci
fourteen and Robert fifteen. Just married in 1945, Robert could
find no work in Fairmont as a farmer, so they had travelled to
Connecticut, worked and saved, and returned to Fairmont to buy
their first home. To support their children, they became maid and
gardener for the town's doctor, working long hours in his large
residence. The doctor eventually retired so Pocahontas and Robert

then moved their children to New York and worked in a big hotel, as maid and porter-cum-concierge. They saved every cent then returned to Fairmont, only to buy the doctor's residence and there raise those of their children who remained at home. They were now retired and in their mid-seventies.

Poci, softly spoken, reserved and a little shy was very much the homemaker. Robert, also reserved, was fairly tall and reminded me very much of my mentor Freddie Paris in style and manners. Robert also had a fantastic singing voice, similar to Freddie's, which I had noticed at the Thanksgiving reunion. He had never sung professionally but each Sunday lifted his voice in praise to God, along with Pocahontas, in the Fairmont First Baptist Church choir. Both Robert and Poci loved music; he particularly liked Johnny Mathis and Nat King Cole and she, the jazz greats — just as it seemed all my family did, including me, thanks to Ellie.

As they drove me around the town showing me places of interest, Robert and Poci explained Fairmont's history. Apparently, the first settlers in the area were loggers who produced lumber and turpentine and pitch for ships but by the late 1800s, a flourishing tobacco market had been established. I realised it was during this time Jefferson and Susan had married and started their own farm just a few miles away.

I found out Fairmont was first founded as Ashpole in 1899, then Union City and finally Fairmont in 1907. Apparently, with the ideal conditions, tobacco became the major crop in the area and by the mid-1950s, Fairmont was considered one of the major tobacco markets in the world. Interestingly, in the early days the town's population was predominately white but over the years, as members of my Killens family along with other sharecroppers' and farmers' children had moved into town, the balance had now shifted to nearly fifty-nine per cent African-American.

SUNDAY MORNING, I stood outside the Fairmont First Baptist Church waiting for Aunt Decie to arrive. Pocahontas and Robert were already inside preparing with the choir. To me, the beautiful Southern church looked just like a picture postcard. Six tall white columns supported a square front portico, behind which, over the main building with its pitched grey roof, stood a small tower supporting a very tall and decorative white steeple. The building looked to be covered in a coffee-coloured render and, in contrast, all the building's trim and the three large mouldings over the front door were painted a pristine white.

Aunt Decie arrived at the kerb as though she was Queen of Fairmont, chauffeured by Albert in his sparkling Cadillac. Albert ran around to the passenger side and opened the door and Aunt Decie stepped from the car, a picture of style. From her extensive wardrobe of clothes, she had chosen a deep blue suit with fur collar and cuffs, smart shoes and bag, hat and gloves and appropriate jewellery. She had certainly set the standard high that morning. People were chatting outside and no doubt a few of Decie's contemporaries had been waiting to see 'what is Decie wearing today?' The Baptist church in my father's hometown was overflowing with well-wishers as many in the congregation had known my father. The word had spread that Decie's long-lost niece from Australia, who had been on television, had turned up in Fairmont for a visit. I proudly walked down the aisle with Aunt Decie and Albert, to whispers and greetings and sat between them in the family pew. Aunt Decie pointed out a cornerstone, dedicated to my father's brother Thomas, then leaning forward she whispered to me their preacher was the Reverend King, a nephew of *the* Reverend Martin Luther King Jr.

Reverend King appeared in his flowing black robes and opened the service then the choir sang like angels. Before he began his sermon, the Reverend said he had an announcement. 'A miracle is happening here today,' he said in a deep booming voice, gesturing towards a beaming Aunt Decie and me, sitting beside her. 'We are welcoming a lost daughter into our family. A daughter lost to us a long time ago but has been found and today we welcome her back into her family.' With that, he looked up and threw his hands heavenward. 'Praise the Lord!' The congregation in a hundred different voices all called out, 'Praise the Lord!' and 'Hallelujah!' and 'A miracle!'

I was stunned. A prickly sensation rushed up my back and spread in a hot flush across my face. But not a flush of shame. It was of joy and pride and love.

I had fought and begged for years to be accepted and part of a blond-haired, blue-eyed family who had rejected me because of the colour of my skin and the circumstances of my birth, which they found unacceptable. I had been hidden, shunned and locked away. But this American family had welcomed me with open arms and loved me, unconditionally. I took Aunt Decie's hand and squeezed it, then grinning broadly, looked around at all the smiling faces.

Aunt Decie and I walked down the aisle, arm in arm at the end of the service. It took a while to reach the front door as we kept being stopped and congratulated every few steps. We were kissed and patted and our hands shaken over and over. At the front door, the large Reverend standing resplendent in his robes, made a fuss of me as we were leaving. He took my hand, then placed his other hand over the top, shaking it warmly and said, 'Child, you are a miracle in progress. God loves you, so don't you ever forget that.' I looked at Aunt Decie's proud and smiling face and I believed him. I thought of how much had happened since I picked up the phone to call Debra for the first time. It *felt* like a miracle.

I finally knew who I was. I had found my roots. My family. I was home.

Heading in the Right Direction: An Epilogue

WITH AGE COMES WISDOM. Eventually you get old enough to understand and forgive some things, but others can never be forgiven.

I have never understood why I was sentenced to Parramatta and Hay. I had never committed a crime and I had never hurt anybody. I was a runaway — that's how I went in — but I came out battered and damaged. I was told I was nothing for so long that I believed it. I lived with the belief and shame of being a bad girl for many years. But I might finally be starting to forgive myself.

Lifelong friendships were formed among the inmates of Parramatta and Hay. Recently, I asked a friend the question we never asked each other when we were in those institutions: 'What are you in for?' It was just a no-no among us. Many Parramatta girls suffer deep shame that they were ever there and live their lives hiding this secret. I know I *was* one of them but not anymore! I now *want* people to know what happened to us, in the hope it will never happen again.*

In 2003, thirty-seven years after I was released, Senator Andrew Murray headed an enquiry into children in care in Australia. I believe it was the first time any government had taken the time to investigate what exactly had been going on in their institutions. Listening to the stories from adults like me, and what we'd endured as innocent children in these places, made many of the politicians

---

* For more information, go to www.TheInconvenientChild.com and click on the 'Parramatta' heading.

weep. The stories and the results of the enquiry were published in a book entitled *Forgotten Australians*.

We were also sharing stories with each other that year, when ex-Parramatta girls joined for a reunion for the first time. It was the first of a number of reunions and marked the beginning of a difficult and challenging journey for many of us.

Actually, 2003 was a year of firsts for me. In June, my son Patrick flew to Los Angeles to represent me at the Las Vegas wedding of my youngest sister Donna and her then-fiancé Ken. I was unable to attend due to ill health but it was a life-changing experience for my son, meeting and getting to know his aunts and uncle. He and Thaddeus had some really good times and bonded easily, being close in age.

Then, on Christmas morning, my cousins Richard and Ellen arrived from North Carolina with their daughter Ronda and her little son Zachary, to visit us and meet my Australian family. It was an emotional day for me, watching my two families come together. Though they had spoken to him on the phone many times, I was so proud to introduce them to my Allan. I felt whole, like a circle had finally been joined, watching my American family embrace Allan, Patrick, my daughter-in-law and grandchildren, Allan's twins and, finally, my mother and Lars.

What could have been an awkward meeting was not, when my precious cousin Ellen reached out with a warm embrace to greet my mother. Ellen, with her usual radiant smile said, 'Well, look at how beautiful you are Grace! Come here and give me some sugar, honey.' They walked into my home arm in arm, laughing.

It was a day filled with joy and magic as we sat down to a full Christmas lunch with all the trimmings, despite the heat — it must have been one hundred degrees. As my mother kissed me goodbye she said, 'Sharyn, your American family is lovely.'

'They are not my family, they are our family. I wouldn't have them if it were not for you,' I replied. She flashed me a dismissive smile and got into the car. As they drove off, I wondered how long it would be before the realisation of what I had said dawned on her.

The family stayed for two weeks and I proudly showed them the Central Coast, Sydney Harbour and my life. Ellen has become my confidante, my advisor and my treasured close friend. We speak almost daily.

Aunt Decie and I spoke each week, too, until she died that year, at the age of eighty-six. She was my only direct living connection to my father, his sister — of the same genetic make-up — which to me was a wondrous thing. Touching Aunt Decie was like touching my father. She had known him since he was born and could tell me of the boy Thaddeus. Through Aunt Decie I also learned who I am. As my family's history was slowly revealed, I realised how blessed and honoured I was to know the last surviving child of Susan and Jefferson. My sons and grandchildren now have a legacy to leave to their future generations — their heritage. I'm sure they will be as proud as I am.

I occasionally call and exchange Christmas cards with many of the cousins I met at the reunion but most often I keep in touch with Pocahontas, in addition to Ellen and Richard. It was they, along with the rest of my American family, who encouraged me when in 2004 I officially changed my name by deed poll to Sharyn Killens, in honour of my father and the family who have enfolded me into their heritage. But I still sing and entertain under the name of Sharyn Crystal.

In 2006, I again flew to Los Angeles and spent three weeks visiting my sisters and brother. Donna and I spent a memorable morning at her local beauty shop where I had my hair straightened and saw how those beautiful and intricate braided hairstyles are created. The atmosphere was festive, girlie and very social and I met some very outrageous and 'bootylicious' women. I speak to all the girls at least once a week, sometimes more, and now, using the Internet, it's so easy to exchange emails and photos. We talk constantly about Daddy and their mother: I am still hungry for every scrap of information about him. We laugh, we cry and we console each other. To discover these precious sisters and brother has been a gift from God. They are the most wonderful people in the world.

And where would I be without my music? It is amongst my earliest of memories, has been my comfort and motivation during distress and challenging times and has given me my dream come true — a singing career. I believe fellow entertainers accept and embrace each other for their talent, and your past is of little consequence. Combine that with the love you feel flooding across the footlights from your audience, that admiration when you walk onto a stage, and what better career to choose for a damaged girl needing love?

I SANG AT HAY in March 2007, when a two-day reunion was held at Hay Institution for Girls, the site of what is now the Hay Gaol Museum. Of the three hundred and sixty-five girls who served time there, about fifteen of us returned to the place of our nightmares. We were now mothers and grandmothers and had not seen each other for more than forty years, yet many could not face it alone and had brought along family and friends for support. On a specially chartered bus, we all travelled to Hell together — the place to which we'd vowed we would never return.

To walk through the gates for the first time, many of us held hands for courage — most could not venture inside without shedding tears. Inside, we were greeted by the organisers and each handed a rose and told to 'have a look around'. We did — for the first time! I remember taking my first step into the main cell block and shuddering as an icy chill ran through me. I swear I could smell my fear as I broke out in a cold sweat. It was strange that the place still *felt* the same, considering it was the first time I had actually seen it. A long-forgotten sense of anxiety, abandonment and isolation rushed back, the memories of abuse and humiliation hitting me in the face as I walked down the centre aisle between the cells. By the time I got to my cell door I was a quivering mess, my stomach heaving. I glanced inside then turned and ran out into the sunshine.

Back in the cell block, at one end we were asked to be seated in chairs to watch an enactment of the daily cell routine by high school students. A whistle blew and teenage girls dressed in a replica of our uniform, appeared at the doors from inside the cells — I froze, almost unable to breath. As officers yelled and girls stamped, we all sat and sobbed. Was it cathartic? I'm not sure, but they meant well.

The people of Hay then came to meet us. They had no idea what had gone on behind the high walls and were visibly upset, listening while many of us told our shocking stories of abuse. They had been told we were criminally insane! Photos were on display for everyone to see and the locals were shocked to realise we had been just teenage girls. It wasn't surprising, really: while researching my story, I was informed by a Department of Community Services Officer that 'Hay never existed'. When I insisted it had — I was an ex-inmate — I was told, 'It was so embarrassing for the Department,' meaning the NSW Department of Child Welfare, the one responsible at the time, 'they didn't acknowledge it because it had been an experiment on teenage girls that had gone wrong.' Shame on them!

The Hay community were courteous and hospitable, many literally reaching out to embrace us and tell us how extremely sorry they were that we had all suffered such atrocities.

A ceremony was held in the Hay Gaol yard, the same area where we used to be drilled in the gruelling exercises. As leading politicians read speeches of apology, acknowledgement and offered support, for the first time I could look around at the buildings: the high prison walls, the watchtowers, the sinister isolation cell building. In commemoration and in the very garden where we girls had laboured, a rose bush was planted beside a plaque which read *Let No Child Walk This Path Again*. To mark the closing of the ceremony, I had been asked to sing 'I Am Woman'. My throat tight and aching as I tried to hold back unshed tears, I sang it with a lot of help from the other Hay girls.

On the Sunday morning, a church service was held by the community in our honour. Prayers of forgiveness were offered in accordance with the sermon's theme. Then children from the congregation presented each of us with an olive branch. Over the weekend, the Hay ladies of the town prepared yummy breakfasts, lunches and dinners.

It was marvellous to meet up with a few of my old friends again. Some had passed away and many, like me, had lived through periods of self-destruction including the abuse of drugs and alcohol. All are survivors. The women who left after that weekend were a different bunch to those who arrived. The healing process had begun and I was ready to move on. I understand now that I was never a bad girl, just a neglected, unloved and unwanted child.

Parramatta was opened, too, on a day in March 2008 during renovations — only for four hours and for ex-inmates and their families to revisit and walk through. I couldn't go so my close friend Lindsay went alone, to represent me and to see for herself. Though a building site filled with rubble and workmen, she said, nothing could disguise the oppressive atmosphere of Parramatta or hide the horrors that had happened there. She watched women wander through the buildings singly or in small groups, peering through doors, discovering rooms and staircases they hadn't known existed and looking out of barred windows, all of them talking quietly — almost whispering — as if no one wanted to awaken sleeping monsters. Although the dungeon shower room was filthy and derelict, evidence of the regime was plain to see. She said she could almost smell the humiliation, and that the dungeon isolation cell was just plain evil — a shackle ring left over from the convict era was still embedded in the old sandstone-block wall.

LINDSAY AND I went to Saint Martha's together. As I walked down that same garden path to the front office forty-eight years after leaving, I noticed much of the gardens had been turned into a parking area. The little chapel hadn't changed and the statue of the Virgin Mary still stood in the shady grotto in the main garden. Walking up the stairs to the dormitories, a familiar feeling of dread made me drag my feet. I needn't have worried: it was hardly recognisable now as partitioned offices. Though a convent and orphanage until 1977, the place is now the Sydney Catholic Education Office. The dining room is a library/book shop and that hateful shower room is now storerooms (but it still made my skin crawl).

Some things you can't forgive. I realise now that Sister Lucifer's shocking beatings had little to do with my wet bed. She beat me because she could, and used me as her whipping post to vent her own frustrations and wage war on her inner demons. That nun was a child abuser.

Some details of her abuse have remained my terrible secret, kept to myself all my life, even into adulthood. In fact, I had buried my shame and self-loathing so deep that it was an extremely painful experience reliving it. Who would believe I could do such a disgusting and dirty thing as drink from the toilet? But I forget that I was just a child, deprived of a basic necessity. Recently, I read of another woman who was driven to the same desperation, as a child in a similar institution. I realised then that I was not alone and I believe others will empathise, and understand that they too are not alone.

I NEVER RESOLVED MY RELATIONSHIP with my mother. For a few years, my mother and I spoke on the phone frequently and enjoyed pleasant trips to the movies or a morning's shopping followed by lunch, usually at her home. Mum and I occasionally shared a bottle of wine over lunch but our days of heavy drinking together were over. For long stretches of time, our relationship was warm and, I believe, loving. I also encouraged Patrick, who lives near us all on the Central Coast, to take his children to visit her and Lars. Their great-grandchildren splashed around in their pool and went for walks on the beach with their great-grandfather, who enjoyed them immensely.

Unfortunately, the good times didn't last as my mother's tolerance of me was tested. Without warning she would become impatient, cold and distant. I helped her as often as I could and reasoned that, being the principal carer for my stepfather, who had developed Alzheimer's, she was under great stress.

I kept inviting her to the theatre, to the cinema and to lunch at my home, offering to pick up her and Lars then drive them home afterwards. All outings were politely refused. She was too tired; too busy; liked staying home; not this week, it was inconvenient; whatever. I tried to understand but was often offended when I heard they had gone to the theatre show anyway and had accepted various invitations for outings with my cousins.

In December 2006, I called to ask what plans she had for Christmas. She informed me my cousins may have plans for them but she wasn't sure.

'Would you like to have Christmas lunch with us? See the great grandchildren —'

'No, no, no,' she interrupted, 'Nothing like that. Maybe your cousins have plans for us. Maybe I will stay home.'

'Well if I get up early on Christmas morning I could come and just stay long enough to have a cup of tea and give you your presents,' I said.

'No, no. No, no, no.' I felt that hideous feeling of rejection once again.

'Well, Grace,' I answered 'That's alright. Don't worry about it.' We chatted about other things for a short while then I put down the phone. We were invited to Christmas lunch with a friend and her family and I accepted. A week later I received a call from my mother.

'Hello, this is your mother calling.' As if I didn't know who she was. 'Just thought I'd invite you to Christmas lunch . . .' she said airily.

Why did she always do this to me? I was getting so tired of it and of her. 'No, thank you. I have made other plans,' I said and put down the phone. She had never considered that her rejection was like a slap in the face to me.

I kept in touch and still drove her shopping and we often had lunch together. She enjoyed herself but I could tell she felt uncomfortable alone with me in public. We were having coffee and cake in a café when a woman arrived whom my mother knew. As she and Leonie talked I listened and smiled, then picked up the bill the waitress had left on the table.

'While you two are catching up, I'll pay the bill,' I said.

'No,' said my mother, 'leave it. I will fix it up.' We argued good-naturedly for a moment till finally, with an exasperated smile, I stood, picked up the bill and turned to Leonie. Cheekily I said, 'Wouldn't you think a mother would let her daughter pay the bill once in a while?' With that I turned and headed to the counter.

Immediately I realised my mistake. I had called her 'Mother' in public! She would be furious with me. She hated the look on people's faces when they tried to figure out how she, the pretty little blonde, had a tall black daughter. Now I was in trouble and felt mortified, instantly the bad little girl again. I paid the bill and reluctantly headed back to the table. Leonie was staring at me with admiration.

'So you're Grace's daughter? Oh, I have heard so much about you. You are the singer. You sing on cruise ships all over the world. How wonderful! That must be fantastic.' I stammered something, smiled and we left. I drove my mother home in frosty silence and helped her carry her bags inside. Then I dutifully kissed her cheek and headed home.

During the drive, the realisation of what I had just witnessed dawned on me. So that's how she did it! She did not actually deny me to her friends and strangers but told them she had a daughter who sang on ships. The convenient daughter — when I was the successful singer. Oh, how proud she must have been telling people that; just as long as people didn't see me and didn't make the connection. I was so upset I had to pull the car over to the kerb.

It still hurt so much that my mother refused to own me, was still ashamed of me. I sobbed, leaning on the steering wheel for support. Now I understood why my mother surrounded herself with relatives whenever we went out together. She had been doing it for years. She had not worried about me on the ship or shopping trips because she knew I would never call her Mum, just Grace. But this time I had slipped up — badly.

I tried to put myself in her shoes. As a beautiful young woman, she must have attracted many suitors, yet she had lived at home caring for her ageing mother and nieces and nephews. She would have wanted a good husband to father her children but had unexpectedly met a handsome and charming black American and fallen pregnant. My prejudiced grandmother had so shamed my mother at that crucial time that she had not only hidden the pregnancy but hidden the child as well. My mother saw me, her black daughter, as her shame — every time she looked at me she saw her mistake.

Yet I had spent a lifetime trying to impress this woman into loving me. I thought about the extent to which I would go, the times I would work myself into a frenzy whenever she came for a visit. I'd knock myself out obsessively cleaning. Well into the night, I'd still be re-lining shelves in my cupboards and tidying shoe closets. It drove Allan crazy but everything always had to be perfect for her.

In the car that day, I realised it was time I lived my life for me. I had to find a place of peace. In that moment I knew I had finished running this race with my mother and now I was backing out. I would give her what she had wanted since the day I was born. I would disappear from her life. I would have no more contact with her. The charming, warm and caring woman she showed the world was not always the woman she showed me. I would not allow myself to be unloved, unwanted, disrespected and treated like crap any longer.

Not long after I had made that decision, my mother became very ill and was taken to hospital. I received a message she did not want to see me — did not want me to visit. A few days later in September 2007, she died. Sadly, five months later, Lars also passed away.

I have never stopped loving my mother. She was always my Princess Mummy. I want to believe my mother loved me — just not in the way that I needed her to.

PERHAPS IT'S NOT SURPRISING that a bad bout of the flu I caught in late 2006, caused irreparable damage to my already weak and struggling heart. I was hospitalised and after extensive tests and the permanent insertion of a defibrillator in my chest, I am being assessed for a heart transplant. New medication seems to be keeping everything under control, though I now officially suffer from severe heart failure. My heart is damaged, is too big and struggles to beat — but as long as it does, that's all that matters.

I am cared for by the brilliant heart team at the Victor Chang Cardiac Research Institute at St Vincent's Hospital in Sydney plus several wonderful local doctors to whom I owe my life. This illness is genetic and, I believe, was passed on to me by my father. I have passed it on to my eldest son but, as the line goes on, we can only hope the effects of the disorder are lessening.

Anthony lives in Queensland with his partner and has for many years. His health is deteriorating as Marfan attacks his body but he remains positive in attitude. We are doing all we can to help him and life goes on. Anthony has recently blessed me with another baby granddaughter. Patrick has five wonderful children. My sons have grown into fine, responsible men and I am so proud to be their mother.

My greatest friend is my wonderful Allan, who loves me completely and unconditionally. We are happy and content in our home and Allan is still the best 'tradie' in town. We have loved and cried, laughed and screamed, in anger and in joy. I love this man and am eternally grateful he walked into my life. He saved me from a lifetime of bad choices. He taught me to appreciate a beautiful sunset and woke me to show me an unforgettable sunrise. He persisted until I found my American family and got that photo of my father. He is the love of my life.

I recently turned sixty and I am delighted. I regard this as a milestone considering my life's experiences and family history, not to mention my health. Reliving and revisiting the places of my life has been a cathartic and life-changing experience. The journey with my beloved friend and confidante Lindsay has been emotional, painful and many times joyous but that's another story . . .

I believe your childhood is what makes you the adult you are. And I know life was harder for me because of my circumstances and life's events.

But now I have solved the mysteries of my past, I look forward to a brilliant future.

Acknowledgments

LOOKING BACK, at times the story of my life may appear unbelievable but the truth is powerful and honesty has been my first priority. It was never my intention to hurt or embarrass anyone and I apologise if I have inadvertently done so. Also, for this reason, we have changed many of the names in my story.

Although it is impossible to list all the special people who have contributed to my life's journey, please know I remember and appreciate you. But there are some too important not to mention.

To the love of my life Allan: how can I ever thank you for your unconditional love, support, generosity and encouragement?

To my two beautiful sons: without you, I would not be here. Your love inspired me to walk down the road to a better life for us all. Thank you.

Thank you to Wayne 'Charlie' Moore, the quiet achiever with the big heart. I am grateful for your kindness of spirit, understanding, generosity and your expertise in making this book a reality. I will treasure the journey, our in-depth conversations, the friendship and your delicious lamb cutlets and potato bake.

To Lindsay Lewis, my treasured friend of twenty years, thank you. God knew what He was doing when He gave me, you. That fateful day we met, you were organising a benefit concert for a friend in need. You are always there emotionally, spiritually and financially to assist those needing help. You have cheered me on through the good times and stayed up with me through nights of crying shame and endless heartache. Bravely you have retraced the steps of my life, including the time I led you through the streets of

Kings Cross. We clung to each other and wept as we stood in the filthy, vile black hole of the isolation cell in Hay Institution for Girls. You have socialised with my mother and stepfather and travelled to Los Angeles and had lunch with my sister. Your compassion, understanding, patience, tolerance, caring and gentleness with my feelings and emotions during the creation of this book will live with me forever. Your knowledge, attention to detail and professionalism have led you from the stages of the world as an entertainer to the boardrooms of the corporate world and to your life now, as an extraordinary author. I have yet to mention that you are a plane crash survivor. Who better to write the story of my life?

Thank you to my three sisters and my brothers for your unquestioning love and acceptance. I am forever grateful to my wonderful cousins Dr Richard Killens and his wife Ellen for their unwavering love and support, and assistance with the historical background of my American family. Thank you also to cousins Pocahontas and Robert and to all of my Australian and American family.

HOW DO WE THANK our extraordinary editor, Selena Hanet-Hutchins? With integrity, empathy and professionalism you patiently guided and encouraged us to believe 'yes we can'. Your editorial skills and knowledge are amazing — thank you for sharing your expertise, wisdom and your delightful sense of humour. You are the third Angel.

Our special love and thanks to our 'other sister' Janie Bartlett, for your invaluable advice, support, enthusiasm and candid comments. Thank you also to Den Parker, and to Janno Darling and Maggie Polglase for your tireless attention to detail.

'SEND MY LOVE' and thank you to my Parramatta and Hay sisters. You are wonderful women of great strength and integrity and I am so proud to be your friend. Let no girl walk this path again.

Thank you for the special love and support from these great friends: Carter Edwards and Francine Bell, to Wilma Robb, Diane Kearney and Pat Cook for helping me remember when I could not face it, to Maggeh Harrison, Margaret Heard, Jan Magain, Linda Sharpe, David Grose, Robyn Sperling and Brian Cowan.

My heartfelt thanks for the support of my friends in the Australian entertainment industry, particularly those who have encouraged this book. You know who you are.

THERE IS A LONG LIST of friends and colleagues who have encouraged and supported us on our journey. Please know that we acknowledge and appreciate your love and contribution and will be forever grateful for the cups of tea, glasses of wine and Kleenex. Now come and celebrate with us.

Authors' Note

THE INCONVENIENT CHILD is the true story of Sharyn Killens' life. In the interests of truth and honesty, all events and conversations have been recounted as faithfully as memory will allow; however, while all the people portrayed in the book are real, we have used pseudonyms for most in order to protect their privacy. So, while some readers may recognise Hay Institution for Girls or Parramatta Girls' Home, the girls' names have been changed and they'll see we have used the generic address 'Sir' or 'Miss' instead of the officers' names; while the buzz of Surf City and the colour of the Bourbon and Beefsteak might still feel like yesterday for many readers, many of the 'characters' of the Cross (equally colourful), the cruise ships and other entertainment milieus will not be so familiar. Having said that, there are of course some stars of the industry who we could present as no one else but themselves.

Articles in the media, including those quoted from the *Sydney Morning Herald*, *Daily Telegraph* and *Riverine Grazier* newspapers, have been terrific for getting a flavour of the different historical times in the book and for understanding how 'the outside' saw Hay and Parramatta. Parliamentary Hansard records and girls' accounts of the institutions have also been invaluable, if horrifying. Academic theses 'An Experiment in the Rehabilitation of Incorrigible Girls:

the Rhetoric and the Reality' by Lynette Aitken and 'Unenlightened Efficiency: The Administration of the Juvenile Correction System in New South Wales 1905-1988' by Peter Quinn were also very important resources.

It's impossible to describe the feeling of seeing Susan Killens' letter in print in *The Robesonian*. What that must have meant in those times! Then to discover and follow the family's progress through copies of the hand-written Census of the United States: Population Schedules was astounding. Thank you to Ancestry.com for access to this and other vital information. Of course none of this would have been possible if not for Worldwide Tracers, who found Thaddeus Killens.

For information on times not our own (we're still too young to remember World War II, let alone the nineteenth century!) and just occasionally to check facts we thought we knew, we were daily thankful for the Internet. We're grateful to Wikipedia (on everything from soldiers' R&R entertainment to local rationing and jobs during the Second World War; from slavery to the Civil Rights Movement; from Hippies, to Marfan's to 1940s boxing), it's always a great research springboard, and to the American Merchant Marine at War website, (www.usmm.org). The following books were also useful for creating the feel of the times and place: Robert Drane's *Fighters by Trade*, *Meet Me at the Trocadero* by Joan Ford, Carlotta's *I'm Not that Kind of Girl* and *The Usual Suspect: the life of Abe Saffron* by Duncan McNab; we'd recommend them to any readers interested in the history of Kings Cross and the East Sydney area. Lyrics from *Let My People Come* appear courtesy of lyricist and composer Earl Wilson Jr. The efforts of helpful staff at the New South Wales State Records Centre, National Archives of Australia, the National Maritime Museum and the State Library of New South Wales were also appreciated.

We would like to give thanks and acknowledge the significant contribution of Kerri-Anne Kennerley and *Midday with Kerri-Anne* (transcript courtesy of *Midday with Kerri-Anne* and Nine Network Australia) and Gordon Elliott and *The Gordon Elliott Show* (courtesy of CBS Entertainment, USA). Our appreciation also goes to the Department of Community Services (DoCS) for permission to use the photos of Parramatta Girls' Home and Hay Institution for Girls.

What we realised during the writing of this book is that one life can cover a lot of topics of interest. If you'd like to know more about Sharyn Killens or any of the places or subject matter in this story, please drop by the website www.TheInconvenientChild.com.

Reading Groups and Book Clubs

To download discussion notes and background to the writing of the book please go to www.TheInconvenientChild.com and click the heading Book Clubs.

•

SHARYN KILLENS' love of music and her driving ambition to become a singer entertainer enabled her to fulfil her dream of singing on stages and cruise ships around the world, under the name of Sharyn Crystal. She has also worked as a publicist and entertainment booking agent and manager, and has served on the Australian Ladies Variety Association Committee. Sharyn has also been nominated for a prestigious Australian Entertainment MO Award for her performance. More recently, she has been a talent quest judge, teaches stage presentation and has produced children's theatre shows.

•

LINDSAY LEWIS began her career in a major record company before running her own businesses. In 1992, after many years working in key Sydney advertising agencies, she moved into publicity then began her own successful textile design and manufacturing company with her husband. Lindsay also spent many years as a professional singer and entertainer and was prominent on the Australian Entertainment MO Awards Committee. She now runs an Internet marketing business.

Sharyn and Lindsay have been close friends for twenty years and *The Inconvenient Child* is the result of their close collaboration.